Philadelphia
Almanac

AND CITIZENS' MANUAL

for
1994

For Aunt Miriam and Uncle Lew

Christmas, 1993

Kenneth Finkel, Editor

The Library Company of Philadelphia, 1993

D0775784

Editor: Kenneth Finkel
Associate Editor: Janice Fisher
Designer: Lesley MacLean, AdamsGraphics, Inc.

Project Volunteers:
Louise B. Beardwood; Carl G. Karsh; Selma P. Kessler

Contributors:
Carolyn Belardo; Michael J. Darcy; Len Davidson; Henry Glassie; Libby Goldstein; Charles Hardy III; Theodore Hershberg; Seth Itzkowitz; Richard L. James; Ricky Jay; Norman Johnston; Linda Z. Jucovy; Margaret O. Kirk; Marta McCave; Michael McGettigan; Patricia McLaughlin; Martin McNamara; Phran Novelli; David O'Neil; Harold M. Rosner; Chris Spurgeon; Joy Stocke; Geoffrey Wilson

Publisher: The Library Company of Philadelphia

This project is funded by the William Penn Foundation.

❖

Cover: Frontispiece from *Journal of My Forty-fifth Ascension, being the first performed in America, on the Ninth of January, 1793* (Charles Cist, 1793). J. P. Blanchard ascended from the yard of the Walnut Street Prison, Sixth and Walnut Streets, and remained aloft for 46 minutes before landing safely in Deptford, New Jersey. Copy photography by Will Brown.

Illustrations: Eighty-two of the historic maps, sketches, prints, photographs, sculptures, and title pages illustrated in this almanac are from the collections of the Library Company of Philadelphia. Other institutions and individuals to be credited and thanked are: The Historical Society of Pennsylvania (p. viii); Cleveland Museum of Art (p. 9); Michael McGettigan (pp. 52, 53, 108, 130); Haverford College Library (top, p. 110); Annenberg Research Institute (middle, p. 110); The Free Library of Philadelphia Rare Book Department (bottom, p. 110); College of Physicians Library (top right, p. 111); Temple University Library (bottom right, p. 111); Atwater Kent Museum (bottom, p. 127); The Franklin Institute (p. 135); the collection of William Rau Haden (top, p. 157); Len Davidson (pp. 188, top and bottom 189, 190, 191, 192, 193).

Grateful acknowledgment is made for permission to reprint the excerpt on p. 177 from *Black Ice* by Lorene Cary (Alfred A. Knopf, 1991).

The Philadelphia Almanac and Citizens' Manual
may be ordered in quantity for educational uses directly from:
The Library Company of Philadelphia
1314 Locust Street
Philadelphia, PA 19107
(215) 546-3181

Contents

Acknowledgments

Many, many people and institutions helped in many ways. Thanks to the Atwater Kent Museum for the opportunity to speak on almanac history. Dr. Bernard C. Watson and the William Penn Foundation offered the vision, faith, and guidance needed to turn an idea into the almanac you hold in your hands.

Market research by Bruce Makous and A. J. Bubnis helped this almanac to know itself from the start. Bill Marr freely shared his time and talent to make a most impressive prototype. Thanks to Borders Bookshop for allowing us access to their customers to test it. And thanks to the scores of people who responded to our questionnaires and gave time to our focus groups. The Wharton School of the University of Pennsylvania generously provided us with facilities in which to work.

The Library Company of Philadelphia, the city's oldest repository of information, feels a natural affinity to the almanac idea and seemed comfortable in its role as midwife. Thanks to the Board of Directors, to Librarian John C. Van Horne, and to the staff: especially Eileen Shapiro, Margaret Jones, Gordon Marshall, Phil Lapsansky, Jim Green, Karen Nipps, Jennifer Woods, and Sue Lee. Mary Anne Hines and Denise Larrabee brought to my attention valuable material on many critical occasions. Susan Oyama and Sarah Weatherwax were especially patient during those times when this project and building renovation made everyday work a challenge.

Thanks to the crew of dedicated, hardworking volunteers, the best anyone could ask for: Louise B. Beardwood, Carl G. Karsh, and Selma P. Kessler. They compiled, checked, wrote, and rewrote to make this a stronger and more worthwhile product.

Janice Fisher's keen eye and constant enthusiasm ensured consistent and much improved content. Bob Seabert turned the prototype into the makings of a book. Lesley MacLean and Sandy Oestreich made the book, always turning out attractive and very readable pages.

We cannot thank by name the staffs of dozens of libraries and museums in the Philadelphia area who assisted in the job of compiling and checking. They always helped, to a one. I would like to thank Val Gonzales, of the Fels Planetarium of the Franklin Institute, for expertly calculating astronomical data, the core of the ancient and venerable almanac tradition.

Thanks to the excellent crew of contributors who are listed elsewhere and the many others who helped: Dave Adams, Robert Altman, Joe Anderson, Ed Bacon, David Baldinger, David Bartlett, Lenora E. Berson, Charles Blockson, Rich Boardman, Bill Bolger, Carole Boughter, Blake Bradford, George Brightbill, Will Brown, Harry E. Cerino, Frank L. Chance, Brendan Clark, the late Dennis Clark, Cathryn Coate, Bud Cook, Harriet Dawson, Richard Donagher, Ed Dougherty, Geraldine Duclow, James Duffin, Ellen Dunlap, David C. G. Dutcher, Joseph Eckhardt, W. D. Ehrhart, Bob Eskind, Tom Ferrick, Charles Field, Ned Finkel, Nancy Goldenberg, Bill Good, Stanley Greene, Mike Hardy, Pat Henning, Steve Hershey, Hayes Hibberd, David J. Holmes, David Hunt, Major Jackson, Ed Jutkowitz, David Kairys, Allan S. Kalish, Bob Kaufman, Ira Kauderer, Linda King, Damon Kletzian, Gayle Koster, Gerald S. Lestz, Allen Liss, Cindy Little, Pam Magidson, Anne Meyers, Danny Miller, Jefferson Moak, Ruth Molloy, Peter Moor, David T. Moore, Nancy Moses, Tybie Moshinsky, Gloria H. Murphy, Ted Newbold, Bernard F. Pasqualini, Maryanne Promos, Frank P. Righter, Jr., Neil Roseman, Steven Rothman, Dan Rottenberg, Glen Ruh, Scott Schultz, Ed Schwartz, Susan Seifert, Elliot Shelkrot, Bill Siemering, Harry Silcox, R. C. Staab, Kate Stover, Maryann Surla, Mary-Anne Thompson, Fasaha Traylor, Richard Tyler, Robin Warshaw, David Weinberg, M. L. Wernecke, Maxwell Whiteman, Scott Wilds, Geoffrey Wilson, and Ben Yagoda.

To my particularly patient and talented wife Margaret, who encouraged me to go on, I am especially grateful.

Kenneth Finkel

Introduction

I n a country where old often means dusty and dusty usually means irrelevant, Philadelphia has always been
uniquely positive about its past. So much of our infrastructure—our neighborhoods, buildings, institutions, material culture—is of times gone. And infrastructure is too clini-
cal and objective a term. In Philadelphia, we are married to
the past for better, worse, richer, poorer. Our mission as
Philadelphians is to come to terms with our particular frag-
ments of the ongoing collision between past and present.

But how? In the mid-1980s, at the convivial luncheon
table of the Franklin Inn Club, talk would sometimes turn to
the then long-gone *Bulletin Almanac*. Former editor Izzy
Lichstein had to restrain his sadness while observing the rit-
ualistic lament (shared by all). Many others besides Izzy still
felt pangs for that amputated literary limb. Philadelphians
had rubbed the paper covers off of their now-brittle copies
of the last, lamented edition for 1976. Great cities *always*
had almanacs! What an unfortunate and telling flaw!

In the summer of 1990, the Atwater Kent Museum asked
me to plan a lecture for December to follow, and I suggested a
talk on Philadelphia's almanac history. This, I figured, might
provide an opportunity to get the long-simmering almanac
idea off the ground. It did. With the enthusiastic assistance of
editor Lorraine Branham, my stiff and hurried lecture turned
into an article on the commentary page of the *Philadelphia
Inquirer:* "Philadelphia Is in Need of Another Almanac."

Before long, with the encouragement of Dr. Bernard C.
Watson and the William Penn Foundation, discussion led to
generous commitment, first in the form of a grant for planning and research, and then, in August 1992, for the project
itself. The continuing faith and support of the William Penn
Foundation is the reason this almanac exists.

❖

If the almanac idea is as old as publishing itself, traditional publishing is today hobbled by the evolving concept of
the information highway. Somehow, book literacy is no
longer considered as essential as computer literacy. Educated
people own and use books filled with printed words but work
amidst scanned words. With the black and white of the printed page making way for the blue and white of a computer
screen (the colors in which this editor processes words, as
well), books have begun to look antiquated, to seem a bit
anachronistic. But they have also acquired an appealing fla-
vor they didn't have before. In the information age, books are
friendlier relics, precious objects from simpler times. They're
hardly dead. Rather, books have finally found their niche.

When Benjamin Franklin, publisher of the *Pennsylvania Gazette,*
offered his first *Poor Richard's
Almanac* in December 1732, the run
sold out immediately. By late January
he had printed two more editions for
a total of about 3,500 copies. Franklin
sold about 2,500 of these copies in
Philadelphia, a city of approximately
9,000 people—one almanac for every
3.6 citizens.

Contrary to popular belief,
Franklin was the 10th almanac printer
in Philadelphia, not the first. Why
hadn't his predecessors succeeded on
this scale? Competitor Titan Leeds, for
example, who first published an
almanac three years before Franklin,
was perhaps a bit too serious.
Franklin's first *Poor Richard's* predict-
ed Leeds' death on October 17, 1733
at exactly 3:29pm. It was not an original prediction: Jonathan Swift had
perpetrated a similar hoax on an
adversary 25 years earlier. Franklin, it
turned out, was a public relations
genius and the success of his first
almanac hung on this stunt. A defen-
sive Leeds started off the preface to
his next almanac by calling Franklin "a
fool and a liar." Franklin now had reason to counter-attack. In a subsequent
almanac, he declared that Leeds was
indeed deceased "but pretends he is
still living."*

By 1758, *Poor Richard's* had perfected its populist voice. That almanac
offers "a plain clean old man with
white locks" named Father Abraham,
who while waiting for an auction to
begin spouts what we now know is
classic Franklinian wit. Father
Abraham comments at length on the
times and how to better live them. At
the end of the harangue Poor Richard
notes that the audience approved of
Father Abraham's advice "and immediately practiced the contrary."

After Franklin, almanacs would
never be the same.

*Provocations of this sort would be
prohibited today by lawyers' fees
and court costs.

Words along the information highway are searchable images, unlimited in their capacity to bombard us. These words, though, are only mundane servants. With computers, modems, CD-ROMs, and fiber optics, transmitted words dissipate almost as soon as they appear. In 1994, we finally realize, we can have it—and want it—both ways. We need transmitted data, but we want printed words.

This publication is a revival of the oldest genre of old-style print: the almanac. Before we set out to compile and edit it, we looked at the range of *Bulletin Almanacs*, starting with the 224-page, 1924 model, called *The Bulletin Year Book and Citizens' Manual*, which inspired our title. That almanac spoke to a "modern" readership with a formula that expanded during its run of 52 years, but didn't evolve very much.

We studied the earliest Philadelphia predecessors, going back past the *Comic Almanac for 1858*, which included a caricature of a taxpayer dressed in rags; past *The Franklin Almanac for 1826*, which informed readers how to prevent toothaches and how to cure hiccups; past Lydia Bailey's *Rittenhouse Almanac for 1815*, which reviewed the War of 1812 and advised on the grafting of budding trees; past

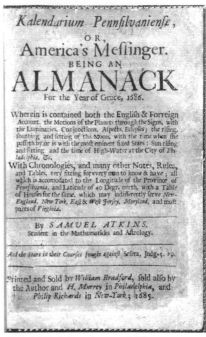

Philadelphia's first almanac, 1685.

Johnson's Pennsylvania and New Jersey Almanac for the year 1808, which printed an "Ode to Taciturnity"; past even Benjamin Franklin's first *Poor Richard's Almanac* in 1732. We went all the way back: 308 years, to 1685 and Samuel Atkins' *Kalandarium Pennsilvaniense*, the first book printed in Philadelphia.

Atkins had "journeyed in and through several places...and [heard] people generally complaining, that they scarcely knew how time passed, nor that they hardly knew the Day of rest, or the Lord's day, when it was for want of a Diary, or Day Book, which we call an Almanack." He was "really troubled." So Atkins provided folks with basic information: from the days of the upcoming year as they relate to astronomical and astrological events all the way to a general chronology from "the flood of Noah" (3,979 years before) to "the first founding of this City of Philadelphia" (four years before).

The charm and value of this long-forgotten kind of almanac is its catchall attitude and serendipitous arrangement. As a perch for ephemeral information, the revived, old-style almanac you now hold is a reference, but it is also a rest stop on the information highway.

Time, which erodes just about everything else, adds patina to that which is already old and imperfect. With every passing day, the past expands in scope and grows increasingly valuable. One of the challenges of being a Philadelphian is learning how to adapt to the present while balancing countless bits and pieces of the city's rich past.

In this slim, single volume, we have chosen to include as much from yesterday as from today. Some sections came to us as logical, even inevitable. Still others were serendipitous. For every entry, another group of equally appealing ideas was set aside for future editions. Over time, we will ignore no subject, so long as it has to do with Philadelphia. Rest assured—we will never run out of material.

As we compile, edit, and check, we know that omissions and errors are inevitable. We invite your suggestions, criticisms, corrections, and clarifications. And we want to know what you think should be in future editions of our almanac. Please send your comments and ideas to: Almanac Editor, The Library Company of Philadelphia, 1314 Locust Street, Philadelphia, PA 19107.

K.F.

Putting "Yo!" in Its Place

We know the rocky road from South Philadelphia to Hollywood for "Yo!" Then, somehow, "Yo!" became geographically displaced. In the summer of 1993, the *New York Times* claimed the now famous street cry, but one letter writer with Philadelphia origins (and a Northern New Jersey address) wrote in to set the matter straight. "Yo!" evolved from *gualgione*, or "young man." In Neapolitan dialect, the pronunciation was guahl-YO. It's a short story for a long-used, and very meaningful, expression.

The sounds of the city and its streets are very much worth listening to, and they have often been the subject of journalistic comment and even scholarship. But nothing in the study of the Philadelphia street cry tops the evening of January 6, 1920, when local historian Kate H. Rowland re-enacted before the Philadelphia City History Society dozens of collected cries. There was no "Yo!" But from Mrs. Rowland's work we know the proper intonation for pretzels. Early street vendors relied on occasional wit, tireless lungs, and, preferably, some musical ability. They barked and sang and made their way along the city's sidewalks and narrow streets to the rhythm of their distinctive calls, selling fish, soap, soup, coal, crabs, and brooms. Itinerant workers offered to sand your floors (with real sand), clean your chimneys, recycle your old rags and bottles, or sharpen your knives. Through open windows poured the appeals—some might say cacophony—of the multitude. All of which sound much more appealing and less inhibited than present-day street vendors who flatly command the passerby to "Check it out." ∎

An-y rags, an-y bones, an-y bottles to-day, An-y shoes or old tin cans.

Ca - at fish.

Cat - fish, buy an - y cat - fish?

Shad - oh, Fine sweet fish, shad - oh.

Hom - i - ny fresh from the Na- vy - yard.

Hom-i-ny, hom - i - ny, hom - i - ny, Who will buy my hom-i-nee?

Accent

Sweep - oh.

Corn, hot corn, hot corn, hot corn.

Lav - en - der two cents a pack, two cents a pack for Lav - en - der.

Old rigs, old rigs, bits of i - ron, bits of brass, old rigs, old rigs.

Pep - per - ry pot, smok-ing hot, Five cents a bowl.

Pretz - els.

Sam, Sam the soap fat man.

Soft soap, soft soap.

Straw - ber - ries, red ripe straw -ber - ries.

Waf - fles, waf - fles, fresh baked waf - fles.

Twelve o 'clock and all is well.

2

The Urge to Preserve

D ue to an act of official vandalism, part of Independence Hall is a facsimile, even maybe a kind of a fraud. In 1816, the city of Philadelphia removed interior paneling. What we see there today never reflected light onto Washington's tight curls or Franklin's great forehead. The newer panels might have been saplings where Revolutionary soldiers slogged, if they were lucky.

As the city's older fabric slipped away, some took notice and a few actually lamented the losses. In 1818, *The Port Folio*, Philadelphia's literary magazine, commented on the passing of an early brick Chestnut Street house built by David Breintnall. "We believe that edifice to have been the last *specimen* in this city, toward which the curious inquirer in these matters, might have been directed," wrote the editor, who for all of his sympathy didn't take a very hard look around. In the next decade, John Fanning Watson identified the house where William Penn had lived on 2nd Street near Walnut Street, and pleaded its case. As Watson considered the Slate Roof House in all its authentic antiquity, his sensibilities became overpowered. An irrepressible "poetry of feeling" stole over him. Europeans regularly protect places with powerful associations, Watson argued. "Who can estimate...value...of so much brick and mortar!" Rescue it; preserve it. "There is a generation to come who will be grateful."

The Slate Roof House survived Watson, but only briefly. Its replacement, a Commercial Exchange, burned almost immediately—"cosmic retribution," according to one historian. Generations that would have been grateful have come and gone and come again. And the Slate Roof House, along with scores of other buildings that "progress" (or whatever they're calling it these days) did not absolutely stand in the way of, are simply gone—simply forever. ■

Sources: Charles B. Hosmer, Jr., *Presence of the Past* (G. P. Putnam's Sons, 1965); John Fanning Watson, *Annals of Philadelphia* (Philadelphia, 1830); Richard J. Webster, *Philadelphia Preserved* (Temple University Press, 1976).

PRESERVATION GROUPS

In truth, the only asset in the Philadelphia area that seems to grow—no matter what—is history. And the most apparent expression of the past is architecture and planning, from the city's few remaining cast-iron sidewalks, to blocks of rowhouses, to mansions, public buildings, and boulevards dating from times before "cost effective" meant anything to anyone.

Preservationists have always managed their uphill struggle against well-financed odds. Organization helps, of course, and several regional groups are dedicated to the principles and action of preservation. Here are a few:

- The Foundation for Architecture, 1 Penn Center, Suburban Station, Philadelphia, PA 19103. 546-3187.
- Philadelphia Historic Preservation Corporation, 1616 Walnut Street, Philadelphia, PA 19103. 546-1146.
- The Preservation Coalition of Greater Philadelphia, 250 S. 16th Street, Philadelphia, PA 19102. 546-0531.

THREATENED BUILDINGS

Baptist Temple, Broad and Berks Streets (Thomas P. Londale, 1891); Bleakley House (Cannon Ball House), Fort Mifflin Road (ca. 1720); Calvary Methodist Church, 48th Street and Baltimore Avenue (Dull & Peterson, 1904); Commandant's House (at Fort Mifflin), Fort Mifflin Road (Pierre Charles L'Enfant, ca. 1800); Greater Straightaway Baptist Church (formerly Congregation Adath Jeshurun), 1705-13 N. 17th Street (J. Franklin Stuckert, 1886); Mercantile Library, 1021 Chestnut Street (Martin, Stewart, & Noble, ca. 1952); Ridge Avenue Farmers' Market, 1810 Ridge Avenue (Davis E. Supplee, 1875); St. Edward's Catholic Church, 7th and York Streets (William and George Audsley, 1903); U.S. Naval Asylum, Grays Ferry Avenue at 24th Street (William Strickland, 1833); Victory Building, 10th and Chestnut Streets (Henry Fernback, 1875; enlarged by Philip W. Roos, 1892)

Lost Philadelphia

This chronological list inventories buildings of significant historical or aesthetic interest demolished over the course of nearly 200 years. Construction and demolition dates are noted. Architects are indicated when known.

- **Robert Morris residence, Chestnut Street between 7th and 8th, ca. 1794–ca. 1800, Pierre Charles L'Enfant.** The financier of the American Revolution couldn't quite finish L'Enfant's extravagance, which came to be known as "Morris's Folly."

- **Greater Meeting House, 2nd and Market Streets, 1755–ca. 1804.** Philadelphia's 18th-century conscience resided here.

- **Benjamin Franklin's house and print shop, Market Street between 3rd and 4th, 1765–1812.** The home and shop of the American original, designed by him.

Benezet House

- **Benezet House, Chestnut Street between 3rd and 4th, ca. 1700–1818.** One of the city's earliest houses with style, and home to an early champion of abolitionism.

- **Pump House, Center Square, 1799–1828, Benjamin Henry Latrobe.** An interpretation of Philadelphia as the "Athens of America" by the man who invented the phrase.

Pump House, Center Square

- **President's House, 9th Street south of Market, 1792–ca. 1829.** The first White House.

- **Pagoda and Labyrinth Garden, Fairmount Avenue, near Fairmount, 1828–ca. 1830, John Haviland.** A Chinese-influenced pleasure garden by an architect of prisons.

- **Walnut Street Jail, Walnut Street between 5th and 6th, 1773–ca. 1835, Robert Smith.** Where prison reform began.

- **Town Hall (Courthouse), 2nd and Market Streets, 1707–1837.** This first City Hall (like the current one) occupied the middle of the street. But here, the style was late-English medieval.

Walnut Street Jail

- **Cooke's Building (Cooke's Folly), 3rd and Market Streets, ca. 1792–ca. 1838.** Before this, businesses didn't have an architecture to call their own, making do with old houses.

- **Masonic Hall, Chestnut Street between 7th and 8th, 1808–1853, William Strickland.** Early Gothic Revival originally with a fanciful wooden tower.

- **Second Chestnut Street Theater, Chestnut Street above 6th, 1822–1856, William Strickland.** Replacement after a fire of Philadelphia's cultural center. Only William Rush's sculptures of Comedy and Tragedy survive.

Town Hall (Courthouse)

Architecture

- **Sedgeley, East Bank of the Schuylkill River (near what is now Girard Avenue), 1799–1857, Benjamin Henry Latrobe.** First American residence in the Gothic Revival.

- **High Street Market, Market Street between Front and 8th Streets and 15th and 17th Streets, ca. 1680s–1860.** So influential in the life of the city, for so long, that officials finally renamed High Street after it.

Sedgeley

- **Slate Roof House, 2nd and Sansom Streets, 1699–1867, James Porteus.** Not only did William Penn and his family reside here, but so did James Logan, John Adams, and William Trent, the founder of Trenton.

- **Bank of Pennsylvania, 2nd Street above Walnut Street, 1801–1867, Benjamin Henry Latrobe.** Its designer later claimed that this building gave Philadelphia architecture "a breadth of effect and a repose vainly sought in other cities."

- **Standpipe of the West Philadelphia Waterworks, west side of the Schuylkill River near 35th and Sycamore Streets, ca. 1855–ca. 1870, Birkinbine & Trotter.** A tour de force in decorative cast iron.

- **Wire Suspension Bridge, Schuylkill River near Fairmount, 1842–1874, Charles Ellet, Jr.** An early, successful test of the American-invented suspension bridge.

- **Main Building, Centennial Exhibition, Fairmount Park, 1874–1876, Henry Pettit and Joseph M. Wilson.** A temporary iron-and-glass showcase of giant (and meaningful) size: 1,876 feet long.

- **The Library Company of Philadelphia, 5th and Library Streets, 1790–1884, William Thornton.** The first permanent home of America's oldest cultural institution.

- **Phil-Ellena (House of George W. Carpenter), Germantown Avenue and Carpenter Street, 1844–1894, George W. Carpenter.** A single suburban estate replaced by an entire neighborhood: Pelham, in Germantown.

- **Dundas-Lippincott Mansion, Broad and Walnut Streets, 1839–1902, Thomas U. Walter.** A single urban estate now the site of an office tower: the Fidelity-Philadelphia Trust Building.

The Library Company

- **Continental Hotel, 9th and Chestnut Streets, 1860–1923, John McArthur, Jr.** The legendary hotel in a city at the peak of its commercial and industrial influence.

- **Rodeph Shalom Synagogue, Broad and Green Streets, 1869–1925, Fraser, Furness & Hewitt.** A Victorian masterpiece updated in the 1920s with a dignified beige box of relatively little character.

- **Philadelphia Record Building, 917–919 Chestnut Street, 1888–1932, Willis G. Hale.** Victorian exuberance replaced by International Style calm: Paul Philippe Cret's Federal Reserve Bank.

- **Broad Street Theater, Broad Street south of Locust, 1876–ca. 1937.** Its onion domes and Moorish arches offered serious counterpoint to the staid Academy of Music, just across the street.

- **The Library Company of Philadelphia, Locust and Juniper Streets, 1878–1940, Frank Furness.** Even the oldest cultural institutions can be swayed by the pendulum of public taste. Alas!

- **Broad Street Station, Pennsylvania Railroad, Market Street west of City Hall, 1881–1953, John M. Wilson and Furness & Evans.** A palace for the railroad conceived during America's Iron Age.

- **Store of Dale, Ross & Withers, 219 Market Street, 1857–ca. 1955, Stephen D. Button.** One of the many sacrifices to the suburban vision that we know as Independence Mall.

5

Architecture

- **Horticultural Hall, West Fairmount Park, 1875–1955, Hermann Joseph Schwarzmann.** A case of demolition by neglect (and excuse), after damage from a storm.

- **Drexel Building, 5th and Chestnut Streets, 1885–1955, Wilson Brothers & Co.** Its iron, A-frame construction spelled engineering triumph. Its proximity to Independence Hall spelled defeat.

- **Jayne Building, 84 Chestnut Street, 1850–1958, William L. Johnston and Thomas U. Walter.** All skyscrapers owe genealogical respect to this building, not to anything in Chicago.

- **Hotel Walton, southeast corner of Broad and Locust Streets, 1895–1966, Angus S. Wade.** Beneath turrets and mansard roofs, a melange of polished marble, potted palms, and tooled leather ceilings. Now the site of a concrete-and-carpet hotel.

Jayne Building

- **Philadelphia County (Moyamensing) Prison, 10th and Reed Streets, 1835–1967, Thomas U. Walter.** "Old Moko" was part Gothic and part Egyptian. Now the site is part Acme and part State Store.

- **Benjamin Rush Residence, Red Lion and Academy Roads (10801 Keswick Road), ca. 1700–1969.** This home of a signer of the Declaration of Independence was accidently demolished by Philadelphia's Department of Licenses. Honest.

- **Whitemarsh Hall (Edward T. Stotesbury residence), Wyndmoor, Pa., 1917–ca. 1975.** More than a big estate: a small, luxurious town with a large staff.

- **Art Club, Broad and Chancellor Streets, 1888–1975, Frank Miles Day.** Fallen to our just about insatiable appetite for convenient parking.

- **20–30 S. 21st Street, 1890–1984, Addison Hutton.** If Renaissance Venice had rowhouses, they would have looked something like these.

Art Club

- **Bulletin Building, northeast corner of Juniper and Filbert Streets, 1908–ca. 1984, Edgar V. Seeler.** Commercial architecture leaning toward play. Most memorable for its polychrome, glazed dome at the corner nearest City Hall.

- **Midvale Steel Works, Wissahickon and Roberts Avenues, ca. 1890–1985.** Industry was the engine that drove Philadelphia. Here was one of the biggest.

- **Octavius V. Catto House, 814 South Street, ca. 1815–1989.** Schoolteacher Catto led desegregation on streetcars in the 1860s and was a promising leader until his murder during Election Day riots in 1871.

- **The Dunbar Stores, 920–922 Chestnut Street, 1851–1990, Stephen D. Button.** When the heart of commercial Philadelphia resided in Chestnut Street, buildings such as these maintained a dignified rhythm and scale.

- **Municipal Stadium (John F. Kennedy Stadium), Broad Street and Pattison Avenue, 1926–1992, Simon and Simon.** Event promoters and politicians agreed that this mammoth stadium—the site of a landmark boxing match, a Papal Mass, and a benefit rock concert—simply had no future. ■

Sources: John Andrew Gallery, ed., *Philadelphia Architecture: A Guide to the City* (Cambridge, Mass. and London, 1984); George B. Tatum, *Penn's Great Town* (University of Pennsylvania Press, 1961); Richard J. Webster, *Philadelphia Preserved* (Temple University Press, 1976); Theo B. White, *Philadelphia Architecture in the Nineteenth Century* (Philadelphia Art Alliance, 1953); Philadelphia Historical Commission files.

Furness Lost

No architect in the history of Philadelphia has been quite so loved, and then so hated, as Frank Furness (1839–1912). The generations of the 1870s, 1880s, and even 1890s sought out his immense talent; the next generations couldn't knock it down fast enough.

This flip-flop is no accident, according to historian George Thomas, who identified Furness's work as a creative burst for the red brick–Quaker City set. Furness revitalized nostalgia for a failing breed of Philadelphian. He gave them a confident look, without pretense and the "honorific display" of white marble. Philadelphians preferred Furness's approach, wrote Thomas, partly because it was unique, partly because it worked, and partly "because it was incomprehensible to the nouveau-riche."

By the time Furness's incomprehensible red brick had turned black with soot, the 20th century needed rubble from which to rise. It was no accident that the rubble was partly from 70 freshly felled Furness structures, about half of which had stood in Center City. Here are some selected losses, dated to their year of construction:

Rodeph Shalom Synagogue, Broad and Green Streets (1869); Lutheran Church of the Holy Communion, Broad and Arch Streets (1870–75); Bloomfield H. Moore House, 510 S. Broad Street (1872–74); Guarantee Trust & Safe Deposit Co., 316–320 Chestnut Street (1873–75); Jefferson Medical College Hospital, 10th and Sansom Streets (1875–77); Provident Life and Trust Company, 409 Chestnut Street (1876–79); DeForrest Willard House, 1601 Walnut Street (ca. 1878); Library Company of Philadelphia, Locust and Juniper Streets (1878–80); Francis Fassitt Store Buildings, 1207–09 Market Street (1881); Commercial Union Assurance Co., 330 Walnut Street (1881); Reliance Insurance Co., 429 Walnut Street (1881–82); George B. Preston House, 2135 Walnut Street (1881–83); Penn National Bank, 7th and Market Streets (1882–84); Bailey, Banks and Biddle Factory, 12th and Sansom Streets (1886); Philadelphia Terminal, Baltimore and Ohio Railroad, 24th and Chestnut Streets (1886–88); Provident Life and Trust Company, 401 Chestnut Street (1888–89); Lippincott, Johnson and Company Store, 629 Market Street (1892); Additions to Broad Street Station, Broad and Market Streets (1892–93); West End Trust Company Building, 1404 S. Penn Square, at Broad Street (1898); 8th Ward Settlement House, Hutchinson and Locust Streets (1900); Arcade Building and Pedestrian Bridge, 15th and Market Streets (1901). ■

Source: George E. Thomas, Michael J. Lewis, and Jeffrey A. Cohen, *Frank Furness: The Complete Works* (Princeton Architectural Press, 1991).

THE LOUVRE OFF LUDLOW STREET

Will the Victory Building, pictured here before ailanthus trees were allowed to sprout from its eaves, live up to its name and survive—or fail and be demolished?

For a long time, Victory's standing in architecture has been more secure than its place on the northwest corner of 10th and Chestnut, just a parking garage south of lowly Ludlow Street. The seven-story office building was built in stages (1873 and 1891) by two New York architects—Henry Fernbach and then Phillip W. Roos—for the Mutual Life Insurance Company of New York. They spared nothing on either go-round. Business boomed, so they (literally) raised the mansard roof.

The building was built by New Yorkers, for New Yorkers—and it looked it. Originally, the 234-foot-long, Rhode Island granite façade might have been too outgoing for local tastes. Today, its engaged columns, pilasters, balustrades, arcades, arched windows, wreathed medallions, parapets, and corner urns are far more eclectic than the florid dreams of a post-modern architect. Here's the commercial equivalent of the Second Empire style (seen locally on Philadelphia's City Hall) that originated in Paris during the reign of Napoleon III. Could such bald worship of European royalty by monied New Yorkers on the plain streets of Philadelphia be just too forthright for its own survival—even a century later? Isn't Philadelphia finally worldly enough, or resourceful enough, to keep it?

CITY HALL STATS

Construction	1871–1901
Intended cost	$10,000,000
Actual cost	$20,368,273
Dimensions	470 feet by 485.5 feet
Site	4.5 acres
Floor space	14.5 acres
Rooms	750
Clock height	361 feet
Clock dial	26 feet diameter
Total height	547 feet, 3.5 inches

PENN SCULPTURE

Sculptor: Alexander Milne Calder

Calder's assistant: John Cassini

Cast by: Tacony Iron and Metal Works

Date placed in City Hall courtyard: November 6, 1892

Date tower installation completed: November 28, 1894

Time from conception to installation: 22 years

Weight of Penn statue: 53,348 lbs.

Length of Penn's foot: 6 feet

Penn's waist: 26 feet

Diameter of coat buttons: 6 inches

Width of Penn's eyes: 10 inches

Dimensions of hat: 3 feet by 7 feet

OTHER SCULPTURES

Total sculptures: 250

On tower: Indians and Swedes

On center pavilion dormers: America, Europe, Asia, and Africa

Doorway spandrels: Civilization and Barbarism; Engineering and Mining

Stairway panels: Youth, Science, and Agriculture

Impost panels of windows: Agriculture, Navigation, Mechanics, and Horticulture

Art

Which Way, William Penn?

William Penn's reign began a century ago. In November 1894, the 37-foot-tall bronze statue of Penn was installed atop the tower of Philadelphia's City Hall. During the final two years of construction, the gigantic Quaker stood at ground level, an attraction in City Hall courtyard. When the tower was complete, Penn was disassembled, hoisted up, and finally reassembled 548 feet above the city's skyline.

City Hall's architectural style had grown out of fashion during the project's three decades of construction. One critic tagged it an "artistic failure." Walt Whitman thought the place "weird," if "beautiful." One Mayor joked about his "white elephant." None of this apparently affected the oversized statue, which developed a following all its own as it hovered over the city. English essayist G. K. Chesterton saw in Penn "the graven figure of a god who had fashioned a new world."

In 1886, after years of sculpting hundreds of allegorical figures, caryatids, and decorative panels, sculptor Alexander Milne Calder's studio turned to the image of Penn. Earlier renditions depicted the founder as a somewhat overweight, middle-aged English aristocrat—which is what Penn was. As an icon for America's rising urban industrial center, the commission called for something more youthful, more stylish. In Calder's three studies, Penn grew progressively slimmer, prouder in stance—and decidedly more clothes-conscious. Those once fearful of historical truth feared no more.

Calder's redesign delighted city boosters. But then, in a fit of jealousy, the architect installed Penn backwards. With shoulders turned toward the sun, Penn appears to look away from active Broad Street South. Architect W. Bleddyn Powell (John McArthur, Jr.'s successor—he died before the job was finished) overrode the original plans. Calder later revealed that the spiteful Powell had purposely turned Penn the wrong way. Never mind that the tower's footing had been prepared for a southerly gaze. The architect explained that he oriented Penn toward Shackamaxon, where (according to myth) the proprietor and the Indians had signed a treaty. There was something to this reasoning. But sense or no sense, this assured that Philadelphia's most visible symbol was, in the words of Calder's interviewer, "condemned to eternal silhouette." ∎

Source: Fairmount Park Art Association, *Sculpture of a City: Philadelphia's Treasures in Bronze and Stone* (Walker Publishing, 1974).

Art

The Wissahickon School?

William Trost Richards' June Day, 1870, at the Cleveland Museum of Art

Benjamin Franklin never waxed nostalgic about the picturesque Wissahickon Creek. Instead, he proposed to build a dam where it flowed into the Schuylkill. The whole of the valley would then become a lake—and Philadelphia's supply of fresh water.

If the Wissahickon had been more powerful than meandering, it certainly would have been shown less mercy by industry. But as it gently flowed, a couple of dozen millers' dams scarcely squeezed enough power from the muddy waters to turn their wooden wheels. The proximity to the rising industrial city, increasingly dependent upon the steam engine, made the dark and rugged 6½-mile ravine seem downright quaint—in a Victorian, woodsy way.

Long before the place became parkland in the late 1860s, folks had escaped to the valley for recreation, relaxation, history, and lore. When the mills were closed to preserve the city's water supply, moss and vines reclaimed their ruins and added to the romantic imagery. Visitors reinvented, for purposes of memory, the rustic old millers, the 1694 settlement of alchemist/scholar Johann Kelpius and his cult of mystical messiah-watchers. They remembered the natives whose arrowheads still littered the ancient paths through groves of hemlock and poplar.

Edgar Allan Poe, George Lippard, and others romanced the place in prose and verse. Nowhere else so near a city offered such scenery. "The softest light I ever beheld," wrote actress Fanny Kemble. Painters, sketchers, and then photographers campaigned in their own ways to popularize Philadelphia's most picturesque setting. The Pennsylvania Academy of the Fine Arts hung more than 60 paintings at its annual exhibitions. In the 15-year span between 1854 and 1869—after Wissahickon's annexation to Philadelphia and preceding its inclusion in Fairmount Park—no less than 30 paintings made the craggy, forested outcroppings of Wissahickon schist over the shallow creek an image as famous as any Alpine or Yellowstone scenery had yet been or still would be. ∎

THE OTHER PHILADELPHIA AWARD

The Medical College of Pennsylvania/Gimbel Philadelphia Award is conferred annually upon a distinguished woman from the Greater Philadelphia area in recognition of her outstanding service to humanity. It began in 1932 as the Gimbel Philadelphia Award, established by Ellis Gimbel. In 1987, after Gimbel Brothers Department Store closed, the Medical College of Pennsylvania assumed sponsorship.

Hundreds of clubs, organizations, professional societies, religious groups, service institutions, and organizations are invited to submit nominations; a selection committee comprising former award recipients makes the selection. The recipient receives a citation and monetary gift. In 1992, the award went to Sister Mary Scullion.

RICHEST PRIZE

The largest science prize offered in the United States is in our own backyard. Since 1990, the Benjamin Franklin National Memorial at the Franklin Institute has presented the Bower Award and Prize for Achievement in Science. Recipients receive a gold medal and cash prize in excess of $250,000. The 1992 award recipient, Denis Parsons Burkitt, received $373,000 for his work on Burkitt's lymphoma and his advocacy of dietary fiber's importance. Previous winners were Solomon Halbert Snyder, for his research into the brain's opiate receptors, and Paul C. Lauterbur, for his pioneering work in nuclear magnetic resonance imaging. The prize is made possible by a $7.5 million bequest from Philadelphia chemical manufacturer Henry Bower.

❖

When the Bellevue-Stratford reopened under new ownership and management in 1979 as the Fairmont, some Philadelphians were enraged by the changes, notably carpeting in both lobby and ballroom and, of course, the name.

Awards

The Philadelphia Award

For longtime *Ladies' Home Journal* editor, socialite, and social reformer Edward W. Bok, the "ideal of service" was a test of good citizenship. Bok thought to keep that ideal "constantly before the minds of the people of Philadelphia in general and the young in particular" by putting his money where his beliefs were. In 1921 he established the annual Philadelphia Award, "in recognition of some service rendered by a resident of Philadelphia or its environs which shall have redounded to the good of the City or its environs."

Award Recipients, 1921–1992

1921: Leopold Stokowski, the internationally styled conductor who developed the Philadelphia Orchestra to worldwide recognition.

1922: Russell H. Conwell, the minister whose acclaimed lecture "Acres of Diamonds" became a metaphor for Philadelphia in general and Temple University in particular.

1923: Samuel S. Fleisher, founder of the innovative and informal Graphic Sketch Club, where adults and children enjoyed art.

1924: Charles Curtis Harrison, University of Pennsylvania Provost, for advancing culture and education.

1925: Samuel Yellin, master craftsman in iron, for the work from his prolific shop in West Philadelphia.

1926: Chevalier Jackson, inventor of the bronchoscope, which removes foreign objects from the throat.

1927: Rev. W. Herbert Burk, who advocated a national monument to George Washington at Valley Forge.

1928: Eli Kirk Price, for his role in the development of Fairmount Park and the Philadelphia Museum of Art.

1929: Cornelius McGillicuddy (Connie Mack), "for setting a high example of sportsmanship" for the youth of Philadelphia.

1930: Paul Philippe Cret, world-famous architect and Professor of Design at the University of Pennsylvania.

1931: The Unknown Citizen, "who has made the best of his troubles...for courage in economic warfare as great as that of the Unknown Soldier on the battlefield." The award was made available to the needy through the Committee on Unemployment Relief.

1932: Earl D. Bond, for his long research in psychiatry that revolutionized the treatment of mental illness.

1933: Lucy L. W. Wilson, Principal of South Philadelphia Girls High School, for her work in public education to provide "what the most progressive private schools are able to give their children."

1934: Charles M. B. Cadwalader, Director of the Academy of Natural Sciences, for organizing 105 expeditions into remote areas to bring "the ends of the earth to the Parkway."

1935: Francis Fisher Kane, lawyer and "friend of the friendless," for founding the Voluntary Defender Association, a group of lawyers who aided indigent defendants in criminal cases.

1936: George W. Wilkins, head of the Shelter for Homeless Men, for taking care of 73,000 disheartened men over a six-year period, providing food, clothing, shelter, medical attention, and hope.

1937: Alfred Newton Richards, Professor of Pharmacology at the University of Pennsylvania, for making possible more accurate diagnosis and successful treatment of kidney disease.

1938: Rufus M. Jones and Clarence E. Pickett, Chairman and Executive Director of the American Friends Service Committee, for organizing homesteading for unemployed miners in Western Pennsylvania and Virginia and supervising their retraining in agriculture.

1939: Thomas Sovereign Gates, for his contribution to education as President of the University of Pennsylvania.

1940: Marian Anderson, singer, for her contributions to music.

1941: No award

1942: William Loren Batt, President of Smith Kline and French Industries, for leading the industrial mobilization for war with the War Production Board.

1943: James M. Skinner, for his work as Vice President and Chairman of the Industry and Finance Committee of the United War Chest Campaign.

1944: William Draper Lewis, lawyer, editor, and Dean of the University of Pennsylvania's School of Law, for his work as Director of the American Law Institute, which educated the legal profession.

1945: Owen J. Roberts, U.S. Supreme Court Justice and early champion of strong world government, who had served as a prosecutor in the Teapot Dome scandal and as an investigator into the responsibility for the disaster at Pearl Harbor.

1946: Marjorie Penney and Maurice B. Fagan, Executive Director and Founder of Fellowship House and Director of the Philadelphia Fellowship Commission, for providing local training for community crisis management.

1947: Samuel S. Fels, for endowing a planetarium at the Franklin Institute as well as research into the study of physical and personality development, gastric ulcers, infantile paralysis, pneumonia, science, education, and sociology.

1948: No award

1949: Frederick H. Allen, child psychiatrist, for work as Director of Child Guidance Clinic.

1950: Fiske Kimball, director of the Philadelphia Museum of Art, particularly for the acquisition of the Arensberg Collection of pre-Columbian and modern art.

1951: Franklin H. Price, for forging the Free Library of Philadelphia into the third largest in the nation, with (among other achievements) a telephone-reference service and a vast collection of books in Braille.

1952: Francis Bosworth, Executive Director of Friends Neighborhood Guild, for developing a plan to help 32,000 Philadelphians from 44 different ethnic groups in lower North Philadelphia to rehabilitate their homes.

1953: George Wharton Pepper, U.S. Senator, lawyer, educator, and author, "for outstanding service to his fellow man."

1954: Esmond R. Long, Director of the Henry Phipps Institute for the Study, Treatment and Prevention of Tuberculosis, University of Pennsylvania, under whose guidance early detection of the disease became possible.

1955: Joseph S. Clark, Jr., Mayor and U.S. Senator, "for his leadership in the drive for reform in city government" and for his work with downtown revitalization.

1956: Isidor S. Ravdin, world-renowned surgeon, Hospital of the University of Pennsylvania.

1957: Catherine Drinker Bowen, writer of best-selling biographies.

1958: Helen C. Bailey, the second woman to serve as Assistant Superintendent of the Philadelphia Public School System.

1959: Harry A. Batten, co-founder of the Greater Philadelphia Movement, which led a drive to reform city government by obtaining a new City Charter in 1951.

1960: Allston Jenkins, President of Philadelphia Conservationists, Inc., for acquiring and preserving the 1200-acre Tinicum Wildlife Preserve in Southwest Philadelphia.

1961: Edwin O. Lewis, prime mover in the development of Independence Mall and Independence National Historical Park.

1962: George W. Taylor, veteran labor arbitrator who gained national fame for settling the bloody strike at Philadelphia's Aberle Hosiery Mill.

1963: John H. Gibbon, Jr., Jefferson Medical College surgeon who invented the heart-lung machine.

1964: Gaylord P. Harnwell, President of the University of Pennsylvania, for inspiring the creation of the University City Science Center and the Science Institute.

1965: Rev. Leon H. Sullivan, Pastor of the Zion Baptist Church and founder of the Opportunities Industrialization Center, which helped those without job skills gain economic independence.

1966: Lessing J. Rosenwald, art collector and public benefactor, who established the Alverthorpe Gallery in Jenkintown, expanded the Rare Book Department of the Free Library, and developed the Print and Drawing Department of the Art Museum.

1967: Richardson Dilworth, former Mayor of Philadelphia, for his "intensely spirited public service, particularly his work as Head of the School Board."

1968: Marcus Albert Foster, principal of Simon Gratz High School, "for transforming the school from one of the city's academically poorest into one of its most effective and dynamic."

1969: Eugene Ormandy, for "bringing to culmination the acknowledged worldwide pre-eminence of the Philadelphia Orchestra."

1970: Louis I. Kahn, architect and University of Pennsylvania Professor of Architecture.

1971: Franklin C. Watkins, for his painting of the human figure and for his contributions to art education at the Pennsylvania Academy of Fine Arts.

1972: John W. Mauchly and J. Presper Eckert, for developing the first all-electronic digital computer at the University of Pennsylvania's Moore School of Electrical Engineering.

1973: Ruth Patrick, the first scientist to develop a comprehensive method of measuring the ecological health of rivers and streams.

1974: William Henry Hastie, President Judge of the U.S. Third Circuit Court of Appeals, for his work in civil rights, including winning (with Thurgood Marshall) a Supreme Court decision that struck down segregation in interstate passenger transportation.

1975: Eight individuals were recognized for their distinguished service to young people:
- Robert W. Crawford, Philadelphia Commissioner of Recreation and President of the Fairmount Park Commission.
- Perry C. Fennell, Jr., a dentist who founded Interested Negroes Inc., which provided career counseling to junior high school students.
- Rev. Melvin Floyd, founder of Neighborhood Crusades Inc., which sought to help reduce gang violence.

- John C. Haas, Chairman of the Board of Rohm and Haas Co. and Chairman of the Board of the Boys Club of Metropolitan Philadelphia.
- Ruth W. Hayre, former District Superintendent of School District 4 in North and West Philadelphia.
- Floyd L. Logan, founder and Executive Director of the Educational Equality League, a civil rights organization.
- Sol Schoenbach, Director of Settlement Music School.
- Irving W. Shandler, President of the Diagnostic and Rehabilitation Center, which treated drug and alcohol addicts and developed preventive programs.

1976: Jonathan E. Rhoads, Professor of Surgery at the University of Pennsylvania.

1977: R. Stewart Rauch, Jr., the driving force behind the development of the Urban Coalition.

1978: Michael J. Sherman and Stephen Shutt, teachers at Vaux Junior High School and Douglass Elementary School, who coached their student championship chess teams.

1979: Robert Austrian, Professor and Chairman of the Department of Research Medicine at the University of Pennsylvania, for development of a pneumonia vaccine for the elderly.

1980: William M. Sample, the police officer whose Sunshine Foundation raised funds to fulfill the dreams of critically ill youngsters.

1981: Edwin Wolf, 2nd, librarian of the Library Company of Philadelphia, for rejuvenating America's oldest cultural institution.

1982: Carolyn L. Johnson, founder and Executive Director of the Adoption Center of Delaware Valley (now the National Adoption Center), for placing children with special needs into permanent family environments.

1983: Edmund N. Bacon, for his long and celebrated tenure as Executive Director of the Philadelphia Planning Commission.

1984: Jennifer A. Allcock, Executive Director and Medical Director of Covenant House Health Services, which provided outpatient and social services regardless of financial status.

1985: Rev. Paul M. Washington, Pastor of the Church of the Advocate, who made the entire city his ministry and became a focus for community activists seeking to better the city.

1986: Willard G. Rouse III, developer of Liberty Place and civic leader whose work included the creation of the Freedom Award.

1987: Elaine Brown, founder of Singing City, "a multi-nation and multi-cultural chorus that combined musical excellence with the goal of improving human conditions."

1988: G. Stockton Strawbridge, in recognition of his civic contributions, including his efforts on behalf of Market Street East.

1989: Hilary Koprowski, virologist and longtime Director of the Wistar Institute.

1990: Herman Mattelman, President of the Board of Education of the School District of Philadelphia credited with helping create a more positive perception of the School District.

1991: Sister Mary Scullion, leader and advocate for the homeless and mentally ill.

1992: Robert Venturi and Denise Scott Brown, architects and theorists of Manayunk, for introducing history into modern architecture. ∎

CITIZENS' MANUAL

The Philadelphia Award's Board of Directors, which reviews nominees near year's end to select a winner, encourages nominations from the public. Write to the Board of Directors, The Philadelphia Award, 239 Arch Street, Philadelphia, PA 19106. The award is presented each May and carries a $20,000 cash prize.

The Liberty Bell's Old Testament inscription, Leviticus (25:10), is part of God's detailed instruction to Moses (while still in the desert) for the conduct of the free life in Israel. The 50th anniversary was to be a jubilee of freedom. "Ye shall return every man unto his possession, and ye shall return every man unto his family."

After the British victory at Brandywine in September 1777, Congress ordered the city's bells removed to prevent their possible conversion to enemy cannons. Bells were removed from the city's steeples, and one day before the British marched into Philadelphia, a wagon train hauled 23 bells to Allentown, where they wintered beneath the floor of Zion High Reformed Church.

U.S. officials anticipated 45 million visitors to Philadelphia for the Bicentennial of the Declaration of Independence in 1976. Officials expected the huge number of visitors would wear out Independence Hall and tax the city's waste water treatment facilities. The bell was relocated to a new pavilion for the event, and Water Commissioner Guarino pronounced the city ready for anything.

Bells

Silent Symbol

I t's more billboard than bell. And the cast message— "Proclaim liberty throughout all the land to all the inhabitants thereof"—commemorated the 50th anniversary of William Penn's Charter of Privileges to settlers. If the bell was thought of at all in July 1776, it was thought of for its unpleasant tone and the dangerously rickety tower in which it hung, just away from the public's eyes and ears.

In another generation, its verse would appeal to abolitionists who adopted the bell as an icon of freedom. This poignant, ironic repackaging proved effective. To this day, the Liberty Bell speaks to 1.5 million annual visitors.

The bell arrived from England late in 1752 and cracked at its very first ringing. John Pass and John Stow offered to recast it at their Second Street foundry. They added copper, hoping for a less brittle bell; but the copper soured the new bell's tone. Back at the forge, they added some silver, aiming for sweetness. A third, somewhat brittle, and still slightly sour bell—but hardly as bad as before—finally went to work.

From mid-1753 to at least 1775, the bell summoned to session members of the Pennsylvania Assembly. Latecomers were fined a shilling. But rot in the tower soon presented the Assembly with a curious challenge: collect shillings and risk collapse, or forgo them and meet in safety. Future calls were silent. So too, apparently, was the proclamation for which the bell seemed destined. It's possible that at the signing of the Declaration of Independence, the bell stood mute— more witness than celebrant.

What caused the bell's famous crack remains a mystery. Quite possibly, every subsequent use—at the triumphal return of the Marquis de Lafayette in September 1824, George Washington's birthday in 1832, the death of Supreme Court Chief Justice John Marshall in 1835—contributed to the bell's demise. Every time an occasion seemed suitable, the failing bell was called upon. The worse the crack grew, the more noble and melodramatic (and possibly pathetic) the sound. Finally, in 1846, when City Council wanted the bell rung for Washington's birthday, William Eckel drilled out and "repaired" its crack, creating the crooked line we know today. Eckel's work also rendered the bell useless, although he did sweep up the filings to made a miniature, souvenir bell.

The contrast between silence and function, crack and inscription, made the bell an icon, a shrine, talisman, and national symbol. All at once, it speaks of the city's founder, the nation's liberators, our continuing ideals, and the constant challenge to keep liberty both real and meaningful. ∎

❖ Philadelphian Samuel Wetherill first began manufacturing white lead in 1789 for use in paint.

Bells

A Bell Well Traveled

August 1752: Arrives in Philadelphia from Whitechapel foundry in England.

September 1777: Escapes capture by British army. Taken to Allentown and hidden beneath the floor of Zion High Reformed Church.

June 1778: Returns to the State House.

January 1885: Travels on special railroad flatcar to World's Industrial and Cotton Centennial Exposition in New Orleans. Crowds cheer the bell at 13 stops.

April 1893: Leaves via Broad Street station for summer-long stay at World's Columbian Exposition in Chicago. John Philip Sousa composes "The Liberty Bell March" in its honor.

October 1895: Is sent to Atlanta for the Cotton State and International Exposition. Despite objections that the bell is too fragile to travel, it makes 40 stops on its way.

January 1902: Off to Charleston, South Carolina, for the Carolina Inter-State and West Indian Exposition.

June 1903: To Charlestown, Massachusetts, for the 128th anniversary of the Battle of Bunker Hill, making 49 stops, each approximately 10 minutes.

June 1904: Encouraged by petition signed by 75,000 St. Louis schoolchildren, City Council votes to send the bell to the Louisiana Purchase Exposition. Its train makes scores of stops along the way to the fair's Pennsylvania state building, where the bell stands draped in the flag.

October 1908: Mounted on a float and paraded around Philadelphia during the 225th anniversary of the city's founding.

July 1915: Most extensive tour to date. A special train carries the bell to residents of 16 states during its 11-day trip to the Panama-Pacific International Exposition in San Francisco.

November 1915: From the San Francisco exposition, on to San Diego for several days at their Panama-California Exposition. Enthusiastically greeted in 13 more states on the return trip to Philadelphia.

January 1, 1976: After a hiatus of 60 years, the bell moves from Independence Hall to a special pavilion on Independence Mall. ∎

WHEN THEY HEARD IT

April 15, 1783: Ratification of the Treaty of Paris ending the Revolutionary War and marking the start of a recognized United States

July 13, 1783: Triumphant return of George Washington

August 1784: First visit by the Marquis de Lafayette

September 18, 1787: Benjamin Franklin's presentation of the proposed Constitution to the Pennsylvania Assembly

December 6, 1790: Assembly of the first U.S. Congress

December 1799: Death of George Washington

...AND A TOUCH OF ARSENIC

Circumference around lip: 12 feet

Circumference around crown: 6 feet, 11¼ inches

Lip to crown: 3 feet

Height over crown: 2 feet, 3 inches

Thickness at lip: 3 inches

Thickness at crown: 1¼ inches

Weight: 2,080 pounds

Length of clapper: 3 feet, 2 inches

Weight of clapper: 44½ pounds

Weight of yoke: 200 pounds

Composition of yoke: American elm

Composition of bell: 65% copper; 25% tin; 3% lead; 1% zinc; and traces of gold, silver, antimony, iron, and arsenic

15

Migrating birds return to the Philadelphia area in this general order:

Late February: robin, bluebird

March: purple grackle, meadowlark, mourning dove, red-winged blackbird, flicker, cowbird, phoebe, field sparrow

April: chipping sparrow, purple martin, ruby-crowned kinglet, tree and barn swallow, hermit thrush, black-crowned night heron, myrtle warbler, towhee (some of these last four remain all winter), chimney swift, house wren, spotted sandpiper, green heron, brown thrasher, black and white warbler

May: Maryland yellowthroat, yellow warbler, whippoorwill, ovenbird, catbird, wood thrush, redstart, crested flycatcher, Baltimore oriole, kingbird, Kentucky warbler, scarlet tanager, bobolink, yellow-breasted chat, red-eyed vireo, rose-breasted grosbeak, blue-winged warbler, yellow-billed cuckoo, black-billed cuckoo, veery, nighthawk, indigo nunting, wood pewee, ruby-throated hummingbird, black-poll warbler

Source: The Academy of Natural Sciences.

FURTHER READING

• Allen, Thomas B., et al. *Field Guide to the Birds of North America.* Washington, D.C.: National Geographic Society, 1983.

• Bull, John and John Farrand. *The Audubon Society Field Guide to North American Birds, Eastern Region.* New York: Alfred A. Knopf, 1977.

• Harding, John J. and Justin J. Harding. *Birding the Delaware Valley Region.* Philadelphia: Temple University Press, 1980.

• Peterson, Roger Tory. *A Field Guide to the Birds East of the Rockies.* New York: Houghton Mifflin, 1980.

• Robbins, Chandler S., et al. *Birds of North America.* New York: Golden Press, 1983.

Birds

Landscaping for Looking

Even before Charles Willson Peale displayed his stuffed birds on the second floor of Independence Hall, Philadelphia was big on ornithology. Birdwatchers organized in 1890 to form the Delaware Valley Ornithological Club, one of the oldest birding clubs in the United States (for information, write to the Club c/o Academy of Natural Sciences, 19th Street and the Parkway, Philadelphia, PA 19103-1195). Many townships in the area also offer Audubon chapter meetings and events.

For birders of a more scientific bent, the Academy of Natural Sciences houses a collection of 150,000 specimens, including all of the bird species found in North America and most of those found elsewhere. The collection is available by appointment to anyone wishing to view it, and staff members can aid you in identifying difficult species.

Also housed at the Academy is VIREO, or Visual Resources for Ornithology—the world's largest collection of bird photographs. More than half of the bird species in the world are represented in VIREO's slides, which are available for purchase or examination, by appointment. These images are frequently used by birders, bird clubs, artists, educators, publishers, and television producers for identification and portrayal of both common and exotic species.

Close to 400 species have been recorded in the Philadelphia area, and many are found in the city. Suitable habitats and food sources will make these species welcome in your garden. The plants listed below grow well in this area and are attractive to birds as well as people.

Flowers: bee balm or Monarda (red is best), Impatiens, petunias, tall Phlox, common evening primrose, sunflowers

Shrubs: bayberry (male and female needed), bearberry, blueberry, Cotoneaster, American elder, Mahonias, autumn olive, privet, Pyracantha, meadow rose, multiflora rose, rugosa rose, serviceberry, shadbush, sumac, Viburnum, Virginia rose, winterberry, wintergreen

Trees: arborvitae, Korean mountain ash, sweet or cherry birch, river birch, Chamaecyparis, flowering crabapples, tart or pie cherry, pagoda or algernate-leafed dogwood, kousa dogwood, cornelian cherry dogwood, Douglas fir, fringe tree (male and female needed), hawthorne, holly (male and female needed), juniper, oak, Austrian pine, Japanese black pine, white pine, spruce

Vines: bittersweet (male and female needed), Boston creeper, Virginia creeper, grape, honeysuckle (red is best), porcelain berry, trumpet vine ∎

Industrial Philadelphia— Sixty Years Ago

I t's been said over and over: Philadelphia now has a service-based economy. What was one of the leading manufacturing cities in the world now depends on the economic strength of businesses that provide services—medical, legal, financial, retail, entertainment, educational, cultural, hospitable, comestible—and on the much-improved convention business.

Statistics tell the story. In 1937, nearly 293,000 people worked in the city's industries; in 1987, that figure had dropped to approximately 99,000 industrial workers; and in 1993, manufacturing accounted for only 66,100 of the city's total 674,500 jobs, according to the Bureau of Labor Statistics.

If you could tour industrial Philadelphia in its manufacturing heyday, what would you see? Such a tour was conjured up in the depths of the Great Depression by the Federal Writers' Project, funded by the Works Progress Administration (WPA). From the remarkable 1937 *WPA Guide to Philadelphia*, here are sketches and scenes from tour number nine, "Through Industrial Philadelphia":

"Today, the only forests are factory chimneys of steel, brick and cement, and the gloom of smoky streets replaces the dim wilderness trail. Most of the city's vast industry is concentrated in Frankford and Kensington, although no section of Philadelphia is without its variety of industrial establishments, sprouting up in the midst of residential or mercantile areas. ...

"At Montgomery Avenue...[at 4th Street] are the several brick buildings of the *John B. Stetson Plant.* ...John B. Stetson made a better hat, the world beat a path to his door...this location today is one of the world's largest hat-producing factories, with an annual output of more than three million hats...the Stetson plants extend over six acres of land and contain 30 acres of floor space. In busy times employees number 2,500 men and 1,000 women. ...Stetson preferred to manufacture everything that went into his hats as well as the hats themselves. He controlled his raw supplies, made his own blocks, ribbons, and boxes. His name stands for hat. ...

"Nine squares north of the Stetson plant, cutting through the heart of Kensington, at A Street and extending to B [on Lehigh Avenue] is one of the largest centers for the manufacture of rugs, lace and lace curtains

THE TEN OLDEST SURVIVING PHILADELPHIA-AREA BUSINESSES

They've merged, acquired, and been acquired. They've changed addresses but kept their names. They've been around for at least 200 years and can therefore claim the rarified title, Oldest Surviving Philadelphia-Area Businesses.

Great Valley Mills, RD 3, Box 1111, Barto, PA 19504. Mail-order stoneground mixes and Pennsylvania Dutch foods. Founded in 1710 by Thomas Jerman.

Covenant Life Insurance Company, 1050 Westlakes Drive, Berwyn, PA 19312. Life insurance; formerly Presbyterian Ministers' Fund. Founded in 1717 by the Synod of Philadelphia.

The Rowland Company, 4900 N. 20th Street, Philadelphia, PA 19144. Now dealing in heavy-duty power transmission products and industrial equipment. Founded in 1731 by Benjamin Rowland.

Philadelphia Contributionship for the Insurance of Houses from Loss by Fire, 212 S. 4th Street, Philadelphia, PA 19106. Homeowners and fire insurance. Founded in 1752 by Benjamin Franklin and others.

Kirk & Nice Inc., 6301 Germantown Avenue, Philadelphia, PA 19144. Funeral directors. Founded in 1761 by Jacob Knorr.

Barnett Laundry & Dry Cleaning Supply Co. Inc., 9275 Commerce Highway, Pennsauken, NJ 08110. Institutional laundry supplier. Founded in 1780 by Ben, Cellers, and William Barnett.

CoreStates First Pennsylvania Bank (First Pennsylvania Bank Corporation), Philadelphia, PA 19101. Financial institution. Founded in 1782 by Robert Morris and acquired by CoreStates Financial Corporation in 1990.

Rawle & Henderson, One South Penn Square, Philadelphia, PA 19107. General practice of law. Founded in 1783 by William Rawle.

Mutual Assurance Company / The Green Tree Group, 414 Walnut Street, Philadelphia PA 19107. Homeowners insurance. Founded in 1784.

Lea & Febiger, 200 Chester Field Parkway, Malvern, PA 19355. Publishers of books in the health sciences. Founded in 1785 by Mathew Carey.

CITIZENS' MANUAL

HAGLEY MUSEUM AND LIBRARY

The sights and sounds of John Bromley's century-old looms at the Quaker Lace Company are gone. The heart of North Philadelphia's grand old textile industry disappeared in 1993—auctioned off to the highest bidder, or scrapped. But in the archives of the Hagley Museum and Library, an educational institution near Wilmington, Delaware, the history of Quaker Lace, and of many other companies, can still be imagined.

Photographs of the Quaker Lace factory, documents and papers, film of workers running the looms, and samples of the vintage lace products are all at Hagley, which specializes in documenting and preserving the history of American business and technology. And while Hagley's main strength is in the Middle Atlantic region, its archival business collection includes over 1,000 firms with national and international impact: the Du Pont Company, Philadelphia and Reading Railroad, the Sun Company, Bethlehem Steel, Philadelphia National Bank, Pennsylvania Power and Light Company.

Hagley's manuscript collections often contain the personal papers of the entrepreneurs who helped create these businesses. The research library was founded in 1953 by Pierre S. du Pont as the Longwood Library, primarily for the collection of the Du Pont Company and family archives. Eight years later it merged with the Hagley Museum and moved to the site of the original Du Pont Company powder works.

Research collections are open to the public. The library is open Monday–Friday 8:30am–4:30pm and the second Saturday of every month. Appointments are required for researchers. For more information, call (302) 658-2400.

❖

The Franklin Printing Company, founded in 1728 by Benjamin Franklin, closed in 1993.

Business

in the country—the *Mill of John Bromley & Sons, Inc.* Founded in 1863, it now covers an entire city block and rises to a height of five stories. ...Seventy-five looms are used in the manufacture of lace and lace curtains. Artists make all the designs, creating various patterns for this department. Products are graded according to weave, the quality of the materials being the same...the weaving of rugs and carpets is done on 30 broad looms and 20 narrow looms. The wool used is purchased in the chief wool-raising centers of the world. The cleaning, mixing and combing of the wool, and its transformation into yarn are all done in the mill. There are facilities for dyeing the yarns, and artists make all the designs and number the various yarn colors that are to be used. The rugs and carpets produced here are of many dimensions, but of only two types: Axminster and broadloom...the plant employs approximately 800 workers.

"At Milnor Street [in Tacony] is *Henry Disston & Sons, Inc., Plant*...today the plant is the largest saw works in the world, employing 2,600 workers in 68 buildings that cover 65 acres. ...The simple handsaw involves more than 80 progressive operations. Steel is made in the company's steel mill using the latest electric furnaces, steam hammers and rolling mills; there are also pyrometers that control furnace heat, testing apparatus, chemical and physical laboratories. ...'Smithing-in-the-black'—the skillful hammering of the saw blade to straighten and flatten it—requires the highest development of the new maker's skill. In a room 430 feet long, where the operation is performed, the line of men fades away in the distance, while the rhythmical tapping of their hammers sounds like the regular vibrations of some gigantic machine. A man lifts a blade, sights along it toward the light to learn from the shadows on the blade just where the hammer should fall. The wavering nature of artificial light makes daylight essential for this kind of work. ..."

Of the 10 industries covered in the WPA's Industrial Tour, none exists today. Stetson closed in 1971. Bromley, later called the Quaker Lace Company, shut down its looms in 1985, though it continued to bleach, dye, and treat lace at its huge mill in North Philadelphia until the company filed for Chapter 11 bankruptcy in November 1993. The last vestiges of this industrial jewel, including some of its looms, were sold at auction in 1993. And Disston gradually shifted its operations out of the city during the 1950s. ∎

Source: The WPA Guide to Philadelphia (University of Pennsylvania Press, 1988; originally published in 1937 as *Philadelphia: A Guide to the Nation's Birthplace).*

From Chestnut Street to Cherry Hill

I t was the early 1960s, and a powerful new vision of the American dream was nearly complete. The boom of middle-income housing just beyond the major cities provided that popular American icon and emblem of success: the suburban, domestic retreat. The mature American automobile, powerful and extravagant, roared for change and propelled development in sprawling new patterns. Those patterns defied the tight, traditional grid of Philadelphia, which flexed from pedestrians to public transportation—but could flex no more. The new highways of the Eisenhower administration provided crucial links between work and home. Grime and crime were left behind, but so was the bustling, unrivaled downtown shopping district. Suburban strip shopping centers simply could not match the experience offered by the shop-lined streets of the city.

The new suburbanites did not have long to wait before a few retailing innovators saw a ripe business opportunity in those new, spiraling subdivisions. A fully enclosed, climate-controlled shopping mall made its East Coast debut in 1961 with the mall at Cherry Hill.

Despite the sameness and mediocrity of today's malls, Cherry Hill was a daring, innovative leap. The brainchild of developers The Rouse Company and Strawbridge & Clothier, designed by architect Victor Gruen, Cherry Hill Mall was an approach to shopping that matched the new way of living. It catered to the car-bound citizen, to the latest rise in consumerism, to the new American homogeneity, and to the demand for whatever was fast and clean. Cherry Hill suited the suburbs.

Cherry Hill's design set it apart from old-style street shopping. Wide corridors provided more space than you'd find on Chestnut Street; the main atrium sported a tropical paradise with plants that, in a city, car exhaust would have quickly killed—but cars, which enabled this commercial Shangri-La, were conveniently lined up on nearby asphalt fields. Storefronts were erased to leave enormous, welcoming entrances, with displays generously spilling out onto the public corridor. Shoppers would drift into a store before they knew they had, much as they would move about in a giant, climate-controlled department store.

In the thirty years since the invention of the mall, the design has been amended and, most recently, completely overhauled. And though Cherry Hill Mall may no longer be the largest, flashiest, or toniest in the region, the precedents it set have directed the course of the region's retailing. ∎

OTHER BUSINESS FIRSTS

In 1739, Plunket Fleeson of Philadelphia stamped a design on paper, joined the sheets together, and painted them; he called the innovation wallpaper.

In 1757, Benjamin Franklin started the first street-cleaning service, "to be paid by each house."

In 1761, the first American venetian blinds were reportedly installed in St. Peter's Church, 3rd and Pine Streets.

On March 11, 1791, an enterprising Philadelphian named Samuel Mulliken received four patents for machines that threshed grain, broke hemp, cut and polished marble, and raised the nap on cloth.

In 1795, Sarah Waldrake and Rachael Summers became the first women employees of the federal government. For 50 cents a day they weighed gold coins at the U.S. Mint.

In 1816, George E. Clymer of Philadelphia introduced the first printing press of a new design to be made in the United States.

In 1816, the Philadelphia Saving Fund Society became the first such institution to receive money on deposit.

In 1825, in a factory at 6th and Chestnut Streets, William Ellis Tucker produced the nation's first successful hard porcelain.

In 1838, William S. Otis of Philadelphia invented the steam shovel to construct railroad roadbeds.

On March 30, 1858, the first pencil with an eraser attached was invented by Philadelphian Hyman L. Lipman.

On March 23, 1858, the first cable car, driven by an underground cable in a tunnel beneath the tracks, was patented by Philadelphian Eleazer A. Gardner.

In 1867, plate glass insurance was first written by the United States Plate Glass Insurance Company of Philadelphia.

On January 21, 1888, long-lasting typewriter "copy" ribbon was patented by Jacob L. Wortman of Philadelphia.

In 1893, the first "self-healing" bicycle tire was made by the B. F. Goodrich Company and exhibited at the 1893 Philadelphia Cycle Show.

January 1994

There are three things
extremely hard: steel, a diamond,
and to know one's self.

—Benjamin Franklin, January 1750

		Rises	Sets
1	Saturday	7:22	4:46
2	Sunday	7:22	4:47
3	Monday	7:22	4:47
4	Tuesday	7:22	4:48
5	Wednesday	7:22	4:49
6	Thursday	7:22	4:50
7	Friday	7:22	4:51
8	Saturday	7:22	4:52
9	Sunday	7:22	4:53
10	Monday	7:21	4:54
11	Tuesday	7:21	4:55
12	Wednesday	7:21	4:56
13	Thursday	7:21	4:57
14	Friday	7:20	4:58
15	Saturday	7:20	4:59
16	Sunday	7:20	5:01
17	Monday	7:19	5:02
18	Tuesday	7:19	5:03
19	Wednesday	7:18	5:04
20	Thursday	7:18	5:05
21	Friday	7:17	5:06
22	Saturday	7:16	5:07
23	Sunday	7:16	5:09
24	Monday	7:15	5:10
25	Tuesday	7:14	5:11
26	Wednesday	7:14	5:12
27	Thursday	7:13	5:13
28	Friday	7:12	5:14
29	Saturday	7:11	5:16
30	Sunday	7:10	5:17
31	Monday	7:09	5:18

The coldest month of the year. In 1984, all 31 days averaged below freezing.

January 22–24, 1935 The strongest January winter storm in Philadelphia weather record history; 16.7 inches of snow covered the ground.

January 25, 1958 A wind gust of 61 miles per hour whistled through the bare winter trees and became the record wind for the month.

Last Quarter	4th
New Moon	11th
First Quarter	19th
Full Moon	27th

February 1994

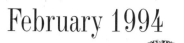

		Rises	Sets
1	Tuesday	7:09	5:19
2	Wednesday	7:08	5:20
3	Thursday	7:07	5:22
4	Friday	7:06	5:23
5	Saturday	7:05	5:24
6	Sunday	7:04	5:25
7	Monday	7:02	5:26
8	Tuesday	7:01	5:28
9	Wednesday	7:00	5:29
10	Thursday	6:59	5:30
11	Friday	6:58	5:31
12	Saturday	6:57	5:32
13	Sunday	6:55	5:34
14	Monday	6:54	5:35
15	Tuesday	6:53	5:36
16	Wednesday	6:52	5:37
17	Thursday	6:50	5:38
18	Friday	6:49	5:39
19	Saturday	6:48	5:41
20	Sunday	6:46	5:42
21	Monday	6:45	5:43
22	Tuesday	6:44	5:44
23	Wednesday	6:42	5:45
24	Thursday	6:41	5:46
25	Friday	6:39	5:47
26	Saturday	6:38	5:49
27	Sunday	6:37	5:50
28	Monday	6:35	5:51

*Don't after foreign food
and clothing roam,
But learn to eat
and wear what's raised at home.*

—Benjamin Franklin, February 1748

The last month of winter. Signs of spring are soon to be found.

February 2 The world celebrates International Meteorological Day. Top-hatted Punxitawnians stimulate a hibernating rodent to learn a long-range weather forecast—even though cloudiness early in the month has never been shown to correlate with the temperatures of the next six weeks.

February 11–12, 1983 The single heaviest snowfall ever recorded strikes Philadelphia. Snow shovel sales soar after the 21.3-inch accumulation.

February 13, 1899 The greatest accumulated snow depth on the ground is recorded at 26 inches. There must be something in the mid-month air.

February 14 The average high temperature is 41° F and the average low is 25° F. Candy is dandy, but wool is warmer.

February 28 The average daytime high is 50° F, 11 degrees higher than the February 1 average high of 39° F.

Last Quarter	3d
New Moon	10th
First Quarter	18th
Full Moon	25th

March 1994

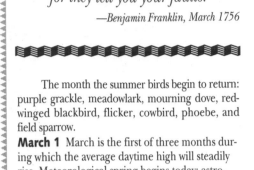

		Rises	Sets
1	Tuesday	6:34	5:52
2	Wednesday	6:32	5:53
3	Thursday	6:31	5:54
4	Friday	6:29	5:55
5	Saturday	6:28	5:56
6	Sunday	6:26	5:57
7	Monday	6:24	5:58
8	Tuesday	6:23	5:59
9	Wednesday	6:21	6:00
10	Thursday	6:20	6:02
11	Friday	6:18	6:03
12	Saturday	6:17	6:04
13	Sunday	6:15	6:05
14	Monday	6:13	6:06
15	Tuesday	6:12	6:07
16	Wednesday	6:10	6:08
17	Thursday	6:09	6:09
18	Friday	6:07	6:10
19	Saturday	6:05	6:11
20	Sunday	6:04	6:12
21	Monday	6:02	6:13
22	Tuesday	6:01	6:14
23	Wednesday	5:59	6:15
24	Thursday	5:57	6:16
25	Friday	5:56	6:17
26	Saturday	5:54	6:18
27	Sunday	5:52	6:19
28	Monday	5:51	6:20
29	Tuesday	5:49	6:21
30	Wednesday	5:48	6:22
31	Thursday	5:46	6:23

The month the summer birds begin to return: purple grackle, meadowlark, mourning dove, red-winged blackbird, flicker, cowbird, phoebe, and field sparrow.

March 1 March is the first of three months during which the average daytime high will steadily rise. Meteorological spring begins today; astronomical spring arrives 20 days later.

March 3 Woodcocks begin their courtship dances in the fading light of dusk. The male "timberdoodle" is famous for its 200-foot freefall during the final stages of its attempt to attract a female.

March 11–12, 1881 The Blizzard of 1881 deposited 10.5 inches of snow, establishing the standard for spring storms.

March 12, 1888 March's strongest wind, a gust of 60 miles per hour, was measured on this date during the Blizzard of 1888.

March 13, 1993 The Blizzard of 1993 was not the "Storm of the Century," but it did set a number of March weather records, including the lowest barometric pressure (28.43 inches) and a new snow/sleet record (11.7 inches).

March 20 3:29pm marks the arrival of the vernal equinox—spring in the Northern Hemisphere. With the sun appearing to be directly overhead at the Equator, daylight and darkness are equally divided.

March 22 Earth Day. Philadelphia's first celebration, on a warm sunny day in 1970, was held on Fairmount Park's Belmont Plateau.

March 29, 1945 The warmest day in March reached a daytime high temperature of 87° F.

Last Quarter	4th
New Moon	12th
First Quarter	20th
Full Moon	27th

April 1994

		Rises	Sets
1	Friday	5:44	6:24
2	Saturday	5:43	6:25
3	Sunday	6:41*	7:26*
4	Monday	6:40	7:27
5	Tuesday	6:38	7:28
6	Wednesday	6:36	7:29
7	Thursday	6:35	7:30
8	Friday	6:33	7:31
9	Saturday	6:32	7:32
10	Sunday	6:30	7:33
11	Monday	6:29	7:34
12	Tuesday	6:27	7:35
13	Wednesday	6:26	7:36
14	Thursday	6:24	7:37
15	Friday	6:23	7:38
16	Saturday	6:21	7:39
17	Sunday	6:20	7:40
18	Monday	6:18	7:41
19	Tuesday	6:17	7:42
20	Wednesday	6:15	7:43
21	Thursday	6:14	7:44
22	Friday	6:12	7:45
23	Saturday	6:11	7:46
24	Sunday	6:10	7:47
25	Monday	6:08	7:48
26	Tuesday	6:07	7:49
27	Wednesday	6:06	7:50
28	Thursday	6:04	7:51
29	Friday	6:03	7:52
30	Saturday	6:02	7:53

Eastern Standard Time to Daylight Savings Time

He that can compose himself is wiser than he that composes books.

—*Benjamin Franklin, April 1737*

In 1823, Scottish chemist Charles Macintosh bound two layers of fabric with a solution of naphtha and rubber to invent the raincoat. They were later called slickers and rain skins, but small children still won't wear mackintoshes and galoshes.

April 1 April showers may bring May flowers, but the month is actually drier than March, which averages 3.86 inches of rainfall compared to April's 3.47 inches. The wettest April on record was 1874, when 9.78 inches filled the rain gauges of Philadelphia weather watchers.

April 3–4, 1915 The heaviest snowfall ever recorded in April, 19.4 inches, dwarfed the monthly average of .3 inch.

April 3–4, 1974 On this date the largest known outbreak of tornadoes within a 24-hour period, 148, hits the Midwest, killing 315 people. April has fewer tornadoes than May, but April tornadoes take more lives because they tend to be more severe.

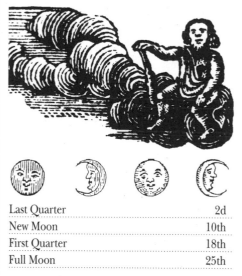

Last Quarter	2d
New Moon	10th
First Quarter	18th
Full Moon	25th

May 1994

Blessed is he that expects nothing, for he shall never be disappointed.

—*Benjamin Franklin, May 1739*

		Rises	Sets
1	Sunday	6:00	7:54
2	Monday	5:59	7:55
3	Tuesday	5:58	7:56
4	Wednesday	5:57	7:57
5	Thursday	5:56	7:58
6	Friday	5:54	7:59
7	Saturday	5:53	8:00
8	Sunday	5:52	8:01
9	Monday	5:51	8:02
10	Tuesday	5:50	8:02
11	Wednesday	5:49	8:04
12	Thursday	5:48	8:05
13	Friday	5:47	8:06
14	Saturday	5:46	8:07
15	Sunday	5:45	8:08
16	Monday	5:44	8:09
17	Tuesday	5:43	8:10
18	Wednesday	5:42	8:11
19	Thursday	5:42	8:12
20	Friday	5:41	8:13
21	Saturday	5:40	8:14
22	Sunday	5:39	8:14
23	Monday	5:39	8:15
24	Tuesday	5:38	8:16
25	Wednesday	5:37	8:17
26	Thursday	5:37	8:18
27	Friday	5:36	8:19
28	Saturday	5:35	8:19
29	Sunday	5:35	8:20
30	Monday	5:34	8:21
31	Tuesday	5:34	8:22

The Greeks gave their god Iris credit for rainbows, but we know them as refracted sunlight passing through the curtain of raindrops at the back of a thunderstorm. May averages four thunderstorm days each year, and we credit May as rainbow month.

May 1 May Day. A high holy day in the Celtic religion, one of the few cultures that marked seasons by life events rather than movements of the sun and stars. The May Pole represents the tree of life, symbol of the spring renewal.

May 4 After today, the planet Mercury is transformed from the morning star to the evening star.

May 10–11 The great migration of warblers makes its way through Philadelphia, sending bird watchers into the woods to gaze up at these tiny, brilliantly colored star maps.

May 15 The woodland flowers are reaching their prime. Skunk cabbage, jack-in-the-pulpit, May apples, trout lilies, trillium, and solomon seal cover the woodland floor before the dark shade of late May closes out the sunshine until next October.

May 19 On Rogation Day, landowners walk property boundaries accompanied by the youngest child. When did you last walk your boundaries?

May 28–31 Our most unsettled weather of the year occurs now, and our annual tornado is likely to appear.

Last Quarter	2d
New Moon	10th
First Quarter	18th
Full Moon	24th

June 1994

		Rises	Sets
1	Wednesday	5:34	8:22
2	Thursday	5:33	8:23
3	Friday	5:33	8:24
4	Saturday	5:32	8:24
5	Sunday	5:32	8:25
6	Monday	5:32	8:26
7	Tuesday	5:32	8:26
8	Wednesday	5:31	8:27
9	Thursday	5:31	8:27
10	Friday	5:31	8:28
11	Saturday	5:31	8:29
12	Sunday	5:31	8:29
13	Monday	5:31	8:29
14	Tuesday	5:31	8:30
15	Wednesday	5:31	8:30
16	Thursday	5:31	8:31
17	Friday	5:31	8:31
18	Saturday	5:31	8:31
19	Sunday	5:31	8:32
20	Monday	5:31	8:32
21	Tuesday	5:32	8:32
22	Wednesday	5:32	8:32
23	Thursday	5:32	8:32
24	Friday	5:32	8:32
25	Saturday	5:33	8:33
26	Sunday	5:33	8:33
27	Monday	5:33	8:33
28	Tuesday	5:34	8:33
29	Wednesday	5:34	8:33
30	Thursday	5:35	8:33

At 20 years of age the will reigns; at 30 the wit; at 40 the judgment.

—Benjamin Franklin, June 1741

The month of the new generation of birds and the first month of meteorological summer (the year's three hottest months begin with June). Hurricane season begins on the first of June and ends November 30. Call the first hurricane Alberto.

June 11, 1958 The highest wind speed ever recorded in June reached 73 miles per hour from the Northwest. Leaves on trees frequently act like sails in summer windstorms and break off great branches. As it turns out, the autumn leaf fall is a valuable adaptation trees made millions of years ago.

June 21 The solstice at 10:49am marks the beginning of astronomical summer. This is the day the sun reaches its highest point in Philadelphia's sky, making your shadow the shortest of the year; 15 hours of sunlight makes it the longest day. The ancient spirits play in the dark shadows of the mid-summer's night.

Last Quarter	1st
New Moon	9th
First Quarter	16th
Full Moon	23d
Last Quarter	30th

July 1994

		Rises	Sets
1	Friday	5:35	8:32
2	Saturday	5:36	8:32
3	Sunday	5:36	8:32
4	Monday	5:37	8:32
5	Tuesday	5:37	8:32
6	Wednesday	5:38	8:31
7	Thursday	5:38	8:31
8	Friday	5:39	8:31
9	Saturday	5:40	8:31
10	Sunday	5:40	8:30
11	Monday	5:41	8:30
12	Tuesday	5:42	8:29
13	Wednesday	5:42	8:29
14	Thursday	5:43	8:28
15	Friday	5:44	8:28
16	Saturday	5:45	8:27
17	Sunday	5:45	8:26
18	Monday	5:46	8:26
19	Tuesday	5:47	8:25
20	Wednesday	5:48	8:24
21	Thursday	5:49	8:24
22	Friday	5:50	8:23
23	Saturday	5:50	8:22
24	Sunday	5:51	8:21
25	Monday	5:52	8:20
26	Tuesday	5:53	8:20
27	Wednesday	5:54	8:19
28	Thursday	5:55	8:18
29	Friday	5:56	8:17
30	Saturday	5:57	8:16
31	Sunday	5:57	8:15

The hottest month of the year. Look for insects and mammals at night.

July 4 The night, according to the Native Americans, of the Thunder Moon. The full moon of July is named for its growling, prowling thunderstorms.

July 10, 1936 The highest daytime temperature ever recorded in Philadelphia: 104°. No one dared to measure the humidity.

July 15 St. Swithin's Day. If rains this day, so it shall for the next forty; if it be fair, stock up on sunscreen. The good English saint wished to be buried outside Westminster Cathedral; when authorities tried to move his body indoors, the rains began and continued for the next forty days.

July 20, 1969 Neil Armstrong leaves the first human footsteps on our satellite—the moon. It rained in Philadelphia.

July 27–28, 1969 The wettest 24 hours in July, when 4.26 inches of rain opened the late summer fungus festival.

New Moon	8th
First Quarter	15th
Full Moon	22d
Last Quarter	30th

August 1994

*Old boys have their playthings
as well as young ones;
the difference is only in the price.*

—*Benjamin Franklin, August 1752*

		Rises	Sets
1	Monday	5:58	8:14
2	Tuesday	5:59	8:13
3	Wednesday	6:00	8:12
4	Thursday	6:01	8:10
5	Friday	6:02	8:09
6	Saturday	6:03	8:08
7	Sunday	6:04	8:07
8	Monday	6:05	8:06
9	Tuesday	6:06	8:04
10	Wednesday	6:07	8:03
11	Thursday	6:08	8:02
12	Friday	6:09	8:01
13	Saturday	6:10	7:59
14	Sunday	6:11	7:58
15	Monday	6:12	7:57
16	Tuesday	6:13	7:55
17	Wednesday	6:13	7:54
18	Thursday	6:15	7:51
19	Friday	6:16	7:50
20	Saturday	6:16	7:50
21	Sunday	6:17	7:48
22	Monday	6:18	7:47
23	Tuesday	6:19	7:45
24	Wednesday	6:20	7:44
25	Thursday	6:21	7:42
26	Friday	6:22	7:41
27	Saturday	6:23	7:39
28	Sunday	6:24	7:38
29	Monday	6:25	7:36
30	Tuesday	6:26	7:35
31	Wednesday	6:27	7:33

Early August is the peak of those hazy, lazy days of summer, or "dog days." The Romans named them for the "dog star" Sirius, the brightest star in the constellation Canis Major and all of the August nighttime sky.

August 1 Lammas Day, set aside to give thanks for the bounty of the earth—an earth day far more ancient than our history records, practiced by farmers.

August 4 The full Maize Moon marks the remarkable growth of corn in the humid days and nights of August.

August 15 The first of the southerly migrating blackbird flocks moves through Philadelphia. Autumn is in the air.

August 15–19 Our first cool air arrives, preceded by thunderstorms. Meteorological summer comes to an end.

August 25 Adult shorebirds migrating from the gathering Arctic autumn reach the coast of New Jersey. They left their young behind—to feed on food too sparse for both generations.

New Moon	7th
First Quarter	14th
Full Moon	21st
Last Quarter	29th

27

September 1994

		Rises	Sets
1	Thursday	6:28	7:32
2	Friday	6:29	7:30
3	Saturday	6:30	7:28
4	Sunday	6:30	7:27
5	Monday	6:31	7:25
6	Tuesday	6:32	7:24
7	Wednesday	6:33	7:22
8	Thursday	6:34	7:20
9	Friday	6:35	7:19
10	Saturday	6:36	7:17
11	Sunday	6:37	7:16
12	Monday	6:38	7:14
13	Tuesday	6:39	7:12
14	Wednesday	6:40	7:11
15	Thursday	6:41	7:09
16	Friday	6:42	7:07
17	Saturday	6:43	7:06
18	Sunday	6:44	7:04
19	Monday	6:45	7:02
20	Tuesday	6:46	7:01
21	Wednesday	6:46	6:59
22	Thursday	6:47	6:57
23	Friday	6:48	6:56
24	Saturday	6:49	6:54
25	Sunday	6:50	6:52
26	Monday	6:51	6:51
27	Tuesday	6:52	6:49
28	Wednesday	6:53	6:48
29	Thursday	6:54	6:46
30	Friday	6:55	6:44

We have lost three hours of daylight. Frost is a month away, though it is still warm.

September 2, 1881 The month's hottest day: 102°.

September 5 Jupiter labors to become the evening planet.

September 23 The first day of astronomical autumn, the autumnal equinox, sneaks up on us at 2:20am.

September 24–26 A series of coastal storms commences—the first to visit us since late May—beginning a period of wet, windy weather.

New Moon			5th
First Quarter			12th
Full Moon			19th
Last Quarter			27th

October 1994

What signifies your patience if you can't find it when you want it?

—*Benjamin Franklin, October 1747*

		Rises	Sets
1	Saturday	6:56	6:43
2	Sunday	6:57	6:41
3	Monday	6:58	6:39
4	Tuesday	6:59	6:38
5	Wednesday	7:00	6:36
6	Thursday	7:01	6:35
7	Friday	7:02	6:33
8	Saturday	7:03	6:31
9	Sunday	7:04	6:30
10	Monday	7:05	6:28
11	Tuesday	7:06	6:27
12	Wednesday	7:07	6:25
13	Thursday	7:08	6:24
14	Friday	7:09	6:22
15	Saturday	7:10	6:21
16	Sunday	7:11	6:19
17	Monday	7:12	6:18
18	Tuesday	7:13	6:16
19	Wednesday	7:14	6:15
20	Thursday	7:16	6:14
21	Friday	7:17	6:12
22	Saturday	7:18	6:11
23	Sunday	7:19	6:09
24	Monday	7:20	6:08
25	Tuesday	7:21	6:07
26	Wednesday	7:22	6:05
27	Thursday	7:23	6:04
28	Friday	7:24	6:03
29	Saturday	7:25	6:02
30	Sunday	6:27*	5:00*
31	Monday	6:28	4:59

* Daylight Savings Time to Eastern Standard Time

Falling leaves whisper that winter is near. No dates for Indian (late) Summer or Squaw (early) Winter—forecasters are not capable of such predictions.

October 19 Shine on, Harvest Moon—the first full moon (8:19am) in the month following the autumnal equinox.

October 19–20, 1940 The heaviest October snowfall on record left 2.2 inches. Philadelphians were calmer about snow in the mid-century; no rush to food stores was reported.

October 23, 1878 A wind gust from the southeast of 75 miles per hour made this the windiest day ever in Philadelphia.

October 31 It is Halloween, or Samhain, the Celtic celebration of harvest's end and winter's beginning. Time to collect the souls of the year's dead and herd them to the gates of the "other world" tended by Druid priests (later called witches). Glowing coals set in turnips eventually became glowering eyes of the jack-o-lanterns.

New Moon	4th
First Quarter	11th
Full Moon	19th
Last Quarter	27th

November 1994

There is much difference between imitating a good man and counterfeiting him.

—Benjamin Franklin, November 1738

		Rises	Sets
1	Tuesday	6:29	4:58
2	Wednesday	6:30	4:57
3	Thursday	6:31	4:56
4	Friday	6:32	4:55
5	Saturday	6:33	4:53
6	Sunday	6:35	4:52
7	Monday	6:36	4:51
8	Tuesday	6:37	4:50
9	Wednesday	6:38	4:49
10	Thursday	6:39	4:48
11	Friday	6:40	4:47
12	Saturday	6:41	4:47
13	Sunday	6:43	4:46
14	Monday	6:44	4:45
15	Tuesday	6:45	4:44
16	Wednesday	6:46	4:43
17	Thursday	6:47	4:43
18	Friday	6:48	4:42
19	Saturday	6:49	4:41
20	Sunday	6:51	4:40
21	Monday	6:52	4:40
22	Tuesday	6:53	4:39
23	Wednesday	6:54	4:39
24	Thursday	6:55	4:38
25	Friday	6:56	4:38
26	Saturday	6:57	4:37
27	Sunday	6:58	4:37
28	Monday	6:59	4:37
29	Tuesday	7:00	4:36
30	Wednesday	7:01	4:36

The last month of autumn. The melancholy days have come, the meadows brown and the forest bare.

November 7, 1977 The wettest November day ever recorded, when 3.99 inches filled basements everywhere.

November 11 St. Martin's Day fixes the winter to be mild if the foliage is still on the trees. If there has been frost, the winter will be cold and bitter. Cue the groundhog.

November 24 The first Thanksgiving was actually celebrated at the end of the harvest in October and featured no turkeys—they were too smart and difficult to catch. Pilgrims and Indians dined on venison, nuts, fruits, fish, and large orange squash (later called pumpkin).

November 26–27, 1898 The snowiest day of the month was covered by 9.2 inches.

November 30 The end of this year's hurricane season.

New Moon	3d
First Quarter	10th
Full Moon	18th
Last Quarter	26th

December 1994

		Rises	Sets
1	Thursday	7:02	4:36
2	Friday	7:03	4:35
3	Saturday	7:04	4:35
4	Sunday	7:05	4:35
5	Monday	7:06	4:35
6	Tuesday	7:07	4:35
7	Wednesday	7:08	4:35
8	Thursday	7:09	4:35
9	Friday	7:10	4:35
10	Saturday	7:11	4:35
11	Sunday	7:11	4:35
12	Monday	7:12	4:35
13	Tuesday	7:13	4:35
14	Wednesday	7:14	4:36
15	Thursday	7:14	4:36
16	Friday	7:15	4:36
17	Saturday	7:16	4:37
18	Sunday	7:16	4:37
19	Monday	7:17	4:37
20	Tuesday	7:18	4:38
21	Wednesday	7:18	4:38
22	Thursday	7:19	4:39
23	Friday	7:19	4:39
24	Saturday	7:19	4:40
25	Sunday	7:20	4:40
26	Monday	7:20	4:41
27	Tuesday	7:21	4:42
28	Wednesday	7:21	4:42
29	Thursday	7:21	4:43
30	Friday	7:21	4:44
31	Saturday	7:22	4:45

I know you lawyers can, with ease
Twist words and meanings
as you please.
—*Benjamin Franklin, December 1740*

The Winter King has come with icy brow to take up his own. The season of hibernation begins this month.

December 1 The day of meteorological winter. In 1963, *all* 31 days were below freezing.

December 10, 1878 A stiff, southeasterly breeze of 63 miles per hour sent hats aloft and people scurrying for cover.

December 21 The first day of the winter solstice, when the sun's highest appearance in the sky is in the Southern Hemisphere. Just over nine hours of sunshine will illuminate the shortest day of the year.

December 25–26, 1909 The whitest Christmas ever, when 21 inches of snow made everything cheery and bright—except for those who had to shovel.

December 31
The average daytime high temperature is 39° F and the low temperature is 25° F. Happy New Year.

New Moon	2d
First Quarter	9th
Full Moon	17th
Last Quarter	25th

President of the United States:

Bill Clinton, The White House, 1600 Pennsylvania Avenue, Washington, DC 20500, White House Comments Line: (202) 456-1111; fax: (202) 456-2461

Governor of Pennsylvania:

Robert P. Casey, 225 Main Capitol Building, Harrisburg, PA 17120, phone: (800) 932-0784; fax: (717) 787-7859 or (717) 783-1396

Governor of New Jersey:

James J. Florio, Office of the Governor, CN 001, Trenton, NJ 08625, phone: (609) 292-6000; fax: (609) 292-3454

Governor of Delaware:

Thomas R. Carper, Carvel State Office Building, 820 N. French Street, 12th floor, Wilmington, DE 19801, phone: (302) 577-3210; fax: (302) 577-3118

U.S. Senators, Pennsylvania:

Harris Wofford, 9456 Federal Building, 600 Arch Street, Philadelphia, PA 19106, phone: 597-9914; fax: 597-4771. 276 Russell Building, Washington, DC 20510, phone: (202) 224-6324; fax: (202) 224-4161

Arlen Specter, 9400 Federal Building, 600 Arch Street, Philadelphia, PA 19106, phone: 597-7200. 535 Hart Building, Washington, DC 20510, phone: (202) 224-4254; fax: (202) 224-1893

U.S. Senators, New Jersey:

Bill Bradley, 1 Newark Center, Newark, NJ 07102-5297, phone: (201) 639-2860; fax: (201) 639-2878. 731 Hart Building, Washington, DC 20510-3001, phone: (202) 224-3224; fax: (202) 224-8567

CITIZENS' MANUAL

Access

Advise and Consent

It's 1994: Do you know where your elected representatives stand?

Governments, the Declaration of Independence says, derive their just powers from the consent of the governed—and, at least on some issues, they also get a lot of advice from them. But do they pay attention?

Ask Zoe Baird—or the Friends of the Free Library.

Inside-the-Beltway types assumed the Senate would confirm Baird as Attorney General, even though she'd hired illegal alien babysitters. But then the folks back home rose up in righteous indignation and started bombarding their senators—and their favorite talk shows—with cards and letters and faxes and phone calls dumping on the $500,000-a-year insurance company lawyer. Within a matter of days, she was a footnote.

When, in the depths of Philadelphia's fiscal crisis, the Rendell administration sought to balance the city's budget by (among other economies) cutting the Free Library's funding, it seemed a foregone conclusion that library staff would be decimated. Some branch libraries would close, and hours at others would be sharply curtailed. Until the Friends of the Free Library swung into action, mobilizing card-carrying library partisans across the city to rally, protest, demonstrate, turn out for Council's budget hearings, and write or phone or fax the mayor and members of City Council. The result: Mayor and Council agreed to buy fewer city cars, cut street resurfacing, tax movie tickets—and leave the Library's subsidy at least partially intact.

The democratic premise comes down to this: The squeaking wheel gets the grease. If there's something you want one of your governments to do—put a stop sign at the end of your block, reform federal campaign laws, clean up the empty lot next door, work to free Tibet, increase funding for Head Start, stop funding a military dictatorship, block imports of goods made by illegal child labor—better squeak up.

You might think politicos get so much mail that one more letter won't make any difference, but they say not. Kevin Feeley, Mayor Rendell's press secretary, said the mayor gets "a ton" of mail, tries to read it all himself, and comes close. Of course, you'd probably look forward to your mail, too, if strangers started sending you $100 checks—as happened to Rendell when, during negotiations with city unions, he told a *Wall Street Journal* reporter that "If I had a hundred dollars for every citizen who tells me to hang in there, we wouldn't have a fiscal problem. ..."

32

**CITIZENS'
MANUAL**

Access

The Clinton White House is so eager to know what you think that the administration has installed voice mail ("Press 1 if you think reducing the deficit should receive the highest priority...") so you can phone in your views, and electronic mail so you can weigh in by computer.

Jennifer Lamson, associate director of grassroots lobbying for Common Cause, says that when it comes to making an impression on government, both quality and quantity count. A congressional office "will take note of massive quantities—even of pre-printed postcards you only have to sign and send in." She says "the letters are tallied up, so there's a sense of what people out in the district care about." But, she says, "well-thought-out letters from folks back home that show knowledge of the issue and an awareness of where it is" in the legislative process have more impact, because they show that people "know what's happening on the issue, care about it, and are watching to see what the senator will do— and will hold him accountable." She says this kind of carefully targeted citizen input—usually letters asking a legislator to vote for a particular bill or against a certain weakening amendment—can be "very effective."

So effective that, now, you can hire it by the hour. In the past couple of years, some Washington lobbyists have begun to specialize in mobilizing apparently spontaneous grassroots outrage. A *New York Times* story told how Jack Bonner, of Bonner & Associates, had orchestrated public outcries against limits on credit card interest rates (for banker clients), against tougher fuel efficiency standards (for auto makers), and against triple-trailer trucks (for a railroad).

Does neatness count? Will messy handwriting and lots of cross-outs reduce your impact on affairs of state? Corliss Clemonts-James, in Congressman Lucien Blackwell's office, says that although "appearance is everything, even in politics," what really counts is persistence. She says Blackwell gets 75 to 100 pieces of mail a day, and "we try not to turn anybody away." But she says that, because it's "impossible to get caught up," whoever bugs you the most eventually gets your attention: "The people who pressure us the most, we'll put everything else on the back burner because we don't want to be bugged." It's the squeaking wheel principle. ∎

❖

Three of the 23 congressional delegates from Pennsylvania to Washington, D.C. would have abolished the National Endowment for the Arts in 1990. Six out of a reapportioned delegation of 21 would do the same in 1993—if given a chance.

U.S. Senators, New Jersey: continued...

Frank R. Lautenberg, Suite 1001, Gateway One, Gateway Center, Newark, NJ 07102, phone: (201) 645-3030; fax: (201) 645-0502. 717 Hart Building, Washington, DC 20510, phone: (202) 224-4744; fax: (202) 224-9707

U.S. Senators, Delaware:

Joseph R. Biden, Jr., 6029 Federal Building, Wilmington, DE 19801, phone: (302) 573-6345; fax: (302) 573-6351. 221 Russell Building, Washington, DC 20510-0802, phone: (202) 224-5042; fax: (202) 224-0139

William V. Roth, Jr., 3021 Federal Building, Wilmington, DE 19801, phone: (302) 573-6291; fax: (302) 573-6434. 104 Hart Building, Washington, DC 20510-0810, phone: (202) 224-2441; fax: (202) 224-2805

U.S. Representatives from Philadelphia, Bucks, Chester, Delaware, and Montgomery Counties

District 1: Thomas M. Foglietta (D), 10402 Federal Building, 600 Arch Street, 19106, 925-6840

District 2: Lucien E. Blackwell (D), 3901 Market Street, 19104, 387-2543 or 2544

District 3: Robert A. Borski (D), 7141 Frankford Avenue, 19135, 335-3355

District 6: Tim Holden (D), Berks Service Center, 1st floor, 633 Court Street, Reading, PA 19607, 371-9931

District 7: Curt Weldon (R), 1554 Garrett Road, Upper Darby, PA 19082, 259-0700

District 8: James C. Greenwood (R), 69 E. Oakland Avenue, Doylestown, PA 18901, 348-7511

District 13: Marjorie Margolies-Mezvinsky (D), 1 Presidential Boulevard, Suite 200, Bala Cynwyd, PA 19004, 667-3666

District 15: Paul McHale (D), 26 E. Third Street, Bethlehem, PA 18015, 866-0916

District 16: Robert S. Walker (R), Exton Commons, Suite 595, Exton, PA 19341, 363-8409 or 8475

Philadelphia Elected Officials

Mayor: Edward G. Rendell (D), Room 215 City Hall, 19107, 686-2181

District Attorney: Lynne M. Abraham (D), 1421 Arch Street, 19102, 686-8700

City Controller: Jonathan A. Saidel (D), 1650 Arch Street, 20th floor, 19103, 686-6680

City Council Representatives
District 1: Wards 1, 2, 5, 14 (Div. 1, 2, 4–11), 18 (Div. 2, 4–7, 10–12), 25, 31, 39 (Div. 1–12, 15–23, 25–28, 30–35, 37–40, 42, 43, 45, 46), 45 (Div. 9–11, 14, 16)
 Joseph C. Vignola (D), Room 404 City Hall, 19107, 686-3458 or 3459
District 2: Wards 8 (Div. 1, 2, 7, 9, 13, 27, 28), 26, 30, 36, 39 (Div. 13, 14, 24, 29, 36, 41, 44), 40, 48, 51 (Div. 3, 8, 9, 22)
 Anna Cibotti Verna (D), Room 405 City Hall, 19107, 686-3412 or 3413
District 3: Wards 3, 6, 24, 27, 44 (Div. 3, 4, 6–18), 46, 51 (Div. 1, 2, 4–7, 10–21, 23–28), 60
 Jannie L. Blackwell (D), Room 408 City Hall, 19107, 686-3418 or 3419
District 4: Wards 4, 21, 34, 38, 44 (Div. 1, 2, 5, 19), 52
 Michael A. Nutter (D), Room 406 City Hall, 19107, 686-3416 or 3417
District 5: Wards 8 (Div. 3–6, 8, 10–12, 14–26, 29, 30), 14 (Div. 3), 15, 16 (Div. 1, 2, 6, 7, 9–11, 13–18), 18 (Div. 1, 3, 8, 9, 13–17), 20, 28, 29, 32, 37 (Div. 1–15, 17–21), 47
 John F. Street (D) [Council President], Room 494 City Hall, 19107, 686-3442 or 3443
District 6: Wards 41, 45 (Div. 1–8, 12, 13, 15, 17–25), 54, 55, 57 (Div. 4–9, 20, 23, 26), 62, 64, 65 (Div. 1–9, 11–23)
 Joan L. Krajewski (D), Room 595 City Hall, 19107, 686-3444 or 3445
District 7: Wards 7, 19, 23, 33, 35, 37 (Div. 16), 42 (Div 1–7, 22, 23), 53, 56 (Div. 1–10, 13–16, 33, 34, 36, 37, 40)
 Daniel P. McElhatton (D), Room 592 City Hall, 19107, 686-3448 or 3449

District 8: Wards 9, 11, 12, 13, 16 (Div. 3–5, 8, 12), 17, 22, 59
 Herbert H. DeBeary, Sr. (D), Room 488 City Hall, 19107, 686-3424 or 3425
District 9: Wards 10, 42 (Div. 8–21, 24, 25), 43, 49, 50, 61
 Marian B. Tasco (D), Room 577 City Hall, 19107, 686-3454 or 3455
District 10: Wards 56 (Div 11, 12, 17–32, 35, 38, 39, 41), 57 (Div. 1–3, 10–19, 21, 22, 24, 25, 27, 28), 58, 63, 65 (Div. 10), 66
 Brian J. O'Neill (R), Room 562 City Hall, 19107, 686-3422 or 3423

Councilmembers-At-Large:
Augusta A. Clark (D), Room 580 City Hall, 19107, 686-3438 or 3439
David Cohen (D), Room 588 City Hall, 19107, 686-3446 or 3447
Happy Fernandez (D), Room 484 City Hall, 19107, 686-3414 or 3415
James F. Kenney (D), Room 586 City Hall, 19107, 686-3450 or 3451
W. Thacher Longstreth (R), Room 594 City Hall, 19107, 686-3452 or 3453
Angel L. Ortiz (D), Room 590 City Hall, 19107, 686-3420 or 3421
Joan Specter (R), Room 582-B City Hall, 19107, 686-3440 or 3441

City Commissioners:
Margaret Tartaglione (D) (Chair), Room 130 City Hall, 19107, 686-3460 or 3461
John F. Kane (R), Room 134 City Hall, 19107, 686-3464 or 3467
Alexander Z. Talmadge, Jr. (D), Room 132 City Hall, 19107, 686-3462 or 3463

Sources (pp. 34–42): Committee of Seventy Election Calendar '93 and Election Calendar '93 Suburban Supplement; The League of Women Voters of Philadelphia 1993 Legislative Reference Directory; *Philadelphia City Government and Related Public Agencies,* July 1992, Campus Boulevard Corporation.

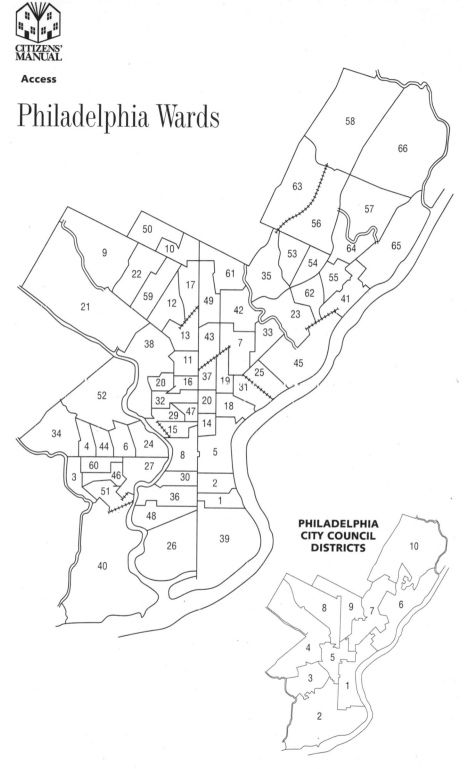

Philadelphia Wards

PHILADELPHIA
CITY COUNCIL
DISTRICTS

Access

CITIZENS' MANUAL

Philadelphia Ward Leaders

Ward 1: George Badame (D), 563-7670 (o), 389-7729 (h); Joseph DiJoseph (R), 468-5259 (h)

Ward 2: Henry J. Cianfrani (D), 463-4500 (o); Charles Santore (R), 627-1273 (h)

Ward 3: Peter D. Truman (D), 726-6555 (h); John Thorne, Sr. (R), 747-3716 (h)

Ward 4: Carol Ann Campbell (D), 471-0511 (o); Melvin C. Howell (R), 831-7128 (o), 477-5453 (h)

Ward 5: Samuel Rappaport (D), 625-9070 (o), 627-3918 (h); John Calabro (R), 336-7847 (h)

Ward 6: Mike Horsey (D), 563-7670 (o), 877-8539 (h); William Dunham (R), 386-3751 (o), 473-8182 (h)

Ward 7: Patricia A. Hughes (D), 426-3668 (o); Mary A. Tierney (R), 423-6710 (h)

Ward 8: Norman S. Berson (D), 893-9300 (o), 732-4070 (h); Suzanne D. Cohen (R), 732-0553 (h)

Ward 9: Patricia Reifsynder (D), 951-2300 (o), 247-2845 (h); Robert G. Bauer (R), 569-9791 (o), 248-9627 (h)

Ward 10: Dwight Evans (D), 549-0220 (o), 549-3397 (h); John LaSane (R), 924-8451 (h)

Ward 11: Alvin Stewart (D), 686-4382 (o), 227-5686 (h); John P. Carsello (R), 223-5579 (h)

Ward 12: Betty Townes (D), 842-1331 (h); Linda Wolfe Bateman (R), 844-6063 (h)

Ward 13: Rosita Youngblood (D), 849-2617 (h); Arianna Gibbs (R), 228-7973 (h)

Ward 14: Benjamin Hassell (D), 232-9087 (h); Michael Smylie (R), 627-7600 (o)

Ward 15: Jane Malloy (D), 563-7670 (o), 232-3508 (h); Myles Wilson (R), 237-1336 (o), 563-7007 (h)

Ward 16: Ann Moss (D), 225-0669 (h); Clarence Thompson (R), 848-2780 (h)

Ward 17: David Cohen (D), 686-3446 (o), 548-2817 (h); John Shirley (R), 247-9896 (o), 927-7398 (h)

Ward 18: Thomas Nilan (D), 426-2980 (h); Leo Kulb (R), 426-5597 (h)

Ward 19: Ralph Acosta (D), 634-1660 (o); Vacant (R)

Ward 20: Shirley M. Kitchen (D), 686-3442 (o), 978-0145 (h); Martha Crawley (R), 232-4975 (h)

Ward 21: Joseph C. Quigley, Jr. (D), 483-2547 (h); M. Joseph Rocks (R), 483-9117 (h)

Ward 22: Joseph E. Coleman (D), 848-4804 (h); Raymond Markloff (R), 757-7646 (o), 848-6221 (h)

Ward 23: Timothy E. Savage (D), 537-4800 (o), 831-0451 (h); Fred Perri, Jr. (R), 535-6082 (h)

Ward 24: Nathaniel Clark (D), 686-7627 (o), 222-4243 (h); Morris Love (R), 476-1789 (h)

Ward 25: Norman Loudenslager (D); 423-6606 (o), 739-5971 (h); John J. Taylor (R), 425-0901 (o)

Ward 26: Ronald R. Donatucci (D), 686-6250 (o); Gus Pedicone (R), 534-5700 (o), 336-2443 (h)

Ward 27: Sheryl George-MacAlpine (D), 387-9372 (o), 386-8780 (h); Matthew Wolfe (R), 387-7300 (o)

Ward 28: Maurice Floyd (D), 387-2543 (o), 228-8659 (h); John W. Baston (R), 226-6857 (h)

Ward 29: Frank L. Oliver (D), 684-3738 (o), 978-7281 (h); Robert R. Byrd (R), 925-5080 (o), 232-8237 (h)

Ward 30: Stanley V. White (D), 925-6840 (o), 732-8387 (h); Frank Murchison, Jr. (R), 755-7405 (h)

Ward 31: Peggy Rzepski (D), 426-4616 (o), 425-6794 (h); Vincent Fenerty, Jr. (R), 634-7120 (h)

Ward 32: Darrell Clarke (D), 686-3442 (o); Edward Griffin (R), 232-1181 (o)

Ward 33: William Stinson (D), 686-3989 (o), 525-0213 (h); Mark Cumberland (R), 686-3409 (o), 425-3586 (h)

Ward 34: Robert A. Brady (D), 472-4488 (o), 241-7804 (h); John J. O'Grady, Jr. (R), 879-8333 (o), 879-6694 (h)

**CITIZENS'
MANUAL**

Access

Ward 35: George Naulty (D), 686-3410 (o); John F. Kane (R), 686-3464 (o), 743-6694 (h)

Ward 36: Anna Cibotti Verna (D), 686-3412 (o), 462-1525 (h); William H. Black (R), 463-3125 (h)

Ward 37: Clem R. Moragne (D), 686-2279 (o), 769-0558 (h); Henry J. Nimmons (R), 225-1379 (o), 225-0396 (h)

Ward 38: Ralph Wynder (D), 223-1312 (h); Christopher A. DiGeorge (R), 482-9551 (h)

Ward 39A: Rosanne Pauciello (D), 468-5109 (o), 468-3866 (h); Mario D'Adamo (R), 934-3783 (o), 468-7641 (h)

Ward 39B: Joseph Howlett (D), 465-1211 (o), 334-3880 (h); Connie McHugh (R), 468-1077 (h)

Ward 40A: Robert J. Avellino (D), 563-7670 (o), 365-5398 (h); Michael Gallagher (R), 492-0157 (h)

Ward 40B: Thomas F. Gehret (D), 686-2230 (o), 492-8265 (h); Patricia M. Hardy (R), 259-0700 (o), 724-4686 (h)

Ward 41: Nicholas Stampone (D), 332-4515 (h); Harry Checcio (R), 333-6161 (o)

Ward 42: Linda Mathews (D), 455-4867 (h); Mary Anderson (R), 324-7062 (h)

Ward 43: William W. Rieger (D), 223-1501 (o), 229-6980 (h); José Hernandez (R), 423-7619 (o)

Ward 44: Vincent Hughes (D), 471-0490 (o); Mary White (R), 472-7968 (h)

Ward 45: Gerry Kosinski (D), 537-1070 (h); Kevin Pasquay (R), 426-0176 (h)

Ward 46: Lucien E. Blackwell (D), 387-2543 (o), 222-1105 (h); Daniel Bonner (R), 387-3734 (o), 622-5461 (h)

Ward 47: Helyn Cheeks (D), 232-5009 (o), 763-5975 (h); Clarence Thompson (R), 848-2780 (h)

Ward 48: Nicholas Maiale (D), 546-5515 (o); William Schaps (R), 389-0128 (o), 463-5450 (h)

Ward 49: Shirley Gregory (D), 324-9410 (o), 276-0995 (h); John Helo (R), 342-7141 (h)

Ward 50: Marian B. Tasco (D), 686-3454 (o); Frank DiCicco (R), 927-3812 (o)

Ward 51: Vivian Miller (D), 686-4280 (o), 474-3097 (h); Lawrence R. Watson, II (R), 665-1886 (o), 879-5220 (h)

Ward 52: Michael A. Nutter (D), 686-3416 (o), 477-2132 (h); Bernice T. Rosenfeld (R), 561-1929 (h)

Ward 53: Christine Solomon (D), 728-1484 (h); Jack Kelly (R), 745-0850 (h)

Ward 54: Allen Butkowitz (D), 745-8461 (o); Bill Brady (R), 676-2600 (o), 673-2592 (h).

Ward 55: Francis E. Gleeson, Jr. (D), 624-6049 (o), 331-0135 (h); Alfred J. Recupido, Sr. (R), 338-3311 (h)

Ward 56: John Sabatina (D), 342-6576 (h); Chris R. Wogan (R), 342-1700 (o)

Ward 57: Francis R. Conaway (D), 676-6298 (o); Angela Wechter (R), 698-9399 (h)

Ward 58: Michael J. Stack (D), 735-6500 (o), 677-5137 (h); George T. Kenney (R), 934-5144 (o)

Ward 59: David P. Richardson, Jr. (D), 849-6896 (o), 849-6592 (h); Joseph L. Messa, Sr. (R), 843-1009 (o), 844-4926 (h)

Ward 60: Isadore A. Shrager (D), 299-2022 (o), 474-2308 (h); George Frambes (R), 473-8108 (h)

Ward 61: Bridget A. Murray (D), 548-5311 (o), 549-6166 (h); John Patrick Walsh (R), 549-4438 (h)

Ward 62: Margaret Tartaglione (D), 686-3460 (o), 535-0409 (h); George C. Bloom, Sr. (R), 535-8925 (h)

Ward 63: Christopher Drumm (D), 342-1596 (h); Frank P. Buzydlowski (R), 677-0607 (o, h)

Ward 64: Rudolph J. Ries (D), 624-1734 (h); John M. Perzel (R), 331-2600 (o), 338-1535 (h)

Ward 65: Joan L. Krajewski (D), 686-3444 (o), 624-6906 (h); Sharon Mattia (R), 824-1992 (h)

Ward 66A: Frank Dillon (D), 351-0252 (o), 632-4557 (h); Joseph J. Duda (R), 561-0650 (o), 637-4696 (h)

Ward 66B: Michael McAleer, Jr. (D), 563-7670 (o), 632-2350 (h); Joseph J. Duda (R), 561-0650 (o), 637-4696 (h)

37

CITIZENS'
MANUAL

Access

Local Pennsylvania State Representatives

To determine in which district you reside, call one of these numbers:
Philadelphia Board of Elections, 686-3469
Bucks County Board of Elections, 348-6154
Chester County Voter Services, 344-6410
Delaware County Bureau of Elections, 891-4120
Montgomery County Board of Elections, 278-3275

Philadelphia County

District 169: Wards 57 (Div. 1–3, 8–19, 21–28), 65 (Div. 10), 66 (Div. 3, 10, 11, 14, 15, 17–21, 23–33, 35–40, 42–46)

Dennis M. O'Brien (R), 9811 Academy Road, 19114-1715, 632-5150

District 170: Wards 58 (Div. 1–8, 10–12, 14–16, 18–44), 66 (Div. 1, 2, 4–9, 12, 13, 16, 22, 34, 41)

George T. Kenney (R), 10104 Bustleton Avenue, 19116, 934-5144

District 172: Wards 55, 62 (Div. 5, 8, 9, 12, 13, 15–26), 64

John M. Perzel (R), 3532 Cottman Avenue, 19149, 331-2600

District 173: Wards 41, 62 (Div. 1–4, 6, 7, 10, 11), 65 (Div. 1–9, 11–23)

Michael P. McGeehan (D), 7153 Torresdale Avenue, 19135, 333-9760 or 9763

District 174: Wards 53 (Div. 11, 12, 15, 17–19, 22), 54, 56 (1, 2, 5, 6, 11–13, 15–18, 20–32, 34–41), 57 (Div. 4–7, 20), 63 (Div. 15, 22)

Alan L. Butkovitz (D), 7067 Castor Avenue, 19149, 745-8461

District 175: Wards 5 (Div. 1, 2, 16, 17, 21), 18 (Div. 1, 2, 4–7, 9–12), 23 (Div. 14–23), 25 (Div. 1, 3, 4, 7, 8, 13, 16), 31 (Div. 1, 3, 4, 7–12), 45 (Div. 1–7, 9, 10, 12, 15–20, 22–25)

Marie A. Lederer (D), 2319 Margaret Street, 19137, 533-5552; 326 E. Girard Avenue, 19125, 426-6604

District 176: Wards 35 (Div. 1–14, 16–23, 25, 27, 31, 32), 53 (Div. 20, 21), 56 (Div. 3, 4, 7–10, 14, 19, 33), 58 (Div. 9, 13, 17), 63 (Div. 1–14, 16–21, 23–25)

Chris R. Wogan (R), 6533 Rising Sun Avenue, 19111, 342-1700

District 177: Wards 7 (Div. 22), 23 (Div. 1–9, 13), 25 (Div. 2, 5, 6, 9–12, 14, 15, 17–24), 31 (Div. 5, 6, 13–19), 33, 42 (Div. 1), 45 (Div. 8, 11, 13, 14, 21)

John J. Taylor (R), 2633 E. Monmouth Street, 19134, 425-5667 or 0901

District 179: Wards 37 (Div. 16, 21), 42 (Div. 2–17, 19–25), 43 (Div. 1–4, 8–17, 19–25), 49 (Div. 1–3, 6, 9, 13, 14, 19)

William W. Rieger (D), 3815 N. 9th Street, 19140, 223-1501 or 229-6980

District 180: Wards 7 (Div. 1–21, 23), 18 (Div. 3, 8, 13–17), 19, 31 (Div. 2), 37 (Div. 13–15, 17–20), 43 (Div. 5–7, 18)

Ralph Acosta (D), 2460 N. 5th Street, 19133, 634-1660

District 181: Wards 5 (Div. 3–6, 12, 13, 15, 18–20, 23), 14, 20, 32 (Div. 2, 5–9, 11, 12, 15–17), 37 (Div. 1–12), 47

W. Curtis Thomas (D), 1348–50 W. Girard Avenue, 19123, 232-1210

District 182: Wards 1 (Div. 10, 16), 2 (Div. 1–5, 8–27), 5 (Div. 7–11, 14, 22), 8, 30 (Div. 3, 7, 8, 16)

Babette Josephs (D), 1229 Chestnut Street, Box B, 19107, 977-7732

District 184: Wards 1 (Div. 4, 5, 8, 11, 17–19, 21), 39, 48 (Div. 1, 5, 6, 8, 13, 14, 17, 18, 20)

William F. Keller (D), 1531 S. 2nd Street, 19147, 271-9190

District 185: Wards 26, 40 (Div. 1, 4, 6, 14–19, 22, 27–31, 38–40, 42–46, 49–51), 48 (3, 4, 7, 9, 10, 12, 15, 16, 19, 21, 22), parts of Delaware County

38

**CITIZENS'
MANUAL**

Access

Robert C. Donatucci (D), 1615 Porter Street, 19145, 468-1515 or 1518

District 186: Wards 1 (Div. 1–3, 6, 7, 9, 12–15, 20), 2 (Div. 6–7), 27 (Div. 19), 30 (Div. 1, 2, 4–6, 9–15, 17), 36, 48 (Div. 2, 11, 23), 51 (3, 8)

Harold James (D), 1423 Point Breeze Avenue, 19146, 462-3308

District 188: Wards 27 (Div. 2–5, 7, 8, 12, 15–18, 22), 46, 51 (Div. 1, 2, 4–7, 9–23, 25–28)

James R. Roebuck (D), 4627 Baltimore Avenue, 19143, 386-9099

District 190: Wards 4 (Div. 1–3, 7, 8, 12), 6 (Div. 1–4, 6, 10–12, 16), 27 (Div. 1, 6, 9, 10, 13, 14, 20, 21, 23), 44 (Div. 1, 3, 4–6, 8–18), 52 (Div. 1), 60

Vincent Hughes (D), Urban Education Foundation, 4601 Market Street, 1st floor, 19139, 471-0490

District 191: Wards 3, 40 (Div. 2, 3, 5, 7–13, 20, 21, 23–26, 32–37, 41, 47, 48), 51 (Div. 24), parts of Delaware County

Anthony Hardy Williams (D), 835 S. 59th Street, 19143, 472-3775

District 192: Wards 4 (Div. 4–6, 9–11, 13–21), 34, 44 (Div. 2, 7, 19), 52 (Div. 5, 14, 15, 20)

Louise Williams Bishop (D), 1991 N. 63rd Street, 19151, 879-6625

District 194: Wards 21 (Div. 1, 2, 4–22, 26–29, 31, 32, 35–38, 40–42), 38 (Div. 9, 10, 19), 52 (Div. 2–4, 6–13, 16–19, 21–28)

Kathy Manderino (D), 6239 Ridge Avenue, 19128, 482-8726, or 2053 N. Wanamaker Street, 19131, 879-8533

District 195: Wards 6 (Div. 5, 7–9, 13–15, 17, 18), 15, 24, 27 (Div. 11), 29, 32 (Div. 1, 4, 10, 31)

Frank L. Oliver (D), 1205 N. 29th Street, 19121, 684-3738

District 197: Wards 11, 13 (Div. 25), 16, 28, 32 (Div. 3, 13, 14, 18–30)

Andrew J. Carn (D), 2015 N. 29th Street, 19121, 765-0806 or 560-5326

District 198: Wards 9 (Div. 3, 9–15), 12 (Div. 8, 11, 15–20, 22–24), 13 (Div. 1–6, 16–24), 21 (Div. 23–25), 22 (Div. 1–3), 38 (Div. 1–8, 11–18, 20,

21), 59 (Div. 17, 18, 20)

Robert W. O'Donnell (D), Park Drive Manor, 633 W. Rittenhouse Street, Suite C4, 19144, 849-2200

District 200: Wards 9 (Div. 1, 2, 4–8, 16 17), 21 (Div. 3, 30, 33, 34, 39, 43–45), 22 (Div. 4–7, 11, 12, 16–26), 50

Gordon J. Linton (D), 1521 E. Wadsworth Avenue, 19150, 242-0472

District 201: Wards 12 (Div. 1–7, 9, 10, 12–14, 21), 13 (Div. 7–15), 17 (Div. 1, 15–17, 22–25, 28, 29), 22 (Div. 8–10, 13–15, 27–29), 59 (Div. 1–16, 19, 21–25)

David P. Richardson, Jr. (D), 6345 Germantown Avenue, 19144, 849-6592, 6896

District 202: Wards 17 (Div. 4, 5, 11–14, 18–21, 26, 27), 23 (Div. 10–12), 35 (Div. 15, 24, 26, 28–30), 42 (Div. 18), 49 (Div. 4, 5, 7, 10–12, 15–17, 21–23), 53 (Div. 1–10, 13, 14, 16, 23), 61 (Div. 1–5, 7, 8, 10), 62 (Div. 14)

Mark B. Cohen (D), 6001 N. 5th Street, 2nd floor, 19120, 924-0895, 3690

District 203: Wards 10, 17 (Div. 1–3, 6–9), 49 (Div. 8, 18, 20, 24, 25), 61 (Div. 6, 9, 11–28)

Dwight Evans (D), 7174 Ogontz Avenue, 19138, 549-0220

Bucks County

District 18: Robert Tomlinson (R), 2307 Bristol Pike, Bensalem, PA 19020, 638-1777

District 31: David J. Steil (R), 8 N. State Street, Newtown, PA 18940, 968-3975

District 140: Thomas C. Corrigan, Sr. (D), 9187 New Falls Road, Levittown, PA 19054, 736-9600

District 141: Anthony J. Melio (D), 4211 Wistar Road, Fairless Hills, PA 19030, 943-8669

District 142: Matthew N. Wright (R), 760 N. Woodbourne Road, Langhorne, PA 19047, 757-8538

District 143: David W. Heckler (R), 39 W. State Street, Doylestown, PA 18901, 348-0600

District 144: Tom Druce (R), 1410 W. Street Road, Warminster, PA 18974, 675-0732, 674-0500

39

District 145: Paul I. Clymer (R), 311 N. 7th Street, Perkasie, PA 18944, 257-0279

District 152: Roy W. Cornell (R), 19 Byberry Avenue, Hatboro, PA 19040, 674-3755

District 178: Roy Reinard (R), 130 Buck Road, Suite 202, Holland, PA 18966, 364-3414

Chester County

District 13: Arthur D. Hershey (R), P.O. Box 69, Cochranville, PA 19330, 593-6565

District 26: Timothy F. Hennessey (R), 1 City Hall Place, Coatesville, PA 19320, 380-8660

District 155: James W. Gerlach (R), P.O. Box 293, Uwchland, PA 19480, 458-8010

District 156: Elinor Z. Taylor (R), 13 W. Miner Street, West Chester, PA 19382, 436-4433

District 157: Carole A. Rubley (R), 500 Chesterbrook Boulevard, E-2A, Lower Level, Wayne, PA 19087, 640-2356

District 158: Joseph R. Pitts (R), 905 Mitchell Farm Lane, Kennett Square, PA 19348, 444-4581

District 167: Robert J. Flick (R), 229 W. Lancaster Avenue, Devon, PA 19333, 688-8002

Delaware County

District 159: Thaddeus Kirkland (D), 29 E. 5th Street, Chester, PA 19013, 876-6420

District 160: Kathrynann W. Durham (R), Brookhaven Borough Municipal Building, Brookhaven Road and Edgemont Avenue, Brookhaven, PA 19015, 874-1358

District 161: Thomas P. Gannon (R), 310 Amosland Road, Holmes, PA 19043, 461-5543

District 162: Ron Raymond (R), 1337 Chester Pike, Sharon Hill, PA 19079, 534-1002

District 163: Nicholas A. Micozzie (R), 411 N. Springfield Road, Clifton Heights, PA 19018, 259-2820

District 164: Mario J. Civera, Jr. (R), 232 Long Lane, Upper Darby, PA 19082, 352-7800

District 165: William F. Adolph, Jr. (R), 312 S. Bishop Avenue, Springfield, PA 19064, 623-3033 or 3525

District 166: Greg Vitali (D), 1001 E. Darby Road, Havertown, PA 19083, 789-3900

District 167: See Chester County

District 168: Matthew J. Ryan (R), 214 N. Jackson Street, Media, PA 19063, 566-2000

District 185: See Philadelphia County

District 191: See Philadelphia County

Montgomery County

District 53: Robert W. Godshall (R), 1702 Hatfield Valley Road, Hatfield, PA 19440, 368-3500

District 61: Joseph M. Gladeck, Jr. (R), 1515 DeKalb Pike, Suite 106, Blue Bell, PA 19422, 277-3230

District 70: John W. Fichter (R), 40 W. Germantown Pike, Suite 70, Norristown, PA 19401, 272-9164

District 146: Robert D. Reber, Jr. (R), 426 King Street, P.O. Box 777, Pottstown, PA 19464, 326-9563

District 147: Raymond Bunt, Jr. (R), 105 Memorial Road and Route 29, Schwenksville, PA 19473, 287-4181

District 148: Lita Indzel Cohen (R), 112 Fayette Street, 2nd floor, Conshohocken, PA 19428, 397-0505

District 149: Ellen A. Harley, Courtside Square, Suite 116, 570 W. DeKalb Pike, King of Prussia, PA 19046, 962-8179

District 150: John A. Lawless (R), 3126 W. Ridge Pike, Eagleville, PA 19403, 631-5100

District 151: George E. Saurman (R), 360 Mattison Avenue, Ambler, PA 19002, 643-7819

District 152: See Bucks County

District 153: Martin L. Laub (R), Easton and Edge Hill Roads, Abington, PA 19001, 885-3500

District 154: Lawrence H. Curry (D), 115 West Avenue, Jenkintown, PA 19046, 572-5210

State House Districts in Philadelphia

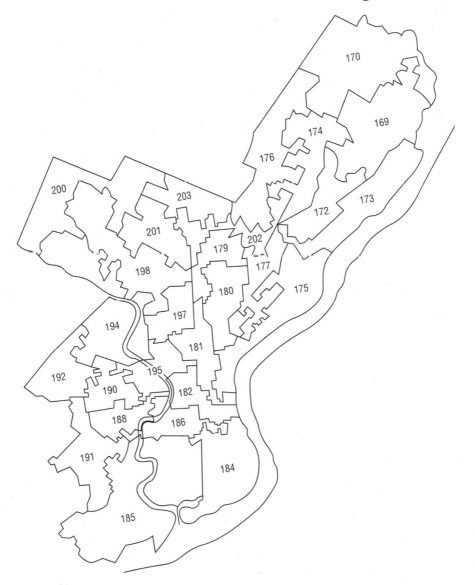

Local Pennsylvania State Senators

Philadelphia County

District 1: Wards 1, 2, 5, 8, 14, 15 (Div. 1–6, 8, 9, 12–19), 18 (Div. 1, 2, 4–7, 9–12), 25, 26 (Div. 9–12, 16, 17, 19, 21, 22), 31, 33 (Div. 15, 17–24), 36 (Div. 1, 2, 9–11, 29, 31, 34–41), 39

Vincent J. Fumo (D), 1208 Tasker Street, 19148, 468-3866

District 2: Wards 7, 18 (Div. 3, 8, 11, 13–17), 19, 20 (Div. 1, 2, 4, 8), 23 (Div. 1–9, 13–23), 33 (Div. 1–14, 16), 37 (Div. 13, 15, 16, 18–21), 42 (Div. 2–4, 6, 7, 16, 17, 20, 21, 24, 25), 43 (Div. 2–8, 11–13, 16–21, 25), 49 (Div. 1, 9, 13), 53 (Div. 6–22), 54, 55, 56 (Div. 1–22, 26, 32–34, 36, 37, 39, 40), 61 (Div. 1), 62

Open following death of Francis J. Lynch (D); election to be held November 2

District 3: Wards 11 (Div. 1, 3–20), 13 (Div. 1, 2, 6–25), 15 (Div. 7, 10, 11), 16, 20 (Div. 3, 5–7, 9, 10), 23 (Div. 10–12), 29, 32, 35, 37 (Div. 1–12, 14, 17), 42 (Div. 1, 5, 8–15, 18, 19, 22, 23), 43 (Div. 1, 9, 10, 14, 15, 22–24), 47, 49 (Div. 2–8, 10–12, 14–25), 53 (Div. 1–5, 23), 61 (Div. 2–28)

Roxanne H. Jones (D), 2330 W. Allegheny Avenue, 19132, 228-1120

District 4: Wards 9, 10, 12, 17, 21 (Div. 3, 24, 32, 34, 38, 39, 43, 44), 22, 50, 59, 63, parts of Montgomery County

Allyson Schwartz (D), 27 E. Durham Street, 19119, 242-9710

District 5: Wards 41, 45, 56 (Div. 23–25, 27–31, 35, 38, 41), 57, 58, 65, 65, 66, parts of Montgomery Country

Frank (Hank) A. Salvatore (R), Academy Shopping Center, 3330 Grant Avenue, 19114, 676-2600

District 7: Wards 4, 6, 11 (Div. 2), 13 (Div. 3–5), 21 (Div. 1, 2, 4–23, 25–31, 33, 35–37, 40–42, 45), 24, 27 (Div. 1, 2, 4–7, 9, 10, 12–17, 23), 28, 34, 38, 44, 52, 60 (Div. 1–5, 12, 23)

Chaka Fattah (D), 4104 Walnut Street, 19104, 387-6404

District 8: Wards 3, 26 (Div. 1–8, 13–15, 18, 20, 23, 24), 27 (Div. 3, 8, 11, 18–22), 30, 36 (Div. 3–8, 12–28, 30, 32, 33), 40, 46, 48, 51, 60 (Div. 6–11, 13–22), parts of Delaware County

Hardy Williams (D), 3801 Market Street, Suite 202, 19104, 662-5700

Bucks County

District 6: H. Craig Lewis (D), 50 Trenton Road, Fairless Hills, PA 19030, 322-0600 or 943-2700

District 10: David W. Heckler (R) elected July 13 to fill seat vacated when James C. Greenwood moved to U.S. House of Representatives; may not be sworn in until Senate session November 22, 1993

District 12: Stewart J. Greenleaf (R), 27 N. York Road, Willow Grove, PA 19090, 657-7700

Chester County

District 9: Clarence D. Bell (R), 280 N. Providence Road, Media, PA 19063, 565-9100

District 19: Earl M. Baker (R), 209 W. Lancaster Avenue, Paoli, PA 19301, 296-7828

District 44: Frank A. Pecora (R), 95 S. Hanover Street, Pottstown, PA 19464, 323-5080

Delaware County

District 8: See Philadelphia County

District 9: See Chester County

District 17: Richard A. Tilghman (R), 406 Gatcombe Lane, Bryn Mawr, PA 19010, 525-7674

District 26: F. Joseph Loeper (R), 403 Burmont Road, Drexel Hill, PA 19026, 284-3577

Montgomery County

District 4: See Philadelphia County

District 5: See Philadelphia County

District 12: See Bucks County

District 17: See Delaware County

District 24: Edwin G. Holl (R), 427 W. Main Street, Lansdale, PA 19446, 368-1500

District 44: See Chester County

State Senate Districts in Philadelphia

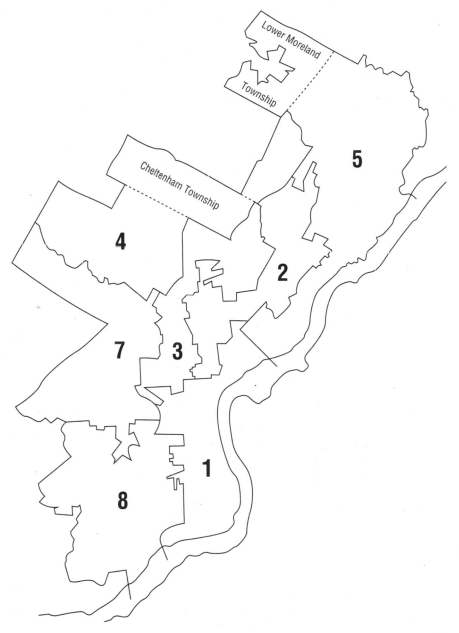

FREE CULTURE

Admission prices for theater, dance, music, and film events have risen sharply in recent years. Trading volunteer time for tickets is more popular than ever.

Most of the theater and dance spaces in the city use some volunteers to handle ushering and general duties on performance nights. While saving money and helping support the arts, volunteers get to see the action backstage and before the show. You may have to stand, but you'll see the show–and it's often possible to usher one show in exchange for tickets to the next one.

Most local museums are also eager to trade admissions or memberships for volunteers' help. To be sure of getting into a volunteer slot, call ahead. The Greater Philadelphia Cultural Alliance (GPCA) publishes and sells an annual guide to about 200 member cultural organizations, from the Academy of Vocal Arts to the Zero Moving Dance Company. GPCA is at 320 Walnut Street (440-8100).

Philadelphia is also home to several music schools: the Curtis Institute, Temple University, and the University of the Arts. At their free student recitals you can hear fine young musicians whom you'll have to pay to see in a few years.

REDUCED SEATS AND DOORS

Both the Philadelphia Orchestra and the Pennsylvania Ballet have, for years, offered "rush" seats.

You arrive just before the performance, when the last open seats are sold at discount prices. It's a great way to see the show, and you're likely to be in good company–music lovers and professional musicians and dancers on a budget.

For the Philadelphia Orchestra, rush tickets are sold for $6 and are available 30 minutes before the curtain.

For the Pennsylvania Ballet, you can buy tickets at half-price one hour before the performance, and you must have a student ID.

Many other groups offer similar discounts. Call for details.

44

CITIZENS' MANUAL

Coping

Getting Help

It's no secret that Philadelphia has a lot of unemployed and underemployed people. About 164,000 of us were counted among the unemployed at the end of 1992. Philadelphia has an extensive network of programs, grants, and services to help those in need, with many designed specifically for children, parents, and the elderly. The back of Bell of Pennsylvania's White Pages directory lists human services and programs.

• Welfare monthly payments from the state of Pennsylvania are available to anyone. The basic payment for a single adult is $205 per month, plus $100 in food stamps and a medical card, which can cover anything from prescriptions to surgery. Many hospitals are reluctant to treat people with medical cards, but they are required to by law. If you are applying for welfare, remember that any income or property can make you ineligible for help. It takes about 15 days to get your first welfare check, though in some cases you may be eligible for food stamps within five days—ask about Food Stamps Now. Both welfare and food stamp programs are limited to about six months, though these limits may be exceeded in cases of proven need. For more information, call the Philadelphia County Public Assistance Office at 560-2547, or the County Assistance Helpline at (800) 692-7462.

• The Low Income Home Energy Assistance Program (LIHEAP) will pay a portion of your gas, electric, or oil heating bills. The program is available to all low-income persons. You'll need a lease or proof of home ownership, your Social Security card, and your utility bills. LIHEAP can contribute to only one form of heating. You can apply to the program from November through January. LIHEAP's office is at 1326 Buttonwood Street; call 560-2970.

• Community Legal Services offers legal help to low-income individuals. Their main office is at 1324 Locust Street (893-5300). They also have branch offices: North Central, 3638 N. Broad Street, 227-2400; Northeast, 3207 Kensington Avenue, 427-4850; South, 1226 S. Broad Street, 271-2500; and West, 5219 Chestnut Street, 561-6383.

• The University of Pennsylvania's Dental School at 4003 Locust Street (898-8965) offers the latest techniques—at fixed rates—done by students under supervision. An initial visit, which includes a complete dental exam and X-rays, costs $53. Fillings cost $20 to $55, and more involved procedures, such as root canal work, cost $170 to $300. The Dental School offers a 10% discount to senior citizens. ∎

Coping

Jobs and Housing

- The University of Pennsylvania is Philadelphia's largest private employer and the source for more than 22,000 jobs. *The Compass*, a biweekly newsletter published from September through May and monthly in June and July, carries extensive job listings. Find a copy at offices on campus, or visit their office at 3624 Market Street (898-1426). The University's Job Opportunities Hotline (898-JOBS) records assorted recent openings.
- The Philadelphia Unemployment Project offers help with referrals, résumés, and career changes. Their office is at 116 S. 7th Street, Room 610, Philadelphia, PA 19106; call 592-0933.
- There are acceptable alternatives to high-priced housing. Many neighborhoods, especially those near the University of Pennsylvania and Temple University, have long had many group homes. Advertisements for house shares can be found on local bulletin boards and in the city's weeklies and college newspapers.
- Dignity Housing, an independent nonprofit organization, works in conjunction with the Philadelphia Office of Services for Homeless Adults to provide housing for formerly homeless people. You must first register with OSHA, 1340 Cherry Street (686-6782), and then contact Dignity Housing at 7208 Germantown Avenue (242-3140).
- Habitat for Humanity, a national, nonprofit organization, aims to provide affordable housing for low-income families that make a small down payment and work 500 hours to help rehabilitate their house. Habitat then provides an interest-free mortgage of 20 to 30 years. They have two offices in Philadelphia: North, 1828 N. 19th Street (765-6000), and West, 4948 W. Stiles Street (477-4639).
- "Urban homesteading"—squatting—has become increasingly popular as people decide to take advantage of the city's more than 20,000 abandoned houses. They research the ownership first, then force the door and set up housekeeping. Squatters target homes owned but left vacant by the Department of Housing and Urban Development and the City of Philadelphia. You can research deeds at the city's Department of Records, City Hall Room 153, Monday–Friday, 8am–2:30pm. Successful squatters consider their risks, such as the state of the building and the reactions of neighbors. Other homesteaders will offer advice. ∎

❖ Anthony Faas of Philadelphia received patent number 11,062 for his accordion in January 1854.

"CHLORONOUS, MUSTY AND EARTHY"

Some love it, some can't stand it, some avoid it altogether. It's Philadelphia water, and the Water Department's Bureau of Laboratory Services officially describes it as "chloronous, musty and earthy." The taste is due largely to algae in the water's sources, the Delaware and Schuylkill Rivers. Treatment plants remove all living organisms from the water, but there will always be a residual taint—particularly in dry springs, when algae are most florid. (One species that grows in a reservoir 250 miles from Philadelphia makes the Delaware taste slightly like cucumbers.) In the 1970s, a switch from chlorine to chloramines was designed to leave less chemical taste behind, but some is inevitable. Add a hint of your own corroded household pipes (the Water Department claims those are the worst offenders) and you have the potable classic: Philadelphia water.

Experience affects opinion. Those who live where drinking water smells of sulfur or is even slightly brackish treasure ours. Conversely, to those who vacation alongside crystalline mountain streams, a sip of Philadelphia water hastens the return to reality. Considering how many people and industries our water has already cycled through, drinkability seems no slight achievement. And our flavorful stuff is safer by far than that of scores of smaller municipalities.

❖

Car-Free in Philadelphia: The Regional Public Transit Guide (Robert J. Ravelli, ed., Camino Books, 1993) notes that conductors rarely check tickets between the crowded 30th Street and Market East station stops on SEPTA's commuter rail trains.

Both the YMCA and the YMHA make allowances for low-income memberships. A respectful, written request is recommended. YMCA main office: 1429 Walnut Street, 963-3705. YMHA main office: Broad and Pine Streets, 545-4400.

$.25

$.30

$.85

❖

July 1956: The Pennsylvania Railroad offers the City of Philadelphia air rights over the tracks to the north of 30th Street Station in return for vacant industrial land. Considered use: a 60,000-seat sports stadium.

Cost of Living

What's It Got to Do with the Price of Pretzels?

Some people manage to get by on baloney and some think they can't live without Beluga and some really can't live without kidney transplants, which makes their costs of living like apples and oranges—there's no comparison. Even if you could put the world on bread and water, you'd be comparing Evian ($1.29 for 1½ liters) to Perrier ($.95 a liter) to Wissahickon Spring ($.69 a gallon) to Philadelphia tap (either $2.13 per 100 cubic feet or $11.53 per 1,000 cubic feet, according to two different people at the Department of Water Revenue). A loaf of whole wheat costs $1.50 at Jack's Firehouse Bakery in Spring Garden, $2.95 at the French Bakery in Chestnut Hill, $.69 at the Stroehmann Bakeries Thrift Store in South Philadelphia—so which one do you compare to the three loaves Ben Franklin spent his last three cents on the day he got here?

And, given this incomparability, how does the Consumer Price Index manage to measure the cost of living? The short answer is: It doesn't.

Even though it's used to calculate cost-of-living adjustments to the incomes of people on Social Security, food stamps, and military and Civil Service pensions, the Consumer Price Index doesn't even try to measure the cost of living, and it admits this right up front. One of the many useful publications the Bureau of Labor Statistics is happy to send to curious citizens explains that, "although it is often called a cost-of-living index (and is sometimes used as one), the CPI is an index of price change only." It tells you how much the prices of things go up—or down, as they did here in 1921, '22, '27, '28, '30–'33, '38, '39, '49, and '55—but not how many things people actually buy at those increased or decreased prices. The Bureau suspects that when the price of caviar skyrockets, a lot of people buy clam dip instead, so their cost of living actually goes down. But the Bureau doesn't know for sure, because it doesn't track what people buy, only how much things cost.

Which things? The CPI tracks the prices of about 250 categories of consumer goods, parceled into seven major groups: food, housing, apparel and its upkeep, transportation, health care, entertainment, and "other." That last category includes such heterogeneous items as haircuts and college tuition, which may not be as incomparable as they sound. As tuition rises, the parents of college students get fewer haircuts, right? ■

Renters: Know Your Rights

Philadelphia tenants—and there are more than 200,000— have very few rights, according to the Tenants' Action Group of Philadelphia. In conflicts between landlords and tenants, the deck is stacked against the tenant. Before signing a lease, read it and learn your rights. The Tenants' Action Group offers two free classes, one on tenants' rights and another on eviction self-defense. Each is offered several times a week at 21 S. 12th Street. Call 575-0700 for details.

A written lease is best, although oral agreements for periods of up to three years are not unheard of. Written leases are most commonly for one year or sometimes for thirty days. Regardless of the length of the lease, if when it ends your landlord chooses not to renew it, you have no recourse unless you (a) are a victim of discrimination or landlord retaliation, (b) were not given proper notice, or (c) were paid up on the rent and the landlord has housing code violations on the property.

Perhaps the best commercially available lease in the city is "Form 78" (available for $2.00 at John C. Clark, Stationer, 1326 Walnut Street). The lease does, however, contain two clauses that the Tenants' Action Group considers "anti-tenant." One allows the landlord to "pass through" increased expenses to the tenant, therefore permitting the landlord to raise the rent in the middle of the lease. Another requires a landlord to give a tenant only five days' notice in beginning eviction proceedings for nonpayment of rent.

Pay special attention to the following aspects of the lease: lease price, rent due dates, number of dwellers allowed, whether pets are permitted, appliances included, whether you are responsible for legal fees for eviction, notice required to end the lease, notice required in an alleged breach of lease, and any provisions you are unable or unwilling to keep.

While a tenant is bound by the terms of a lease, some lease terms *cannot* be enforced in court. For example, a tenant cannot be (a) made to take a dwelling "as is," (b) made responsible for all repairs or all repairs over or under a certain amount of money, or (c) prohibited from representing himself or herself in court. The lease cannot allow a landlord to (a) seize the possessions of a tenant who is behind in rent without going through a legal process, (b) change the locks and seize a tenant's possessions if the tenant breaks the lease, or (c) prohibit the tenant from suing the landlord.

Legally enforceable clauses sometimes found in leases include: (a) the tenant agrees to pay whatever legal and other expenses the landlord incurs during eviction for nonpayment of rent; (b) the tenant agrees not to sublet the apartment without written consent of the landlord; (c) any additions or improvements made by the tenant become the property of the landlord; (d) the landlord can require the tenant to remove additions or bill the tenant for the cost of doing so; and (e) the tenant agrees to pay all rent due for the remaining portion of the lease if he or she breaks the lease.

Any promises a landlord makes—such as making repairs after a renter moves in—may pass by the wayside if they are not mentioned in the lease. On rare occasions, the interpretation of a lease may be in a tenant's favor. For example, if a lease says nothing about pets, pets are allowed. But why have to go to court to keep your cat? It's best to get it in writing. ■

Source: Tenants' Action Group of Philadelphia, *The Tenant Survival Book.*

Buying a House: Settlement Costs

Closing the sale, or settlement, is the end of the home-buying process and the beginning of a new set of responsibilities. Both buyer and seller pay dearly to consummate this legal act—usually conducted by a broker, lender, title company, or attorney—in which the title of the property passes from seller to buyer. Here are the estimated settlement costs for both parties for an average Philadelphia rowhouse costing $60,000 in the Lower Northeast. The buyer has obtained a conventional, $54,000, 30-year mortgage for 7.5% and is prepared to make a down payment of 10%, or $6,000.

Buyer's Estimated Settlement Costs	$ 6,193.58
Closing	*4,347.00*
Title Insurance	494.00
Realty Transfer Tax (2.115%)	1,269.00
Recording of Deed and Mortgage	60.00
Notary Fees	15.00
Mortgage Application Fee	325.00
Mortgage Document Preparation Fee	200.00
Private Mortgage Insurance	269.00
(insurance against loss by lender in case borrower defaults)	
Points—Mortgage Service Fee	1,620.00
(3% of mortgage)	
Endorsements #100, #300	45.00
(fee to ensure property lines)	
Water and Sewer Adjustment	50.00
Accruals	*1,846.58*
Tax Accruals (1 yr.)	1,300.00
Tax Accruals (2 mo.)	216.67
Fire/Homeowner's Insur. (1 yr.)	250.00
Fire/Homeowner's Insur. Accruals (2 mo.)	41.67
PMI Accruals (2 mo.)	27.00
1 Day's Interest	11.25
Total Due at Settlement	**$ 66,193.58**
(Less Total Amount Financed	54,000.00)
Cash Required at Settlement	**$ 12,193.58**

Seller's Estimated Settlement Costs	$ 5,029.00
Realty Transfer Tax (2.115%)	1,269.00
(total 4.23% tax is usually shared by seller and buyer)	
Notary Fees	15.00
Termite Certification	75.00
City Certification	50.00
Disbursement Fee	20.00
Mortgage Payoff	—
Broker's Commission	3,600.00
(Total Net Proceeds to Seller	**$54,971.00)**

Some Estimated Monthly Costs of Running that $60,000 Rowhouse:	
Principal and Interest	$ 377.58
PMI Insurance Fee	13.50
Taxes	108.33
Fire/Homeowner's Insurance	20.83
Water/Sewer	40.00
Electric (non-electric heat)	70.42
Gas	74.00
Total	**$ 704.66**

Sources: Jackson-Cross Company Realtors; Summit Financial Mortgage Corporation; PGW; PECO; Philadelphia City Planning Commission; Water Revenue Bureau.

▼▼

MORTGAGE SAVVY

In working with a mortgage company or a mortgage broker, you'll be surprised to learn how many fees are negotiable—if you just ask. For instance:

The Disbursement Fee is merely a $20 bonus charged by the mortgage company to write the checks. Isn't this their job?

If you shop around for your own title insurance, you can usually get the same coverage for 20 percent less than what a mortgage company will charge to get it for you.

Make sure your mortgage application fee is applied toward the closing costs (for such fees as credit report and appraisal), or get a full refund at settlement.

Private mortgage insurance is not required if your down payment is 20 percent or more.

Points are always negotiable.

Water and sewer adjustments are not necessary if the proper work is done before settlement. Ask for this fee back at closing.

Questions and Answers

Where can I get a copy of the Philadelphia City Charter?

To get a copy of the City Charter as it has stood since April 17, 1951, go to Room 250, 16th and Arch Streets, pay your $10, and tote the tome home—all 230 pages of it. Be prepared to buy another, revised charter soon, though.

What about a copy of the City Building Code?

As long as you are there, why not pick up a copy of the entire City Code? It provides every ordinance, rule, and nuance for everything from plumbing to electricity for $90 (the price does not include a binder). This and the City Charter are both also available by mail (call 686-4755).

What's a constable?

A constable is a locally elected official whose origin is in English common law. In William Penn's Pennsylvania, the constable kept the peace, executed warrants, and prevented unruly crowds from gathering. Today constables still have the authority to make arrests, but they spend most of their time serving summonses and other legal documents for district justices. The office was abolished in Philadelphia in 1970.

Has the one-horse open sleigh passed me by?

Wait for a good layer of snow on the ground—at least a few inches—then call Bob Dougherty, the last of the rent-a-sleighs, at 248-4490 to make a reservation. The sleigh departs Valley Green Inn on Forbidden Drive (motorists are forbidden to drive there) along the romantic and craggy Wissahickon. You'll enjoy a one-hour ride through the darkest and loveliest section of Fairmount Park on a winter's day or evening for $50 (a four-person sleigh) or $100 (the 10-passenger model).

Where do I go to register to vote?

To the nearest state store, or post office, or library, or many other city offices. Large quantities of registration forms (for registration campaigns) are available at 520 N. Delaware Avenue, 5th floor, as are absentee ballots. For more information, call 686-1505. The Registration Office is always open until midnight on the final day to register (a month before the election) to give you every last chance to register and drop off filled-in forms.

Can I rent a Renoir?

No, but you can rent or buy paintings from the Philadelphia Museum of Art Sales and Rental Gallery (787-5451). Become a member of the Museum, take a look at

ELECTRICITY Q & A

- **How do you turn on the lights?**
  Start with a phone call. There are three PECO "sectors" in Philadelphia and one for each surrounding county; check the phone book to determine the number to call. If you don't have a phone book handy, call the folks at PECO's main number, 841-4000. They'll ask for your Social Security number and will send a PECO worker to your home within three days (someone must be home to let the worker in). A $6.00 charge will show up on your first bill.

- **How can I avoid the ongoing meter readings?**
  You can't, entirely. You must let meter readers in twice a year for verification. If the meter is mounted on the exterior of your house or the building in which you live, you don't need to be home when they cut the juice. If you find it largely impossible to be home for regular meter readings, ask about an automatic reader that can be installed at PECO's suggestion. You read this meter yourself and call in the information. Or you can get a card to fill out and display in your window for the meter reader to copy.

LEAVING TOWN?

- **Can I get a passport without going to the Federal Building at 6th and Arch Streets?**
  There's a passport office in each of the county courthouses:

  Doylestown (Bucks County), 348-6191

  West Chester (Chester County), 344-6310

  Media (Delaware County), 891-4399

  Norristown (Montgomery County), 278-3783

  You must apply for a passport in person unless you're renewing an expired passport within 12 years of the date of issue. In that case, you can apply by mail.

STREETS Q & A

- **How do I make a pothole?**
Hire a plumber. Their ditches for water pipe repairs make the best chassis-wrackers. Patched areas often settle and sink, leaving troughlike holes. During winter months, water expands as it freezes in the cracks. Salt, cinders, studded snow tires, and chains broaden innocent cracks into potholes that proliferate in early spring, like crocuses.

- **Now that I've made a pothole, how do I get it filled?**
In Philadelphia, call 686-5508. A Streets Department repair crew will be out as soon as possible—which means about 15 working days, at best. If you see an especially large or dangerous pothole, call your local police precinct and ask that a warning marker be set out.

- **How do I get a street light repaired?**
Call 592-5683, and you'll get a speedy response. Problems called in before 7:30pm are checked by 4:30am. The office is available by phone 21 hours a day (closed from 4am to 7am).

- **How do I get a traffic light or stop sign installed?**
Good luck. The city has been removing traffic lights to save money. But go ahead and make a case to your representative City Councilperson. To get an existing traffic light repaired, call 686-5530.

IT'S NOT ELEMENTARY

- **How old does a child have to be to enroll in kindergarten?**
It depends on the school district. In Upper Darby, a prospective kindergartner must be 5 by August 31; in Lower Merion, by September 1; in Central Bucks, by September 15; in Upper Merion and Medford, October 1; in Wallingford-Swarthmore, October 31; and in Haverford, January 31. Prospective kindergartners in Philadelphia must turn 5 by February 1.

CITIZENS' MANUAL

How To

their collection of contemporary paintings and photographs by local artists, and make your decision. They'll take your credit card imprint and other vital information. The charge is 10% of the value of the work per month; there is a two-month rental minimum for your home, four months for your company. Rental fees can be applied toward the purchase price.

Where do I play golf without joining a country club?
Several courses within the city limits are available for a nominal greens fee. At Walnut Lane Golf Course (482-3370), Henry Avenue and Walnut Lane, more than 30,000 players enjoy the game each year. You can play from 6am to 8pm Monday to Friday for $14 per round, Saturday and Sunday for $16. Call ahead to reserve tee times for weekends, which are assigned on a first-come first-served basis. Club rentals are $9 a round, and if you need some tips the club pro is available for $30 per half-hour, five lessons for $120.

Can anyone march in the Thanksgiving Day Parade?
Well, not anyone. You have to have *some* talent. Ask WPVI-TV (Channel 6), the parade sponsors, for an application (581-4507). The parade producer will review your submission (which may include a video cassette and photographs). WPVI reaches out to lots of local bands, but they're happy to consider applications—and you've got nothing to lose.

I have no talent to speak of. Can I help out in some other way?
Volunteers are needed the day of the parade to do everything from usher in the grandstands to help the bands hit their mark on time. Shifts begin around 5am. Call 581-4507 in advance.

Where can I get free condoms?
Many health centers distribute a free package of 10 condoms, including these clinics, which are open during regular business hours: Health Center One, 1400 Lombard Street (875-5637), Episcopal Hospital, Front and Lehigh Streets (427-7365), and Health Center Five, 20th and Berks Streets (978-2490).

Where can I get a free condom at nights and on weekends?
Procrastination can pay off. Seven days a week, you'll find someone handing out flyers on South Street offering a free condom at Condom Nation, plus a discount on a purchase. The shop, located at 626 S. 4th Street (925-7177), is open daily at 11am and closes Sunday and Monday at 10pm, Tuesday to Thursday at 11pm, and Friday and Saturday at 12:30am.

CITIZENS'
MANUAL

How To

Can I adopt an elephant? How about a rat?

If you're tired of the rats who live on your block, adopt a naked mole rat at the Philadelphia Zoo—$25 covers its nutritional intake for a year. An elephant in the same Zoo Adoption program (call 243-1100, ext. 232) will set you back as much as $2,500. If that's too steep, buy an elephant "Dinner for a Week" for $48. A gorilla, if you prefer, is a still cheaper date at $29. You'll receive a photograph suitable for framing, a Certificate of Parentage, a fact sheet, a newsletter, and an invitation to Parent's Recognition Day. About 2,500 folks help to feed the animals at the "Nation's First Zoo."

Whom do I call to confirm a rumor?

The Philadelphia Commission on Human Relations maintains a "Report a Rumor" line: 686-4670. They'll take your call anonymously, if you wish, and they'll check it out.

Are there still fox hunts?

It's little known outside horse circles, but the public is welcome to tag along by car ("car-following" is the technical term) or on horseback ("hilltopping"). Call a hunt club for details. Radnor Hunt Club (644-9918) is the area's oldest. The season runs from fall to spring.

Where can I bury my dead pet?

Since 1889 the Francisvale Home for Smaller Animals (688-1018) has maintained a locally famous pet cemetery on a hillside at Upper Gulph Road and Arden Road in Radnor Township. Burial fees vary according to the size of the animal. A small dog, for example, would cost about $260. You must make separate arrangements for a headstone.

Where can I take my family for an inexpensive weekend getaway?

Rent a cabin at a Pennsylvania state park. Twenty-four of the state's 114 parks offer cabins that are rented out to residents and non-residents by lottery. Call (800) 637-2757 to get the *Pennsylvania Recreation Guide*, the brochure *Cabins in Pennsylvania State Parks*, and an application.

The closest park with cabins is French Creek State Park in Elverson, Chester County (582-1514).

Can I escape the city lights and do some serious stargazing?

The Strawbridge Memorial Observatory at Haverford College (896-1000) and the Sproul Observatory at Swarthmore College (328-8000) are open to the public one night a month during the school year. An astronomy student or professor explains how to operate the telescopes and what to look for.

What's wrong with the dogwood trees?

Dogwood blight, or anthracnose, has killed thousands of dogwoods on the East Coast since the late 1970s. Anthracnose is a fungus that causes spotted leaves and weakens the tree. If a tree isn't seriously infected, it may recover. Prune away dead twigs and branches. Keep the tree adequately watered and don't over-fertilize. Apply a fungicide in spring.

On a home remodeling project, who's responsible for the building permit?

Most contractors will apply for the necessary building permit, but obtaining one is ultimately the property owner's responsibility. What you must apply for varies from place to place, but a permit is nearly always required for new construction or for renovations costing more than a few hundred dollars. Some townships also require building permits for roofing, fences, or signs. If you are having work done on your house, it's a good idea to ask the contractor for a copy of the filing.

If I dug straight down, clear through the center of the earth, would I end up in China?

No, it's a generations-old urban myth. Philadelphia is listed in the *Rand McNally Illustrated Atlas of the World* as being located at 39°57' north latitude and 75°7' west longitude. Dig a hole clear through to the opposite side and you would be at 39°57' south latitude and 104°53' east longitude—or in the middle of the Indian Ocean. The nearest land is about 700 miles to the northeast: Cape Naturaliste, Australia. ∎

COMMUNITY DROPOFF POINTS FOR PLASTICS

- Center City: Reading Terminal Market, Arch Street between 11th and 12th Streets. Phone: 592-8774. First Saturday only, 11am–1:30pm.
- Northwest Philadelphia: Weaver's Way Recycling, Unitarian Church Parking Lot at rear of 6511 Lincoln Drive. Phone: 884-2488. Every third Saturday, 9:30am–1:30pm.
- South Philadelphia: South Philadelphia Environmental Coalition, 12th and Reed Streets. Phone: 467-3377. First Saturday only, 10:30am–12:30pm.
- West Philadelphia: The Firehouse Farmers Market, 50th Street and Baltimore Avenue. Phone: 724-7660. First and third Saturdays, 10am–1pm.

CITY DROPOFF POINTS FOR PLASTICS:

19111: Northeast High School, Cottman and Algon Avenues. Saturdays 1–4pm.

19116: Washington High School, 11000 Bustleton Avenue. Saturdays 9am–noon.

19128: Streets Department Station, 330 Domino Lane. Saturdays 1–4pm.

19136: Lincoln High School, Rowland and Ryan Avenues. Saturdays 1–4pm.

19144: City Parking Lot, Chew Avenue and Washington Lane. Saturdays 9am–noon.

19154: Rush Middle School, Knights and Fairdale Roads. Saturdays 9am–noon.

Source: Philadelphia Recycling Office.

❖

The biggest source of pollution in Philadelphia is *you*—in your car. Auto exhaust is the city's number-one environmental problem, a trait Philadelphia shares with other major urban areas. Nationwide, automobiles are responsible for one-half of the carbon monoxide, one-third of the nitrogen oxides, and one-quarter of the hydrocarbons released into the atmosphere.

CITIZENS' MANUAL

Recycling

Forgoing Plastics

Philadelphia's curbside recycling program is scheduled to be operating citywide by March 1994, but recycling plastics will still be a do-it-yourself affair.

Budget constraints forced officials to drop plastics from the curbside collections and scale back pickups from weekly to biweekly. Unless the economy improves, no policy change is in sight.

City crews collect newspapers, metal, and glass curbside from blue recycling buckets every other week. The mandatory program, which began in January 1989 in the city's Northwest and then expanded, serves household residences, except those with six or more units. Recycling guidelines for businesses and apartment buildings are scheduled to take effect in 1994.

The crews won't take empty plastic milk jugs and liter soda bottles. Residents who wish to recycle plastic items must take those items to one of ten dropoff sites, four run by community groups and six by the city.

The city spends $140 to collect and dispose of a ton of trash. As of April 1993, the city spends $107 for every ton of recyclables. If the city collected plastics at curbside, recycling costs would soar to an estimated $700 per ton, says Thomas Klein, the program's director of education and promotion.

"In a waste management world that is measuring everything by weight, plastic is just too light for its volume to be cost-effectively handled. You drive around with a truck that's loaded to the gills, but it doesn't bring in much tonnage because there's so much plastic, which is essentially air."

Klein says the city's Saturday-morning dropoff points draw a steady low-level stream of traffic in plastics recycling, mostly of empty gallon milk jugs and liter soda bottles.

"I don't think any city has been able to make [curbside plastics recycling] work," he says. "The reason plastics continue to be collected in city recycling programs is the public wants it and the program managers either have enough money to pay for it or they don't know how much they pay for it."

But plastic isn't the only recycling challenge. The new biweekly pickups have taken a big toll on participation. As long as curbside pickup was weekly, between 80 and 90 percent participated. Now it's down to 50 percent, which raises the age-old question: Is the jug half empty or half full? ∎

CITIZENS' MANUAL

Recycling

Big Trash

One person's trash can be another's treasure, but here's how to get rid of what nobody (around here) seems to want:

Large appliances, mattresses, furniture, etc.: Put these out with your regular trash; the city will send a special truck, usually the following day. Call a charitable organization or thrift store to see if they can use the items.

Tires: No more than two can be put out with trash. Many tire dealers will, for a small fee, accept them for recycling. There are also two local commercial recycling centers. Domino Salvage, 1251 Conshohocken Road in Conshohocken (277-6670), charges $1 per tire; Waste Management of North America, Inc., at Milner and Bleigh Streets in Philadelphia (335-0330), charges $1.50 per tire.

Car batteries: All dealers who sell new batteries must accept the old one for recycling. (If they don't, call the Department of Environmental Resources at 1-800-346-4242.) A few businesses will pay you a nominal fee for your car batteries: William G. Smith & Sons, 2948 N. 2nd Street (763-5528); East Coast Recycling, 3301 Tulip Street (634-2030); National Temple Recycling Center, 1201 Glenwood Avenue (787-2760); Jack's Paper Stock & Scrap Metal, 3615 Emerald Street (535-7588); Charles Piacentino Scrap Metal, Swanson and Ritner Streets (389-4434).

Trees, shrubs, etc.: Leave them curbside. Tie branches together in bundles four feet long and two feet in diameter; do the same for logs and tree branches.

Motor oil: *Don't* pour used oil down the storm sewer; it's illegal. Pep Boys stores accept used motor oil, as do many Exxon service stations (for the nearest one, call Exxon at 800-732-1100). Many other gas stations also accept used oil.

Building material and construction debris: Although the city won't accept these materials, here are three Philadelphia companies that will charge you by the ton or by the load: Richard S. Burns Company, 4300 Rising Sun Avenue (324-0519); Winzinger Recycling, Delaware and Allegheny Avenues (425-4422); Delaware Valley Recycling, Inc., 3107 S. 61st Street (724-2244). ■

❖ **WORD RECYCLING: Here are 44 words of four letters or more composed from the word "Philadelphia":** aide, ailed, aped, aphid, appall, appeal, apple, applied, dale, deal, dell, dial, dill, hail, hale, hall, head, heap, held, hell, help, hide, hied, hill, ideal, idle, ladle, laid, lapel, lead, leap, lied, paid, pail, pale, pall, peal, pied, pile, pill, plaid, plea, plead, plied

SUBURBAN RECYCLING

Under the state law requiring recycling, municipalities and townships of more than 4,000 population must recycle at least three materials out of a list of ten. Among the communities that do more than the minimum are Upper Moreland and Abington Townships in eastern Montgomery County.

Upper Moreland collects clear, brown and green glass, aluminum and tin cans, newspapers, and yard waste. Set out in biodegradable bags, residents' lawn clippings, leaves, and other yard waste are collected every Monday and taken to a township compost site, where they are free for the taking by residents and non-residents alike.

In the five years since the program was expanded to include compost, the township has cut by half the trash tonnage it pays to incinerate—no small savings. Public spiritedness keeps the program going, but the township also conducts spot checks on neighborhoods and issues warning letters to non-recyclers, according to public works director Jack Snyder.

Neighboring Abington Township's recycling program—one of the oldest—dates back to 1970. Besides glass, cans, newspapers, and lawn waste, Abington also collects junk mail.

"It's second nature to all the people," says public works director Ed Micciolo, who estimates that the township recycles 39 percent of its trash. "The more you recycle, the more it saves you in the long run."

JURY DUTY

To serve on a county or federal jury panel you must be a U.S. citizen; over 18; able to read, write, and understand English; and able—physically and mentally.

Jury selection for Philadelphia Court of Common Pleas:

Jury Assembly Room 111, City Hall, Philadelphia, PA 19107

Jury Selection Commission: 686-4658

Questionnaires mailed to city residents each year seeking background information: 300,000

Percent rejected based on questionnaire: 35–40%

Prospective jurors summoned each day: 350–500

Percent of that pool actually picked for a trial: 30–50%

Length of service: One day or one trial

Compensation for jurors: $9 per day for first three days; $25 per day thereafter

Jury selection for Federal District Court (Eastern District of Pennsylvania):

Room 2609, U.S. District Court, 601 Market Street, Philadelphia, PA 19106, 597-7728

Questionnaires mailed each year: 30,000

Location of residents receiving questionnaires: 10 Eastern Pennsylvania counties

Percent rejected based on questionnaire: 35%

Prospective jurors summoned each week: 470

Percent of that pool selected each week to serve: 30%

Length of service: Two days or one trial

Compensation for jurors: $40 per day, plus parking and mileage ($.25 per mile)

Public Meetings

This schedule of Philadelphia Boards and Agencies' public meetings provides the essentials of democracy in action. For information on public meetings outside of Philadelphia, call your city or town clerk's office.

Art Commission. First Wednesday each month. Time varies. 1600 Arch Street, 12th floor. 686-4463. Submit proposals ahead.

City Council. Every Thursday except in July, August, first week of January, Thanksgiving and Christmas weeks. 10am, City Hall, Room 400. 686-3410.

City Planning Commission. Usually first and third Thursday each month, except only once in July and August. 1pm, 1717 Market Street, 15th floor conference room. 686-4606. Call ahead to address meeting.

Commission on Human Relations. First Wednesday each month. 9:30am, 34 S. 11th Street, 4th floor. 686-4675. Call ahead to address meeting.

Delaware River Port Authority. Third Wednesday each month. 9am, Administration Building, Ben Franklin Bridge, Camden. 925-8780.

Delaware Valley Regional Planning Commission. Third Thursday each month. 10:30am, The Bourse, 21 S. 5th Street, 8th floor. 592-1800, ext. 175. Regional Citizens Committee of the DVRPC: Third Tuesday each month. Noon or 1pm, same location and telephone.

Fairmount Park Commission. Second Wednesday each month, except July and August. 3pm, Memorial Hall, Fairmount Park. 685-0000. Submit in advance drawings for review.

Gas Commission. First or second Tuesday each month, except July and August. 10am, 1401 Arch Street, Suite 1226. 563-6928.

Historical Commission. Second Wednesday each month. 10am, City Hall, Room 401. Architectural Committee: last Thursday each month. 2 or 3pm, 1401 Arch Street, 13th floor. 686-4543. Submit drawings in advance.

Redevelopment Authority. Second and fourth Tuesday each month. 4pm, 1234 Market Street, 8th floor. 854-6582. Call ahead to address meeting.

Southeastern Pennsylvania Transportation Authority. Fourth Thursday each month, except November and December, third Thursday. 3pm, 714 Market Street, 3rd floor. 580-7330. Call ahead to address meeting.

Zoning Board of Adjustment. Hearings every Tuesday at 8:30am and every Wednesday at 3:30 and 5pm, 1321 Arch Street. 686-7878. ∎

CITIZENS' MANUAL

Rights, Privileges, and Obligations

Taxes

No matter where (or just about how) you live, you can't get away without paying taxes—at least not here. Here are the many city taxes a Philadelphia resident or business person must cough up each year.

City and county taxes:

- Gross Receipts Tax (for businesses): 3.25 mills on taxable gross receipts
- Hotel Room Rental Tax: 5% of room rate
- Net Income Tax (for businesses): 6.5% on taxable net income
- Net Profits Tax (for businesses; corporations exempt): 4.96% on net profits
- Personal Property Tax: 4 mills on assessed valuation of taxable items
- Real Estate Tax: $3.745 per $100 assessment
- Real Estate Transfer Tax: 3.23% through June 30, 1994; 3% thereafter
- Sales and Use Tax: 1%. Exemptions to state and city sales and use taxes: food not consumed on premises, many household supplies, clothing, medical supplies and devices, textbooks, fuel and utility services.
- Wage Tax (withheld) or Earnings Tax (not withheld): 4.3125% for non-residents, on taxable gross earnings; 4.96% for city residents
- Water and Sewer Tax: charge based on meter, size, and use

Other city taxes passed on to consumers:

- Amusement Tax: 5% of ticket price and/or 2.5% on gross receipts (now includes movie theaters)
- Departure Tax (Passenger Facility Charge): $3 per airline passenger
- Mechanical Amusement Device Tax: $100 per year per device (on coin- or token-operated devices such as videogames, jukeboxes, and peep shows)
- Parking Tax: 15% of amount charged

Philadelphia public school taxes:

- Business Use and Occupancy Tax: $4.62 per $100 of assessed value of real estate used for business purposes
- School Income Tax: 4.96% on taxable income
- School Real Estate Tax: $4.519 per $100 assessment

Sources: Pennsylvania Economy League; Philadelphia Code; Philadelphia Department of Revenue.

YOUR VOTE

To vote you must be a citizen of the United States, 18 years old by the day after the election, and a resident of your election district for at least 30 days before the election.

HOW TO REGISTER:

In person: In Philadelphia, register at the Voter Registration Division, Riverview Place, Delaware Avenue and Spring Garden Street, 5th floor; or at City Hall, Room 138. In the suburban counties, register at your county courthouse.

By mail: Obtain an application from your post office, library, or state liquor store. Complete the application and mail it in (the postage is free). Your county voter registration office will notify you when you are officially registered.

Re-register if you

- change your name for any reason (including marriage)
- have not voted at least once in the past five elections
- needed a court order to vote in the last election

For more information:

Philadelphia Voter Registration Division: 686-1505

County Board of Elections: 686-3469

To obtain an absentee ballot: City Hall, Room 138, 686-3469

Pennsylvania State Bureau of Elections: (717) 787-5280

Committee of Seventy: 545-0104

League of Women Voters:
Philadelphia: 977-9488
Bucks County: 598-3663
Montgomery County: 836-1099
Chester County: 692-0275
Delaware County:..........449-0977
Camden County:...(609) 429-1027
N.J. League: ....(609) 394-3303

Sources: Committee of Seventy; State Bureau of Elections; League of Women Voters.

55

This Is a Recording

T he very good news about living in the age of touchtone phones and automation is that you can get detailed information 24 hours a day. Tape recordings often provide you with more information than you ever thought to ask for. What's more, these user-friendly mechanisms will repeat their messages endlessly, rarely if ever leave anything out, and don't get huffy if you hang up mid-sentence. Here's a list of some favorite touchtone linkups for fast, reliable information.

U.S. Postal Service, 382-9201

Wander through this voice-mail system and you'll never have to wait in line at your local post office (plus the number's always open). Hear about postal rates, preparing and sending packages, mail order tips, mail fraud, proof of mailing or delivery, post office and self-service locations and hours, sending valuables, moving and vacation information, and stamp collecting. There's a large library of three-digit codes (to hear the directory, just hit 328), and the system responds quickly, allowing you to interrupt one message and move on to another immediately.

Note: If it's the middle of the night—or day—and you find you're out of stamps, call (800) STAMP-24 and you can charge up to $85 on your VISA, Discover, or MasterCard for just a $3 service charge. The stamps show up in your mailbox in three to five business days. (If you do stop by your post office, you can also pick up a "Stamps-by-Mail" envelope—there's no handling fee to order stamps that way.) If you have stamps delivered at home and calculate your postage costs by phone, you can avoid post office lines forever.

WRTI-FM JAZZLINE, 204-5277

Dial this service of Temple University's jazz station to learn about current performances, as well as the names and addresses of local restaurants and clubs where live jazz is a regular feature. You can also get the scoop about recent programming on JAZZ 90, station membership information, and—for some odd reason—the "National Park Report," a short feature about visiting selected national parks. And, if you press 8, you'll have the current time.

TEL-MED, 829-5501

It's 3am and you're worried about a medical problem; whom can you call? TEL-MED is sort of like calling a friend who's a nurse—but you don't have to wake anyone up. You'll hear solid information about all kinds of ailments, from headaches to hemorrhoids; you choose from over 30 categories and several sub-topics of each. Each recording takes you through a description, followed by common diagnostic procedures and various treatment options; the message often ends with names and addresses of organizations and support groups. After it's all over, you may leave your name or request that a brochure be sent to you.

A non-intrusive mention is made that this is a service of the Pennsylvania Hospital, and they offer the number of their physician referral service. Once you've listened to the tape, maybe you'll be able to rest easier. (Press 122 to hear all about sleep.)

WDAS Datebook Hotline, 477-9327

Updated weekly, the hotline lists concerts, celebrations, events, and activities, primarily sponsored by local churches. Addresses, further information, numbers, and contact names are given. To have your activity listed, send the information in advance to WDAS-FM, Belmont and Edgely Roads, Philadelphia, PA 19131, or call 477-WDAS.

Amtrak, 824-1600

It's fast. For unreserved fare information, push different buttons to hear about trips to New York, Washington, Baltimore, Boston, Lancaster, and Harrisburg—and back again. You'll be asked to punch in times and dates of your expected arrivals and departures.

CITIZENS'
MANUAL

Telephone

Better Business Bureau, 448-6100

When a business treats you badly or you don't get the service you've been promised or paid for, speak up. The Better Business Bureau will take your complaints, investigate, push for resolution, and help future customers by keeping a report on file.

To hear an automated telephone report about a company in question, call this number and follow the instructions to enter the company's area code and phone number. You'll hear current information, learn if there are outstanding complaints against the company, and hear how the company handles complaints brought to its attention. (This service's automated voice pattern sounds like a dyspeptic computer. You'll get the feeling you've crossed over into a consumer-conscious Twilight Zone.)

Greater Philadelphia Film Office, 686-3663

Ought to be in pictures? The Greater Philadelphia Film Office coordinates and facilitates movie making in the city, and this number is a 24-hour hotline of jobs that are available on area film projects—everything from open casting calls to a slew of production jobs, including gaffers, grips, best boys, and all the other credits that only the most dedicated moviegoers—and mothers—read. It's updated weekly, and the listings are very detailed, even specifying whether there's money upfront to pay you for your work.

Social Security Administration, (800) 772-1213

When you call the Social Security Administration, the first thing you're told is how many minutes it will be before an operator can take your call. (Isn't that a nice feature?) And if you don't want to wait for a real live person, make use of the automated service. With touchtone prompts and voice messages,

you can request a new Social Security card, a record of your earnings and estimate of future benefits, proof of payments, information about how working affects your payments, or a general information booklet. And when you're done, you can hang on to talk to an operator, if you need further assistance.

IRS at Your Service, 627-1040

This IRS tape system called TELE-TAX helps you figure out your tax return. You can even get your current year's refund status right on the phone; just have your Social Security number, filing status, and the refund amount when you call.

The IRS information tapes cover a broad range of tax topics. You control the tapes by pressing the "#" key to repeat the part of the tape you just heard (giving you time to write things down) and pressing the "*" key to move on to another category. A list of the tapes and their corresponding numbers comes with your tax package, but you can also press 323 to hear the directory of topics.

Pennsylvania Convention Center, 418-4700

Convention Center officials are still trying to decide when it's appropriate to use its "Auto Attendant" service. Is it better to talk to a live person or a super-sophisticated telephone answering system? For now, callers to the Convention Center will reach real people during regular business hours and tap into Auto Attendant only if they are on hold for more than 45 seconds. Callers after 5pm can expect the automated system to direct them to Sales and Marketing, Exhibitor Services, Personnel, or the Convention Center Calendar for that week. Callers are provided not only with event dates and times but directions to the most appropriate entrance: "Enter on the north side of 12th Street, at Arch." ■

❖

In March 1877, a Philadelphia audience heard a concert performed in New York, transmitted by long-distance telephone. The program included "Yankee Doodle," "Home Sweet Home," and "The Last Rose of Summer."

Wireless telegraphers held a national contest in Philadelphia on February 23, 1910, to test speed and accuracy in receiving and transmitting signals.

CHECK YOUR ATTIC

So you're thinking about collecting baseball cards? Think it's the perfect way to combine nostalgia and low-pressure leisure time? Think again. According to baseball card expert and author Alan Rosen of Montvale, N.J., collecting has become a "billion-dollar industry."

"Collecting baseball cards is like buying a piece of the past, and collectors are so eager, the business is recession-proof," Rosen said before the first major auction of "sports memorabilia" at Christie's last year. At that sale, a ca. 1910 baseball card featuring one-time Philadelphia Nationals and Philadelphia Americans player Sherwood Magee sold for $28,600. The Magee card was particularly unusual because the player's name was misspelled "Magie."

At these prices, it's no wonder that baseball cards, printed on stock only slightly better than shirt cardboard, are handled like precious art. The Conservation Center for Art and Historic Artifacts in Philadelphia has treated, not-so-old baseball cards featuring Mickey Mantle, Pee Wee Reese, and Ernie Banks. Described as "worn but not a wreck," these cards required crease reduction, slight mending, and some cosmetic work to repair minor image loss. The cost for conservation: hundreds of dollars.

Well, it sounded like fun and relaxation—for a while, anyway.

CHECK YOUR SHOES

If you're looking to pay practically zip for collectibles how about joining the International Sand Collectors Society? This gritty group of 100 active members collects sand from all over the world and writes home about it. How about that incredibly purple sand from Nepal? (It's gorgeous.) Or beach sand from the Arkansas (pronounced ar-KAN-sas) Avenue beach in Atlantic City? (It's just good, old Jersey sand.) Membership costs $5 a year and includes a newsletter. Write to William S. Diefenbach, 43 Highview Avenue, Old Greenwich, CT 06870.

Collectibles

Painted Saws in the Pine Barrens

I n the heart of the Pine Barrens, in a red frame farmhouse situated in a field just after the paved road turns to sand, there lived a folk art painter named Margaret Bakely.

She never had an agent. She never had a gallery show. But when she died in Vincentown in 1993 at the age of 59, the oil and watercolor paintings by this former blueberry picker could be found in homes, restaurants, hunting lodges, and businesses throughout this rural slice of southern New Jersey.

Bakely painted exactly what she saw. The cranberry bogs, capturing the exquisite flame-red colors of the floating harvest. The blueberry packing houses. Deer galloping across open fields and snow-covered meadows. Farm houses with wisps of smoke coming out of chimneys. Birds, fish, flowers, sometimes people.

Her paintings could be impressionistic (some say surreal). And while her earlier work was done on paper, sketchbooks, and canvas, Bakely spent the last five or six years of her life painting on saws. Circular saws, big and small. Hand saws, including the Disston model pictured here. Six-foot-long logging saws that folks bought to hang over their fireplaces.

During her lifetime, Bakely (known as Lee or Liz) sold painted saws for $20 to over $100. Advertising was never an issue. People found her work through friends, the annual Cranberry Bog Festival, or Thompson family members who own the cranberry operations and land where Bakely lived with her husband, Vernon "Pudgy" Bakely. Remembers Pudgy: "Sometimes folks would just knock on the door and say, 'Are you the woman who paints saws?'"

Pudgy and their two children still have a collection of Bakely's painted saws, not to mention a stock of unpainted saws in a shed behind the house. Watercolors and oil sketches representing Bakely's lifetime of work are carefully stacked inside a cabinet, an arm's reach from the formica kitchen table and chair where Bakely always sat down to paint.

And while the family still sells an occasional saw or painting, Pudgy claims he wants to keep the last dozen or so saws hanging in the farmhouse where Margaret Bakely lived.

A tribute to this native Pinelands folk artist was held at the 1993 Cranberry Bog Festival in Chatsworth, where a special exhibit featured the work of Margaret Bakely. ∎

Road Map Warrior

Did you know that...

- one of the first road maps, published in 1914 by Gulf, was a vest-pocket book with modest lines and dots connecting Pittsburgh with nearby towns?
- the 1935 Esso Road Map of Washington, D.C., includes flags for each embassy, including the German flag of the Nazi Third Reich?
- the 1939, 1940, and 1941 Esso Road Maps of Tennessee indicate the town of Polaski, the birthplace of the Ku Klux Klan, with depictions of hooded Klansmen?
- "a more intellectual crowd" in the Northeast, ranging from civil engineers to map curators, subscribes to Noel Levy's monthly titled "The Map Catalogue"?

Levy, a road map collector/dealer from Dallas and Baltimore, maintains that "the average redneck...can't read a map. He can't fold a map." Levy claims that "there are maybe a couple of hundred map collectors across the country." His catalogue offers some 5,000 road maps for sale from $1 to $15 each. A one-year catalogue subscription is $30. Write to P.O. Box 595699, Dallas, TX 75359.

One client made a historical record of road development in the western half of the country, collecting only road maps for areas west of the 90th meridian. Others hunt maps from the year and the state of their birth. Some collect entire series of maps issued by specific oil companies, like Texaco or Esso. Still others cotton to maps with special covers—like scenic pictures or tourist destinations. "It's a new kind of hobby. It's really in its infancy," says Levy.

When asked how he got started in map collecting, Levy responds with an ordinary-is-extraordinary answer. "My parents piled us four kids in a station wagon and we'd go on long road trips and stop for gas and to go to the bathroom and what would be interesting to a kid was a road map and I would stuff them in the back seat.

"But I really didn't do much with it until about 10 or 11 years ago," admits this former public relations, advertising, and business professional who one day noticed road maps in an antique store. That started him thinking about a new career as a dealer in early road maps. Today, his collection includes national and international road maps from 1900 to the present.

"I think a historian once said that there are laborers, inquisitors, intellectuals and warriors," says Levy. "I think I'm a warrior for the intellectual." ■

❖

"E Pluribus Unum" (out of many, one) was first seen on coins from the Philadelphia Mint in 1795.

Pennsylvania Train Wrecks, 1856–1980

July 17, 1856: Fifty-nine die and twice that number are injured—many of them school children bound for a picnic—in a head-on crash near the quiet town of Wissahickon in Montgomery County. A Quaker widow named Mary Johnson Ambler heroically tends the injured. In 1888, the town is renamed in her honor.

July 15, 1864: A coal train collides with another transporting 800 Confederate prisoners of war near Shohola in Pike County. Ten Union guards and 67 prisoners die.

October 4, 1877: A reunion of the descendants of Heinrich Pennypacker, an early settler of Chester County, turns into a disaster when a torrential storm washes out 60 feet of track near Kimberton. The train is derailed; seven die and dozens are injured.

April 5, 1878: A freight train rear-ends a line of 40 stopped tank cars filled with oil. The resulting explosions and a spectacular fire threaten the town of Slatington in Lehigh County. Six die and 50 are injured.

October 10, 1888: In a crash at "Mud Run," between Hazleton and Scranton, wooden passenger cars collapse like a telescope, killing 64.

September 19, 1890: One coal train rams another, stopped on a curve near Shoemakersville in Berks County. Within a few minutes, the evening express to Pottsville plows into the wreckage. The engine and cars tumble into the Schuylkill, killing 22 and injuring 30.

October 24, 1892: Just north of the Flat Rock tunnel across the Schuylkill River from Manayunk, a passenger express collides head-on with an outbound freight. Seven die.

December 1893: When Lehigh Valley Railroad workers strike on November 18, over wages and other grievances, management hires inexperienced workers. Several wrecks follow. The worst is at White Haven when a fire following a crash nearly engulfs the town. The strike ends when Mary Cummings, daughter of the railroad's founder, sides with the workers.

May 12, 1899: Twenty-nine die and dozens are injured when the second section of a Philadelphia-bound express crashes into the first section, stopped at Lorane, south of Reading. An antiquated signaling system is blamed.

August 13, 1900: During a heavy thunderstorm, a funeral procession of several horse-drawn omnibuses approaches a grade crossing near Slatington, Lehigh County. The first omnibus passes, just ahead of a westbound train. The second does not, and 13 of 28 mourners die. (In the 20th century,

DEATH IN THE DELAWARE: 1856

At eight o'clock on Saturday evening, March 15, Captain Corson cast off lines from the ferry *New Jersey*, moored at the foot of Walnut Street. The Delaware still flowed thick with ice. Near mid-river, from the engine room, Corson heard the cry of "fire" and turned back to Philadelphia. The brick boiler had collapsed and the entire ferry was soon aflame with Corson and the pilot house at the center of the inferno. A crowd gathering on the waterfront witnessed the self-illuminated disaster. "One by one—sometimes five or six at a time," noted one eyewitness, "they made the fearful leap from the burning wreck into the scarcely less likelihood of death amid the icy water." Rescuers among the floes of ice, including members of the Vigilant Engine Company, saved 46. Sixty-one died; 30 bodies were never recovered.

grade-crossing fatalities will far outnumber fatalities of railroad passengers.)

May 11, 1905: Theatrical magnate Sam S. Shubert and 22 others die near Harrisburg when the Cleveland-bound express sideswipes a derailed freight car loaded with explosives. Damages paid per victim average $250.

December 5, 1921:

The 1943 Congressional Limited wreck.

Twenty-six die as two older, wood-body commuter coaches meet head-on in a deep cut near Bryn Athyn. In response, the Reading Railroad switches to steel cars.

September 9, 1943: Eighty die on Labor Day as an axle of the Pennsylvania Railroad's proud Congressional Limited fails on a curve in the Frankford section of Philadelphia. Several cars are ripped open as they ram a signal tower.

May 18, 1951: In the bright sunshine of an early morning, a Red Arrow Express engineer rounds the curve near the Rosemont Station to see a stopped Philadelphia Night Express. Two sleeping cars are demolished as nine die and 60 are injured.

July 28, 1962: Faulty rail alignment is to blame for the derailed Harrisburg-to-Philadelphia "baseball special" at Steelton. Three cars roll down an embankment into the Susquehanna River. Nineteen die; 116 are injured.

November 11, 1978: More than 1,000 are routed overnight from their homes in Sharon Hill when a Conrail derailment leads to a sulfuric acid spill.

July 17, 1980: Seventy persons are injured when a commuter train, stopped near North Wales for mechanical problems, is struck from behind by another. SEPTA, heir to a consolidated, 490-mile aging network of rails, finds 24 bridges unsafe, 434 bridges in need of repair, and 350 functioning passenger cars in dire need of repair. ■

Source: Charles J. Adams III and David J. Seibold, *Great Train Wrecks of Eastern Pennsylvania* (Exeter House Books, 1992).

DESTRUCTION ON BROAD STREET: 1923

At 11:20pm on Sunday, June 10, a locomotive fireman arriving on the Pittsburgh train spotted smoke curling from under the platform of the Broad Street Station train shed. Ten minutes later, station firemen ripped open the decking in search of the elusive source. Ross B. Davis, chief engineer of the fire bureau, crawled along the greasy floor feeling for hot spots. He found them. Paint, deck planking, asphalt, and oil that had dripped from cars and locomotives for decades fed the flames. Seven alarms were struck by 1:06am; more than half the city's fire equipment responded as the 300 x 600 foot shed, the world's largest, was destroyed. Remarkably, the following day's 530 trains carrying 80,000 passengers were largely unaffected. Stations at North and West Philadelphia accommodated the rail traffic. In extinguishing the blaze above ground, however, workers deluged the Market Street subway and put it out of service.

**Undergraduate
Enrollment, 1991–1992**

Temple University	19,336
West Chester University of Pennsylvania	9,961
University of Pennsylvania	9,541
Drexel University	8,341
Villanova University	6,858
Widener University	5,400
LaSalle College	4,820
St. Joseph's University	3,815
Philadelphia College of Textiles and Science	2,852
Immaculata College	2,120
Holy Family College	2,119
Gwynedd-Mercy College	1,787
Philadelphia College of Pharmacy and Science	1,598
Swarthmore College	1,320
University of the Arts	1,269
Cabrini College	1,251
Bryn Mawr College	1,243
Cheyney University of Pennsylvania	1,215
Eastern College	1,209
Neumann College	1,207
Delaware Valley College	1,204
Beaver College	1,168
Haverford College	1,113
Ursinus College	1,017
Hahnemann University	917
Chestnut Hill College	856
Philadelphia College of Bible	685
Rosemont College	653
Moore College of Art and Design	500
Gratz College	240
Curtis Institute of Music	132
Academy of the New Church	116

Local Colleges and Universities Ranked

Percentage of Applicants Admitted

1. Swarthmore College 26
2. Hahnemann University 42
3. Haverford College 43
4. University of Pennsylvania 47
5. West Chester University of Pennsylvania 53
6. Philadelphia College of Bible 54
7. LaSalle College 60
8. Bryn Mawr College 61
9. Widener University 61
10. Philadelphia College of Pharmacy and Science 67

Scholastic Aptitude Test Scores of Entering Freshmen
(perfect score = 1600)

1. Swarthmore College 1335
2. Haverford College 1280
3. University of Pennsylvania 1269
4. Bryn Mawr College 1260
5. Villanova University 1108
6. Widener University 1076
7. LaSalle College 1060
8. Philadelphia College of Pharmacy and Science... 1030
9. Drexel University 1020
10. St. Joseph's University 1010

Percentage of Freshmen Who Return the Following Year

1. Haverford College 99
2. Swarthmore College 98
3. University of Pennsylvania 97
4. Bryn Mawr College 96
5. Villanova University 93
6. LaSalle College 91
7. Rosemont College 90
8. St. Joseph's University 90
9. Widener University 90
10. Moore College of Art and Design 89

Most Expensive (Tuition, Room, and Board for 1993–1994)

1. Swarthmore College $24,782
2. University of Pennsylvania $24,442
3. Bryn Mawr College $23,960
4. Haverford College $23,902
5. Villanova University $20,240
6. Ursinus College $19,165
7. Moore College of Art and Design $18,944
8. Drexel University $18,192
9. St. Joseph's University $17,700
10. Beaver College $17,660

Education

Least Expensive (Yearly Tuition, Room, and Board)
1. Cheyney University of Pennsylvania .... $ 5,794*
2. West Chester University of Pennsylvania........ $ 6,458*
3. Temple University.. $ 9,437*
4. Philadelphia College of Bible $10,594
5. Hahnemann University................................ $12,360
6. Philadelphia College of Pharmacy and Science $13,106
7. Gwynedd-Mercy College.............................. $13,125
8. Eastern College... $13,286
9. Chestnut Hill College.................................. $13,400
10. Immaculata College..................................... $13,650

* For Pennsylvania Residents.

Largest Endowments (in Millions of Dollars)
1. University of Pennsylvania................................. 974.4
2. Swarthmore College... 342.4
3. Bryn Mawr College.. 163.8
4. Academy of the New Church............................ 143.8
5. Haverford College... 89.0
6. Drexel University.. 72.9
7. Temple University... 42.6
8. Villanova University.. 30.0
9. St. Joseph's University.. 28.0
10. LaSalle College.. 18.0

Largest Libraries	Number of Volumes	Periodical Subscriptions
1. University of Pennsylvania	3,756,762	32,118
2. Temple University	2,107,910	15,414
3. Bryn Mawr College*	890,000	1,980
4. Swarthmore College*	776,000	2,700
5. Villanova University	583,000	2,855
6. Drexel University	500,000	4,800
7. West Chester Univ. of Pa.	470,000	2,800
8. Haverford College*	400,000	1,257
9. LaSalle College	345,000	1,650
10. St. Joseph's University	299,000	1,750

* Library Consortium.

Sources: The Chronicle of Higher Education Almanac, 1992; Peterson's Four-Year Colleges, 1993; The Insider's Guide to the Colleges; Barron's Profiles of American Colleges (19th ed.).

❖

Philadelphia cabinet-maker and upholsterer Henry Peres Kennedy received a patent for a reclining chair in 1841.

THE UNIVERSITY OF PENNSYLVANIA

In June 1993, billionaire communications magnate Walter H. Annenberg gave $120 million to the University of Pennsylvania. The funds, one of the largest gifts this or any other university has ever received, will further enhance Penn's rankings among the nation's educational institutions.

HOW THE UNIVERSITY OF PENNSYLVANIA RANKED AMONG U.S. COLLEGES AND UNIVERSITIES IN 1990–1991

4th leading fundraiser: $143,384,123

6th largest number of foreign students enrolled: 3,122

15th largest endowment: $825,601,000

16th highest number of doctoral degrees conferred: 449

20th in spending on research and development for science and engineering: $189,390,000

24th largest library: 3,756,762 volumes

37th in number of freshmen who are National Merit Scholars: 46

Source: The Chronicle of Higher Education Almanac, 1992.

❖

Just south of 12th and Market Streets, John Bill Ricketts erected in 1792 a building designed for his circus. President Washington attended a performance on April 22, 1793.

In 1864, Philadelphian Charles P. Hatch introduced oil tank cars—flatbeds with three upright tanks. Rain dissolved the glue coating and caused problems with leakage.

Non-credit classes designed to combat the influence of Communism were offered in December 1935 by St. Joseph's College; more than 1,200 students enrolled.

Philadelphia School District Compared

Student Performance on the Standardized TELLS Test

Until recently, when the state adopted a new standardized test, Testing for Essential Learning and Literacy Skills, or TELLS, was administered to all Pennsylvania public school students in grades 3, 5, and 8. The tests measure the percentage of students whose reading and math skills are appropriate for their current grade level. While many educators argue that standardized tests have limited usefulness, the TELLS scores provide one of the few available ways to compare student performance in school districts around the state.

Tells Test*

	Chester		Lower Merion		Philadelphia		Pittsburgh		Radnor	
	Math	Reading	Math	Reading	Math	Reading	Math	Reading	Math	Reading
Grade 3	54	55	98	98	48	49	63	66	98	98
Grade 5	50	51	98	97	56	41	65	58	98	91
Grade 8	43	47	98	97	51	51	57	58	100	99

* Percentages indicate students at or above current grade level.

Government Funding and Higher Education

Like other large urban districts throughout the nation, the School District of Philadelphia faces the challenges of tight budgets, increasing costs, and the varied needs of its students. The chart below compares school revenue in Philadelphia and four other school districts. Philadelphia is by far the largest of these districts—five times larger than Pittsburgh and 75 times larger than Radnor.

Cost per Student

	Chester	Lower Merion	Philadelphia	Pittsburgh	Radnor
Local	$2352	$7462	$2394	$4694	$8299
State	$3187	$ 945	$2823	$2694	$ 994
Federal	$ 420	$ 26	$ 595	$ 384	$ 290
Total	$5959	$8433	$5812	$7772	$9583
% Who Go on to Other Schools*	32.1	93.6	63.1	62.2	92.6

* Community colleges and other two-year colleges, four-year colleges and universities, and non-degree programs.

Source: Pennsylvania Department of Education.

❖

The College Access Program, a project of the Philadelphia Schools Collaborative and the School District of Philadelphia, offers assistance in choosing and applying to colleges and universities—and in finding financial aid. They have offices in the Gallery II and in West, North, and Northwest Philadelphia. For more information, call 299-7279.

Education

Total School Enrollment in the Philadelphia Five-County Area, 1990–1991

The education of school-age children in the five-county Philadelphia region is an enormous enterprise, with more than 460,000 public school and nearly 175,000 private school students. They account for 27% of all public school and 50% of private school students in the state. Public schools in the region employ more than 27,000 classroom teachers.

County	Elementary		Secondary		Total
	Public	Private	Public	Private	
Bucks	43,304	14,961	34,807	5,528	98,600
Chester	30,221	7,697	23,038	3,101	64,057
Delaware	35,050	18,698	25,486	8,245	87,479
Montgomery	44,662	24,168	33,908	11,174	113,912
Philadelphia	111,560	60,682	79,418	20,168	271,828

Public School Classroom Teachers and their Salaries in the Five-County Area, 1991–1992

County	Total	Male	Female	Salary*
Bucks	4,542	1,642	2,900	$51,695
Chester	3,113	1,038	2,075	$42,420
Delaware	3,627	1,214	2,413	$44,142
Montgomery	5,066	1,803	3,263	$46,890
Philadelphia	10,990	3,194	7,796	$41,826

* Full-time average.

School Districts with the Highest Teacher Salaries in the Five-County Area, 1991–1992*

Centennial, Bucks County:	$56,219
Abington, Montgomery County:	$56,032
Council Rock, Bucks County:	$55,490
Colonial, Montgomery County:	$54,951
Bensalem Township, Bucks County:	$52,289

*These five school districts also have the highest teacher salaries in the entire state.

School Districts with the Lowest Teacher Salaries in the Five-County Area, 1991–1992

Oxford Area, Chester County:	$34,286
Avon Grove, Chester County:	$36,365
Spring Ford Area, Montgomery County:	$37,022
Southeast Delco, Delaware County:	$37,617
Coatesville Area, Chester County:	$38,285

Source: Pennsylvania Department of Education.

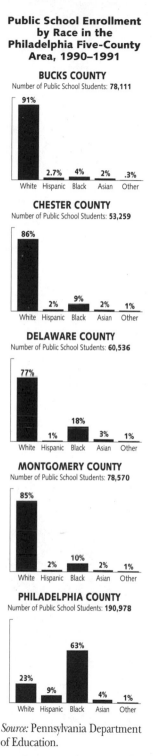

Public School Enrollment by Race in the Philadelphia Five-County Area, 1990–1991

BUCKS COUNTY
Number of Public School Students: **78,111**
91% White, 2.7% Hispanic, 4% Black, 2% Asian, .3% Other

CHESTER COUNTY
Number of Public School Students: **53,259**
86% White, 2% Hispanic, 9% Black, 2% Asian, 1% Other

DELAWARE COUNTY
Number of Public School Students: **60,536**
77% White, 1% Hispanic, 18% Black, 3% Asian, 1% Other

MONTGOMERY COUNTY
Number of Public School Students: **78,570**
85% White, 2% Hispanic, 10% Black, 2% Asian, 1% Other

PHILADELPHIA COUNTY
Number of Public School Students: **190,978**
23% White, 9% Hispanic, 63% Black, 4% Asian, 1% Other

Source: Pennsylvania Department of Education.

65

CITIZENS' MANUAL

HOW TO ADDRESS THE SCHOOL BOARD

Philadelphia School Board meetings are held twice a month, on alternate Mondays, from September through June. From October through April, one meeting a month is held at 1:30pm in the Board Room of the Administration Building, 21st Street and the Parkway; the other meeting is held at 7pm in various schools around the city. In September, May, and June, all meetings are held at 1:30pm in the Board Room.

If you want to speak at a Board meeting, register by calling the School District's Office of Communications, 299-7850, by 4:30pm on the Friday before the meeting. Let them know what you want to speak about.

There is no limit on the total number of people who can speak at a meeting, but there is a limit of six speakers on any particular subject. Speakers are allowed three to five minutes for their presentations. You should also prepare 25 copies of your statement to hand out at the meeting.

The public is also invited to attend open conferences, held at 10:30am in the Board Room, on the Monday morning before every Board meeting. Subjects include administrative matters, educational programs, and updates on school issues.

Philadelphia Board of Public Education Administration Building

School Voices

A t the end of each regularly scheduled meeting of Philadelphia's Board of Education, parents, teachers, students, and other members of the community can address the Board and the Superintendent about their concerns. The following excerpts from the official Board minutes record a few of the recurring themes.

March 23, 1992

A.F., from the Home and School Association, stated that the Roberto Clemente Middle School is beyond repair. It is impossible to provide a safe and secure school environment in the present building. He identified the following areas of concern: auditorium, gym, cafeteria, elevators, and ventilation and air conditioning systems. A.F. requested the encumbrance of funds for a new school building and the establishment of a committee to address the school's immediate needs. He offered the assistance and support of the Clemente Home and School Association.

M.M., Potter-Thomas Home and School Association, expressed gratitude for the many facility improvements made to the Potter-Thomas School.

B.H., parent, asked that teaching of the Health Education curriculum be immediately suspended.

V.C. and U.C., students at Roberto Clemente Middle School, described their school as being without heat periodically, described students being bused to a recreation center for physical education, and described dilapidated student lockers. They requested a new school building.

The Superintendent [Constance E. Clayton] stated she agreed about the condition of the Clemente School building, but that she must implore the students not to make it any worse and not to jeopardize the lives of others. She further stated that it is her understanding that there are two facilities being explored as possible sites for the Clemente School.

June 29, 1992

D.S., parent, disclosed that the Horticultural Department at Swenson Skills Center is closing due to insufficient enrollment. She indicated that many of the program participants are learning-disabled and mentally and/or physically handicapped. She indicated that this program has enabled special needs students to develop self-confidence and to learn a marketable skill. She advocated a stay for this program.

N.B., of Act-Up, demanded: the development of a comprehensive plan for students to receive condoms in every high school by the end of the 1993 school year, budget appropriations for the purchasing of condoms, salaries for employees in the Drop-In Centers, and safer-sex pamphlets and informational brochures.

Education

A.P., speaking on behalf of the Asian parents of Kirkbride School, expressed concern that the proposed budget cuts would mean the elimination of a kindergarten teacher there. She enumerated the advantages of a kindergarten experience for Asian students.

August 18, 1992

W.L. and D.S., parents, stated that although they have been informed that the Horticultural Program at Swenson will be open for one additional year, they would ask that the program remain open indefinitely.

September 8, 1992

G.H., student, indicated that she has been dropped from the Franklin Learning Center's student rolls because of excessive absences. She attributed these absences in part to being a single parent and illnesses. She indicated that a newly created family support system will enable her to attend school on a regular basis.

October 13, 1992

R.P., parent of a student attending AMY 6, stated that his daughter has been late for school since the beginning of this school year because of her bus route. The school bus that transports his daughter and approximately 35 other students begins at 7:15am, makes 13 stops, travels approximately 20 miles, and arrives at the school between 9:00 and 9:15am. He indicated that he has tried on numerous occasions to have this route rescheduled, but to no avail. He believes that the route is unreasonably long, and he implored the members of the Board to assist him in obtaining a more reasonable route. He further indicated that one of the requirements for admission to a magnet high school is student punctuality. He asked that the lateness recorded on his daughter's record for this school year be waived. He asked for an immediate resolution to the transportation problem.

March 22, 1993

C.T.L., H.S.T., and Y.Y.C. asked that a school bus be provided for the children who reside in Chinatown and attend McCall School. They offered examples of the hazards encountered by the children as they walk to and from school.

March 29, 1993

J.A., V.D., B.R., and D.H., parents, enumerated their concerns regarding the Comegys Elementary School. They asked that school security be improved, for the assignment of a crossing guard at the corner of 51st Street and Chester Avenue, and for the repair of a sewer problem at 51st and Kingsessing Avenue that forces the children to walk in the street after a heavy rain.

T.N., grandmother of two students, fervently opposed the current adolescent sexuality curriculum and the distribution of condoms. She advocated the implementation of abstinence training programs. ■

Source: Philadelphia School Board Meeting Minutes.

PAYING FOR PRIVATE

Almost 30 percent of Philadelphia school-age children attend private school, including parochial schools, Friends schools, and other sectarian and non-sectarian institutions.

The decision to bypass public education can be an expensive one. These are the costs of 17 years of private schooling for two children: one who was born in 1972 and will graduate from college in 1994, and another who was born in 1988 and will graduate from college in 2009. They include tuition at a Friends school in Philadelphia and tuition, room, and board at a private college in New England.

1977–1994		1993–2009
$ 1,675	Kindergarten	$6,870
$ 1,970	Grade 1	$7,565
$ 2,275	Grade 2	$8,136
$ 2,735	Grade 3	$8,671
$ 3,210	Grade 4	$9,759
$ 3,730	Grade 5	$10,740
$ 4,170	Grade 6	$11,853
$ 4,885	Grade 7	$12,826
$ 5,215	Grade 8	$13,622
$ 6,015	Grade 9	$15,606
$ 6,490	Grade 10	$16,558
$ 7,235	Grade 11	$17,386
$ 7,870	Grade 12	$18,255
$ 19,915	Freshman	$61,838
$ 21,290	Sophomore	$66,476
$ 22,700	Junior	$71,463
$ 23,880	Senior	$76,822
$145,260	**Total**	**$434,446**

The projected tuition at primary and secondary levels is based upon an annual inflation rate of 5 percent. The projected university tuition is based upon an annual 7.5 percent inflation rate, the 1993 rate for college tuition costs.

Sources: Germantown Friends School (base cost); College Savings Bank, Princeton, N.J. (projection).

AVERTING SHUTOFF

An energy crisis is deepening for many low-income Philadelphians. In 1992, there were more than 75,000 shutoffs of water, gas, or electric service, and at least 30,000 customers weren't reconnected. Shutoffs can lead to housing abandonment and home-lessness. Programs such as weatheriza-tion, conservation, fuel assistance, and energy-related home repair can help avert that downward slide.

Philadelphia's Energy Coordinating Agency (854-8030) coordinates programs for low- and middle-income Philadelphians. Seven walk-in Neighborhood Energy Centers offer help with fuel assistance, conservation, and education programs:

- Belmont Improvement Association, 4087 Lancaster Avenue (382-6107), serving West Philadelphia
- Diversified Community Services, 1920 S. 20th Street (336-3511), serving Southwest Philadelphia and South Philadelphia, west of Broad Street
- Friends Neighborhood Guild, 1529 N. 7th Street (235-9026), serving North Philadelphia, east of Broad Street
- GRACE (Germantown Residents Acting to Conserve Energy), 5020 Wayne Avenue (844-2244), serving Germantown and Logan
- New Kensington Community Development Corporation, 2513 Frankford Avenue (427-0350), serving the Kensington area
- St. Elizabeth's Housing, 1845 N. 23rd Street (235-7000), serving North Philadelphia, west of Broad Street
- United Communities, 2029 S. 8th Street (467-8700), serving South Philadelphia, east of Broad Street

Customers facing shutoff should first contact the appropriate utility. Various fuel assistance programs provide limit-ed grants to help qualified residents pay their bills. Some are federally funded; some are privately funded. PECO's Customer Assistance Program combines assistance with conserva-tion: PECO sets up a monthly pay-ment agreement for customers who agree to keep electric consumption at a certain usage level.

Source: Energy Coordinating Agency.

CITIZENS' MANUAL

Energy

Conserve at Home

Here are a dozen ways to save energy:

1. Take your water heater's temperature. If you turn your water heater down so that the water is 120 degrees, it'll still be hot enough for bathing, laundry, and most dishwashing.

2. Dust off your refrigerator. All those coils behind or under-neath it are what actually do the cooling. If they're clean, they work more efficiently.

3. Tune up your heater. A heating technician can do a checkup for usually less than $100. Often, you'll end up sav-ing more than that in reduced fuel bills.

4. Get a damper. Your boiler may be operating at the low effi-ciency level of 50 to 60%. That can be dramatically improved by adding a motorized, tight-closing automatic vent damper that will cut off unnecessary air flow up your chimney and out of your house while the heater is off.

5. Get a smart thermostat. A thermostat that turns down the heat after you go to bed and turns it on again before you get up can quickly pay for itself. Set the nighttime temperature back 10 degrees to save about 12% on your winter heating bill.

6. Fix your faucets. One drop per second wastes 700 gallons of water a year. And if it's hot water, you're wasting energy, too.

7. Shade your house. Awnings, shades, and drapes can block the sun during the hottest part of the day. Large, leafy trees on the south and west sides of your house can keep it as much as 15 degrees cooler in summer.

8. Is anyone watching? Do you really want that unique atmos-phere only an unwatched television provides? Turn it off!

9. Check that flame. If the color of the flame on your gas range isn't blue, it's not operating efficiently—the burners are probably clogged with food. Try using pipe cleaners to clear the passages.

10. Go fluorescent. The new, compact fluorescent bulbs are one of the recent miracles of energy conservation. A 15-watt fluorescent puts out as much light as a 60-watt incandescent. It will also outlast a dozen incandescent bulbs.

11. Buy smart. Major appliances now have large yellow and white labels with information about their energy efficiency. Spend a few extra dollars for a more efficient refrigerator, water heater, washer, or dryer. You'll save in the long run.

12. Take advantage of free information on energy conserva-tion from PECO ([800] 521-5353) and PGW (684-6720). ∎

Sources: Philadelphia Electric Company; Philadelphia Gas Works; Institute for Human Development.

Community Organizations

Here are some of the many environmental groups active in the Philadelphia area. Most offer membership in their organizations, and they happily welcome volunteers.

Bicycle Coalition of the Delaware Valley, P.O. Box 8194, Philadelphia, PA 19101. Phone: 242-9253 (BICYCLE).

BCDV lobbies to make bicycling easier and safer in the region. They also publish a regional map of recommended bicycling routes.

Clean Air Council, 1909 Chestnut Street, 2nd floor, Philadelphia, PA 19103. Phone: 567-4004; fax: 567-5791.

The Council, this region's oldest citizen-based advocacy organization (founded in 1967), works to reduce air pollution from automobiles and industry. They're also active in indoor air quality, waste reduction, government oversight, and citizen advocacy.

Clean Water Action, 1518 Walnut Street, #1304, Philadelphia, PA 19104. Phone: 735-8409.

CWA is a national organization with strong local presence that deals with water quality, toxin reduction, public education, and more.

Delaware Valley Rainforest Action Group, 3900 Ford Road, 14-K, Philadelphia, PA 19131. Phone: 473-5131.

The DVRAG promotes conservation of the world's tropical forests.

Friends of Philadelphia Parks, P.O. Box 12677, Philadelphia, PA 19129-0077. Phone: 879-8159.

FoPP promotes the care and appreciation of the city's parks.

The Nature Conservancy (Pennsylvania Chapter), 1211 Chestnut Street, 12th floor, Philadelphia, PA 19107. Phone: 963-1400.

The Nature Conservancy is an internation-al organization with a pragmatic approach to conservation. They buy up parcels of threatened habitat, thereby saving them from development or other destruction. The Conservancy has purchased more than 36,000 acres in Pennsylvania.

Pennsylvania Environmental Council, 1211 Chestnut Street, Suite 900, Philadelphia, PA 19107. Phone: 563-0250.

PEC is a statewide organization, working on issues of land use, growth management, transportation, and air and water pollution.

Penn State Urban Gardening Program, 4601 Market Street, 3rd floor, Philadelphia, PA 19139. Phone: 560-4166.

The program has helped start more than 500 gardens in vacant lots and other abandoned grounds. They're also a great source of advice for beginning backyard gardeners.

Pennsylvania Resources Council, P.O. Box 88, Media, PA 19063. Phone: 565-9131.

The PRC is best known for their work in recycling and waste reduction. They have a number of publications on topics such as organizing a recycling program and becoming a more environmentally conscious shopper.

Sierra Club (Southeastern Pennsylvania Group), 623 Catherine Street, Philadelphia, PA 19103. Phone: 592-4063.

This local branch of one of America's largest and oldest environmental organizations deals with a wide variety of regional environmental issues. The group also plans local outings and conservation projects. ∎

EARTH TALK

WHYY-FM (91 FM) features two weekly programs dealing with environmental concerns. "EarthTalk" is a one-hour show covering everything from global warming to the state of the Delaware River. The show mixes news, feature reports, call-in segments, and interviews with people ranging from Al Gore to Captain Sewer. "EarthTalk" is hosted by Mike Weilbacher, an environmental educator, speaker, and author. The show can be heard Saturday at 11am and Tuesday at noon.

"Living on Earth" is National Public Radio's weekly look at environmental issues. The show, produced in Boston, is global in scope, with reports from around the country and around the world. It airs Sunday mornings at 7:30.

Expositions

The Centennial

The Hotel at 52nd Street and Elm (now Parkside Avenue).

Philadelphia's first public relations genius was John L. Campbell, a professor from Wabash College in Indiana who in 1866 urged Mayor Morton McMichael to celebrate America's 100th birthday as a Centennial Exposition. In spite of (perhaps because of) residual economic and political unrest in the aftermath of the Civil War, the notion of a giant, nationalistic celebration caught on.

Among the ranks of volunteers who worked for project leader John Welsh was Elizabeth Duane Gillespie, who created a women's committee and quickly raised $40,000. When it became clear that the all-male exposition leadership would not display women's work, Gillespie summoned her forces and raised an additional $30,000. And for the first time, a World's Fair had a building by and for women.

The Centennial was enormously popular and visitors returned home impressed, not so much with American history, but with American machinery and manufacturing. This perception shaped Philadelphia's emerging identity as the "Workshop of the World."

Only its shareholders did not perceive the Centennial as an all-around success. They received 23 cents on each dollar invested—in part because the U.S. government, claiming its $1.5 million contribution was a loan rather than a gift, sued to get it back. ∎

The Sesquicentennial

Politicians strong-armed the site selection process and insisted on a May 31, 1926 opening day, even though the buildings were certain to be incomplete. They were, and it rained and rained—only mud lay between the construction sites. Not enough visitors came—and those who did left to spread the bad news. A few foreign countries abandoned their exhibits early. Never again would Philadelphians feel comfortable hosting a World's Fair.

Oh, there were interesting exhibits. Electrical displays and fountains lit with pastel colors mitigated the effects of mud. A facsimile of old Philadelphia, with re-creations of the city's earliest buildings, foreshadowed Williamsburg.

But the perfect combination of timely messages was *outside* the fairgrounds, near Broad Street and Oregon Avenue. All the visitors rode or walked beneath it on their way in, and again on their way out.

It was Philadelphia's temporary, therefore little-known, yet far-reaching contribution to American popular culture: a giant, glowing, light bulb–covered Liberty Bell. ∎

The Great Bell

- **Location:** Over the plaza on Broad Street south of Oregon Avenue, north of main entrance to grounds
- **Height:** 80 feet
- **Weight:** 80 tons of steel
- **Foundations:** Wooden pilings 30 feet deep, capped by concrete
- **Bell:** Steel framework covered with sheet metal
- **Illumination:** 26,000, 15-watt lightbulbs at six-inch intervals
- **Bulb colors:** "Amber" lights; "ivory" highlights; "old rose" shadows
- **Visibility:** From City Hall (especially when illuminated) and from other vantage points throughout the city
- **Inside the bell:** A blue, star-studded interior of the dome lit by eight, 200-watt projectors in the clapper
- **Cost:** $100,000
- **Completion time:** 47 days

Source: E. L. Austin and Odell Hauser, *The Sesqui-Centennial Exposition* (Current Publications, 1929).

Phillywood

B etween 1897 and 1916, Russian immigrant Siegmund "Pop" Lubin developed a Philadelphia-based cinema dynasty that at one point included over 3,000 films, four studios, and the first motion picture theater and theater chain in Philadelphia—not to mention a reputation as a mass marketing/advertising entrepreneur.

Amazingly, Lubin's career began at a time when movies were still largely viewed as novelties, pioneered in Philadelphia by the likes of Coleman Sellers, Eadweard Muybridge, and Thomas Eakins. But movies were becoming big business. And if the entire movie industry hadn't picked up and moved to the West Coast in the early 1900s, Philadelphia and people like Lubin might very well have been at the heart of the industry we now know as Hollywood.

Today, Philadelphia's post-*Rocky* reputation as a town for films with gritty urban settings could be considered a rebirth of the early film days. Then, as now, the city's streets, parks, and neighborhoods routinely found their way into productions.

Despite his many successes, Lubin remains somewhat obscure in American film history. Perhaps the reason is Lubin's streak of bad luck. Every master negative Lubin made was destroyed when his vaults blew up during a fire at the 20th Street and Indiana Avenue studio on June 13, 1914. Today, only one-twelfth of Lubin's estimated 3,000 films survive, many of them still on unstable, nitrate-based film. In 1917, facing bankruptcy and other business problems related to the fire, Lubin sold his Betzwood Studio (near Valley Forge), where major works had been produced since 1912. And while for a time the new owners continued to make films there under Lubin's Liberty Bell trademark, they closed and sold the studio in 1922, a year before Lubin died at his Ventnor, New Jersey home.

When Joseph P. Eckhardt heard that the Betzwood Studio and the Betzwood Mansion were being torn down in 1962, he began to wonder about the man behind the movie studio stories. Eckhardt began to collect Lubin stories. There was the time, for instance, that Lubin was trying to film a scene of Christ walking on water, using smudge pots to simulate mist in a gulch strung with a tightrope. But after days of preparation, Lubin's Christ, a "human fly" hired from a local carnival, lost his focus. "That damn Christ of mine got drunk and fell off a cliff and broke his legs!" Lubin reportedly screamed.

Eckhardt, associate professor of history at Montgomery County Community College, is writing a book about Lubin. He's helped coordinate the installation of a historical marker for Betzwood Studio. And every first weekend in May since 1989, Eckhardt has been producer of the Betzwood Film Festival—featuring such Lubin classics as the Toonerville Trolley series and the filmmaker's oldest surviving film, *Impersonation of Fight*, dating back to 1899—the story of a boxer.

Eckhardt argues for the preservation of Lubin's home at 1608 N. 15th Street (perhaps the oldest surviving film location) and his still-extant 20th Street and Indiana Avenue studio. After all, says Eckhardt, "Lubin made *Rocky* before *Rocky*." ■

▼▼

THE BETZWOOD SERIES

The 26 films listed below were made at Lubin's Betzwood Studio, not far from Valley Forge National Park, from 1912 to 1922. The films made during or before 1916 were produced by Lubin; films made at Betzwood after 1917, the year Lubin sold the studio to the Wolf Brothers, were directed and produced by Lubin's son-in-law, Ira M. Lowry.

1912: *Twixt Love and Ambition; In the Service of the State; The Sheriff's Mistake; The Bank Cashier*

1913: *The Price of Victory; A Country Girl*

1914: *A Partner to Providence; The Vagaries of Fate; Michael Strogoff, or The Courier of the Czar*

1915: *Where the Road Divided; The Exile; Sweeter than Revenge; Tillie's Tomato Surprise*

1916: *Race Suicide*

1918: *Sandy Burke of the U-Bar-U; Oh, Johnny; High Pockets;* untitled concert film with sing-along words

1919: *A Misfit Earl*

1920: *The Skipper's Narrow Escape; Toonerville's "Boozem" Friends*

1921: *Toonerville Follies; Toonerville Tactics; The Skipper's Scheme; The Skipper's Flirtation*

1922: *Breaking Home Ties*

The Philadelphia Cinema Scene

Two of the Largest Film Festivals:

Philadelphia Festival of World Cinema. Produced by International House, this city-wide, 12-day festival each May screens new films and celebrates independent film artists as well as other film producers. Festival Director: Linda Blackaby, 895-6593.

The Philadelphia International Film Festival and Marketplace (PHILAFILM). Started in 1977, PHILAFILM is the oldest film festival in the city. In 1994, it will be held July 20–23. Festival Director: Lawrence L. Smallwood, Jr., 977-2831.

Other Festivals and Screenings:

• Betzwood Film Festival, featuring classic films from the early 1900s by Betzwood Studio owner/producer Siegmund "Pop" Lubin. First weekend in May. Montgomery County Community College, Cultural Affairs Office, Joseph P. Eckhardt, 641-6505.

• Ebony Film Series, featuring films and documentaries throughout the year. Ebony Theater, Afro-American Historical and Cultural Museum, 574-0380.

• Feminist Film Series, featuring six yearly Friday night screenings of films and videos related to women's issues. Community Education Center, 387-1911.

• Film Forum Philadelphia, screening classic feature films and comedies on Saturday nights. Philadelphia Center for Older People, David Grossman, 732-7704.

• Jewish Film Festival, featuring films and lectures on Jewish topics. New season, November 1993–April 1994. Jewish Community Centers of Greater Philadelphia, 545-0153.

• Latino Film Festival, featuring films to preserve and present Puerto Rican and Latin American cultural traditions. Tentatively scheduled in 1994 through Taller Puertorriqueño, Johnny Irizarry, Executive Director, 423-6320.

Philadelphia Filmmaker Resources:

Greater Philadelphia Film Office. Promotes the city and region for films, television, documentaries, and commercials, responding to over 500 queries each year concerning film projects in the Philadelphia area. Provides resources for the Philadelphia production community. Sharon Pinkenson, Executive Director, 686-2668.

The office offers a hot line with up-to-date information on production activity and film/video events and opportunities throughout the region (686-3663). It also publishes the *Greater Philadelphia 1993 Film and Video Production Guide* (available through the office and selected bookstores), with 500 paid listings to help promote city services and local talent when film production crews come to town.

Independent Film Makers Series. An annual competition sponsored by WHYY Channel 12 for Delaware Valley film makers. For deadline and entry information call WHYY–TV12, Independent Images, 351-0508.

Philadelphia Independent Film/Video Association (PIFVA). An association of over 360 independent media artists, designed to provide informational, practice, and moral support for film, video, and audio makers as well as other artists, students, and educators, other media arts centers, and those working in the commercial industry who support independent media. David Haas, Coordinator, 895-6594.

And Fond Farewells in 1993 to:

Temple Cinematheque. Where film fans could view those classic and European works ignored by commercial screens. Despite a last-minute wave of loyal moviegoer support, Temple University closed it on July 1.

Video and Film Center at the Free Library of Philadelphia. Over two thousand 16mm films have now been turned over to the Pennsylvania Public Library's Film Center in University Park, Pennsylvania, which is part of the state library system. These films, ranging from features to documentaries, can still be reserved and acquired through the Free Library by calling 686-5367; a two-week lead time is required. The library's collection of educational videos remains at the Free Library and is available by reservation. As always, videos ranging from entertainment to opera to instructional can still be borrowed by library cardholders. ∎

The Farm Market as Oasis

Reedbirds and canvasbacks aren't hanging by their legs in open stalls any longer, but there are more markets than ever in Philadelphia—and more are coming. City markets, suburban markets, neighborhood markets, farmers' markets, farmerless farmers' markets, markets in old supermarkets, country markets, big and old, small and new—there's a market for nearly everyone.

Philadelphia's market heritage goes back to the city's beginnings in the 1680s. But why are half of the markets listed here less than 20 years old? Today, there are few farmers, fewer farms; the Schuylkill and Delaware are no longer bounteous providers of fish. And good luck if you go searching for arbutus or wild mushrooms in a nearby hardwood forest.

Renewed interest in markets is driven by a desire to regain our community, our link with the past. In markets, the transaction between consumer and producer regains significance as we seek to

reconnect with the natural world, the seasons, the food chain. Markets ground us. They're our escape into reality.

The sense that we are participating in our own sustenance and our own community economy only reinforces the satisfaction. When local farmers thrive they remain, stemming the tide of tract development that has obliterated much of our regional agricultural base. On their own small scale, markets strengthen ecology.

It's not easy, though. The traditional market farmer leads a precarious life. Only last year, Philadelphia City Council forced indoors perhaps the last truck farmer who drove in daily from Skippack, Montgomery County, to sell sweet corn on a side street in Roxborough. For centuries, government and corporate officials have been chasing farmers. Ever since the first markets on the dock and the open sheds (they were called shambles) on Market Street, farmer and merchant have been the target of railroads needing right of way, health inspectors, and fussy planners who see sensory-loaded activities as nuisances unbefitting the neat and tidy modern metropolis.

Well, the citizens see things differently. Folks like the hubbub and gentle chaos of the marketplace. They like the rough edges, the salmon sliding from a cart across a sand-dusted aisle. They like the sensory barrage of exotica from near and far. The market is the last great common ground where boundaries and delicacies, bar none, invite all to nourish both stomach and soul.

Of course, markets have changed. Most are enclosed. They are heated and air conditioned. Refrigerated display cases have replaced the wooden counter piled high with dressed poultry. Gourmet products and prepared foods feed busy families who cook less often. Fruits from Chile are as common as the Perkasie peach. New vendors from Asia, young entrepreneurs, and growing backyard businesses have replaced many of the farmers.

But much is the same—and blessedly so. Throughout history, markets are oases of civility. And in a world of rapid-fire changes and increasing hostilities, folks don the mantle of civility as they enter the market. There, all seems well again, or at least not as bad. ■

Farmers' Markets

Note: Except where indicated, all are accessible to handicapped persons, have restaurants on the premises, have public seating and restrooms, and are heated and air conditioned.

Philadelphia:

The Amish Farmers Market
1100 S. Delaware Avenue, South Philadelphia
Manager: Aaron Stoltzfus, 334-7450
Hours: Wednesday–Friday 8am–6pm; Saturday 8am–4pm
Vendors: 2
Parking: Ample and free
Founded: 1990
Size: 2,600 sq. ft.
Comments: No restrooms, public seating, or restaurants

Chestnut Hill Farmers Market
8229 Germantown Avenue
Manager: Ceridwyn Chase, 242-5905
Hours: Thursday and Friday 9am–6pm; Saturday 8am–5pm
Vendors: 17
Parking: 70-space free lot
Founded: 1983
Size: 5,000 sq. ft.
Comments: Limited public seating; no restaurants

Dutch Country Farmers Market
2031 Cottman Avenue, Northeast Philadelphia
Manager: 745-6008
Hours: Wednesday 9am–3pm; Thursday and Friday
8am–6pm; Saturday 8am–5pm
Vendors: 9
Parking: Ample and free
Founded: 1991
Size: 4,000 sq. ft.
Comments: No restrooms, public seating, or restaurants

Firehouse Farmers Market
50th Street and Baltimore Avenue, West Philadelphia
Manager: Bill Coleman, 724-7000
Hours: Monday–Saturday 8am–7pm
Vendors: 8
Parking: Non-metered street parking
Founded: 1988
Size: 4,000 sq. ft.
Comments: Limited public seating

AMERICAN MARKETS AS SEEN BY A VISITOR

Front and Market Streets

"Markets are held in the broadest streets, for which purpose, market-houses are built in the middle of the streets in arcade form. In these markethouses, meat-, vegetable- and fruit dealers offer their wares for sale, all of which makes a pleasant sight. In these market streets, there seems to be a fair all year long, at least one notices the same crowd at the fairs in Leipzig or Frankfurt. The buying and selling is endless and lasts until nearly midnight, until which time the booths and stores are wonderfully illuminated.

"A peculiar custom, which at first seems improper to us Germans, concerns the buying of victuals. This job is usually left to servants in Germany, but here, it is not considered a disgrace for even the richest merchant to go to the market himself and buy butter, eggs and such things and then to carry home his purchases. Often one sees wealthy and respected men walking homeward with plump fish in their hands. Usually, however, they take a servant with them to carry the purchases. What a ridiculous figure a [German] businessman would cut by doing such a thing!"

Source: Anonymous, *Nordamerica* (Tubinbgen, 1818). Translated by Glenys A. Waldman.

FOLK FOODLIFE

Bread, central to every colonial meal, reflected one's status in life. French rolls requiring finely ground flour were favored by the wealthy; "middlin'" or brown bread (rye) was for the rest.

London cookbooks, the standard of good taste, usually were on the shelves of Philadelphia bookstores within a month of publication.

Benjamin Franklin demonstrated electrical cooking in 1749. He killed a turkey by electric shock, then roasted it over a fire started by his "electrified bottle."

England's Chelsea buns became known here as cinnamon buns.

Spicy African gumbos were called olios or pepperpots by English-speaking colonists of blander palate.

Melons and cantaloupes, grown from seed brought from Tripoli, were first grown in the United States at a residence in Germantown in 1818.

In the 1839 book *Aristocracy in America*, British author Francis Grund wrote that Philadelphians "have more taste, and have the best cooks in the United States."

Philadelphian John Landis Mason's invention of the hermetically sealed Mason jar revolutionized and simplified home food preservation.

"Centennial cake," introduced at the 1876 exposition, lives on as "shoo-fly pie." It is now associated with the Pennsylvania Dutch.

The Centennial made popular the "hokey-pokey man," a street vendor selling ices, sandwiches, sausages, fresh bread, "zoologicals" (Philadelphia baker Walter G. Wilson's animal crackers), and small antipasto salad.

When Gilbert and Sullivan's operetta "H.M.S. Pinafore" opened here in 1879, bakeries produced a long loaf called the pinafore. Entrepreneurial "hokey-pokey men" sliced the loaf in half, stuffed it with antipasto salad, and sold the world's first hoagie.

Food / Farmers' Markets

Italian Market

South 9th Street, between Wharton and Christian Streets, South Philadelphia

Manager: no market office; information available from Mariella at Fante's, 922-5557

Hours: Vary by store; generally, market is closed Monday, open Tuesday–Saturday 9am–5:30pm; on Sunday, stores close about midday

Vendors: 150 stores and street stalls

Parking: Street parking and pay lots; free lots on Ellsworth Street between 9th and 10th Streets and on 8th Street between Carpenter Street and Washington Avenue

Founded: More than a century ago when people began selling in front of their homes

Size: 6 blocks long, or 2,000 sq. ft.

Comments: No public seating or restrooms; difficult handicapped access; restaurants include Italian, Vietnamese, sandwich shops, and cheesesteak and hoagie shops

Lancaster County Farmers Market

5942 Germantown Avenue, Germantown

Manager: George Schneider, 843-9564

Hours: Tuesday 6am–4pm; Friday 5am–6pm

Vendors: 21

Parking: Free lot with 50 spaces

Founded: 1940

Size: 8,000 sq. ft.

Comments: No public seating; a few lunch counters; no ramp for wheelchairs, but steps are low

Lancaster Farmers Market

5317 N. 5th Street, Olney

Manager: Mr. Eberly, 457-3521

Hours: Wednesday and Saturday 6am–3pm; Friday 7am–3pm

Vendors: 16

Parking: Street spaces

Founded: Over 75 years ago

Size: Unknown

Comments: No public seating; no air conditioning

Manayunk Farmers Market

4120 Main Street

Manager: Harry Renner, 483-1363

Hours: Thursday–Saturday 8am–7pm; Sunday 9am–3pm

Vendors: 25

Parking: Ample and free

Founded: 1993

Size: 18,000 sq. ft.

Comments: Outside deck with river view

Food / Farmers' Markets

Reading Terminal Market
12th and Arch Streets, Center City
Manager: Bill Gardiner, 922-2317
Hours: Monday–Saturday 8am–6pm
Vendors: 70
Parking: Limited street parking; discount from merchants in
  nearby garages
Founded: 1892
Size: 75,000 sq. ft.
Comments: Many lunch counters and ethnic specialties

Other Area Markets:

Allentown Fairgrounds Farmers Market
17th and Chew Streets
Managers: Norman Ziegler and Daniel Wuchter, 432-8425
Hours: Thursday 10am–8pm; Friday 8am–8pm;
  Saturday 8am–6pm
Vendors: 40
Parking: Ample and free
Founded: 1935
Size: 90,000 sq. ft.

Ardmore Farmers Market
Suburban Square Shopping Center
Manager: Kimberly J. Ross, 896-7560
Hours: Thursday–Saturday 7am–6pm
Vendors: 15
Parking: Ample and free
Founded: 1982
Size: 6,500 sq. ft.
Comments: Restaurants in shopping center

Berlin Farmers Market
41 Clementon Road, Berlin, NJ
Manager: (609) 767-1246
Hours: Thursday and Friday 11am–9:30pm; Saturday
  10am–9:30pm; Sunday 10am–6pm
Vendors: 90 indoors, 700 flea market vendors outdoors
Parking: Ample and free
Founded: 1947
Size: ¼-mile indoor shed
Comments: Market is primarily non-food

Booths Corner Farmers Market
Routes 261 and 491, Boothwyn, PA
Manager: John Chelucci, 485-0774
Hours: Friday 10am–10pm; Saturday 10am–9pm
Vendors: 90 indoors; more outdoors in season
Parking: Ample and free
Founded: 1940
Size: 15 acres

FOLK FOODLIFE

continued...

The soft pretzel, a Philadelphia street tradition, was introduced in the early 1820s.

Scrapple—sliced fried loaf of pork scraps cooked in broth thickened with cornmeal, buckwheat flour, and spices—was inspired by the native *balkenbrij* or "rafter pudding" of thrifty settlers from Holland and northern Germany.

The now-locally endangered oyster was consumed in such quantities in the 19th century that discarded shells were used to pave streets and build wharves along the Delaware.

Philadelphia confectioner Elizabeth Coane Goodfellow (1767–1851) gave America its first lemon meringue pie.

A better peanut butter grinder was patented in 1893 by A. W. Straub & Co.

Philadelphia wine merchant Lorenz Seckel (1747–1823) found tasty hard pears, believed to be a natural hybrid, growing wild on his farm along the Delaware. We call them Seckel pears.

Philadelphia was known for vegetarian cookery through the 18th and 19th centuries. The spiritual center of vegetarianism was the Bible Christian Church, Third Street above Girard Avenue—a building later demolished to make way for a slaughter house.

The first commercial ice cream freezer was patented by Philadelphia Quaker Eber C. Seamen in 1848.

Source: Mary Anne Hines, Gordon Marshall, and William Woys Weaver, *The Larder Invaded: Reflections on Three Centuries of Philadelphia Food and Drink* (The Library Company of Philadelphia and the Historical Society of Pennsylvania, 1987).

300 YEARS OF PHILADELPHIA BEER

Back in the 1680s, taverns did more than purvey food and drink. They were community centers, full of educational and entertainment oppor-

Brewing in the 1790s

tunities. Over the course of time, they displayed whale bones, Asian tigers, and a six-year-old mathematical wizard from Vermont. They hosted business meetings and took overnight accommodations. The whole experience was lubricated by beer. No mere coincidence that William Frampton, the owner of the Blue Anchor, the city's first tavern, on Front Street, south of Walnut, was also Philadelphia's first brewer.

English-style malt liquors—ale, stout, and porter—reflected the city's English origins. But Philadelphia porter was preferred to its London counterpart. George Washington imported Philadelphia porter to Mount Vernon.

Then in 1844, a Bavarian immigrant smuggled in a pocketful of the lager yeast. Before long, Philadelphia had 40 new breweries, all with Teutonic owners who catered to the tastes of a huge number of recent German-speaking arrivals. By January 19, 1919, when Prohibition took effect, Philadelphia had nearly 100 breweries. In 1933, when the 18th Amendment was repealed and Prohibition ended, most of these breweries did not reopen.

Modern technology produces a beer more manufactured than brewed. It's more about chemistry, bottling, and transportation than the ancient craft of brewing. Gone, too, is the tradition of a fetching a bucket or "growler" from the corner tavern. Of Philadelphia's eight breweries at the end of World War II, four were left by the early 1960s. One by one, they closed. Schmidt's was the last to go flat—just as the brew pub revival was taking root in Center City.

Food / Farmers' Markets

Amish Farmers Market at the Downingtown Market Place
Business Route 30, 3½ miles west of Exton
Manager: Henry Esh, 269-4050
Hours: Friday 9am–9pm; Saturday 9am–8pm
Vendors: 18
Parking: Ample and free
Founded: 1956
Size: 15,000 sq. ft.

Green Dragon Farmers Market and Auction
955 N. State Street (2 miles north of Ephrata, PA)
Managers: Bill Rohrbach and Larry Loose, (717) 738-1117
Hours: Friday 9am–10pm (hay auction 10am,
  cattle auction 11am, dry goods/produce auction 4pm,
  new items auction 7pm)
Vendors: 400
Parking: Ample and free
Founded: 1932
Size: 10 acres
Comments: No air conditioning

Flourtown Farmers Market
920 Bethlehem Pike
Manager: Greg Bushu, 233-5303
Hours: Thursday 8am–6pm; Friday and Saturday 7am–5pm
Vendors: 20
Parking: Ample and free
Founded: 1985
Size: 8,000 sq. ft.
Comments: No public restrooms or restaurants;
  public seating on outside benches

Zern's Farmers Market
Philadelphia Avenue (Route 73), Gilbertsville, PA
Manager: John Specca, 367-2461
Hours: Friday 2pm–10pm; Saturday 11am–10pm
Vendors: 500
Parking: Ample and free
Founded: 1922
Size: 12 acres
Comments: No air conditioning; country market with eight
  different auctions—including auto, animals, eggs, and
  household—and a giant flea market

Jenkintown Farmers Market
The Bridge at Foxcroft Square, 323 Old York Road
Manager: Caren Fox Fires, 886-2000
Hours: Wednesday–Friday 8am–7pm; Saturday 7am–6pm
Vendors: 20
Parking: Ample and free
Founded: 1991
Size: 12,000 sq. ft.

Food / Farmers' Markets

Central Market
Penn Square, Lancaster, PA
Manager: Donald Horn, (717) 291-4723
Hours: Tuesday and Friday 6am–4:30pm; Saturday 6am–2pm
Vendors: 82
Parking: Nearby garages, $.70 per hour
Founded: In the 18th century; located in current building
    since 1889
Size: 20,000 sq. ft.
Comments: Oldest inland market in the United States;
    no restaurants in market and no public seating; no air
    conditioning

The Market Place at Lansdowne
2 W. Baltimore Pike
Manager: 284-9907
Hours: Wednesday–Friday 7am–7pm; Saturday 7am–6pm;
    Sunday 8am–3pm
Vendors: 14
Parking: Public lots, $.25 per hour
Founded: 1993
Size: 9,000 sq. ft.
Comments: No restaurants; market is in restored 92-year-old
    bank building

Leesport Farmers Market
8 miles north of Reading on Route 61
Managers: Woody and Bill Weist, 926-1307
Hours: Wednesday 9am–8pm
Vendors: 80 indoors; 150 in open sheds;
    400 in outdoor flea market
Parking: Ample and free
Founded: 1947
Size: 35 acres
Comments: Livestock auction every market day beginning
    1pm; craft show five times a year; no air conditioning

Montgomeryville Farmers and Discount Marketplace
Route 63 between Routes 309 and 202
Manager: Al Hoffman, 628-3276
Hours: Friday 11am–9:30pm; Saturday 10am–9:30pm;
    Sunday 11am–5pm
Vendors: 142
Parking: Ample and free
Founded: 1992
Size: 62,000 sq. ft.
Comments: Mostly general merchandise; not much food

MAJOR PHILADELPHIA BREWERS OF THE 1890S

Goodbye to the Lager

Arnholt & Schaefer Brewing Company, 30th and Thompson Streets

J. & P. Baltz Brewing Company, 31st and Thompson Streets

Louis Bergdoll Brewing Company, 29th and Parrish Streets

Bergner & Engel Brewing Company, 32nd and Master Streets

John F. Betz & Son, Crown and Willow Streets

Class & Nachod, 1732 Mervine Street

Continental Brewing Company, 21st Street and Washington Avenue

George Esslinger, 415 N. 10th Street

Fred Fiel, 2207 N. 6th Street

Theodore Finkenauer, 1716 Germantown Avenue

John Hohenadel, 3506 Queen Street

Jacob Hornung, 22nd and Clearfield Streets

Liebert and Obert, 156 Oak Street

F. A. Poth Brewing Company, 31st and Jefferson Streets

Rieger & Gretz, 1538 Germantown Avenue

Frederick Schaefer, 338 Brown Street

Peter Schemm & Son, 25th and Poplar Streets

C. Schmidt & Sons, 113 Edward Street

Robert Smith India Pale Ale Brewing Company, Girard Avenue and 38th Street

Weisbrod & Hess, Frankford Avenue and Adams Street

Albert Wolf, 212 N. 3rd Street

John J. Wolf, 929 N. 5th Street

Source: Tovey's Official Brewers' and Maltsters' Directory, 1892–1893.

THERE WENT PHILADELPHIA'S SPINE

The Market Street Markets in 1799

An account of the High Street (or Market Street) markets from 1809 published in a literary magazine called *The Port Folio* included the suggestion that the markets, which then stretched from the Delaware to Fourth Street, be extended:

"Since the visits of the Yellow Fever, the building tide has flowed westward with new and wonderful force, and the completion of the market between the two rivers will probably take place in the present generation." The writer commented on the modest choice of a site "that will deprive this edifice of any pretensions to magnificence" but admired the grandiose, finished Philadelphia Market as "a uniform, open arcade mathematically straight, two miles in length, perfect in its symmetry, gracefully broken by the water building [in its middle, at Center Square]...and by the intersecting streets, and open onto a noble bridge, lying in the same line, at Schuylkill."

The anonymous writer claimed that the finished market would "never be a contemptible object" and hoped that "no pragmatical architect will destroy this symmetry, by adopting new dimensions as to height or breath, and taking a different curve for his arch."

By the 1850s, the market shambles had extended to Eighth Street and west of Broad, from 15th to 17th Streets. But the city's widest right of way was soon yielded to the rising railroads. Arguing that Philadelphia's unique spine of markets was a health nuisance, the railroads had vendors shuffled to a series of new indoor market halls. By "modernizing" Philadelphia's markets, the railroads opened the center of Market Street—and Center City—to a new kind of commerce, and a new kind of grade-level danger.

Food / Farmers' Markets

Narberth Farmers Market
104 Essex Avenue
Managers: Steve and Anna Lapp, 664-9274
Hours: Tuesday 7am–5pm; Friday 7am–6pm;
  Saturday 8am–4pm
Vendors: 4
Parking: Street and meter
Founded: 1970
Size: 3,600 sq. ft.
Comments: No restrooms, public seating, or restaurants;
  no air conditioning

The Market at Albrecht's
701 Montgomery Avenue, Narberth, PA
Manager: Metropolitan Management Co., 667-1700
Hours: Wednesday–Friday 8am–7pm; Saturday 7:30am–6pm
Vendors: 14
Parking: 55 free spaces; non-metered street parking
Founded: 1993
Size: 5,000 sq. ft.
Comments: No public seating or restaurants

Pennsylvania Dutch Farmers Market
2150 S. Eagle Road, Newtown, PA
Manager: 860-7788
Hours: Monday–Saturday 9am–6pm; Amish section
  Thursday–Saturday only
Vendors: 15
Parking: Ample and free
Founded: 1991
Size: 13,000 sq. ft.

Reading Farmers Market
800 Penn Street
Manager: Levi Wegman, 372-4986
Hours: Thursday and Friday 6am–5pm; Saturday 6am–noon
Vendors: 19
Parking: Free lot across street
Founded: In current location since 1970
Size: 16,000 sq. ft.

Sharon Hill Farmers Market
1220 Chester Pike
Manager: Henry Gehman, 583-7900
Hours: Thursday–Saturday 7am–4pm
Vendors: 12
Parking: 50 free spaces
Founded: 1934
Size: 4,000 sq. ft.
Comments: One luncheonette

Food / Farmers' Markets

Springfield Farmers Market
The Shops at Springfield Park, 910 E. Woodland Avenue
Manager: Kim Ross, 642-5445
Hours: Thursday and Friday 8am–6pm; Saturday 7am–5pm
Vendors: 10
Parking: Ample and free
Founded: 1986
Size: 4,300 sq. ft.
Comments: No public seating or restaurants

Lancaster County Farmers Market
389 W. Lancaster Avenue, Strafford, PA
Manager: Sam Neff, 688-9856
Hours: Wednesday, Friday, Saturday 6am–4pm
Vendors: 31
Parking: Ample and free
Founded: 1951; in current location since 1977
Size: 10,000 sq. ft.

Black Horse Farmers Market
701 N. Black Horse Pike, Williamstown, NJ
Manager: (609) 728-7996
Hours: Thursday 10am–5pm; Friday 9am–8pm;
   Saturday 8am–3pm
Vendors: 10
Parking: Ample and free
Founded: 1993
Size: 10,000 sq ft.
Comments: Non-food market is connected to Amish market;
   no public seating

Cowtown Farmers Market
U.S. Route 40, 8 miles east of Delaware Memorial Bridge,
   Woodstown, NJ
Manager: Bob Becker, (609) 769-3202
Hours: Tuesday and Saturday 8am–4pm
Vendors: 600
Parking: Ample and free
Founded: In current location since 1942
Size: 38 acres
Comments: No public seating; no air conditioning;
   many non-food vendors; cattle auction

❖

September 1967: A new school year begins with the announcement that, owing to higher food costs and salaries for cafeteria workers, prices of school lunches have increased by five cents, to 35 cents for elementary pupils and 40 cents for higher grades.

September 1975: Penn Fruit Co., a major food retailer with 61 stores, declares bankruptcy. Within a month 26 stores close and 1,500 workers are laid off.

CITIZENS'
MANUAL

WHAT TO DO

There's a weedy, nasty vacant lot in your neighborhood. You and your neighbors have all seen community gardens around town and decide you want one, too. What do you do next?

Call Neighborhood Gardens Association/A Philadelphia Land Trust (625-8264). Ask for the publication *How to Obtain Permission to Garden on a Neighborhood Vacant Lot.* NGA can help you negotiate a lease with the owner (if necessary) or even help acquire the land.

You will need the exact address of the lot, which you can determine by context or by consulting official maps. Get the owner's permission, preferably in writing.

Call Philadelphia Green (625-8280). They can help you with things like fencing, soil, and tools.

Call Penn State's Urban Gardening Program (560-4167). They offer great advice, as well as publications, on just about everything from organizing your gardeners to building fences with recycled lumber. Ask for the *Garden Coordinator's Handbook.*

Write down your rules so that all participants know what's expected of them.

Enrich your plot with organic matter. Free compost is available at Fairmount Park Recycling Center (685-0108); you can get mushroom compost (not free) from Joe Leo, Inc. (444-3892). Don't forget manure from the carriage companies and riding academies (in the phone book).

Plant.

Gardening

Farm Out: Community Gardening in Philadelphia

In the 1990s gardening is more than a great way to keep vacant lots clean, more than a source of food and flowers. It's a successful strategy for neighborhood improvement and organization.

Public gardening comes and goes in Philadelphia—sometimes even on the same plot of ground. Nearly a century ago, the Vacant Lot Cultivation Association encouraged cultivation in West Philadelphia, Logan, and Germantown. In 1897, the Association divided four open acres at 56th and Haverford into fifth-acre plots to encourage self-sufficiency among Philadelphians in economic "distress." The site was eventually developed for housing. But in 1976, when some of that housing was demolished, a half-acre was reopened, and with help from the Penn State Urban Gardening Program it bloomed again. In 1989 developers claimed the site for housing a second time, continuing the land-use give and take.

The government advocated vegetable gardening during both World Wars. The more folks raised, the more farm products they could send to the military. Not far from the old Woodside Amusement Park, in Fairmount Park, Philadelphia families cultivated 200- to 300-square-foot plots, each enough—barely—to feed a family of four.

In 1953, Louise Bush-Brown organized settlement house workers and garden clubs into the Neighborhood Gardens Association, which sponsored beautification programs in low-income neighborhoods and public housing projects. According to Bush-Brown, South Philadelphia's 700 block of Mercy Street became "the first Garden Block in America" after residents worked together to install and plant window boxes. In 1960, vacant lot gardens were added through the leadership of County Agent William A. White. Some of today's active community gardeners, such as Alta Felton and Mabel Wilson near 25th and Reed Streets, began their public gardening careers with the Neighborhood Gardens Association. By its 25th anniversary in 1978 (shortly before merging into the Pennsylvania Horticultural Society's Philadelphia Green Program), the Association could claim the planting of 850 city blocks.

Vacant lot "farming out" revived in the Green '70s with Recreation Department programs that helped turn vacant lots into flower and vegetable gardens, tot lots and basketball courts. The Pennsylvania Horticultural Society initiated community vegetable gardens; the Penn State Urban Gardening Program provided technical assistance. By the late 1980s, more than a thousand lots throughout the city had been transformed. ∎

Gardening

The Southwark/ Queen Village Story

I n the 1970s, as Queen Village began reemerging from years of disinvestment and abandonment, community gardeners began to quietly cultivate a vacant lot at the northeast corner of 2nd and Catherine Streets. But community renaissance also meant community rebuilding, and bulldozers soon chased community gardeners from the land.

A larger lot was staked out at 311-333 Christian Street, where the Henry Berk School had once stood. The government, having dropped its plans for a health center on the site, reclassified the land as excess federal property, slated for sale. Fear set in. But the opportunity presented itself: this site could yet become a permanent community garden and open space.

As the threat of sale loomed, State Senator Henry J. Cianfrani aided the improvement of the site by seeing to the removal of thousands of square feet of concrete (an old school yard). Twenty more garden plots and an orchard bloomed.

At the request of the Queen Village Neighbors Association (QVNA), U.S. Congressman Thomas M. Foglietta introduced QVNA gardeners to representatives of several related federal agencies, including Housing and Urban Development and the Department of Agriculture. The gardeners had learned of a program at the National Park Services permitting a transfer of "surplus property" to municipalities for recreational use; they planned to request such a transfer of the property from the General Services Administration.

Then, in the mid-1980s, the city agreed to apply for the property if QVNA wrote the application. Architects, lawyers, and activists produced the required documents, including plot plans and letters of support from the entire Philadelphia congressional delegation, the governor, the mayor, and most of City Council, among others. In order to get an interim lease, QVNA resolved to sacrifice the neighborhood's only parking lot and assured the city that it would not be liable for injuries or for maintenance costs.

A decade and a half of politicking had paid off. With the help of the Neighborhood Gardens Associations/A Philadelphia Land Trust, this community-managed open space of Southwark/Queen Village Garden became permanent. Both process and product represent the blooming of a city community. ■

PIGEON PEAS AND BANANA TREES

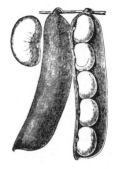

You can see the world's people in their plants and gardens. Fava beans arose in Egypt and migrated to China, Italy, and Britain. Gardeners with roots in all those countries grow them here.

Some Southeast Asians brought seeds with them to Philadelphia in the 1970s. They plant lemon and Thai basil in "crazy mixed-up" beds with mustards, gingor, gourds, and beans. Their gardens, and many more, can be seen at Common Ground Community Garden at Island Avenue and Bartram Road in Southwest Philadelphia. Farther along Island Avenue are traditional Southern Italian gardens.

At 64th and Market, you can see African American and Korean gardens and their interplay. Korean garden beds often include hot peppers, huge radishes, and a profusion of greens. Many African Americans plant peanuts, collards, and sometimes cotton or tobacco on raised rows, West African–style. This is "for the kids to see and remember."

Natives of Puerto Rico near 2305-13 N. Palethorpe Street have a poultry *casita* and containers with pigeon peas and, yes, bananas. On 6th Street just below Lehigh, Filipino gardeners mix bitter melons on overhead trellises with yard-long beans.

Philadelphia gardens, like their gardeners, spring from diverse roots.

83

Arboretums, Gardens, and Preserves

Awbury Arboretum Association, 6000 Chew Street, Philadelphia, PA 19138. Phone: 849-2855. Hours: Daily 9am–7pm. Free admission.

Philanthropist and shipping magnate Henry Cope established this as his family's summer residence before the Civil War, when Germantown was still a railroad suburb. In 1916, the arboretum was dedicated to the public. Among its 55 acres are diverse ecosystems maintained as outdoor laboratories: wetlands, upland woods, and spectacular English-style vistas from the Cope House, the center for arboretum activities. Of special interest are champion specimen trees, pond habitats, and the still-intact, mid-19th-century garden designed by landscape architect William Saunders.

Bartram's Garden, 54th Street and Lindbergh Boulevard, Philadelphia, PA 19143. Phone: 729-5281. Hours: May–October Wednesday–Sunday noon–4pm; November–April Wednesday–Friday noon–4pm. Admission $2.

About 1730, John Bartram (1699–1777) established on 44 rolling acres along the Schuylkill River in Southwest Philadelphia what is now the oldest botanic garden in the country. Bartram collected plants while exploring the colonies and brought them back to Philadelphia. King George III titled him "Botanizer Royal for America." And the setting where John and son William Bartram studied, propagated, and introduced into cultivation approximately 200 native American trees and shrubs is preserved with the restored 18th-century buildings: house, barn, stable, carriage house, ice house and seedhouse. There is also a 15-acre wildflower meadow and river's edge trail.

Bowman's Hill Wildflower Preserve, Washington Crossing Historic Park, P.O. Box 103, Washington Crossing, PA 18977. Phone: 862-2924. Hours: Monday–Saturday 9am–5pm, Sunday noon–5pm, closed major holidays. Donations accepted.

Plants native to Pennsylvania are featured in the 26 trails. Guided tours, lectures, and films are presented. A small research library is available by request.

Briar Bush Nature Center, 1212 Edge Hill Road, Abington, PA 19001. Phone: 887-6603. Hours: Building open Monday–Saturday 9am–5pm, Sunday 1–5pm; nature trails open sunrise–sunset; closed major holidays. Free admission.

Outdoor attractions include a pond fed by windmill pump, an active beehive, and a crawl-through cave, as well as live animal displays, woodland plants, and trails. Exhibits emphasize the ecology of the mid-Atlantic region, and educational programs for children and adults are conducted. The center's building houses a library, meeting rooms, and gift shop. Guided tours, lectures, and films are available.

Hagley Museum and Library, Route 141, P.O. Box 3630, Wilmington, DE 19807. Phone: (302) 658-2400. Hours: March 15–December daily 9:30am–4:30pm; January–March 14 Saturday and Sunday 9:30am–4:30pm. Admission $8.

Hagley—the original du Pont mills, estate, and gardens—is set amid 230 acres of trees, flowering shrubs, and wildflowers. It includes the first du Pont family home (built in 1802), a restored flower and vegetable garden in the French tradition, a workers' community, and mill buildings with working water turbine, steam engine, and a 19th-century machine shop. The complex offers diverse restorations, exhibits, and live demonstrations.

Haverford College Arboretum, 370 Lancaster Avenue, Haverford, PA 19041. Phone: 896-1101. Hours: Daily dawn–dusk. Free admission.

Between 1834 and 1845, English landscape gardener William Carvill developed a plan for Haverford College, including a 216-acre arboretum set on gently rolling land with open spaces, woodland, streams, majestic trees, and special gardens. Of interest are a traditional Japanese Zen garden, sculpture gardens, and the Smith-Magill Memorial Gardens planted near the original Carvill Arch.

The Highlands, 7001 Sheaff Lane, Fort Washington, PA 19034. Phone: 641-2687. Hours: Tours of mansion and garden Monday–Friday 9am–4pm; gardens open all year (appointment preferred). Admission $1.

Built in 1796 by Anthony Morris, this country seat includes an elegant late Georgian mansion with nine outbuildings. Later owners enlarged both mansion and gardens, chronicling the history of families who occupied the property for nearly two centuries. In the gardens are examples of the Federal-style picturesque landscape, scientific farming, and grape culture of one-time owner George Sheaff, and Colonial Revival gardens.

The Horticulture Center, Northwest Horticultural Drive, West Fairmount Park, Philadelphia, PA 19131. Phone: 685-0096. Hours: Daily 9am–3pm. Admission $2. Japanese House and Garden: Hours: Wednesday–Sunday 11am–4pm. Admission $1.

A fenced-in portion of Fairmount Park, where the great glass Horticultural Hall once stood, the center includes the Japanese House and Garden. Seasonal gardens are maintained near walking paths; the 32,000-square-foot greenhouse is used for display and production. Both Asian and North American trees are featured.

Jenkins Arboretum, 631 Berwyn Baptist Road, Devon, PA 19333. Phone: 647-8870. Hours: Daily dawn–dusk. Free admission.

On the grounds of the former home of H. Lawrence Jenkins and Elisabeth Phillippe Jenkins, the arboretum is a public park and wildlife sanctuary, with an emphasis on azaleas, rhododendrons, and wildflowers. Located on a remnant of Southeastern Pennsylvania's hardwood

85

forest, the arboretum consists predominantly of a canopy of oaks, with tulip-poplar, hickory, beech, and other species. Visitors can follow the easy paved trails among the trees or along the stream, see birds and other wildlife, and observe nature's moods and seasons.

Longwood Gardens, Route 1, P.O. Box 501, Kennett Square, PA 19348. Phone: 388-6741. Hours: Outdoor gardens daily 9am–6pm (until 5pm November–March); conservatories daily 10am–5pm and later for special events. Admission $10 adults (Tuesday $6), $2 children 6–15, $6 youth 16–20.

In 1700, Quaker farmer George Peirce purchased this land from William Penn. His grandsons began a 15-acre arboretum in the 1790s, about a century before Pierre du Pont bought the property to preserve the arboretum and construct today's major gardens. Outdoors are Peirce's Park, the Peirce–du Pont House, the 600-foot-long Flower Garden Walk, the Hillside Garden, the Idea Garden, and numerous other areas featuring 11,000 types of plants. Under glass (nearly four acres of it) are 20 gardens with orchids, roses, palms, and seasonal flowers. In addition, Longwood has a 10,010-pipe organ as well as dramatic outdoor illuminated fountains, and it helps sponsor 300 performing arts events and educational programs.

Ebenezer Maxwell Mansion, 200 W. Tulpehocken Street, Philadelphia, PA 19144. Phone: 438-1861. Hours: April–December Thursday–Sunday 1–4pm; other times by appointment. Admission $4 adults, $3 seniors, $2 students.

This suburban villa is the city's first Victorian historic house museum and the focus of a six-block area of restored Victorian structures in Germantown. The restored house, built in 1859, is a tribute to rising suburban/middle-class prosperity and features then-new inventions: gas lighting, central heat, hot and cold running water, and indoor plumbing. The landscape features over 150 varieties of trees, shrubs, herbaceous plants, ferns, and vines that illustrate the range in tastes and plant material of the period.

Morris Arboretum of the University of Pennsylvania, 100 Northwestern Avenue, Philadelphia, PA 19118. Phone: 247-5777. Hours: Monday–Friday 10am–4pm, Saturday and Sunday 10am–5pm. Admission $3 adults, $1.50 students and seniors.

Located in Chestnut Hill, the Morris Arboretum was founded in 1887 as "Compton," the estate of John and Lydia T. Morris, world travelers and avid collectors of artifacts, plants, and garden styles. In 1932, the University of Pennsylvania transformed the estate into a public garden and center for research and education. On 92 acres are many of the area's newest, rarest, and largest trees, all set in a Victorian landscape of winding paths, rolling hills, meadows, streams, and special gardens.

Rockwood Museum, 610 Shipley Road, Wilmington, DE 19809. Phone: (302) 761-4340. Hours: Tuesday–Saturday 11am–4pm, closed holidays. Admission $5 adults, $4 seniors, $1 children.

Delaware merchant-banker Joseph Shipley built Rockwood in 1851 upon his retirement from business in England. The estate features six acres of cultivated grounds and 62 acres of woodlands in addition to the mansion, gardener's cottage, porter's lodge, barn, and outbuildings. Both house and gardens represent the eclectic tastes of owners who made collecting visits to many parts of the world.

Scott Arboretum of Swarthmore College, Swarthmore College, 500 College Avenue, Swarthmore, PA 19081-1397. Phone: 328-8025. Hours: Daily dawn–dusk. Free admission.

Conceived by Arthur Hoyt Scott, the arboretum was established in 1929 with an endowment given by his family. The arboretum is a "garden of suggestions" displaying the best ornamental garden plants for eastern Pennsylvania. Home gardeners can view over 5,000 species of plants on 110 acres. Major plant collections include flowering cherries, hollies, winterhazels, crabapples, lilacs, magnolias, native azaleas, tree peonies, viburnums, wisterias, and witchhazels. Special garden areas include the Entrance Garden, Teaching Garden, Fragrance Garden, Outdoor Amphitheater, Courtyard Garden, Winter Garden, Rose Garden, and Summer Border.

Taylor Memorial Arboretum, 10 Ridley Drive, Wallingford, PA 19086. Phone: 876-2649. Hours: Daily 9am–4pm, closed major holidays. Free admission.

Taylor, an old mill property along the Ridley Creek, is operated by the Natural Lands Trust, Inc. It has an Azalea Trail, Bald Cypress Pond, Anne's Grotto (an old Quarry Site), and a waterfall. Much of its plant collection represents specific wildlife habitats.

The Tyler Arboretum, 515 Painter Road, Media, PA 19063. Phone: 566-5431. Hours: Daily 8am–dusk. Admission $3 adults, $1 children.

William Penn granted this 700-acre tract to Quaker farmer Thomas Minshall, and for eight generations it remained in the family. Two descendants, brothers Minshall and Jacob Painter, planted the initial arboretum in the late 19th century; Laura Tyler bequeathed the land to the public in 1944. Tyler's mature collections, including the Painter Trees, the pinetum, and extensive rhododendron and holly areas, blend into the natural landscape. The arboretum offers a variety of environmental programs incorporating 20 miles of hiking trails, prime bird-watching habitat, and a historic house and library.

Welkinweir Preserve, 7 Prizer Road, Pottstown, PA 19464. Phone: 469-6366. Hours: Daily dawn–dusk. Free admission.

Formerly a private estate, Welkinweir offers panoramic views of a unique blend of horticultural and natural elements, including a dwarf conifer collection and a series of seven ponds. In 1961, Philadelphia conservationists formed the Natural Lands Trust, which currently owns and/or manages 54 preserves with 13,000 acres in the mid-Atlantic states, including the Welkinweir Preserve and the Taylor Memorial Arboretum.

Winterthur, Route 52, Winterthur, DE 19735. Phone: (302) 888-4600. Hours: Tuesday–Saturday 9am–5pm, Sunday noon–5pm. Admission $7.

Beginning in 1811, four generations of du Ponts farmed Winterthur. Henry Francis du Pont, the last private owner, both collected superb examples of American decorative arts and pursued a lifelong interest in horticulture and landscape design. Period room settings in the Winterthur museum and in garden areas are bound together by du Pont's extraordinary eye for color and attention to detail. Winterthur Garden is considered one of the most beautiful and successful naturalistic gardens in the world. The eight-acre Azalea Woods is du Pont's masterpiece of color, harmony, and naturalistic design. Visitors may also sample the museum's treasures with an introductory tour, which does not require reservations. ■

BREINTNALL'S LEAF PRINTS

Joseph Breintnall, according to Benjamin Franklin, was "a good-natur'd middle-ag'd man, a great lover of Poetry, reading all he could meet with, and writing some that was tolerable; very ingenious in many nicknackeries, and of sensible conversation." Breintnall designed the legal forms that were the bread and butter of Franklin's early printing trade, and he engaged in a variety of experiments that made the two fast friends.

For instance, an observation that people in the tropics preferred lighter-color clothing led Breintnall to experiment with solar heat. He devised a special-formula ink. Along with Franklin and others, Breintnall formed the Junto, or "Leather Apron Society," for tradesmen to share ideas beyond the day-to-day. In 1731, Breintnall became the first secretary of the newly formed Library Company of Philadelphia, where his unique leaf prints have resided for more than 250 years.

Breintnall's interests in nature and ink combined in this 11-year project, which began in 1731. He made scores of leaf prints, a few of which we reproduce on these pages. Leonardo da Vinci and others had experimented earlier, but Breintnall set about the problem anew to learn how to obtain the best of the delicate tracery on paper. He improved upon earlier methods of leaf printing both through inks and printing-press techniques developed specifically for the work. Franklin later adapted some of these discoveries to print paper currency that defied counterfeiters.

Rethinking the Regional Economy

I n order to find our niche in the global economy, we need a new regional identity. We need to understand the changes that have transformed the region's economy and appreciate the richness of our resources.

What is Greater Philadelphia? The metropolitan area, also known as the Delaware Valley, includes Philadelphia and its neighboring counties in Southeastern Pennsylvania—Bucks, Chester, Delaware, and Montgomery (pop. 3.7 million). The U.S. Census now adds to this New Jersey's Burlington, Camden, Gloucester, and Salem Counties for a new nine-county region (pop. 4.9 million). And viewed most broadly, Greater Philadelphia is the 11-county tri-state region, which embraces New Jersey's Mercer County and Delaware's New Castle County (pop. 5.7 million).

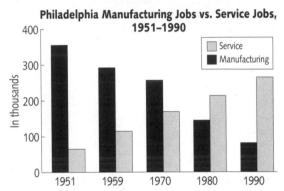

Philadelphia's industrial base and identity as a manufacturing city survived far into the 20th century. Unlike other old regional economies dominated by single industries (coal and steel, shoes, textiles, or tires) that collapsed in the middle third of the century, Philadelphia's broadly diversified industrial base persisted into the 1970s. Everything from lace handkerchiefs and cigars to Stetson hats and locomotives once built here gave Philadelphia the nickname "Workshop of the World." Like a snake shedding its skin, Greater Philadelphia has emerged from this recent and painful economic molting process with a new and highly diversified service economy. The region is now well matched with the major economic trends developing within the global economy.

In a future dominated by increased emphasis on "brain intensive" activities—the production of knowledge and the availability of a highly educated labor force—Greater Philadelphia's 83 degree-granting institutions rank it near the top of the nation's metropolitan areas. More than 46,000 students graduated from colleges and universities here in 1990—just about as many as in the famous "college towns" of Boston and Baltimore combined.

Nearly one in five of the nation's physicians has trained in a Philadelphia-area medical school or hospital. The 11-county region boasts leading medical research facilities and the nation's largest concentration of major pharmaceutical firms.

Firms specializing in advanced technology account for an ever-increasing share of growth in the new economy. Availability of organized venture capital in Greater Philadelphia—over $1.5 billion in 35 firms—adds to the synergy among universities, entrepreneurs, and venture capitalists. This augurs well for continued growth, especially in the crescent promoters call America's "High-Tech Main Street": Route 202 from Princeton, New Jersey to Wilmington, Delaware.

Finally, the global economy is stimulating remarkable growth in the hospitality industry—travel, tourism, conventions, hotels, restaurants, food, personal services, retail sales, and transportation. Philadelphia stands to gain substantially by working for a larger share of this $2 trillion sector of the world economy.

As the birthplace of the nation, Philadelphia commands a unique appeal for tourists and conventioneers. Once here they can fan out into the countryside to visit other cultural sites and attractions. The hospitality industry will grow into the local economy's most dynamic sector and will serve as a major source of much-needed unskilled, entry-level jobs.

Greater Philadelphia

The region's future economic well-being depends on the central city's economic health. (Studies of comparable metropolitan areas show that suburbs of relatively well-off cities fare much better than suburbs of suffering cities.) Despite the deconcentration of jobs and population, despite the growing independence of suburban economies, city and suburbs increasingly function as one complex economic matrix:

- Each day, close to 400,000 persons cross Philadelphia's borders on their way to work. About 260,000 enter the city and 130,000 leave.
- Nearly three of every ten dollars in the five-county region's $110 billion gross metropolitan product results from city-county business transactions.

If Philadelphia had a precipitous economic decline, the region would also experience economic pain. The difference between the best- and worst-case scenarios in Southeastern Pennsylvania by the year 2000 is 446,000 fewer jobs, $11.6 billion in lost wages, and $585 million (in 1990 dollars) in lost state corporate net income, personal income, and sales taxes.

Regions, rather than cities, are already the key geographic elements in the American economy, and regions are now emerging as vital units in the global economic competition. Success is measured, in part, by the amount of foreign investment attracted to a region and by the performance of its goods and services in the global marketplace. Cooperation is the logical and critical strategy to foster the perception (and the reality) of Greater Philadelphia as a force in the new economic geography.

Philadelphia, the surrounding counties, and the hundreds of municipalities within these counties must work together to overcome parochialism and ensure that regional resources—labor, transportation, infrastructure, and environment—are developed and managed efficiently. Philadelphia-bashing is old politics. Go-it-alone strategies are outdated economics. Participation in the global economy requires regional cooperation.   —*Theodore Hershberg* ■

Sources: Anita A. Summers and Thomas F. Luce, *Economic Development Within the Philadelphia Metropolitan Area* (University of Pennsylvania Press, 1987); William J. Stull and Janice Fanning Madden, *Post-Industrial Philadelphia: Structural Changes in the Metropolitan Economy* (University of Pennsylvania Press, 1990); *Greater Philadelphia Business Guide to Education and Training* (Greater Philadelphia Economic Development Coalition, 1992); *The Economic Impact of Hospitals in Southeastern Pennsylvania: Regional Summary* (Pennsylvania Economy League, 1992).

Sources for bar chart: For 1951, 1959, 1970, 1980: *County Business Patterns*, U.S. Bureau of the Census; for 1990: *Philadelphia Employment Trends*, 1991, U.S. Bureau of Labor Statistics.

Percent of Employed Persons Working Outside of Their County of Residence

Bucks	46
Burlington	43
Camden	44
Chester	39
Delaware	45
Gloucester	54
Montgomery	35
Philadelphia	20

College and University Degrees Granted in Greater Philadelphia, 1990

Type of Degree	Number of Graduates
Diploma/Certificate	999
Associate	6,981
Bachelor	27,182
Master	7,817
Ph.D.	1,118
Professional	2,876
Total	46,973

Hospital Wages and Salaries by County in Southeastern Pennsylvania

Bucks	$356,000,000
Chester	$258,000,000
Delaware	$528,000,000
Montgomery	$706,000,000
Philadelphia	$3,464,000,000

Hospitals in Southeastern Pennsylvania generate over $5.3 billion in wages, representing approximately 20% of private sector payroll dollars.

Sources: U.S. Census, 1990; *Greater Philadelphia Business Guide to Education and Training*, Greater Philadelphia Economic Development Coalition, 1992; *The Economic Impact of Hospitals in Southeastern Pennsylvania, Regional Summary*, Pennsylvania Economy League, October 1992.

PHILADELPHIA HEALTH DISTRICTS BY RACE

A Health Profile of Philadelphia, 1990

Philadelphia is organized into ten health districts, and, as the data suggest, the health of residents varies dramatically among those districts in areas including infant mortality, syphilis, and lead poisoning. Almost all of the reported cases of lead poisoning are in children, who can suffer permanent damage to their kidneys, liver, and brain from eating chips of lead-based paint.

	White Philadelphians	Philadelphians of Color*
District 1	54,859	24,178
District 2	91,602	45,950
District 3	50,146	115,571
District 4	32,744	103,137
District 5	16,109	79,442
District 6	31,281	42,960
District 7	179,468	11,235
District 8	53,325	143,355
District 9	79,169	152,537
District 10	259,883	18,626

* Includes black and Asian residents and other racial minorities. Hispanic residents are included in either category, depending on their self-definition of race.

Source: U.S. Census, 1990.

Reported Cases of Syphilis and Lead Poisoning

	1990		1985–1989 median	
	Syphilis	Lead Poisoning	Syphilis	Lead Poisoning
District 1	347	26	93	25.5
District 2	433	22	76	30.5
District 3	892	103	291	79.0
District 4	612	70	145	83.5
District 5	1,446	82	286	81.5
District 6	829	34	157	49.0
District 7	105	9	50	10.5
District 8	1,063	94	383	95.5
District 9	785	66	208	73.5
District 10	45	3	24	2.0
Total	6,557	509	1713	530.5

Source: Philadelphia Department of Public Health.

The Ten Most Frequent Causes of Death

	Number of Deaths			Number of Deaths
1. Heart Disease	5,852		6. Pneumonia and Influenza	535
2. Cancer	4,657		7. Homicide and Legal Intervention	490
3. Stroke	1,189		8. Diabetes	451
4. Accidents and Adverse Effects of Drugs	688		9. Septicemia (Blood Poisoning)	448
5. Chronic Obstructive Pulmonary Disease (Asthma, Bronchitis, Emphysema)	586		10. AIDS	327
			All Other Causes	3,752
			All Causes	18,975

Health

Infant Deaths and the Percentage of Pregnant Women Receiving Late or No Prenatal Care

Infant mortality rates measure the number of deaths among infants under one year of age for each 1,000 live births. These deaths are often a result of low birth weight—under 5.5 pounds—which is, in turn, often related to a pregnant woman's lack of prenatal care. The chart gives the percentage of pregnant women who received no prenatal care at all or care that began during their last trimester. In Philadelphia, the infant mortality rate and access to prenatal care vary sharply among races.

	Live Births	Infant Mortality Rate (per 1000)	Percentage of Pregnant Women Receiving Late or No Prenatal Care
District 1			
White Women	438	2.3	4.2
Women of Color	541	22.2	26.6
District 2			
White Women	1,136	7.9	5.6
Women of Color	1,389	20.2	25.7
District 3			
White Women	523	7.6	4.7
Women of Color	2,635	19.7	20.3
District 4			
White Women	257	19.5	4.4
Women of Color	2,282	21.0	22.5
District 5			
White Women	212	0.0	6.8
Women of Color	2,288	23.2	28.1
District 6			
White Women	1,079	9.3	9.8
Women of Color	989	25.3	26.8
District 7			
White Women	2,788	9.3	4.1
Women of Color	264	18.9	15.5
District 8			
White Women	1,886	11.1	9.7
Women of Color	2,990	25.4	18.5
District 9			
White Women	967	3.1	3.0
Women of Color	3,081	16.6	15.0
District 10			
White Women	3,328	5.7	2.4
Women of Color	321	21.8	6.3
Total			
White Women	12,614	7.9	5.0
Women of Color	16,780	22.1	21.0

INFANT MORTALITY IN PHILADELPHIA AND SELECTED NATIONS

A country's infant mortality rate is considered a key indicator of the health of its people. This chart shows how the infant mortality rates (per one thousand live births) for all Philadelphians, white Philadelphians, and Philadelphians of color compared to those of industrialized and Third World nations.

Infant Mortality Rate

Japan	4
Austria	5
Ireland	6
Italy	6
Spain	6
Taiwan	6
Canada	7
Iceland	7
White Philadelphians	**7.9**
Australia	8
Singapore	8
Greece	10
United States	10
Cuba	13
Bulgaria	14
Jamaica	14
Kuwait	15
Philadelphia	**16.0**
Costa Rica	17
Poland	17
Chile	19
Romania	19
Panama	21
Philadelphians of Color	**22.1**
Thailand	24
China	27
Mexico	36
Philippines	40
Guatemala	48
Vietnam	54
Iraq	56
India	88
Ethiopia	114
Bangladesh	118
Laos	124
Afghanistan	164

Philadelphia data are for 1990; other data are for 1991.

Sources: Philadelphia Department of Public Health, World Health Organization.

AIDS in Philadelphia

The demographics of AIDS have been changing consistently since the beginning of the epidemic in the early 1980s. The percentage of total AIDS cases among gay/bisexual males has decreased significantly, while there has been an increase in cases among intravenous drug users. In 1985, more than 81% of reported AIDS cases were among gay/bisexual males and about 7% were among intravenous drug users. By 1992, only slightly more than half of the new cases were among gay/bisexual males, while 29% were among IV drug users. Increasing numbers of people are also becoming infected with HIV through heterosexual contact.

Adult Cases of AIDS, by Year Reported and Risk Factor

Year	1985	1986	1987	1988	1989	1990	1991	1992
Total Cases	122	137	385	366	526	541	619	700
Gay Bisexual Males	99	110	291	259	326	325	342	355
IV Drug Users	9	9	47	47	104	105	162	204
Gay/Bisexual IV Drug Users	7	11	28	40	37	46	52	46
Heterosexual Contact	5	4	9	7	29	26	43	39
Blood Products	1	2	5	5	11	10	4	11
Risk Not Identified	1	1	5	8	19	29	16	45

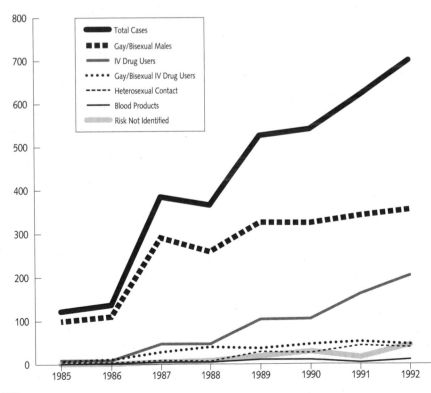

AIDS, Race, and Gender

The percentage of reported AIDS cases among blacks and Hispanics has been consistently increasing. Hispanics accounted for 7% of AIDS cases through the end of 1991 and 11% of cases in 1992. Blacks accounted for almost 56% of cumulative AIDS cases from the beginning of the epidemic through 1991; they accounted for 60% of new cases reported in 1992. AIDS is also increasing among women of all races.

Cumulative through December 31, 1991:

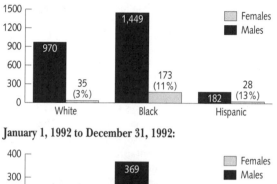

January 1, 1992 to December 31, 1992:

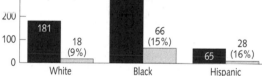

Data for groups other than white, black, and Hispanic are not available.

Cumulative Philadelphia Pediatric AIDS Cases

The increasing numbers of HIV+ women means that increasing numbers of babies are at risk of being born with the AIDS virus. According to the Philadelphia Department of Public Health, a total of 52 pediatric AIDS cases have been reported in Philadelphia. Twenty-four of those children have died.

White	4	7.7%
Black	34	65.4%
Hispanic	14	26.9%

▼▼▼

NATIONAL, STATE, AND LOCAL AIDS CASES AND MORTALITY: Cumulative through December 31, 1992

	Cases	Deaths	% Deaths
United States	242,146	160,372	66.2
Pennsylvania	7,092	4,858	68.5
Philadelphia	3,553	2,346	66.0

CITIZENS' MANUAL

AIDS INFORMATION

The AIDS Library of Philadelphia
32 N. 3rd Street
Philadelphia, PA 19106

Phone: 922-5120

Founded:
1987, by a group of volunteers

Staff:
8 paid employees and about 80 active volunteers

Holdings:
2,200 bound volumes; 90,000 articles and other items in the information files; 200 videotapes; 150 periodical subscriptions

Kinds of information included in the holdings:
AIDS prevention and treatment, statistics, history of the epidemic, coping with loss, legal issues, personal narratives

Library use:
35,000 visitors and phone inquiries in 1991–1992

Library users:
People who are HIV+, high school and college students writing papers, people leading AIDS education programs

Information callers most frequently seek:
Symptoms of AIDS; clinics that give confidential AIDS tests; names of support groups; statistics on AIDS

Information library visitors most frequently seek:
Drugs and other treatments; statistics; the risk of infection through invasive medical procedures; educational programs for targeted groups, such as low-literate adults; how to care safely for someone with AIDS

97 Places to Visit

Having a lot of history is one thing; doing something responsible and intelligent about it is quite another. For sheer quantity and quality of historic sites, Philadelphia and its surrounding counties are unequaled anywhere in the United States. Here is the nation's greatest array of sites, and many of them are interpreted and open to the public.

After years of largely volunteer efforts, sometimes haphazard but often critical to a site's survival, representatives of some 60 of these sites—from a 17th-century cabin to an authentic Japanese villa—met in the spring of 1992 to form a new umbrella organization. The Tri-State Coalition of Historic Places now works for the "preservation and continuing interpretation of historic sites thorough education, advocacy, support, and information services" for those who maintain the sites. In 1993, the still-growing coalition became affiliated with the Museum Council of Philadelphia and the Delaware Valley.

- **American Flag House, 239 Arch Street, Philadelphia, PA 19106. Phone: 627-0591.** Hours: Tuesday–Sunday 10am–5pm. Restored Colonial home of Betsy Ross.
- **American Swedish Historical Museum, 1900 Pattison Avenue, Philadelphia, PA 19145. Phone: 389-1776; fax: 389-7701.** Hours: Tuesday–Friday 10am–4pm, Saturday and Sunday noon–4pm. Founded in 1926 to celebrate Swedish and Swedish-American history.
- **Andalusia Foundation, 1237 State Road, P.O. Box 158, Andalusia, PA 19020. Phone: 639-2077; fax: 639-2078.** Hours: Daily 9am–5pm. Greek Revival country residence (1806–1836) of the Craig and Biddle families.
- **The Athenaeum of Philadelphia, 219 S. 6th Street, Philadelphia, PA 19106. Phone: 925-2688; fax: 925-3755.** Hours: Monday–Friday 9am–5pm. Research library with museum collections in National Historic Landmark building.
- **Barclay Farmstead Museum, 209 Barclay Lane, Cherry Hill, NJ 08034. Phone: (609) 795-6225.** Hours: Tuesday–Friday 9am–4pm. Nineteenth-century Federal brick farmhouse and outbuildings.
- **Barnes Foundation, 300 N. Latches Lane, Merion, PA 19106. Phone: 667-0290; fax: 664-4026.** Hours: Reopens 1995. Post-Impressionist and early modern French paintings, and arboretum.
- **Barns-Brinton House, Route 1, P.O. Box 27, Chadds Ford, PA 19317. Phone: 388-7376; fax: 388-7480.** Hours: May–September Saturday and Sunday noon–6pm. Early 18th-century brick tavern restored as a museum.

- **Bartram's Garden, 54th Street and Lindbergh Avenue, Philadelphia, PA 19143. Phone: 729-5281.** Hours: May–October Wednesday–Sunday noon–4pm; November–April Wednesday –Friday noon–4pm. Oldest surviving botanic garden (1731) in the United States.
- **Belfield Farm at LaSalle University, 1900 W. Olney Avenue, Philadelphia, PA 19141. Phone: 951-1221; fax: 951-1488.** Hours: Daily dawn–dusk. National Historic Landmark home of Charles Willson Peale from 1810 to 1825.
- **Bellaire Manor, 2000 Pattison Avenue, Philadelphia, PA 19145. Phone: 664-8456.** Hours: By appointment. Early (1714) Georgian house in Flemish bond brick, with separate "Bake House" kitchen.
- **Belmont Mansion, Belmont Mansion Drive, West Fairmount Park, Philadelphia, PA 19131. Phone: 878-8844.** Hours: Tuesday–Friday 10am–4pm and by appointment. Early Palladian structure (1746) with later additions and plaster ceiling reliefs.
- **Blue Bell Inn, 7303 Woodland Avenue, Philadelphia, PA 19143. Phone: 365-5914.** Hours: Saturday 1–4pm and by appointment. Colonial tavern and ordinary, scene of a Revolutionary War battle; presently under restoration.
- **Brandywine Battlefield Park, Route 1, Box 202, Chadds Ford, PA 19317. Phone: 459-3342; fax: 459-9586.** Hours: Tuesday–Saturday 9am–5pm, Sunday noon–5pm. Commemorates the Revolutionary War battle of September 10, 1777.

• **Brinton 1704 House, Oakland Road, West Chester, PA 19382. Phone: 793-1582.** Hours: May–October Saturday and Sunday 11am–6pm. National Historic Landmark house on land acquired by William Penn in 1686, with 18th-century furnishings.

• **Pearl S. Buck House, 520 Dublin Road, P.O. Box 181, Perkasie, PA 18944. Phone: 249-0100; fax: 249-9657.** Hours: Tours Tuesday–Saturday 10:30am, Tuesday–Sunday 1:30 and 2:30pm, and by appointment. National Historic Landmark home of the Nobel and Pulitzer Prize–winning author.

• **Burlington County Prison, 49 Rancocas Road, Mt. Holly, NJ 08060. Phone: (609) 265-5958.** Hours: April–November Wednesday 10am–3pm, Saturday 10am–1pm. A county jail used in its original state from 1810 until 1965.

• **Burrough-Dover House, Burrough-Dover Lane and Haddonfield Road, Box 56, Pennsauken, NJ 08110. Phone: (609) 662-9175.** Hours: By appointment. Colonial pioneer farmhouse constructed ca. 1710 of local sandstone.

• **Carpenters' Hall, 320 Chestnut Street, Philadelphia, PA 19106. Phone: 925-0167.** Hours: Tuesday–Sunday 10am–4pm. Site of the First Continental Congress (1774) and birthplace of Pennsylvania.

• **Cedar Grove, Lansdowne Drive, West Fairmount Park, Philadelphia, PA 19131. Phone: 763-8100, ext. 332.** Hours: Tuesday–Sunday 10am–4pm. Quaker farmhouse from the 1740s with 18th- and 19th-century furniture.

• **John Chads House and Barn, Route 100 North, P.O. Box 27, Chadds Ford, PA 19317. Phone: 388-7376; fax: 388-7480.** Hours: May–September Saturday and Sunday noon–6pm; barn Monday, Wednesday, Friday 9am–2pm. Stone house (1725) with a beehive oven; the barn quarters the Chadds Ford Historical Society.

• **Chester Historic Courthouse, 412 Avenue of the States, P.O. Box 541, Chester, PA 19016. Phone: 876-8663.** Hours: 9am–5pm. Oldest public building (1724) in continuous use in the United States.

• **Cliveden (Chew House), 6401 Germantown Avenue, Philadelphia, PA 19144. Phone: 848-1777.** Hours: Tuesday–Saturday 10am–4pm, Sunday 1–4pm. Georgian stone home ca. 1767, site of the 1777 Battle of Germantown.

• **Colonial Pennsylvania Plantation, Ridley Creek State Park, Media, PA 19063. Phone: 566-1725; fax: 566-4424.** Hours: April–November Saturday and Sunday 10am–4pm. Eighteenth-century living history farm museum.

• **John W. Coltrane House, 1511 N. 33rd Street, Philadelphia, PA 19104. Phone: 763-1118; fax: 763-5856.** Hours: Monday–Friday 10am–3pm. National Historic Landmark where Coltrane composed his early works.

• **Concord School House, 6309 Germantown Avenue, Philadelphia, PA 19144. Phone: 843-0943.** Hours: March–October by appointment. One-room 1775 schoolhouse with original artifacts.

• **Darby Library Company, 1001 Main Street, P.O. Box 164, Darby, PA 19023. Phone: 586-7310.** Hours: Monday–Friday 11am–5pm, Saturday 10:30am–noon. Public library founded in 1743, specializing in popular and children's materials.

• **Delaware County Historical Society, 85 N. Malin Road, Room 208, Broomall, PA 19008. Phone: 359-1148.** Hours: Monday, Wednesday, Thursday 9am–3pm, Tuesday 1–8pm. Research library with a display of portraits, documents, and artifacts.

• **Deshler-Morris House, 5442 Germantown Avenue, Philadelphia, PA 19144. Phone: 596-1748.** Hours: April–December Tuesday–Sunday 1–4pm and by appointment. George Washington presided over the new Republic here during the 1793 yellow fever epidemic.

• **Alfred O. Deshong Museum, 1020 Avenue of the States, Chester, PA 19013. Phone: 874-7934.** Hours: Monday–Friday 10am–4pm. Features the Asian art collection of a contemporary Chester artist.

• **Dickinson House, 2130 Sierra Road, Plymouth Meeting, PA 19462. Phone: 828-8111.** Hours: Tuesday and Friday noon–4pm and by appointment. Six-acre Quaker farmstead with 18th- and 19th-century structures.

• **Thomas Eakins House, 1729 Mount Vernon Street, Philadelphia, PA 19130. Phone: 235-8814; fax: 236-4465.** Hours: Tours by appointment. 19th-century, National Historic

Landmark rowhouse owned and occupied by the artist (1844–1916) and family.

- **Elfreth's Alley Association, Inc., 126 Elfreth's Alley, Philadelphia, PA 19106. Phone: 574-0560.** Hours: February 15–December 15 daily 10am–4pm; December 16–February 14 Saturday and Sunday 10am–4pm. America's oldest residential street.
- **Ephrata Cloister, 632 W. Main Street, Ephrata, PA 17522. Phone: (717) 733-6600; fax: (717) 733-4811.** Hours: Monday–Saturday 9am–5pm, Sunday noon–5pm. Radical 18th-century communal society known for crafts and music.
- **Wharton Esherick Museum, P.O. Box 595, Paoli, PA 19301. Phone: 644-5822.** Hours: Tuesday–Friday 10am–4pm, Saturday 10am–5pm, Sunday 1–5pm; call for reservations. Unique studio/home of the craftsman/artist, including sculpture and furniture.
- **Fallsington Village, 4 Yardley Avenue, Fallsington, PA 19054. Phone: 295-6567.** Hours: May–October Monday–Saturday 10am–4pm, Sunday 1–4pm. Seventeenth-century English Quaker settlement, with tours, programs, and museum.
- **Finley House, 113 W. Beechtree Lane, Wayne, PA 19087. Phone: 688-2668.** Hours: Tuesday and Saturday 2–5pm. A basement from 1789 and a 19th-century structure with furnished rooms, library, and artifacts.
- **Fireman's Hall Museum, 147 N. 2nd Street, Philadelphia, PA 19106. Phone: 923-1438.** Hours: Tuesday–Saturday 9am–5pm, closed holidays. Turn-of-the-century firehouse with early American firefighting artifacts.
- **Fonthill Museum, East Court Street, Doylestown, PA 18901. Phone: 348-9461; fax: 230-0823.** Hours: Monday–Saturday 10am–5pm, Sunday noon–5pm. Concrete castle built in 1912 as the home of Henry Mercer.
- **Henry George Birthplace, 413 S. 10th Street, Philadelphia, PA 19147. Phone: 922-4278; fax: 922-7089.** Hours: Monday–Friday by appointment. Restored early American birthplace of the economist and author.
- **Glen Foerd, 5001 Grant Avenue, Philadelphia, PA 19114-3199. Phone: 632-5330.** Hours: Tours Monday–Friday 10am, 2pm, and by appointment. An 1850 country home with 25 furnished rooms, pipe organ, Tiffany skylights, and rathskeller.
- **Graeme Park, 859 County Line Road, Horsham, PA 19044. Phone: 343-0965.** Hours: Wednesday–Saturday 10am–4pm, Sunday noon–5pm. Eighteenth-century homestead of a provincial governor.
- **The Grange Estate, Box 853, Havertown, PA 19083. Phone: 446-4958.** Hours: Tours Saturday and Sunday 1–4pm.
- **Greenfield Hall and Samuel Mickle House, 343 Kings Highway East, Haddonfield, NJ 08033. Phone: (609) 429-7375.** Hours: Monday, Wednesday, Friday 9:30am–12:30pm and by appointment. Mansion dating from 1841 contains Haddonfield Historical Society collections and library.
- **Griffith Morgan House, Griffith Morgan Lane, P.O. Box 522, Pennsauken, NJ 08110. Phone: (609) 665-1948; fax: (609) 665-0082.** Hours: By appointment. Oldest sandstone house (ca. 1693) in Camden County.
- **Harriton House, 500 Harriton Road, P.O. Box 1364, Bryn Mawr, PA 19010. Phone: 525-0201.** Hours: March–December Wednesday–Saturday 10am–4pm and by appointment. The 1704 home of Charles Thomson, Secretary to the Continental Congress.
- **The Highlands, 7001 Sheaff Lane, Fort Washington, PA 19034. Phone: 641-2687.** Hours: Monday–Friday 9am–4pm. Eighteenth-century country estate, outbuildings, and formal gardens.
- **Historic Germantown Preserved, c/o Cliveden, 6401 Germantown Avenue, Philadelphia, PA 19144. Phone: 848-1777; fax: 438-4775.** Hours: Vary according to site. Consortium of historic houses and museums in Germantown area.
- **Historic Houses of Odessa, P.O. Box 507, Odessa, DE 19730. Phone: (302) 378-4069; fax: (302) 378-4050.** Hours: Tuesday–Saturday 10am–4pm, Sunday 1–4pm. Historic house complex depicting 18th-century small town life.
- **Historic RittenhouseTown, 206 Lincoln Drive, Philadelphia, PA 19144. Phone: 438-5711.** Hours: Wednesday–Friday 9am–5pm, Saturday and Sunday noon–4pm. Site of America's first paper mill and the birthplace of David Rittenhouse.

• Historic Yellow Springs, P.O. Box 62, Art School Road, Chester Springs, PA 19460. Phone: 827-7414; fax: 827-1336. Hours: Monday–Friday 9am–4pm. Colonial health spa, Revolutionary War hospital, art school, and National Register village.

• Hope Lodge and Mather Mill, 533 Bethlehem Pike, Fort Washington, PA 19034. Phone: 646-1595; fax: same. Hours: Tuesday–Saturday 9am–5pm, Sunday noon–5pm. Eighteenth-century Colonial house and 20th-century Colonial Revival house compared.

• Hopewell Furnace National Historic Site, 2 Mark Bird Lane, Elverson, PA 19520. Phone: 582-7883; fax: 582-2768. Hours: Daily 9am–5pm except January 1, Thanksgiving, and December 25. Restored charcoal-burning cold-blast iron furnace active 1771–1883.

• Independence National Historical Park, 313 Walnut Street, Philadelphia, PA 19106. Phone: 597-8974; fax: 597-1548. Hours: Daily 9am–5pm. Park sites tell the story of Philadelphia and of the creation of the United States.

• Japanese House and Garden, North Horticultural Drive, West Fairmount Park, Philadelphia, PA 19131. Phone: 878-5097; fax: 878-9577. Hours: May–August Tuesday–Sunday 11am–4pm; September and October, Saturday and Sunday 11am–4pm; and by appointment. Seventeenth-century-style shoin house, with ceremonial teahouse and Momoyama-style garden.

• Thaddeus Kosciuszko National Memorial, Third and Pine Streets, Philadelphia, PA 19106. Phone: 597-8974; fax: 597-1548. Hours: Daily 9am–5pm. Home of the Polish patriot 1797–98.

• Mario Lanza Museum, 416 Queen Street, Philadelphia, PA 19147. Phone: 468-3623. Hours: Monday–Saturday 10am–3:30pm. Memorabilia highlighting the career of the Italian-American actor and tenor.

• Laurel Hill, East Edgely Drive, Fairmount Park, Philadelphia, PA 19131. Phone: 627-1770; fax: 646-4409. Hours: Wednesday–Saturday 10am–5pm. Georgian house, ca. 1767, with furnishings including 19th-century musical instruments.

• Thomas Leiper House, 521 Avondale Avenue, Wallingford, PA 19086. Phone: 566-6365. Hours: Saturday and Sunday 1–4pm and by appointment. The 1785 country estate of the Philadelphia tobacco merchant, patriot, and railroad pioneer.

• Lemon Hill Mansion, Kelly and Sedgley Drives, Philadelphia, PA 19130. Phone: 232-4337. Hours: Wednesday–Sunday 10am–4pm. Adamesque Federal mansion (1799) with 19th-century furnishings.

• Locktender's House, 145 S. Main Street, New Hope, PA 18938. Phone: 862-2021. Hours: Monday–Friday 10am–2pm, Saturday and Sunday noon–4pm. House on Delaware Canal occupied by locktenders 1831–1932.

• Longwood Gardens, Route 1, P.O. Box 501, Kennett Square, PA 19348. Phone: 388-6741; fax: 388-2079. Hours: Daily 9am–6pm, and many evenings. Over a thousand acres of display gardens plus a four-acre indoor conservatory.

• Loudoun Mansion, 4650 Germantown Avenue, Philadelphia, PA 19144. Phone: 685-2067. Hours: Closed for repairs. Federal period home with 18th-century furniture and paintings of original owners.

• A Man Full of Trouble Tavern Museum, 127–129 Spruce Street, Philadelphia, PA 19106. Phone: 922-1759; fax: 744-2470. Hours: Second Sunday each month 1–4pm. Last surviving Colonial inn (1759) in Philadelphia.

• Thomas Massey House, Lawrence Road at Springhouse Road, Broomall, PA 19008. Phone: 353-3644. Hours: Monday–Friday 10am–4pm, Sunday 2–4:30pm. Restored 1696 Quaker house of an indentured servant who became a prosperous landowner.

• Ebenezer Maxwell Mansion, 200 W. Tulpehocken Street, Philadelphia, PA 19144. Phone: 438-1861. Hours: Thursday–Sunday 1–4pm. Victorian house museum and garden depicting 19th-century domestic life.

• Memorial Hall, West Fairmount Park, P.O. Box 21601, Philadelphia, PA 19131. Phone: 685-0113; fax: 878-9577. Hours: Monday–Friday 9am–4pm. Massive display hall built for the 1876 Centennial Exhibition.

• Mercer Museum, 84 S. Pine Street, Doylestown, PA 18901. Phone: 345-0210; fax:

97

230-0823. Hours: Monday–Saturday 10am–5pm, Sunday noon–5pm. Artifacts, tools, and displays of early American life in a National Historic Landmark 1913–16 concrete structure.
• **Moravian Pottery and Tile Works, 130 Swamp Road, Doylestown, PA 18901. Phone: 345-6722; fax: 348-6379.** Hours: Daily 10am–4:45pm. Working history museum producing hand-crafted decorative tiles.
• **Morris Arboretum of the University of Pennsylvania, 100 Northwestern Avenue, Philadelphia, PA 19118. Phone: 247-5777; fax: 248-4439.** Hours: Monday–Friday 10am–4pm, Saturday and Sunday 10am–5pm. Arboretum featuring Victorian landscape, sculpture, and architecture.
• **Mount Pleasant, Mount Pleasant Drive, East Fairmount Park, Philadelphia, PA 19131. Phone: 763-8100, ext. 333.** Hours: Tuesday–Saturday 10am–4pm. Georgian mansion (1761) with ornamental woodwork and Chippendale-style furniture.
• **Muhlenberg House, 201 Main Street, Box 828, Trappe, PA 19426. Phone: 489-8883.** Hours: Tuesday 1:30–3pm and June–August Sunday 1:30–4pm. A museum of 18th- and 19th-century Trappe/Collegeville artifacts in a 1755 house.
• **Ormiston Mansion, Reservoir Drive, East Fairmount Park, Philadelphia, PA 19131. Phone: 763-2222.** Hours: June–August Saturday and Sunday 11am–4pm and events. Georgian house (1798) with a Scottish bake oven and an open fireplace.
• **Pennsbury Manor, 400 Pennsbury Memorial Road, Morrisville, PA 19067. Phone: 946-0400; fax: 295-2936.** Hours: Tuesday–Saturday 9am–5pm, Sunday noon–5pm. William Penn's 17th-century plantation.
• **Pennypacker Mills, 5 Haldeman Road, Schwenksville, PA 19473. Phone: 287-9349.** Hours: Tuesday–Saturday 10am–4pm, Sunday 1–4pm. Colonial Revival summer estate (1901) of Governor Samuel W. Pennypacker.
• **Philadelphia Art Alliance, 251 S. 18th Street, Philadelphia, PA 19103. Phone: 545-4302; fax: 545-0767.** Hours: Monday–Friday 11am–5:30pm, Saturday noon–5pm, Sunday noon–4pm. Nation's oldest multidisciplinary arts center in a Rittenhouse Square mansion.

• **Edgar Allan Poe National Historic Site, 532 N. 7th Street, Philadelphia, PA 19123. Phone: 597-8780; fax: 597-1548.** Hours: Daily 9am–5pm. Home of the author in 1843–44.
• **Pomona Hall, Park Boulevard and Euclid Avenue, Camden, NJ 08103. Phone: (609) 964-3333.** Hours: Monday–Thursday 12:30–4:30pm, Saturday 1–4pm, Sunday 2–4pm. Eighteenth-century house, genealogical library, and museum operated by the Camden County Historical Society.
• **Pottsgrove Manor, West King Street, Pottstown, PA 19464. Phone: 326-4014.** Hours: Tuesday–Saturday 10am–4pm, Sunday 1–4pm. Early Georgian home (1752) of John Potts, ironmaster and founder of Pottstown.
• **Primitive Hall, Greenlawn-Chatham Road, West Grove, PA 19320. Phone: 384-9282.** Hours: By appointment. Brick manor house (1738) built by Joseph Pennock.
• **Caleb Pusey House, 15 Race Street, P.O. Box 1138, Upland, PA 19015. Phone: 874-5665.** Hours: May–October Saturday and Sunday 1–4pm, and by appointment. Original 1683 two-room English dwelling, authentically furnished.
• **Read House, 42 The Strand, New Castle, DE 19720. Phone: (302) 322-8411.** Hours: Tuesday–Saturday 10am–4pm, Sunday noon–4pm, and by appointment. Restored 1801 mansion of George Read with 1840s formal gardens.
• **Rockwood Museum, 610 Shipley Road, Wilmington, DE 19809. Phone: (302) 761-4340; fax: (302) 764-4570.** Hours: Tuesday–Saturday 11am–4pm. Nineteenth-century country estate with manor house, conservatory, and landscape gardens.
• **Schwenkfelder Library, 1 Seminary Street, Pennsburg, PA 18073. Phone: 679-3103.** Hours: Monday–Friday 9am–4pm. Theological and historical library and museum.
• **Stenton, 4601 N. 18th Street, Philadelphia, PA 19140. Phone: 329-7312.** Hours: Tuesday–Saturday 1–3pm. Georgian plantation home (1730) of James Logan, secretary to William Penn.
• **Erwin Stover House, Tinicum Park, River Road, Erwinna, PA 18901. Phone: 348-6098; fax: 348-6379.** Hours: June–September

Friday–Sunday 1–4pm. Restored and furnished Federal estate home (1820) with later additions.

- **Stover-Myers Mill, Dark Hollow Road, Pipersville, PA 18901. Phone: 348-6098; fax: 348-6379.** Hours: June–August Saturday and Sunday 1–4pm. Restored 19th-century grist and sawmill complex with original equipment.
- **Strawberry Mansion, 33rd and Dauphin Streets, Philadelphia, PA 19131. Phone: 228-8364.** Hours: Tuesday–Saturday 10am–4pm. Federal house (ca. 1789) with Georgian and Empire additions plus exhibits of dolls and artifacts.
- **Sweetbriar Mansion, West Fairmount Park, Philadelphia, PA 19131. Phone: 222-1333.** Hours: By appointment. Adamesque 1797 Federal residence.
- **Terracina, 76 S. 1st Avenue, Coatesville, PA 19320. Phone: 384-9282.** Hours: By appointment. Country Gothic home built in 1850 by noted ironmaster Rebecca Lukens.
- **Three Arches Historic Site, 335 Trenton Road, Fairless Hills, PA 19030. Phone: 547-7823.** Hours: Thursday 11am–2pm, Sunday 1–3pm, and by appointment. The 1712 home of John Sotcher, William Penn's steward.
- **Tyler Arboretum, 515 Painter Road, Media, PA 19063. Phone: 566-5431; fax: 891-1490.** Hours: Grounds open daily 8am–dusk. A 650-acre historic arboretum with over a thousand plant varieties.
- **Wagner Free Institute of Science, 17th Street and Montgomery Avenue, Philadelphia, PA 19121. Phone: 763-6529.** Hours: Tuesday–Friday 9am–4pm and weekend programs. National Historic Landmark Victorian natural history museum.
- **Peter Wentz Farmstead, Shearer Road, P.O. Box 240, Worcester, PA 19492. Phone: 584-5104; fax: 584-5112.** Hours: Tuesday–Saturday 10am–4pm, Sunday 1–4pm. An 18th-century farmstead museum; Washington's headquarters in 1777.
- **Walt Whitman House, 328 Mickle Boulevard, Camden, NJ 08103. Phone: (609) 964-5383.** Hours: Wednesday–Sunday 9am–noon and 1–5pm. Greek Revival home of the poet containing furnishings and memorabilia.
- **Whitman-Stafford Farmhouse, 315 E. Maple Street, Laurel Springs, NJ 08021. Phone: (609) 784-1105.** Hours: By appointment. Restored 18th-century farmhouse on two acres with late Victorian furnishings.
- **Woodford Mansion, 33rd and Dauphin Streets, East Fairmount Park, Philadelphia, PA 19131. Phone: 229-6115.** Hours: Tuesday–Saturday 10am–4pm. Georgian house (1756) containing fine 18th-century furnishings.
- **Wyck House, 6026 Germantown Avenue, Philadelphia, PA 19144. Phone: 848-1690.** Hours: April–December Tuesday, Thursday, Saturday 1–4pm, and by appointment. Colonial gardens and Quaker house altered in 1824 by William Strickland. ■

❖

Pound for pound, the Centennial Exposition exhibited machinery to art at a ratio of 9.3 to 1, with 19,542,989 tons of machinery and 2,100,900 tons of art.

Rowhouse Heaven

Philadelphia's basic building blocks are city squares (or blocks) and block-long rows of houses (or rowhouses). The construction of block after block of rowhouses fueled the expanded city in the 19th century and gave Philadelphia a reputation as the "city of homes." No other city was as distinctive, statistically and visibly, for the hundreds of blocks of new two- and three-story houses added each year at the periphery of the city's built-up portion. A lack of geographical constraints to the north, south, and ultimately to the west of the center, survival of the English ground-rent system, the prevalence of building associations, and the relatively skilled nature of Philadelphia's working classes all contributed to the situation where a significant proportion of families could afford their own rowhouse. Philadelphia long had fewer tenements and fewer persons per household than any other large city. ∎

❖

Laundry service, without pressing, began in Philadelphia in 1892.

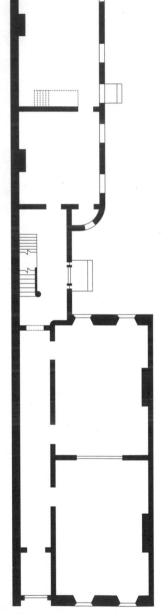

706 Spruce Street , 1830s–1970s

Housing

North from Broad Street and Oregon Avenue.

▼▼▼

GREAT CHANGES

"There have been great changes in the face of the country, in its levels and contour, and in the direction and beds of its watercourses since the days of the Swedes and the early Quakers. Some streams have disappeared, some have changed their direction, nearly all have been reduced in volume and depth by natural silt, the annual washing down of hills, by the demands of industry for water-power, the construction of mill-dams and mill-races and bridges, the emptying of manufacturing refuse from factories, saw-pits, and tan-yards, and by the grading and sewerage necessary in the building of a great city. In this process, old landmarks and ancient contours are not respected, the picturesque yields to utility, and the face of nature is transformed to meet the exigencies of uniform grades, levels, and drainage. The Board of Health, the Police Department, the City Commissioners, and the Department of Highways have no bowels of compassion for the antiquarian and the poet. They are slaves of order, hygiene, of transportation, of progress."

—J. Thomas Sharf and Thompson Westcott, *History of Philadelphia, 1609–1884* (L. H. Everts, 1884).

Carstairs Row: 700 block of Sansom Street.

AFRICAN AMERICAN STATE HISTORICAL MARKERS: PEOPLE

Julian Francis Abele (1881–1950), designer of the Philadelphia Museum of Art, 26th Street and the Benjamin Franklin Parkway; Robert Mara Adger (1837–1910), bibliophile and political activist, 823 South Street; Sadie T. M. Alexander (1898–1989), lawyer and civil rights activist, 700 Westview Street; Pearl Bailey (1918–1990), singer and actress, 1946 N. 23rd Street; Robert Bogle (1774–1848), caterer, 112 S. 8th Street; David Bustill Bowser (1820–1900), artist, 841 N. 4th Street; Cyrus Bustill (1732–1806), baker and Revolutionary War hero, 210 Arch Street; Octavius V. Catto (1839–1871), educator and political organizer, 812 South Street; John W. Coltrane (1926–1967), musician and composer, 1511 N. 33rd Street; Father Divine (1882–1965), religious leader, northeast corner of Broad Street and Ridge Avenue; Crystal Bird Fauset (1894–1965), the first African American woman elected to the Pennsylvania Legislature, 5403 Vine Street; Jesse Redmon Fauset (1886–1961), novelist, poet, and educator, 1853 N. 17th Street; James Forten, Sr. (1776–1842), sailmaker and abolitionist, 336 Lombard Street; Meta V. Warrick Fuller (1877–1968), sculptor, 254 S. 12th Street; Elizabeth Taylor Greenfield (1809–1876), concert singer, 1013 Rodman Street; Frances Ellen Watkins Harper (1825–1911), Underground Railroad conductor, 1006 Bainbridge Street; Billie Holiday (1915–1959), singer, 1409 Lombard Street; Francis "Frank" Johnson (1792–1844), musician and composer, 536 Pine Street; Alain Leroy Locke (1885–1954), philosopher and educator, 2221 S. 5th Street; Robert Purvis (1810–1898), abolitionist, 1601 Mount Vernon Street; Paul Leroy Robeson (1898–1976), actor, singer, and activist, 4951 Walnut Street; Stephen Smith (1797–1873), businessman and philanthropist, 1050 Belmont Avenue; William Still (1821–1902), abolitionist, businessman, and writer, 244 S. 12th Street; Henry Ossawa Tanner (1859–1937), painter, 2908 W. Diamond Street; Laura Wheeler Waring (1887–1948), artist and educator, 756 N. 43rd Street; Jacob C. White, Jr. (1837–1900), educator, 1032 Lombard Street.

Philadelphia's 53 National Historic Landmarks

- **Academy of Music, Broad and Locust Streets. Built 1857.** Don't be fooled by the red brick exterior or disheartened by the brown-painted brownstone. This longtime home of the Philadelphia Orchestra opens up into a lavish opera house, the nation's oldest and acoustically the best. Napoleon Le Brun and Gustave Runge were its architects.

- **American Philosophical Society Hall, 104 S. 5th Street. Built 1789.** Home of America's oldest learned society, founded in 1743. Its founder was Benjamin Franklin, of course.

- **Athenaeum of Philadelphia, 219 S. 6th Street. Built 1845–47.** One of America's first Italianate urban clubhouses in the style of early Victorian London. John Notman introduced brownstone here.

- **John Bartram House, 54th Street and Eastwick Avenue. Built 1731.** Residence and riverbank gardens of one of America's first native botanists, who couldn't have imagined that the flats of the lower Schuylkill would later sprout oil tank farms. One of the city's hidden gems.

- **Boat House Row, 1–15 Kelly Drive. Built 1860–ca. 1920.** Funny thing how Thomas Eakins stole the Schuylkill from the Fairmount Waterworks (see below). Through much of the 19th century, it was the view of the Waterworks that Philadelphians romanticized. Then Eakins painted the calm light only scullers know. Now say "Schuylkill" and we see scullers. Their boathouses are worth seeing, too.

- **Carpenters' Hall, 320 Chestnut Street. Built 1770–71.** Even if the First Continental Congress hadn't met here in 1774, even if it were only a guild hall for the Carpenters' Company of Philadelphia, this building would still be an unparalleled specimen of design and construction.

- **Christ Church, 22–26 N. 2nd Street. Built 1727–54.** The congregation is one year shy of 300 years and in the original center of town. The church tower used to singlehandedly constitute Philadelphia's skyline.

- **Church of St. James The Less, Hunting Park Avenue and Clearfield Street. Built 1846–50.** The Church of England exported more than religion; sometimes it exported churches. Here, an English architect trusted a Philadelphia architect to follow his designs. No accident, then, that this looks like an English parish church of the 13th century. Americans loved the look—and used it everywhere, in every type of building.

Landmarks

- **Cliveden (Chew House), 6401 Germantown Avenue. Built 1763.** Carpenter Jacob Knorr and mason John Hesser blended the look of an English house (derived from a book) and a Germantown house for lawyer Benjamin Chew's country seat. It proved popular with the family, which stayed about two centuries. Now the pediments, cornices, and spacious front hall of this house museum make a fine stage for the annual redo of the Revolutionary War Battle of Germantown.

- **Colonial Germantown Historic District, Germantown Avenue between Windrim Avenue and Upsal Street. Built 18th–19th centuries.** Williamsburg is all reconstruction. Germantown Avenue's surviving buildings from the 18th century are the real thing. Here's the one street in Philadelphia that retains, however modestly, its original character and patina. It all started in 1683, when William Penn invited Germans fleeing religious persecution to settle in Pennsylvania.

- **Edward Drinker Cope House, 2102 Pine Street. Built ca. 1880.** America's premiere 19th-century bone and rock man (geologist and paleontologist) lived here.

- **Thomas Eakins House, 1729 Mount Vernon Street. Built ca. 1854.** America's greatest 19th-century painter lived here all but the first two years of his life.

- **Eastern State Penitentiary, 21st Street and Fairmount Avenue. Built 1823–29.** Before Quaker reformers lost what remained of their political influence in the early 19th century, they convinced the Commonwealth to upgrade the dungeon system of punishment. Architect John Haviland's star-shaped ground plan was a living laboratory for the new Pennsylvania System, an experiment in humane solitary confinement. This was America's largest, most famous, and most influential building.

- **Elfreth's Alley Historic District, 2nd Street between Arch and Race Streets. Built 17th–18th centuries.** Even though William Penn's original plan for the city does not include streets such as this, cut through his original squares by land speculators, Elfreth's Alley claims to be the oldest unchanged and continuously inhabited street in America.

- **Fairmount Water Works, east bank of the Schuylkill River above Spring Garden Street Bridge. Built 1812–22.** A Classical Revival front for buildings that house machinery was part of the city's first waterworks at Center Square. But that was obsolete after about a decade. Fairmount lasted nearly a century and constantly pioneered municipal water technology, from paddle wheels to turbine engines. All of Fairmount Park grew from the seed of its planted grounds.

AFRICAN AMERICAN STATE HISTORICAL MARKERS: PLACES

African Zoar Methodist Episcopal Church, founded in 1794, 4th and Brown Streets; A.M.E. Book Concern, publishing house founded in 1836, 631 Pine Street; Christian Street YMCA, the nation's first for African Americans, 1724 Christian Street; Frederick Douglass Memorial Hospital, the first hospital staffed wholly by African Americans, 1522 Lombard Street; The Dunbar Theatre, built by E. C. Brown and Andrew Stevens, 500 S. Broad Street; First African Baptist Church, first at 10th and Vine Streets, now at 16th and Christian Streets; First African Baptist Church Cemetery, 8th and Vine Streets; First African Presbyterian Church, established by John Gloucester, 42nd Street and Girard Avenue; First Protest Against Slavery, held in 1688 by German Quakers, 5109 Germantown Avenue; Fraunces Tavern, established by George Washington's personal cook, 310 S. 2nd Street; Freedom Theatre, founded by John Allen in 1966, 1346 N. Broad Street; London Coffee House, where Africans were once purchased, Front and Market Streets; Mercy Hospital, founded by Dr. Henry M. Minton, 17th and Fitzwater Streets; Mother Bethel A.M.E. Church, founded in 1787 by Richard Allen, 6th and Lombard Streets; Site of Pennsylvania Hall, built by abolitionists and destroyed by a mob in 1838, 6th and Arch Streets; The Philadelphia Tribune, founded by Christopher Perry in 1884, 520-26 S. 16th Street; Prince Hall Grand Lodge, established in 1797, 4301 N. Broad Street; St. Peter Claver's Roman Catholic Church, site of black literary and dramatic meetings, 1200 Lombard Street; Site of St. Thomas' African Episcopal Church, organized in 1792, 5th Street south of St. James Place; Standard Theatre, where Bessie Smith and Duke Ellington performed, 1126 South Street; Union Local 274, American Federation of Musicians, a segregated union, 912 S. Broad Street.

Source: Philadelphia's Guide: African-American State Historical Markers (The Charles L. Blockson Afro-American Collection/ The William Penn Foundation, 1992).

UNUSUAL MAIN LINE LANDMARKS

The "chicken thief" monument. Chances are you've never noticed this little-known monument near Stop #6 on the driving tour of Valley Forge National Park. Erected around the turn of the century by the Daughters of the American Revolution, it honors an unknown soldier shot by a farmer while poaching.

Ryerss Farm for Aged Equines. This 364-acre farm in northern Chester County (in Coventryville, on Route 23, 2.5 miles west of Route 100) is one of horse country's oldest and oddest institutions. Established in 1888 with the bequest of Anne Waln Ryerss, the retirement home for horses hosts up to 75 equines at a time, most of them beloved family pets.

Purple martin colony, Glen Mills Schools, Concordville. This school for delinquent youths is also home to one of the state's largest breeding colonies of purple martins. It took 26 years to attract the first pair of birds. Now there are 32 martin houses and as many as 600 purple martins in residence every year from April to August.

Christmas light display, 511 Fairfax Street, Drexel Hill. For locals, it's as much a tradition as season's greetings cards to visit the light display that has been mounted by the Pflaumer family for a quarter of a century. There are lights by the tens of thousands. In addition, Santa and his reindeer move along a "monorail" fashioned from an automated dry cleaner's rack.

Valley Forge Dam-Knox Bridge. Of all the quaint covered bridges in Pennsylvania, this one is probably the most photographed and most painted because of its proximity to Valley Forge Park. The bridge, which dates to 1865, has been strengthened with steel girders to carry automobile traffic.

Minquas Trail, Rose Valley. A bronze statue of a beaver marks the site of the old Indian trail leading westward to the Susquehanna River. The statue is across the street from the Hedgerow Theater.

Landmarks

- **First Bank of the United States, 120 S. 3rd Street. Built 1795–97.** By acting on Alexander Hamilton's proposal and chartering the bank, Congress and President Washington took the necessary first steps toward implementing sound national fiscal policy. Now both the building and the debate over policy are nearly 200 years old.

- **Fort Mifflin, Fort Mifflin Road. Built 1772–75, 1798.** At the beginning of the British occupation of Philadelphia during the Revolutionary War, American forces still held Fort Mifflin and controlled access to the city from the Delaware. The Americans yielded only after a brutal three-day siege. In 1798, the fort was rebuilt according to designs by Pierre L'Enfant, planner of Washington, D.C.

- **Founder's Hall, Girard College, Corinthian and Girard Avenues. Built 1833–47.** In 1831, rags-to-riches shipping magnate Stephen Girard died and bequeathed millions for an educational institution for white, fatherless boys. Girard's fortune inspired a dramatic departure from his will. Under the forceful guidance of Nicholas Biddle, a main building that Girard envisioned as modest grew into a monumental Greek Revival temple by architect Thomas U. Walter.

- **Furness Library, School of Fine Arts, University of Pennsylvania, 34th Street below Walnut. Built 1888.** Architect Frank Furness liked patterns in red so much he had shirts made of red-checked cloth. This is Furness's most distinctive major work, recently restored to its original red-brick Gothic Revival brilliance.

- **Germantown (Manheim) Cricket Club, 5140 Morris Street. Built 1890–1907.** Philadelphia's passion for the anglophilic is expressed here in both the game and the architecture. This is the second oldest American cricket club, founded in 1855. Ironically, interest in cricket faded in the 1920s with the rise of one of this club's members: international tennis star William T. (Big Bill) Tilden.

- **Frances Ellen Watkins Harper House, 1006 Bainbridge Street. Built 1870–1911.** Home of Harper (1825–1911), the African American writer, poet, lecturer, women's suffrage and temperance reformer, and Underground Railroad conductor.

- **Hill-Physick-Keith House, 321 S. 4th Street. Built 1786.** President Jackson came to Philadelphia in 1832 to be treated by Philip Syng Physick, the "father of American surgery" who lived here from 1815 to 1837. The house was built not with doctor's fees but rather with the profits derived from the trade of wine importer Col. Henry Hill.

- **Institute of the Pennsylvania Hospital, 111 N. 49th Street. Built 1859.** Thomas Kirkbride believed that insanity should

Landmarks

be treated as an illness and that a hospital for such patients should be aimed at recuperation rather than warehousing. His then-rural hospital, conceived with architect Samuel Sloan, influenced similar institutions throughout America.

• **Insurance Company of North America Building, 1600 Arch Street. Built 1925.** INA has since become CIGNA and moved its headquarters to one of the city's new skyscrapers. Now, as you pay your city taxes here, you may contemplate the many forms of insurance pioneering that once coursed through this building's offices and corridors.

• **James Logan Home (Stenton), 18th and Courtland Streets. Built 1730.** Irish-born Logan was William Penn's secretary, a botanist, and a curmudgeonly classical scholar whose taste in books led Benjamin Franklin and friends to seek his advice as "a Gentleman of Universal learning, and the best Judge of Books in these Parts." His country seat is a rare and refined specimen.

• **Memorial Hall, West Fairmount Park. Built 1876.** Of the large buildings put up for the huge international celebration of the Centennial Exposition, only this—home of the art exhibition—and Horticultural Hall were intended to survive. Now only Memorial Hall exists.

• **Mother Bethel A.M.E. Church, 419 Richard Allen Avenue (6th Street). Built 1889.** Discrimination in seating led a number of African Americans to withdraw from St. George's Methodist Church in 1787 and found the Free African Society. When this group split, former slave Richard Allen led the 1793 formation of the African Methodist Church, later known as "Mother Bethel," America's first church of the African Methodist Episcopal (A.M.E.) Church.

• **Mount Pleasant, East Fairmount Park. Built 1761.** One of the finest examples of late Georgian domestic architecture in the Middle Colonies and certainly the grandest house in Fairmount Park. Once owned (though never occupied) by Benedict Arnold, today it is a historic house museum.

• **New Market, South 2nd Street between Pine and Lombard Streets. Built 1745–1804.** Now and then, a street in Philadelphia is unexpectedly wider than the rest. They were once occupied by long, narrow sheds known as market shambles. Here, the city's unique survivor reminds us of Market Street between Front and 8th, before 1859.

• **Charles Willson Peale House (Belfield), 2100 Clarkson Avenue. Built ca. 1750.** Painter (he painted Washington), archeologist (he excavated a mastodon), and museum entrepreneur (he operated one in Independence Hall), Peale was patriarch of a large family of artists. He lived here from 1810 to 1825.

UNUSUAL MAIN LINE LANDMARKS

continued...

General "Mad" Anthony Wayne's ghost, St. David's Church Cemetery, Radnor. The Revolutionary War hero is buried here, but his ghost reportedly gallops through the cemetery on horseback each year on New Year's Eve.

....

Historic Yellow Springs, Art School Road, Chester Springs. The Revolutionary War military hospital turned fashionable mineral-water spa now hosts art shows and craft festivals. You can see the hospital ruins and the springhouse where singer Jenny Lind once "took the waters."

....

The horse at Bryn Mawr Hardware Store, 903 Lancaster Pike, Bryn Mawr. It just wouldn't be the Bryn Mawr Hardware Store without that big white horse in front. The horse belonged to a saddle shop that stood on the site in the 1890s. And after 100 years it still doesn't have a name.

....

Giant sequoia. Bet you didn't think there were any sequoias in Pennsylvania. But Tyler Arboretum in Lima boasts the oldest giant sequoia east of the Mississippi, a 69-foot specimen that's been certified a champion by the Pennsylvania Forestry Association.

....

Landmarks

Now a century old, the first Baedeker guide to America, *The United States with an Excursion into Mexico* (Karl Baedeker, 1893), recommended to visitors the following things to see and places to visit in Philadelphia: Abraham Lincoln (statue); Academy of Music; Academy of Natural Sciences; Academy of the Fine Arts; American Philosophical Society; Anatomical Museum; Apprentices' Library; Arch Street Episcopal Church; Armory of the State Fencibles; Art Club; Assembly Hall of the German Society of Pennsylvania; Baldwin's Locomotive Works; Baltimore and Ohio Railway Station; Base Ball Grounds; Belmont Mansion; Beneficial Saving Fund Society; Beth-Eden Baptist Church; Blockley Almshouses; Bourse; Boys' Central High School; Broad Street Station; Builders' Exchange; Carpenters' Hall; Cathedral of Ss. Peter & Paul; Chamounix; Chestnut Hill; Chew House; Christ Church; Christ Church Burial Ground; Church of the Epiphany; Church of the Gesu; Church of the Holy Communion; Circus; City Hall Square; College of Physicians; Colonnade Hotel; Commercial Exchange; Cooper's Shop; Cramp's Ship-building Yards; Custom House; Deaf and Dumb Asylum; Drexel Building; Drexel Institute; Eastern Penitentiary; Fairmount Park; Fidelity Safe Deposit Co.; First Baptist Church; First Regiment Armory; First Unitarian Church; Franklin Institute; George's Hill; German Hospital; Germantown; Girard College; Girard Avenue Bridge; Girard Bank; Girard College; Girard Life Insurance Building; Grace Baptist Temple; Historical Society of Pennsylvania; Horticultural Hall; Independence Hall; Johnson House; Lafayette, Bellevue, and Stratford Hotels; Laurel Hill Cemetery; League Island; Lemon Hill; Manhattan Insurance Co.; Mary J. Drexel Home; Masonic Temple; Memorial Hall; Mercantile Library; Merchants' Exchange; Monument Cemetery; New York Mutual Life Insurance Co.; Penn Mutual Life Building; Penn National Bank; Pennsylvania Co. for Life Insurance and Annuities; Pennsylvania Hospital; Pennsylvania Insane Asylum;

- **The Pennsylvania Academy of the Fine Arts, southwest corner of Broad and Cherry Streets. Built 1871–76.** The directors of the Academy, a combination museum and art school founded in 1805, were located on Chestnut Street near 10th, close to architect Frank Furness's banks. He outdid himself in this building, and it's just as well—none of the banks survive.

- **Pennsylvania Hospital, 8th and Spruce Streets. Built 1756.** No United States hospital is older. Another institution credited to the support of Benjamin Franklin.

- **Philadelphia City Hall, Penn Square, Broad and Market Streets. Built 1871–1901.** America's largest and most elaborate city hall, planned in an earlier form for Independence Square. Architect John McArthur, Jr., employed the Second Empire style, which faded from popularity long before the building was complete. The sculpture is by Alexander Milne Calder and his many assistants.

- **Philadelphia Contributionship, 212 S. 4th Street. Built 1835.** In 1752, Benjamin Franklin helped organize the Philadelphia Contributionship for the Insurance of Houses from Loss by Fire, the first fire insurance company in the United States. Architect Thomas U. Walter designed a purposefully modest structure of brick walls, oak joists, and pine floors, costing a thrifty $20,946.

- **Philadelphia Masonic Temple, 1 N. Broad Street. Built 1873.** The exterior of this Norman Romanesque–style building is gray granite. Its interior rooms, some of the most ornate and eclectic of the late Victorian era, are well worth a look.

- **Philadelphia Savings Fund Society, 12 S. 19th Street. Built 1932.** One of the most important American skyscrapers, designed by George Howe and William Lescaze.

- **Edgar Allan Poe House, 530–532 N. 7th Street. Built ca. 1835.** Poe wrote "The Raven" and other of his best-known pieces in this brick rowhouse, his home for two years in the mid-1840s.

- **Reading Terminal and Train Shed, 1115–1141 Market Street. Built 1891–1893.** The fate of the world's largest single-span arched-roof train shed (by Wilson Brothers & Co.) is sealed now that the Pennsylvania Convention Center's ballroom will share the shed with an atrium of sorts. The headhouse, by New York architect Francis H. Kimball, is still empty—and looking emptier.

- **Reynolds-Morris House, 225 S. 8th Street. Built 1786–87.** One of the finest surviving examples of a Georgian Philadelphia row townhouse.

Landmarks

- **RittenhouseTown Historic District, 206–210 Lincoln Drive.** Built 1690–1850. The site of America's first paper mill and birthplace of David Rittenhouse. Its location along the major traffic artery to and from Center City makes this one of the city's most seen and least visited places.

- **St. Mark's Episcopal Church, 1607–1627 Locust Street.** Built 1847–52. Another fine example of the archeological phase of America's Gothic Revival, reflecting the influence of the Anglican reform.

- **Second Bank of the United States, 420 Chestnut Street.** Built 1824–36. The somber, fluted Doric columns and broad entablature here still proclaim this victim's innocence in the 1830s "Bank War" between President Andrew Jackson and Congress. What William Strickland's design talent could do!

- **Thomas Sully Residence, 530 Spruce Street.** Built 1796. During his long life (Sully was born in the Revolutionary War era and died just before the Centennial), he painted portraits that made folks look younger, thinner, and brighter. The commissions never stopped coming.

- **Henry Ossawa Tanner Homesite, 2908 W. Diamond Street.** Built 1871. Boyhood home of the African American painter, whose work earned recognition in Europe and the United States.

- **U.S. Naval Asylum, Grays Ferry Avenue at 24th Street.** Built 1827–44. Architect William Strickland joined the Greek Revival style with a utilitarian design for housing disabled and destitute naval officers.

- **U.S.S. _Becuna_ (SS-319) (submarine), Penn's Landing, Delaware Avenue and Spruce Street.** Built 1944. Who says landmarks need to be on land? This decorated one (the _Becuna_ sunk 3,888 tons of Japanese shipping during World War II) could operate 400 feet below land level.

- **U.S.S. _Olympia_ (cruiser), Penn's Landing, Delaware Avenue and Spruce Street.** Built 1888. Not one older steel-hulled American warship is afloat. The _Olympia_ served as Admiral George Dewey's flagship in the Battle of Manila Bay in 1898.

- **Wagner Free Institute of Science, 17th Street and Montgomery Avenue.** Built 1860. Few, if any, museums have escaped modernization. Dropped ceilings, glass partitions, Lucite labels—all are taken for granted in the nineties cultural experience. Here is a Victorian survivor, a museum of museology.

- **Walnut Street Theatre, 9th and Walnut Streets.** Built 1809, 1828. Architect John Haviland transformed this site, first

BAEDEKER'S PICKS

continued...

Pennsylvania Museum of Industrial Art; Pennsylvania School of Industrial Art; Penn Treaty Monument; Philadelphia Hospital; Philadelphia Library; Pipe Bridge; Post Office; Public Ledger Building; Reading Railway; Ridgway Library; Rittenhouse Square; Schuylkill Arsenal; Schuylkill Falls; Second Reformed Episcopal Church; Singerly Building; Solitude; Spreckels Sugar Refinery; Spring Garden Institute; Statue of William Penn; Statue of Humboldt; St. George's House; Swedenborgian Church; Swedes' Church; Synagogue Rodef Shalom; Terminal Station of the Reading Railroad; Union League Club; United States Mint; United States Navy Yard; University of Pennsylvania; Wanamaker's Store; Washington Square; Water Works; William Penn Charter School; Wissahickon Drive; Wissahickon Heights; Wissahickon Inn; Women's Medical College and Hospital; Young Men's Christian Association; Zoological Garden.

❖

THE POWER OF THE PLAQUE

"The episode of the kite, so firm and fixed in legend, turns out to be dim and mystifying in fact," wrote Carl Van Doren, Benjamin Franklin's biographer. That Franklin didn't make much of his encounter with lightning could be further evidence of his public relations savvy. He wrote nothing under his own name on the episode. Joseph Priestley's account, 15 years after the 1752 event, is the closest we get. "He took the opportunity of the first approaching thunderstorm to take a walk in the fields," wrote Priestley. Franklin confirmed that this was true, but didn't say where he discovered "the Sameness of Electric Matter with that of Lightning." Nonetheless, a small plaque at St. Stephen's Methodist Episcopal Church, 19 S. 10th Street, reads: "This church is built on the site where Benj. Franklin flew his famous kite." And who are we to argue?

On the 3700 block of Chestnut Street.

Set in this city's sidewalks are small landmarkers, bronze business cards that bear the names and addresses of concrete paving contractors. These plaques of pride meant a job well done and an advertisement that would last as long as the pavement—even longer.

But for many neighborhood kids, they meant sore arms. "Punchblocks," as they were known, marked forbidden squares. If you stepped on one, witnesses stiffly punched your arms and shoulders, shouting, "punch block! punch block!" until you could work your way back to the square and spit on it, thereby restoring your immunity. Boys seemed to favor the fading practice.

Today, these markers are slowly vanishing as new pavements are installed. If contractors leave anything behind, they'll emboss their names into the semi-set concrete—decidedly modest, and safe to tread.

❖

Circus elephants Virginius and Bozzarius drowned in 1831 while crossing the Delaware River.

James Dundas raised giant water lilies (*Victoria regia*) in his garden greenhouse at Broad and Walnut Streets in 1850.

In 1856, Joshua Pusey ascended with a hot-air balloon from the garden of a restaurant near 10th and Chestnut Streets. His basket: a rattan eagle with flappable wings.

used for circuses, into one for legitimate theater. It is one of the oldest surviving theaters in the United States.

- **John Wanamaker Store, Juniper and Market Streets. Built 1902–10.** Original home store of one of the major merchandising enterprises in retailing history, designed in the Second Renaissance Revival style by Daniel Burnham & Co. of Chicago.

- **Woodford, southwest corner of Ford Road and Greenland Drive, Fairmount Park. Built ca. 1756, ca. 1772.** The first of the great, opulent, late Georgian mansions erected in the Philadelphia area.

- **The Woodlands, 40th Street and Woodland Avenue. Built ca. 1770, 1788.** On the rise above the 19th-century gravemarkers of Woodlands Cemetery stands William Hamilton's country retreat recast into the refined style of England's Robert Adam.

- **Wyck House, 6026 Germantown Avenue. Built 1690.** During the Revolutionary War, this oldest farmhouse in Germantown served as a British field hospital. Strickland's revision some 170 years later turned it into a respectable country seat for the Haines family, which renovated the place in 1852 and occupied it until 1972. Now it's a historic house museum. ■

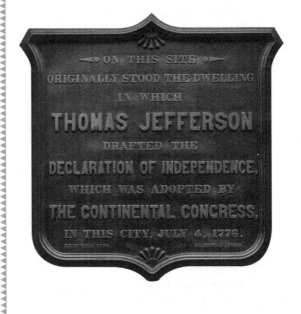

Special Collections

For far too long Philadelphians have not made the most of, boasted of, their civic assets. In fact, haunted by an urban inferiority complex, they have not even themselves searched out what they should be proud of. Among many excellencies—if they only knew about them—they should glory in the remarkable, spinetingling resources of the special collections in the area's libraries. Alas, they don't know that most of them exist. They certainly don't know the quality, variety, and excitement of these libraries' holdings.

Cumulatively, the 20 members of the Philadelphia Area Consortium of Special Collections Libraries (PACSCL) have existed for more than two thousand years. In their collections the rare items exceed 100 million. And to think that many Philadelphians have seen not a one!

As long ago as 1955, on the occasion of the meeting in Philadelphia of the Association of College and Research Libraries, 13 institutions joined in "A Cooperative Exhibition of Rare Books and Manuscripts." Held at the University Museum, "Philadelphia's Riches" was a brave attempt, but it had no local or lasting impact. It was situated too far from the milling crowd; the exhibition was seen chiefly by librarians attending the conference; there was no catalogue printed; and the public at large was not reached through publicity or programs.

By definition, libraries are venerable and sit on hidden wealth. The 1988 exhibition "Legacies of Genius: A Celebration of Philadelphia Libraries," held at the Historical Society of Pennsylvania and the Library Company of Philadelphia, featured only a tiny fraction of the available cultural assets. Yet there was an astounding assemblage of books, manuscripts for the curious to see, the teachers to use for teaching, the scholar to study, and the autodidact to assimilate into his or her store of knowledge. It all came as a surprise to most Philadelphians, to most Americans, and certainly to foreign visitors.

The selection for the exhibition was embarrassed by riches. Items included were limited to manuscripts, books, prints, drawings, and photographs. In age they ranged from a manuscript of the Haggadah (service for Passover), a thousand years old, to John Von Neumann's original 1945 typescript of the first stored computer program. A jewel-like illuminated manuscript Psalter of the 13th century and a Persian epic with colorful miniatures of the 16th were featured, as were important autograph letters of the scientists Galileo Galilei and Isaac Newton. Books printed before Columbus discovered America and the 1493 published announcement of that event shared the shelves with original autograph manuscripts of Charles Dickens's *Pickwick Papers* and Edgar Allan Poe's *Murders in the Rue Morgue*.

Among the many first editions were Dante's *Comedia Divina* of 1472, the famous Shakespeare Folio of 1623, and John Milton's *Paradise Lost* of 1667—all three from Haverford College. There was a copy of Daniel Defoe's *Robinson Crusoe* of 1719 from the Rosenbach Museum and Library, and Beatrix Potter's 1901 *Tale of Peter Rabbit* from the Free Library of Philadelphia.

The American Philosophical Society holds the only known proof of the first printing of the Declaration of Independence. The Historical Society of Pennsylvania is home to James Wilson's draft of the Constitution. Classics of medicine are found at the College of Physicians. We have documents of ground-breaking advances in science, from the earliest pictures of objects under a microscope (Robert Hooke's *Micrographia* of 1665 at Temple University) to an account of the first explosion of an atomic bomb in 1945 (Henry DeWolf Smyth's report at the American Philosophical Society). Birds (in Audubon's famous elephant folio), animals, flowers, and fish in gorgeous colors can be seen in the region's libraries. The whole is a full kaleidoscope of history, literature, science, and art. ∎

Source: Adapted from Edwin Wolf 2nd, ed., *Legacies of Genius: A Celebration of Philadelphia Libraries* (Philadelphia Area Consortium of Special Collections Libraries, 1988).

PACSCL: Philadelphia Area Consortium of Special Collections Libraries

William Shakespeare's main interest was in having his plays performed, not printed. Seven years after his death, in 1623, about half of the plays were gathered and printed. Here is Haverford College's copy.

This 1000-year-old manuscript is considered to be the oldest extant Haggadah, or service for Passover. It is found at the Annenberg Research Institute.

At first, no publisher would accept Beatrix Potter's story. So in 1901, she had it printed privately. The Free Library of Philadelphia's massive collection of children's literature also includes several of Potter's manuscripts.

- **The Academy of Natural Sciences of Philadelphia,** 19th & The Parkway, Philadelphia, PA 19103-1195. Phone: 299-1040; fax: 299-1028. Hours: Monday–Friday 9am–5pm.

- **American Philosophical Society,** 105 S. 5th Street, Philadelphia, PA 19106. Phone: 440-3400; fax: 440-3423. Hours: Monday–Friday 9am–5pm.

- **Annenberg Research Institute,** 420 Walnut Street, Philadelphia, PA 19106. Phone: 238-1290; fax: 238-1540. Hours: Monday–Friday 9am–5pm (by appointment only).

- **The Athenaeum of Philadelphia,** 219 S. 6th Street, Philadelphia, PA 19106. Phone: 925-2688; fax: 925-3755. Hours: Monday–Friday 9am–5pm (library by appointment only; exhibition galleries open to public without appointment).

- **The Balch Institute for Ethnic Studies,** 18 S. 7th Street, Philadelphia, PA 19106. Phone: 925-8090; fax: 922-3201. Hours: Monday, Tuesday, Thursday, Friday 9am–5pm; Wednesday noon–8pm.

- **Bryn Mawr College, Mariam Coffin Canaday Library,** Bryn Mawr, PA 19010. Phone: 526-5271; fax 526-4739. Hours: Monday–Friday 9am–4:45pm.

- **College of Physicians of Philadelphia,** 19 S. 22nd Street, Philadelphia, PA 19103. Phone: 561-6050; fax: 561-6477 and 569-0356. Hours: Tuesday–Friday 9am–5pm.

- **The Free Library of Philadelphia,** 1901 Vine Street, Philadelphia, PA 19103-1189. Phone: 686-5416; fax: 563-3628. Hours: Monday–Friday 9am–5pm. Tours: Monday–Friday 11am.

- **Hagley Museum and Library,** 298 Buck Road, Wilmington, DE 19807. Phone: (302) 658-2400; fax: (302) 658-0568. Hours: Monday–Friday 8:30am–4:30pm; second Saturday of each month 9am–4:30pm.

- **Haverford College Library,** Haverford, PA 19041. Phone: 896-1161; fax: 896-1224. Hours: Monday–Friday 9am–12:30pm and 1:30–4:30pm; Saturday (when college is in session) 10am–1pm.

- **The Historical Society of Pennsylvania,** 1300 Locust Street, Philadelphia, PA 19107. Phone: 732-6201; fax: 732-2680. Hours: Tuesday, Thursday, Friday, Saturday 10am–5pm; Wednesday 1–9pm.

Libraries

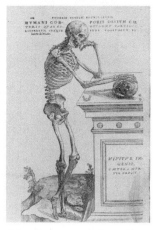

The Free Library of Philadelphia.

- **The Library Company of Philadelphia,** 1314 Locust Street, Philadelphia, PA 19107. Phone: 546-3181; fax: 546-5167. Hours: Monday–Friday 9am–4:45pm.

- **Philadelphia Maritime Museum,** 321 Chestnut Street, Philadelphia, PA 19106-2779. Phone: 925-5439; fax: 625-9635. Hours: Tuesday–Friday 10am–5pm; first Saturday of each month 10am–4pm.

- **The Presbyterian Historical Society,** 425 Lombard Street, Philadelphia, PA 19147. Phone: 627 1852; fax: 627-0509. Hours: Monday–Friday 8:30am–4:30pm.

- **Rosenbach Museum & Library,** 2010 DeLancey Place, Philadelphia, PA 19103. Phone: 732-1600; fax: 545-7529. Hours: Monday–Friday 9am–5pm (by appointment).

- **St. Charles Borromeo Seminary, Ryan Memorial Library,** 100 E. Wynnewood Road, Overbrook, PA 19096. Phone: 667-3394; fax: 664-7913. Hours: Monday–Thursday 8:30am–11pm; Friday 8:30am–5pm and 6:30–10:30pm; Saturday 1–5pm; Sunday 1–11pm.

- **Swarthmore College Libraries, Friends Historical Library,** 500 College Avenue, Swarthmore, PA 19081-1399. Phone: 328-8477; fax: 328-7329. Hours: Monday–Friday 8:30am–4:30pm; Saturday (when college is in session) 9am–noon.

- **Temple University Special Collections Libraries,** 13th and Berks Streets, Philadelphia, PA 19122. Phone: 787-8230; fax: 787-5201. Hours: Monday–Friday 9am–5pm.

- **University of Pennsylvania, Van Pelt Library Special Collections,** 3420 Walnut Street, Philadelphia, PA 19104-6206. Phone: 898-7088; fax: 898-0559. Hours: Monday–Friday 9am–4:45pm.

- **The Henry Francis du Pont Winterthur Museum,** Route 52, Winterthur, DE 19735. Phone: (302) 888-4630; fax: (302) 888-4870. Hours: Monday–Friday 8:30am–5pm. ■

After five years of observations beginning in the late 1530s, Andreas Vesalius inaugurated the study of scientific anatomy with an illustrated book published in Basel, Switzerland. This copy is found at the College of Physicians.

This engraving of a fly from Temple University is one of 38 plates made for Robert Hooke's 1665 Micrographia.

CITIZENS'
MANUAL

Libraries

1987 (21 branches)
Central, Chestnut Hill, Falls of Schuylkill, Fishtown, George Institute, Greater Olney, Haverford Avenue, Kingsessing, Lawncrest, Lovett, Mantua, Northeast Regional, Northwest Regional, Oak Lane, Overbrook Park, Paschalville, Passyunk, Queen Memorial, Richmond, Tacony, Wyoming

1988 (26 branches)
Bushrod, Fox Chase, McPherson Square, Roxborough, Whitman

1989 (29 branches)
Bustleton, Katharine Drexel, Welsh Road

1990 (35 branches)
Holmesburg, Nixon/Cobbs Creek, Southwark, Walnut Street West, West Oak Lane (reactivated), Wynnefield (reactivated)

1991 (39 branches)
Lehigh, C. B. Moore, Ritner, South Philadelphia

1992 (46 branches)
Andorra, Blind & Physically Handicapped, Frankford, Haddington, Kensington, Logan, Widener (reactivated)

1993 (51 branches)
Eastwick, Greenwich, Nicetown-Tioga, Torresdale, West Philadelphia Regional

Source: Friends of the Free Library of Philadelphia.

Free Library of Philadelphia Friends Groups

They fight to keep books, people, and budgets, and then they volunteer to staff libraries on weekends when staff cuts are invariably made. They tend gardens and have plant sales to raise money for everything from computers to draperies to large-print books to best-selling novels. They party, they meet, they organize. And long ago they formed legislative committees, recognizing indeed that their strength is in numbers.

They are the Friends of the Free Library—an alliance of 8,000 people in 51 Branch Friends Groups that represent every branch in the city but two.

In the 20 years since the first Friends group formed, the Alliance of Friends celebrated perhaps its finest political hour only this past year, beginning the moment its members gathered in a skyline room at the Central Branch to watch Mayor Rendell's televised budget address. The prospects were as dismal as expected. But the Alliance was ready. It rallied its members and fought a proposed $2 million cut in the library system's $29 million budget. From one end of the city to the other, Friends circulated petitions urging that the money be restored; well over 20,000 signatures were gathered and presented to City Council. As a result, nearly 66 percent or $1.266 million of the proposed cuts was restored.

The victory was tainted by the news that Greenwich Library on Snyder Avenue would still be closed. Indeed, the Greenwich Friends Group that formed in 1993 to help the neighborhood fight the closing became the first Friends Group to have a life beyond that of its library.

As in any volunteer organization, the 51 different Friends Groups and their contributions vary from branch to branch. While one may need people to make curtains or lobby legislators, another branch may need volunteers so that it can literally have enough people to open its doors.

The Friends attract members young and old. The Central Friends is the oldest and largest group in the Alliance, with 3,500 members. And the newest Friends group is scheduled to begin in the Fall of 1993, at Eastwick.

The Alliance of Friends publishes a newsletter to help its 51 Friends groups stay informed. For more information contact Sheila Whitelaw Ayers, Executive Director, The Friends of the Free Library of Philadelphia, 19th Street and Logan Square, Philadelphia, PA 19103, 567-4562. ■

The Scene

One of the world's oldest traditions—telling and reading stories and poetry—has been revived with a vengeance in Philadelphia. Two decades ago, folks might have attended readings at Robin's Bookshop or the Painted Bride, a defunct bridal shop on South Street. Ever since, the literary scene has expanded and diversified. There's the informative (the City Book Shop's monthly calendar), the provocative (J. C. Dobbs's poetry slamming), and much in between.

Philadelphia has always been known for "bright young writers willing to learn their craft and share it with the public," says poet Herschel Baron, who ran the Moonstone Poetry Series at Robin's beginning in 1981. Moonstone ran its course until 1992, and others followed. We offer this sampling:

- *American Writing: A Magazine.* A twice-yearly publication, edited by Alexandra Grilikhes, featuring writing that takes risks with form, point of view, perception, and the boundaries of consciousness. Subscriptions are $10 a year for individuals, $18 a year for institutions; single issues are $6. For more information, write to 4343 Manayunk Avenue, Philadelphia, PA 19128.

- **Artists for Recovery.** Developed by and for creative/performing artists who are in recovery for emotional hurts or addictions. Open microphone events include readings of original poetry. The group publishes a newsletter and has published an anthology of poetry, prose, and art. For more information, write to 3721 Midvale Avenue, Philadelphia, PA 19129, or call 951-0332.

- **Beathaus, 12th and Ellsworth Streets.** In the spirit of the beatnik coffeehouses of the fifties and early sixties, featuring paintings, music, drama, poetry, and prose. The Beathaus provides a venue for all artists and patrons to meet and discuss new ideas. For more information, call Randy Lee at 465-6106.

- **Borders Book Shop, 1727 Walnut Street.** Offers readings by many local poetry and fiction groups. For more information, call 568-7400.

- **Bothy Club, at the Mermaid Inn, 7673 Germantown Avenue.** Monday evening readings. For more information, call 247-9797.

- *Boulevard.* A nationally distributed magazine dedicated to exceptional fiction, poetry, essays on literature, and other arts. For more information, write to P.O. Box 30386, Philadelphia, PA 19103.

- **Café Kush, 1431 Spruce Street.** Open readings every Thursday night. For more information, call 732-1032.

- **City Book Shop, 1127 Pine Street.** A café atmosphere for weekly readings by new and established poets and writers of fiction, readings from contemporary classics in poetry and fiction, and panel discussions. The shop publishes broadsides featuring local poets. For more information, call 592-1992.

- **Delco Poets Coop.** An organization of Delaware Valley poets and writers who, among other things, run the Mad Poets Full Moon Series at Rose Tree Park in Media. For more information, call Eileen D'Angelo at 586-9318.

- *Dot Dot Dot Magazine.* Dedicated to the universality of art and self-expression. For more information, write to Barry Swift, P.O. Box 54247, Philadelphia, PA 19105.

- **Dot Dot Dot Writers Series, Monday nights at Doc Watson's Pub, 216 S. 11th Street.** Features new and established writers of poetry and prose, followed by an open reading. For more information, call Cecily Kellogg at 925-0113.

- *Drunken Boat.* A bimonthly journal devoted to prose and poetry, with special emphasis on unusual reportage, translations, and literary curiosities. For more information, write to P.O. Box 53615, Philadelphia, PA 19105.

- *Enormous Sky.* Published by and for undergraduate students at Temple University, the magazine accepts all forms of literary expression. For more information, write to P.O. Box 69, 2nd floor, Student Activities Center, Temple University, 13th and Montgomery Avenues, Philadelphia, PA 19122.

Literature

- **Fran's Bookhouse, 6617 Lincoln Drive, Philadelphia, PA 19119.** Features rare, new, and out-of-print adult and children's books, authors, and book-collecting classes. For more information, call Francenia Emory at 438-2729.

- **Giovanni's Room, 345 S. 12th Street.** Known as the "living room" of the feminist/lesbian/gay community. Features fiction, nonfiction, newspapers, maps, guides, and literary criticism from around the world; information about events and newsworthy causes; and regular readings by both new and established authors. For more information, call 923-2960.

- **Gloria's Café Changing Times Jazz and Poetry Series, 29th and Poplar Streets.** Where Afrocentric people and others voice their views through poetry. For more information, call Anwar El at 227-3408.

- *Hellas.* Published twice yearly (subscriptions: $14), *Hellas* features original poetry and scholarly writing, and sponsors monthly poetry readings at both Borders and Barnes & Noble bookstores. For more information, write to Gerald Harnett, 304 S. Tyson Avenue, Glenside, PA 19038, or call 994-1086.

- **The Hole, 15 Bank Street.** Features open readings every Monday night. For more information, write to 15 Bank Street, Philadelphia, PA 19106.

- **Itchy Foot Coffee House, United Methodist Church, 4620 Griscom Street.** Readings, featuring Clear Thoughts Poetry Circle, held every other Saturday night in the church basement. For more information, call Kevin Brown, 333-0965.

- **J. C. Dobbs, 304 South Street.** A bar where poetry slamming (competitive reading) is held the last Thursday of every month. For more information, call 925-4053.

- **Last Drop Coffee House, 1300 Pine Street.** Groove Sessions Performance Series every other Thursday night at 8:30pm features poets, musicians, actors, and other artists. All are encouraged to develop their own form and explore jamming together. For more information, call 893-0434.

- *Lizzie Borden's Axe.* Publishes irreverent, funny, bold fiction and poetry. For more information, write to Crystal Bacon, 247 S. Juniper Street, Philadelphia, PA 19147.

- **Manayunk Arts Center.** Presents six readings a year centered on such themes as "Memories of Philadelphia" and "The Life and Art of William Blake." Also publishes *Schuylkill Valley Journal;* subscriptions are $6 a year. For more information write to Peter Krok, 419 (Rear) Green Lane, Philadelphia, PA 19128, or call 482-3363.

- **Meridian Writers Cooperative.** Dedicated to the empowerment and promotion of emerging writers in the Philadelphia area. Organizes and leads writing and discussion groups and seeks submissions twice yearly for public readings of high-quality fiction. For more information, write to P.O. Box 12376, Philadelphia, PA 19119.

- **North Star Bar Poetry Series, 27th and Poplar Streets.** One of the longest-running poetry series in Philadelphia, presenting the best area poets. For more information, call Dierdre McKee at 222-7020.

- **Painted Bride Art Center.** Works with artists to create and present programs that seek to affirm the intrinsic values of all cultures and art's ability to effect social change. Publishes *The Painted Word* twice yearly (distributed free) and *The Painted Bride Quarterly* (subscriptions: $16 a year, $28 for two years). For more information, write to The Painted Bride, 230 Vine Street, Philadelphia, PA 19106, or call 925-9914.

- **Philadelphia Cultural Council, Northeast Regional Library, Cottman and Oakland Avenues.** Dedicated to reaching out to the community through the arts. Features poetry readings and workshops. For more information, call 685-0500.

- **Poetry Center.** Offers readings and workshops in both poetry and fiction at the Gershman YMCA, Broad and Pine Streets. Has featured local and international poets for more than two decades. For more information, call Jack Israel 527-7900.

- **Poetry Forum—A Collage of Voices.** Eight poets (four women and four men) read their original poetry in 15-minute segments and conclude with a reading open to public participation. Held throughout the city and suburbs; regularly at Barnes & Noble, 835 Old York Road, in Jenkintown (886-5366). For more information, write to Joanne Leva, 1925 Richard Road, Willow Grove, PA 19090.

- *Poetry Plus.* Features both poetry and fiction. Lists information about cultural events throughout Philadelphia. For more information, write to P.O. Box 59312, Philadelphia, PA 19102.

- **Poets & Prophets.** Presents the only year-round Feature & Open Poetry Series in Philadelphia. Saturday-night readings (7pm at the Pen & Pencil Club, 1623 Sansom Street, 2nd floor) are open to all. The first volume of a Poets & Prophets anthology is pending. For more information, write to P.O. Box 4205, Philadelphia, PA 19101, or call 328-POET.

- *Quo Modo Quarterly.* Features information about Philadelphia's "café culture," from performers to habitués, artists to owners. Publishes poetry, fiction, and essays and sponsors a weekly reading series at the Beathaus (see above). For more information, write to P.O. Box 58904, Philadelphia, PA 19102-8904.

- **Robin's Book Store, 108 S. 13th Street.** One of the city's oldest independent bookstores, featuring readings by new and established authors of fiction and nonfiction. Offers an excellent collection of contemporary and classic fiction and nonfiction. For more information, call 735-9600.

- **Singing Horse Press.** One of Philadelphia's oldest independent publishers of poetry; "never free of controversy." Publications include *Her Angel* by Karen Kelly and *Draft X* by Rachel Blau DuPlessis. For more information, write to P.O. Box 40034, Philadelphia, PA 19106.

- *6ix.* Publishes work that crosses boundaries of culture and genre. *6ix's* writing is heretical and playful. For more information, write to 44 W. Washington Lane, Philadelphia, PA 19144.

- **Solomon's Porch Poetry Series.** For more information, call Jourdan Keith at 382-POEM.

- *Synergism.* An anthology of collaborative poetry, poetic prose, and new forms that seeks to document and explore the experiential component of collaborative art. For more information, call Kelly McQuain at 545-6646.

- **University of Pennsylvania Creative Writing Department.** For more information, call 898-7341.

- **Voices of Awareness Poetry Network.** Features readings the third Sunday of each month, plus performances by poets, songwriters, and rappers. Projects include a poetry database, poetry workshops, and programs to send poets into schools to enrich younger poets. For more information, write to P.O. Box 49018, Philadelphia, PA 19141, or call Cheryl Sanders at 276-1210 or RuNett Nia Ebo at 438-1809.

- **Walt Whitman Cultural Arts Center, 2nd and Cooper Streets, Camden.** Since 1976, featuring poetry, fiction, and performance art. For more information, call Lamonte Steptoe at (609) 757-7276. ■

Source: Painted Bride Art Center's City-Wide Poetry Festival Guide, April 18, 1993, compiled by Major Jackson and the Meridian Writers Cooperative.

Almanack will you buy an Almanack?

CITIZENS' MANUAL

You Can't Get There from Here

MAPS AT THE LIBRARY

The Map Collection of the Free Library of Philadelphia contains a lot more than just maps. It has over 5,000 volumes: place-name books, guide books, and reference books on cartography. There are 16th-century atlases and 19th-century gazetteers documenting all nations. Resources run from the expected to the exceptional—from nautical charts for the East Coast to CIA thematic maps of the world. The outstanding collection of Philadelphia, Pennsylvania, and New Jersey maps, views, and atlases includes the most current flood and wetlands maps, updated Sanborne insurance maps for Philadelphia, aerial photographs, and real estate atlases for both city and suburbs.

Over 140,000 individual maps are housed in this department of the Central Library at 19th and Vine Streets, on Logan Circle. None of this rare and wonderful material is available for lending, although some can be photocopied. Hours: Monday - Friday, 9am - 5pm. Call 686-5397.

MAPS AT HOME

The following lists the many current maps of Philadelphia:

ADC's Visitor's Map of Philadelphia Pennsylvania; American Automobile Association—Philadelphia (for exclusive use of members; not for sale); FASTMAP—Philadelphia and vicinity; Franklin's Map of Philadelphia and suburbs; Philadelphia City Map—A Gousha Travel Publication; Hagstrom—Map of Philadelphia Center City, Pennsylvania; Hertz—Philadelphia and vicinity; MapEasy's Guidemap to Philadelphia; Patton's Philadelphia & Suburbs Street & Road Map and Center City; The Philadelphia Inquirer Map & Guide to Center City Philadelphia and surrounding area; Rand McNally—Philadelphia, Pennsylvania; Rand McNally StreetFinder—Philadelphia; SEPTA's Philadelphia Street and Transit Map; SEPTA's Suburban Street and Transit Map; Streetwise Philadelphia Center City.

Don't go looking for Ravine Avenue in Chestnut Hill. Just because it's on every city map doesn't mean it exists.

Maps are rarely error-free, and Philadelphia's maps are no exception. Some errors occur when cartographers rely on government documents, such as the City Plan, showing "paper" streets that were thought of but never built.

According to the City Plan, Ravine Avenue runs between Chestnut Hill Avenue and Hillcrest Avenue. In fact, it doesn't exist. It's a stream bed.

Most maps also incorrectly show Meadowbrook Avenue intersecting Northwestern Avenue in Chestnut Hill. It doesn't. Blame the City Plan again. That's two mistakes, only a few blocks apart.

Colonial cartographers were hardly perfect. Nicholas Scull and George Heap's 1753 map of the city—the best-known map of historic Philadelphia—left out the house of William Allen, the colony's chief justice.

The most reliable recent Philadelphia maps were the ones published by SEPTA's predecessor, the old Philadelphia Transportation Co. (PTC), between the 1940s and 1970s. Back then, the cartographer went out and verified everything. If a street was there, it made the map.

But not all map errors are inadvertent. It's common practice to include deliberate little errors, such as a fictitious or "trap" street, mainly to catch plagiarizers. Some cartographers depict a driveway entrance as a street, others purposely misspell a street name. One Cape May map indicated "Cedar Lane" incorrectly as "Caesar Lane."

A cartographer who finds his or her "trap" street on a competitor's map is apt to sue for copyright infringement, though less predictable turns have been taken. A Texas cartographer put his home driveway on a city map and gave it his last name—only to later find a city crew installing an official sign.

More than a century ago, Philadelphia was the nation's cartography capital, but today there are just two local map publishers: Franklin Maps of King of Prussia and Alfred B. Patton Inc. of Doylestown.

Edward Patton of Patton Inc. says map publishers aren't touchy about their errors. They know their maps are outdated the day they are issued. "I don't think anyone has ever made an entirely 100 percent correct map," he says. "We appreciate knowing about errors so we can correct them." ∎

Philadelphia Postal Zip Codes

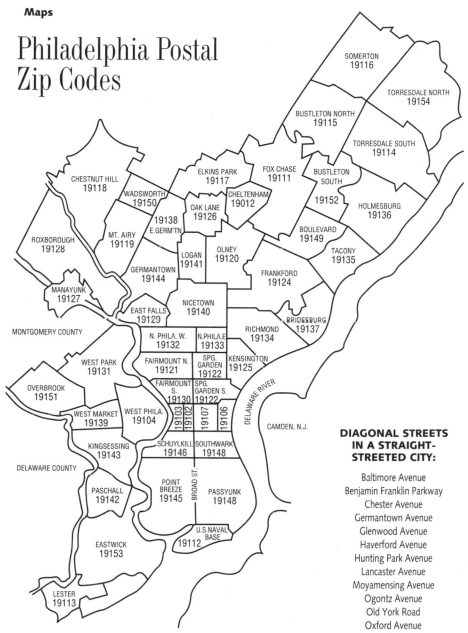

SOMERTON 19116

TORRESDALE NORTH 19154

BUSTLETON NORTH 19115

TORRESDALE SOUTH 19114

CHESTNUT HILL 19118

ELKINS PARK 19117

FOX CHASE 19111

BUSTLETON SOUTH

WADSWORTH 19150

CHELTENHAM 19012

19152

HOLMESBURG 19136

OAK LANE 19126

19138

E.GERM'TN.

BOULEVARD 19149

ROXBOROUGH 19128

MT. AIRY 19119

LOGAN 19141

OLNEY 19120

TACONY 19135

GERMANTOWN 19144

FRANKFORD 19124

MANAYUNK 19127

NICETOWN 19140

EAST FALLS 19129

BRIDESBURG 19137

MONTGOMERY COUNTY

N. PHILA. W. 19132

N.PHILA.E. 19133

RICHMOND 19134

FAIRMOUNT N. 19121

SPG. GARDEN 19122

KENSINGTON 19125

WEST PARK 19131

FAIRMOUNT S. 19130

SPG. GARDEN S. 19122

OVERBROOK 19151

WEST MARKET 19139

WEST PHILA. 19104

19103

19102

19107

19106

CAMDEN, N.J.

DELAWARE RIVER

KINGSESSING 19143

SCHUYLKILL 19146

SOUTHWARK 19148

DELAWARE COUNTY

PASCHALL 19142

POINT BREEZE 19145

BROAD ST.

PASSYUNK 19148

EASTWICK 19153

U.S.NAVAL BASE 19112

LESTER 19113

DIAGONAL STREETS IN A STRAIGHT-STREETED CITY:

Baltimore Avenue
Benjamin Franklin Parkway
Chester Avenue
Germantown Avenue
Glenwood Avenue
Haverford Avenue
Hunting Park Avenue
Lancaster Avenue
Moyamensing Avenue
Ogontz Avenue
Old York Road
Oxford Avenue
Passyunk Avenue
Ridge Avenue
Roosevelt Boulevard
Woodland Avenue

In addition to 33 Philadelphia-born mayors (the first was Charles Read, b. 1726) and 30 English-born ones (the last was John Weaver, b. 1903) is a slew of non-natives. Here are the first stomping grounds of 32 Philadelphia mayors-to-be:

Other countries

Barbados: Samuel Hassell

Germany: Hilary Baker (Bonnheim), Rudolph Blankenburg (Barntrup), John Geyer

Ireland: Thomas Griffitts, James Logan (Lurgan, County Armagh), Robert Strettell

Jamaica: Jonathan Dickinson

Scotland: William Burns Smith (Glasgow)

Wales: Edward Roberts

Other states

Connecticut:
Joel Jones (Coventry)

Delaware:
Charles Gilpin (Wilmington)

Maryland:
William Fishbourn, Richard Hill, Samuel Preston (Talbot County)

Massachusetts:
Edward Shippen (Boston), Samuel Davis Wilson (Cambridge)

New Jersey:
John Inskeep (Marlton), Morton McMichael (Bordentown), Joseph Hampton Moore (Woodbury), Benjamin Wood Richards (Batsto)

New York:
Matthew Clarkson (New York City), Thomas Lawrence, Sr. (Dutch Church), Edward Gene Rendell (New York City), John Morin Scott (New York City)

North Carolina:
Willie Wilson Goode (Seaboard)

Ohio:
John Edgar Reyburn (New Carlisle)

Pennsylvania:
Harry Arista Mackey (Susquehanna), John Barclay (Bucks County), Richardson Dilworth (Pittsburgh), Robert Eneas Lamberton (Bethlehem)

Virginia:
John Gibson (Accomack County)

Mayors

The Philadelphians

Half of the city's history went by before we actually elected a mayor. The first one, Humphrey Morrey, was appointed by William Penn more than 300 years ago, and various versions of the City Charter (beginning in 1701) dictated that the post be filled by appointment. Except for a brief time during the Revolutionary War when the King of England picked the mayor, the responsibility fell to City Council.

Being mayor wasn't much of a job then. And for the longest time, a volunteer had to be found and cajoled to take the unpaid post. Some, like Anthony Morris, avoided it by running away. But that was the 1740s.

Finally, in 1839, Philadelphians were allowed to vote for their mayor in a popular election. Spoiler John C. Montgomery ran with candidates John Swift and John K. Kane. No one claimed a majority. Swift, who had already served six one-year terms, had sided with rioters aimed at the city's abolitionists during his last term, and this gave him the edge. Swift won 49 more votes than Kane, a Yale-educated lawyer who later became a federal judge. Kane, too, was pro-slavery (he later jailed a Philadelphian for helping free a slave), but the voters did not yet have that example for purposes of comparison. The choice for mayor again reverted to City Council, and Swift was granted a seventh term. The electorate later sent him back five more times.

In 1854, when Philadelphia County consolidated and the current boundaries of the city were settled upon, a new charter determined that the mayor would serve two-year terms. In 1861, the term length grew to three years. Finally, in 1885, the current four-year term and the two-term limit were made law.

Entries on the following list are by administration number. The date on which the term began is followed by the mayor's name. Life dates are given in the first entry, including place of birth and death, if known. Election returns for the winner and challenger(s) are included beginning with the 131st administration. Party affiliations are included (as available) beginning with the 136th administration.

According to the current City Charter, the mayor must be at least 25 years old and a city resident for at least three years before election. The two successive term limit is still in effect. If the mayor's office falls vacant, the President of City Council steps in as Acting Mayor. ∎

❖

Theophilus Van Kannel of Philadelphia patented the revolving door in 1888.

Continental Congress held the first national lottery on April 10, 1777.

Philadelphia Mayors, 1691–1993

1. May 20, 1691 **Humphrey Morrey** (b. ?; d. February 2, 1716)
2. October 25, 1701 **Edward Shippen** (b. 1639 Yorkshire, England; d. October 2, 1712)
3. October 24, 1702 **Edward Shippen**
4. October 5, 1703 **Anthony Morris** (b. August 23, 1654, London; d. October 23, 1721)
5. October 3, 1704 **Griffith Jones** (b. ca. 1640/1650; d. 1712)
6. October 2, 1705 **Joseph Willcox** (b. 1669; d. 1721)
7. October 1, 1706 **Nathan Stanbury** (b. ?; d. 1721)
8. October 7, 1707 **Thomas Masters** (b. ?; d. 1724)
9. October 5, 1708 **Thomas Masters**
10. October 4, 1709 **Richard Hill** (b. 1673, Maryland; d. September 9, 1729)
11. October 3, 1710 **William Carter** (b. ?, Wapping, Middlesex, England; d. ca. 1738)
12. October 2, 1711 **Samuel Preston** (b. 1665, Maryland; d. September 10, 1743)
13. October 7, 1712 **Jonathan Dickinson** (b. 1663, Jamaica; d. 1722)
14. October 6, 1713 **George Roch**
15. October 5, 1714 **Richard Hill**
16. October 4, 1715 **Richard Hill**
17. October 2, 1716 **Richard Hill**
18. October 1, 1717 **Jonathan Dickinson**
19. October 7, 1718 **Jonathan Dickinson**
20. October 6, 1719 **William Fishbourn** (b. June 25, 1677, Talbot County, Maryland; d. 1742)
21. October 4, 1720 **William Fishbourn**
22. October 3, 1721 **William Fishbourn**
23. October 2, 1722 **James Logan** (b. October 20, 1674, Lurgan, Ireland; d. October 31, 1751)
24. October 1, 1723 **Clement Plumsted** (b. 1680; d. May 1745)
25. October 6, 1724 **Isaac Norris** (b. July 26, 1671, London; d. June 4, 1735)
26. October 5, 1725 **William Hudson** (b. 1661?, Yorkshire, England; d. December 16, 1742)
27. October 4, 1726 **Charles Read** (b. ca. 1686; d. January 6, 1737)
28. October 3, 1727 **Thomas Lawrence** (b. September 4, 1689, New York; d. April 20, 1754)
29. October 2, 1728 **Thomas Lawrence**
30. October 7, 1729 **Thomas Griffitts** (b. ?; d. 1746)
31. October 6, 1730 **Thomas Griffitts**
32. October 6, 1731 **Samuel Hassell** (b. 1691, Barbados; d. June 13, 1751)

HISTORICAL ODDS ARE...

...0 in 96 that a Philadelphia mayor is a woman or a person of color.

...1 in 96 that a tugboat will be named for a mayor. The *Edwin S. Stuart* used to ply the waters of the Delaware.

...roughly 1 in 20 that a mayor will live to serve out his term. Thomas Lawrence died April 20, 1754, and was replaced five days later by Charles Willing, who died November 30 of the same year. Hilary Baker died September 25, 1798, a victim of the Yellow Fever Epidemic. Samuel Davis Wilson died August 19, 1939, about a week after he resigned due to illness. George Connell served as acting mayor until the election of Robert Eneas Lamberton, who died August 22, 1941, of Lou Gehrig's Disease.

...better than 1 in 15 (in Philadelphia's first century-and-a-half) that a mayor had a mayor for a father or a grandfather. In all, six sons (two from the same family) followed in their fathers' footsteps. There were John Barker and his son James; Thomas Lawrence and his two sons, Thomas and John; Anthony Morris and his namesake son; Clement Plumsted and his son William; Edward Shippen and his namesake grandson; Benjamin Shoemaker and his son Samuel; and Charles Willing and his son Thomas.

❖

Matthew Lawler was a pirate in the Revolutionary War.

Isaac Norris helped rescue William Penn from debtors' prison.

Only one mayor is represented by a full-standing public statue. Morton McMichael, by sculptor John H. Mahoney in the early 1880s, stands on Lemon Hill Drive in East Fairmount Park.

Robert Wharton volunteered as a jailer and lived in the Walnut Street Prison during the Yellow Fever Epidemic in 1793.

119

ASSASSINATION ATTEMPT

Mayor Scott

Philadelphia mayors are well accustomed to verbal potshots, but only one was the object of an actual assassination attempt.

On May 3, 1843, Mayor John M. Scott was seated in his office shortly after one o'clock when the impressively named Adalberte Benedictis Ptolemeis strode up to his desk. A shabbily dressed man in a large dark cloak, Ptolemeis presented the mayor with a lengthy paper, in French, declaring he was "living in the streets" and demanded a position teaching Italian and geometry. Familiar with the request from earlier occasions, Scott offered money, which was refused. The mayor then rose to leave and had reached the doorway to the adjacent office of City Treasurer Cornelius Stevenson when Ptolemeis drew a pistol and shot the mayor in the back.

"I had just entered the Treasurer's office, when I heard a pistol shot," reported witness Charles Poulson. "Mayor Scott entered very pale and said, 'I am shot.' 'Where?' I asked, and the Mayor pointed to his back. I took off his coat, vest and suspenders and on raising his shirt, saw a bruise the size of a quarter-dollar."

The mayor's coat and vest had been penetrated. Only the web of his silk suspenders stopped short the would-be assassin's lead ball, which Treasurer Stevenson retrieved from the office floor.

Mayors

33. October 3, 1732 **Samuel Hassell**
34. October 2, 1733 **Thomas Griffitts**
35. October 1, 1734 **Thomas Lawrence**
36. October 7, 1735 **William Allen** (b. August 5, 1704; d. September 6, 1780)
37. October 5, 1736 **Clement Plumsted**
38. October 4, 1737 **Thomas Griffitts**
39. October 3, 1738 **Anthony Morris** (b. 1682, London; d. ?)
40. October 2, 1739 **Edward Roberts** (b. April 4, 1680, Wales; d. 1741)
41. October 7, 1740 **Samuel Hassell**
42. October 6, 1741 **Clement Plumsted**
43. October 5, 1742 **William Till** (b. ca. 1697; d. 1766, New Castle, Del.)
44. October 4, 1743 **Benjamin Shoemaker** (b. August 3, 1704, Germantown; d. June 25, 1767)
45. October 2, 1744 **Edward Shippen** (b. July 9, 1703, Boston; d. September 25, 1781, Lancaster)
46. October 1, 1745 **James Hamilton** (b. ca. 1710; d. August 14, 1783, New York)
47. October 7, 1746 **William Attwood** (b. ?; d. 1754)
48. October 9, 1747 **William Attwood**
49. October 4, 1748 **Charles Willing** (b. May 18, 1710, Bristol ?, England; d. November 30, 1754)
50. October 3, 1749 **Thomas Lawrence**
51. October 2, 1750 **William Plumsted** (b. November 7, 1708, Philadelphia; d. August 10, 1765)
52. October 1, 1751 **Robert Strettell** (b. 1693, Dublin; d. June 12, 1761)
53. October 3, 1752 **Benjamin Shoemaker**
54. October 2, 1753 **Thomas Lawrence**
55. April 25, 1754 **Charles Willing** Became Mayor at the death of Lawrence.
56. October 1, 1754 **Charles Willing**
57. December 4, 1754 **William Plumsted** Became Acting Mayor at the death of Willing.
58. October 7, 1755 **William Plumsted**
59. October 5, 1756 **Attwood Shute** (b. ?; d. 1758)
60. October 4, 1757 **Attwood Shute**
61. October 15, 1758 **Thomas Lawrence** (b. April 16, 1720; d. January 21, 1775)
62. October 2, 1759 **John Stamper** (b. ca. 1709; d. 1782)
63. October 7, 1760 **Benjamin Shoemaker**
64. October 6, 1761 **Jacob Duché** (b. April 26, 1708, Philadelphia; d. September 28, 1788, England)
65. October 5, 1762 **Henry Harrison** (b. 1708, Lancashire, England?; d. January 3, 1766)
66. October 4, 1763 **Thomas Willing** (b. December 30, 1731, Philadelphia; d. January 18, 1821)

Mayors

67. October 2, 1764 **Thomas Lawrence**
68. October 1, 1765 **John Lawrence** (b. May 30, 1724; d. 1799)
69. October 7, 1766 **John Lawrence**
70. October 6, 1767 **Isaac Jones** (b. July 17, 1716, Philadelphia; d. October 18, 1773)
71. October 4, 1768 **Isaac Jones**
72. October 3, 1769 **Samuel Shoemaker** (b. 1725, Philadelphia; d. October 10, 1800)
73. October 2, 1770 **Samuel Shoemaker**
74. October 1, 1771 **John Gibson** (b. 1729; d. 1782)
75. October 6, 1772 **John Gibson**
76. October 5, 1773 **William Fisher** (b. 1713; d. 1787)
77. October 4, 1774 **Samuel Rhoads** (b. 1711, Philadelphia; d. April 7, 1784)
78. October 5, 1775 **Samuel Powel** (b. October 28, 1738, Philadelphia; d. September 29, 1793)
79. April 11, 1789 **Samuel Powel**
80. April 12, 1790 **Samuel Miles** (b. March 22, 1739; d. December 29, 1805, Cheltenham)
81. April 13, 1791 **John Barclay** (b. January 22, 1749, Bucks County; d. September 25, 1824)
82. April 13, 1792 **Matthew Clarkson** (b. April 15, 1733, New York City; d. October 5, 1800)
83. April 3, 1793 **Matthew Clarkson**
84. April 15, 1794 **Matthew Clarkson**
85. April 6, 1795 **Matthew Clarkson**
86. May 5, 1796 **Matthew Clarkson**
87. October 18, 1796 **Hilary Baker** (b. February 21, 1746, Bonnheim, Germany; d. September 25, 1798)
88. October 17, 1797 **Hilary Baker**
89. October 16, 1798 **Robert Wharton** (b. January 12, 1757, Philadelphia; d. March 7, 1834)
90. October 11, 1799 **Robert Wharton**
91. October 21, 1800 **John Inskeep** (b. January 29, 1757, Marlton, N.J.; d. December 24, 1834)
92. October 16, 1801 **Matthew Lawler** (b. January 1, 1755; d. July 14, 1831, Cincinnati, Oh.)
93. October 19, 1802 **Matthew Lawler**
94. October 18, 1803 **Matthew Lawler**
95. October 16, 1804 **Matthew Lawler**
96. October 15, 1805 **John Inskeep**
97. October 21, 1806 **Robert Wharton**
98. October 20, 1807 **Robert Wharton**
99. October 18, 1807 **John Barker** (b. 1746; d. April 3, 1818)
100. October 17, 1809 **John Barker**
101. October 16, 1810 **Robert Wharton**
102. October 15, 1811 **Michael Keppele** (b. September 9, 1771, Philadelphia; d. February 1821)
103. October 20, 1812 **John Barker**

Mayors

MAYORAL NICKNAMES

Samuel Howell Ashbridge had been coroner without much ado. But while he was mayor, his daughter's huge and ostentatious wedding drew large presents and even larger criticism from the press. Ashbridge thereby earned the title "Boodle Mayor."

....

In the years leading up to the War of 1812, the British made it a practice to attack American ships and seize men from their crews as deserters. John Barker, then a general in the Philadelphia Militia Legion, led enraged young Philadelphians in such companies as "The Young Men of Correct Democratic Principles." The newspaper *Aurora* called an address by Barker "a piece of rhodomontade" and labeled him "Major-General Nightcap."

....

German-born Quaker Rudolph Blankenburg was long involved in municipal reform. (His wife Lucretia was an active suffragist.) While mayor, Blankenburg donated his entire salary to the pension funds of the police, firemen, and teachers. He was known as "Old Dutch Cleanser."

....

William S. Stokley, a confectioner noted for his lack of oldfashioned substance and ungentlemanly image, was called "Sweet William."

....

104. October 19, 1813 **John Geyer** (b. 1778; d. 1835)
105. October 18, 1814 **Robert Wharton**
106. October 17, 1815 **Robert Wharton**
107. October 15, 1816 **Robert Wharton**
108. October 21, 1817 **Robert Wharton**
109. October 20, 1818 **Robert Wharton**
110. October 19, 1819 **James Nelson Barker** (b. June 17, 1784, Philadelphia; d. March 9, 1858, Washington, D.C.)
111. October 17, 1820 **Robert Wharton**
112. October 16, 1821 **Robert Wharton**
113. October 15, 1822 **Robert Wharton**
114. October 21, 1823 **Robert Wharton**
115. October 19, 1824 **Joseph Watson** (b. 1784; d. April 9, 1841)
116. October 18, 1825 **Joseph Watson**
117. October 18, 1826 **Joseph Watson**
118. October 16, 1827 **Joseph Watson**
119. October 21, 1828 **George Mifflin Dallas** (b. July 10, 1792, Philadelphia; d. December 31, 1864) Resigned.
120. April 15, 1829 **Benjamin Wood Richards** (b. November 12, 1797, Batsto, N.J.; d. July 12, 1851) Filled unexpired term of Dallas.
121. October 20, 1829 **William Milnor** (b. June 26, 1769, Philadelphia; d. December 13, 1848, Burlington County)
122. October 19, 1830 **Benjamin Wood Richards**
123. October 18, 1831 **Benjamin Wood Richards**
124. October 16, 1832 **John Swift** (b. January 12, 1790; d. June 9, 1873)
125. October 15, 1833 **John Swift**
126. October 21, 1834 **John Swift**
127. October 20, 1835 **John Swift**
128. October 18, 1836 **John Swift**
129. October 17, 1837 **John Swift**
130. October 16, 1838 **Isaac Roach** (b. February 24, 1786; d. December 29, 1848)
131. October 15, 1839 **John Swift** 3,343 vs. *John K. Kane* 3,294 and *John C. Montgomery* 2,670
132. October 20, 1840 **John Swift** 6,355 vs. *Henry Horn* 4,820
133. October 19, 1841 **John Morin Scott** (b. October 25, 1789, New York City; d. April 3, 1858) 5,658 vs. *Samuel Badger* 4,693
134. October 18, 1842 **John Morin Scott** 6,145 vs. *Richard Vaux* 5,065
135. October 10, 1843 **John Morin Scott** 6,585 vs. *Samuel H. Perkins* 3,976
136. October 15, 1844 **Peter McCall** (Whig) (b. August 31, 1809, Trenton; d. October 30, 1880) 5,506 vs. *Elhanan W. Keyser* (Nat Am) 5,065
137. October 21, 1845 **John Swift** 4,979 vs. *Elhanan W. Keyser* 4,538 and *James Page* 3,946

Mayors

138. October 20, 1846 **John Swift** 5,562 vs. *Richard Vaux* 3,402 and *Peter A. Brown* 3,244
139. October 19, 1847 **John Swift** 6,046 vs. *J. Altamont Phillips* 3,550 and *Peter Fritz* 2,530
140. October 17, 1848 **John Swift** 8,440 vs. *Samuel Badger* 5,079
141. October 16, 1849 **Joel Jones** (Ind) (b. October 25, 1795, Coventry, Conn.; d. February 3, 1860) 6,429 vs. *Charles Gilpin* (Whig) 6,364
142. October 15, 1850 **Charles Gilpin** (Whig) (b. November 17, 1809, Wilmington, Del.; d. October 29, 1891) 7,363 vs. *Joel Jones* 5,081
143. October 21, 1851 **Charles Gilpin** (Whig) 9,275 vs. *John Swift* (D) 3,934
144. October 19, 1852 **Charles Gilpin** (Whig) 8,792 vs. *William Badger* 4,328 and *John S. Warner* 408
145. October 18, 1853 **Charles Gilpin** (Whig) 8,002 vs. *John Thompson* 4,392
146. June 13, 1854 **Robert Thomas Conrad** (Whig) (b. June 10, 1810; d. June 27, 1858) 29,507 vs. *Richard Vaux* (D) 21,011
147. May 13, 1856 **Richard Vaux** (D) (b. December 19, 1816, Philadelphia; d. March 22, 1895) 29,534 vs. *Henry D. Moore* (Am Repub) 25,455
148. May 11, 1858 **Alexander Henry** (People's) (b. April 11, 1823; d. December 5, 1883) 33,868 vs. *Richard Vaux* (D) 28,934
149. May 8, 1860 **Alexander Henry** 36,658 (R) vs. *John Robbins* (D) 35,776
150. January 1, 1863 **Alexander Henry** (R) 34,613 vs. *Daniel Fox* (D) 30,049
151. January 1, 1866 **Morton McMichael** (R) (b. October 20, 1807, Bordentown, N.J.; d. January 6, 1879) 44,617 vs. *Daniel Fox* (D) 39,511
152. January 1, 1869 **Daniel Miller Fox** (D) (b. June 16, 1819; d. March 21, 1890, Atlantic City) 61,517 vs. *Hector Tynsdale* (R) 59,679
153. January 1, 1872 **William S. Stokley** (R) (b. April 25, 1823, Philadelphia; d. February 21, 1902) 58,508 vs. *James S. Biddle* (D -Ref) 50,307
154. January 1, 1875 **William S. Stokley** (R) 60,128 vs. *Alexander K. McClure* (Ind/D) 49,133
155. January 1, 1878 **William S. Stokley** (R) 64,779 vs. *Joseph L. Caven* (D/Ind) 61,913
156. April 4, 1881 **Samuel George King** (D/Cit Comm) (b. May 2, 1816, Philadelphia; d. March 21, 1899) 78,215 vs. *William S. Stokley* (R) 72,428
157. April 7, 1884 **William Burns Smith** (R) (b. November 14, 1844, Glasgow; d. November 23, 1917, Laurel Springs, N.J.) 79,552 vs. *Samuel George King* (D) 70,440

PLACES THAT WOULDN'T BE QUITE THE SAME WITHOUT PHILADELPHIA MAYORS

Norristown, Pa.
(named for Isaac Norris)

Allentown, Pa.
(named for William Allen)

Shippensburg, Pa.
(named for Edward Shippen)

Dallastown, Pa. and Dallas, Tx. (named for George Mifflin Dallas, below)

LONG-SERVING MAYORS

Robert Wharton served 14 one-year terms between 1798 and 1824.

John Swift served 12 one-year terms between 1832 and 1849.

Bernard Samuel served 11 years in all (beginning in 1941, with the final three years of Lamberton's term). Subsequently, Samuel was elected and re-elected.

James H. J. Tate began serving a 10-year stint in 1962, when Richardson Dilworth left to run for the governor's office. Tate was elected in 1964 and re-elected in 1968, narrowly winning (by less than two percent of the votes cast) over his former District Attorney, Arlen Specter.

These mayors are represented in the venerable *Dictionary of American Biography*: William Allen, James Nelson Barker, Rudolph Blankenburg, Robert Taylor Conrad, George Mifflin Dallas, Edwin Henry Fitler, James Hamilton, Richard Hill, Joel Jones, James Logan, Morton McMichael, Anthony Morris, Isaac Norris, Edward Shippen, Richard Vaux, Robert Wharton, Thomas Willing.

❖

Richard Vaux once danced with Queen Victoria. He refused to wear an overcoat or walk past the Union League.

CITY HALL AS A MUSEUM

Throughout City Hall's construction, plaster models of exterior sculpture were exhibited in the "model room" near the south entrance. As early as 1877 some were on loan to the permanent part of the International Exhibition at Memorial Hall, later to become the Pennsylvania Museum and still later the Philadelphia Museum of Art. Other models were loaned temporarily to Spring Garden Institute for classroom use. By 1894, public interest in the casts had so waned that City Commissioners told local institutions to choose what they wanted, after which remaining models would be destroyed to make room for offices. The Evening Telegraph on July 16, 1894, remarked that it would take a half-dozen sturdy men wielding heavy hammers two days to reduce the unclaimed plaster to atoms. None appears to have survived.

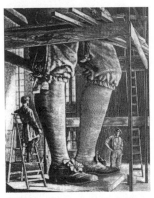

Modeling Penn

City Hall's Southern Entrance

Mayors

158. April 4, 1887 **Edwin Henry Fitler** (R) (b. December 2, 1825, Philadelphia; d. May 31, 1896) 90,211 vs. *George deBenneville Keim* (D) 62,263

159. April 6, 1891 **Edwin Sydney Stuart** (R) (b. December 28, 1853, Philadelphia; d, March 21, 1937) 108,978 vs. *Albert H. Ladner* 69,913

160. April 10, 1895 **Charles Franklin Warwick** (R) (b. February 14, 1852, Philadelphia; d. April 4, 1913) 137,863 vs. *Robert E. Pattison* (D) 79,879

161. April 3, 1899 **Samuel Howell Ashbridge** (b. December 5, 1849, Philadelphia; d. March 24, 1906)

162. April 6, 1903 **John Weaver** (b. October 5, 1862, Worcestershire, England; d. March 18, 1928)

163. April 1, 1907 **John Edgar Reyburn** (b. February 7, 1845, New Carlisle, Oh.; d. January 4, 1914, Washington, D.C.)

164. December 4, 1911 **Rudolph Blankenburg** (Key/D) (b. February 16, 1843, Germany; d. April 12, 1918) 134,680 vs. *George H. Earle, Jr.* (R) 130,185

165. January 3, 1916 **Thomas B. Smith** (R) (b. November 2, 1869, Philadelphia; d. April 17, 1949, Abington, Pa.) 166,643 vs. *George D. Porter* (Frank) 88,135

166. January 5, 1920 **Joseph Hampton Moore** (R) (b. March 8, 1864, Woodbury, N.J.; d. May 2, 1950) 227,739 vs. *Harry Wescott* (D) 30,408, *Joseph S. MacLaughlin* (Chart) 17,900, and *Charles Bauer* (Soc.) 6,320

167. January 7, 1924 **William Freeland Kendrick** (R) (b. June 24, 1874, Philadelphia; d. March 29, 1953) 286,398 vs. *Raymond A. Raff* (D) 37,239

168. January 2, 1928 **Harry Arista Mackey** (R) (b. June 26, 1873, Susquehanna, Pa.; d. October 17, 1938) 296,959 vs. *Joseph Hampton Moore* (Cit) 128,611

169. January 4, 1932 **Joseph Hampton Moore** (R) 362,329 vs. *Michael Donahue* (D) 31,330

170. January 6, 1936 **Samuel Davis Wilson** (R) (b. August 31, 1881, Cambridge, Mass.; d. August 19, 1939) 379,222 vs. *John B. Kelly* (D) 333,825 Resigned shortly before his death.

171. August 19, 1939 **George Connell** (R) (b. November 3, 1871, Philadelphia; d. October 22, 1955) Became Acting Mayor at death of Wilson.

172. January 1, 1940 **Robert Eneas Lamberton** (R) (b. September 14, 1886, South Bethlehem, Pa.; d. August 22, 1941, Longport, N.J.) 398,384 vs. *Robert C. White* (D) 361,143

173. August 22, 1941 **Bernard Samuel** (R) (b. March 9, 1880, Philadelphia; d. January 12, 1954) Became Acting Mayor at death of Lamberton.

174. January 3, 1944 **Bernard Samuel** (R) 346,297 vs. *William C. Bullitt* (D) 282,832

175. January 5, 1948 **Bernard Samuel** (R) 413,091 vs.
Richardson Dilworth (D) 321,469
176. January 7, 1952 **Joseph Sill Clark Jr.** (D) (b. October
21, 1901, Philadelphia; d. January 12, 1990) 448,983
vs. *Daniel A. Poling* (R) 324,283
177. January 2, 1956 **Richardson Dilworth** (D) (b. August
29, 1898, Pittsburgh, Pa.; d. January 23, 1974) 423,035
vs. *W. Thatcher Longstreth* (R) 293,329
178. January 4, 1960 **Richardson Dilworth** (D) 438,278 vs.
Harold Stassen (R) 229,818
179. February 13, 1962 **James Hugh Joseph Tate** (D)
(b. April 10, 1910, Philadelphia; d. May 27, 1983,
Longport, N.J.) Became Acting Mayor when Dilworth
resigned to run for governor.
180. January 6, 1964 **James Hugh Joseph Tate** (D) 401,714
vs. *James T. McDermott* (R) 333,446
181. January 1, 1968 **James Hugh Joseph Tate** (D) 353,326
vs. *Arlen Specter* (R) 342,398
182. January 3, 1972 **Frank Lazarro Rizzo** (D) (b. October
23, 1920, Philadelphia; d. July 16, 1991, Philadelphia)
394,067 vs. *W. Thatcher Longstreth* (R) 345,912
183. January 5, 1976 **Frank Lazarro Rizzo** (D) 311,879
vs. *Charles W. Bowser* (I) 134,334 and
Thomas Foglietta (R) 101,001
184. January 7, 1980 **William Joseph Green, III** (D)
(b. June 24, 1938–) 313,345 vs. *David W. Marston* (R)
174,083 and *Lucien Blackwell* (Cons) 108,447
185. January 2, 1984 **Willie Wilson Goode** (D) (b. August
19, 1938, Seaboard, N.C.–) 396,266 vs. *John Egan* (R)
263,742 and *Thomas Leonard* (I.) 57,146
186. January 4, 1988 **Willie Wilson Goode** (D) 333,254 vs.
Frank Lazarro Rizzo (R) 319,053
187. January 6, 1992 **Edward Gene Rendell** (D)
(b. January 5, 1944, New York City–) 281,751 vs. *Joseph
M. Eagen, Jr.* (R) 130,478 ∎

Sources: The Philadelphia City Archives; Melvin G. Holli and
Peter d'A. Jones (eds.), *Biographical Dictionary of American
Mayors, 1820–1980: Big City Mayors* (Greenwood Press,
1981); Anthony A. Roth, *Collections of the Genealogical Society
of Pennsylvania: Mayors of Philadelphia, 1691–1972. Some
Genealogical Notes* (Manuscript, The Historical Society of
Pennsylvania); *Who Was Who in America: Historical Volume,
1607–1896* (A. N. Marquis Company, 1963).

❖

In 1937, the Philadelphia Museum of Art purchased Paul Cezanne's "The
Bathers" for the record price of $110,000. One newspaper cartoonist
depicted William Penn on City Hall holding out the canvas and saying:
"Lookit! I bought you a pretty picture." Forty thousand homes in
Philadelphia then lacked bathtubs.

Tales of the Great Migration

Northern Liberties, 1923.

As immigration from Europe to the United States dropped during World War I, falling from 1.2 million in 1914 to only 111,000 in 1918, Philadelphia employers recruited African Americans from the rural South. Legend has it that William Atterbury of the Pennsylvania Railroad commissioned the Reverend James Duckrey, a Baptist minister and messenger in his office, as labor agent. Duckrey's successful mission, in the spring of 1916, yielded the first of many trainloads of laborers. By 1929, 300,000 African Americans had left the South for the promise of better lives in the industrialized North. In Philadelphia, between 1910 and 1930, the African American community increased from 84,000 to 219,000. Here are some memories of that time:

"Yeah, I was 8 years old, 9 years old when I started farming. I didn't get much [schooling]. Down south they didn't allow you to send your kids to school. Not in them days. 'Cause if you were a Southerner and a colored fella workin' on your farm and he got a boy around 10, 12 years old, you tell his dad, hey you need that boy to help, you take him out of school. You need him. And they take you out."—*James Plunkett*

"And they [white people] used to come out there to the country and ride through the fields and it would be hot. They had their little old kids with black patent leather shoes on and white socks and things, and we would be out there in the mud and stuff all between your toes and everything. And they would look at you like they thought you was something to be scared of. ...I can't tell you how I felt. I really can't tell you how I felt."—*Marie Mathis*

"And I told my father—we were out in the field picking cotton that day I left home. And I told my father that he had promised me a trip to Philadelphia. And I asked him when I could go when we was talkin' about how little money I had made. And he told me I could go anytime. So I remember I had finished that row of cotton. Left that bag of cotton sittin' at the end of the row. And as far as I know, it's sitting there still."—*David Amey*

"I remember as if it was yesterday. There were thousands of them at the station waiting to get on that train to go north. Like herds of cattle. ...Some of them walked out of their homes and didn't even take nothin'."—*Edgar Campbell*

"They had to do it at a certain time in the dark of night. They had to go to the outskirts of the city on a railroad spur and they had put an old raggedy car on that railroad spur. ...When everything was ready he was going to light a cigarette on the deck of that car, and the men that was hidden—my father was one—hidden in the bushes alongside of that thing, laying in the bushes. ...When he lit that cigarette, all of them jumped right up and got in that car, and everybody was quiet and not a light or anything. What they call a little shifter or a little engine came, hitched onto that car, and the train, the Broadway Limited, was going north."—*William Brown* ■

Source: "Goin' North: Tales of the Great Migration," produced by Charles Hardy III and aired on WHYY 90.9FM, February-March 1985.

How the Orchestra Beat the Mummers

I t was 1952. Democrats had taken City Hall; urban renewal dollars were poised to pour in from Washington; and Philadelphians continued their search for a new identity. A few years before, the Gimbel Brothers Department Store at 10th and Market Streets had sponsored a "Better Philadelphia Exhibition." And now, with the betterment begun, store executives wondered how to celebrate it in a triptych of murals. Possessing a rowhouse-sized blank expanse of wall over a bank of well-traveled store elevators, Gimbels invited a stable of artists to paint something of lasting civic value.

Morris Berd's composite *Industrial Philadelphia—The Workshop of the World* and Harry Gricevics's visionary *Philadelphia of Tomorrow* breezed through the review process. But when the committee saw Alfred Bendiner's study of exuberant twirling and colorful strutting on a chaotic Broad Street, they grew uncomfortable. Although the committee liked Bendiner's style, the Mummers weren't quite dignified enough. Find an appropriate Philadelphia subject, they told him.

The artist was frustrated and furious. He hadn't anticipated that his confident, circuslike rendering of average Philadelphians mocking and mimicking on New Year's Day might fail to fit some unspoken agenda. But the committee's inclination toward white-collar Philadelphia—the more starch the better—was now obvious. They didn't want sequins and feathers. Perhaps top hats and tails?

This shift posed no real problem for the eclectic Bendiner. For years, his sketches of Igor Stravinsky, Jascha Heifetz, Marian Anderson, Sergei Rachmaninoff, and others had accompanied reviews of performances in *The Evening Bulletin,* and he had just come out with his first book, *Music to My Eyes,* a collection of 51 caricatures of performers on stage at the Academy of Music. Bendiner had even dedicated the book to Rachmaninoff, whose high-starch Philadelphia premiere, his Piano Concerto No. 3, Bendiner had witnessed (and sketched) on December 1, 1939. Rachmaninoff "rode his own meddlesome musical steed in a fashion that held his audience spellbound," wrote one reviewer. No Philadelphian, certainly not anyone on the Gimbels committee, would dare find fault with this safe subject.

But in his revision for Gimbels, Bendiner threw a subtle, silent curve. He replaced the profile of Wolfgang Amadeus Mozart in the medallion over the Academy's proscenium arch with one of his wife, Betty. Call it artistic license. Call it sleight of hand. Whichever, Bendiner introduced onto the walls of the Academy (and the staid walls of Gimbels Department Store) a little Mummeresque mockery. ■

1993 Parade Prize Winners

Comic Division

Club	Captain
1. Murray	1. Henny Schultz, Murray
2. Purul	2. Tom Ross, Landi
3. Goodtimers	3. Domenic Rinaldo, Hammond
4. Hammond	4. Bill Wooten, Sr., Goodtimers
5. Landi	5. Larry Meenan, Purul
6. Liberty	6. Bill Dunleavy, Liberty

Fancy Costume Division

Club	Captain
1. Golden Sunrise	1. Mark Wray, Hog Island
2. Oregon	2. Jack Trepts, Oregon
3. Hog Island	3. Dave Shuster, Golden Sunrise

String Band Division

Club	Prize	Theme
1. Quaker City	$7,550	La Quakeracha
2. Ferko	7,350	Barnyard Boogie
3. Fralinger	7,150	Bad Boys
4. Avalon	6,950	Red, White, Rhythm & Blue
5. Uptown	6,750	Next Stop, Pennsylvania Station
6. Polish American	6,550	Come Join The Circus

WHERE WILL THEY STRUT NEXT?

Nineteenth-century Mummers strutted down Chestnut Street. And since 1901, modern Mummers have strutted up Broad Street toward City Hall on New Year's Day. Is it time—again—to spin this Philadelphia tradition right on its heels?

Imagine the Mummers' Parade on New Year's Eve. Imagine 25,000 Mummers strutting down Broad Street from City Hall to Veterans Stadium. Imagine the parade "climaxing in a grand music and fireworks finale... telecast live nationally...searchlights could emblazon City Hall and Veterans Stadium and lasers could connect the two, marking the parade path...."

So envisioned the Philadelphia City Planning Commission in 1993, in a recommendation to "make the Mummers' Parade more attractive to both live and television audiences."

But the Mummers don't quite see their parade being turned around, said Joseph W. Schubert, long-time Mummer and now executive director of the Mummers Museum at Second Street and Washington Avenue. "The majority of the Mummers prefer to have it just as it is now."

However, things do change, Schubert admits. After being discontinued in the 1980s, the Summer Mummers' Parade came back in 1993.

So who knows? If not Vet Stadium, how about a Grand Finale in the Pennsylvania Convention Center? "It's been mentioned," said Schubert. "And politically, it might happen."

Mummers

7. Crean	6,350	Crean's In Full Bloom
8. Woodland	6,150	Woodland Hits Rock Bottom
9. Hegeman	5,950	Caliente In Miami
10. Greater Kensington	5,750	Who Do Voodoo
11. South Philadelphia	5,550	South Philadelphia Goes Scrap Happy
12. Italian American	5,350	All Wrapped Up
13. Trilby	5,150	Tiny Tot Talent Theater
14. Durning	4,950	Durning's Island Adventure
15. Palmyra/South Jersey	4,750	Elves' Winter Workout
16. Greater Overbrook	4,550	Pajammin'
17. Aqua	4,350	Midnight At The Oasis
18. Broomall	4,150	Hobo Junction
19. Duffy	3,950	Sometimes I Feel Like A Nut
20. Ukrainian American	3,750	Clowning In The New Year
21. Ventnor City	3,550	Music, Music, Music
22. Greater Bucks	2,790	All Dat Jazz

Captain

1. Bob Shannon, Jr., Quaker City 4. William J. Speziale, Ferko
2. Jamie Caldwell, Uptown 5. Mike Vaughan, Avalon
3. Bill Bowen, Jr., Fralinger

Fancy Brigade Division

Club	Prize	Theme
1. Shooting Stars	$5,400	Singapore Swing
2. Jokers	4,800	Nonsense On The Nile
3. Clevemore	4,300	Give Me That Old Time Religion
4. Saturnalians	3,800	Midnight In Moscow
5. Golden Crown	3,300	Junglemania
6. Avenuers	2,900	Gotta Minute?
7. Vikings	2,500	Biggest Brigade In The Parade
8. Downtowners	2,300	Hot Wax
9. Merry Makers	2,100	Land Of Mythical Mayhem
10. Strutters	2,000	Old Trash With A New Twist
11. Gallagher	1,800	Off The Wall, A Rock Concert
12. Satin Slipper	1,700	Rain Forest, A Magical Thing
13. Magic	1,600	Smooth Criminal
14. Ring # 1	1,500	Bourbon Street Strut
15. Alpha	1,400	Caribbean Dreamin'
16. Charles Ray	1,300	House Party

Captain

1. Fred Keller (Jokers) 3. Micky Adams (Shooting Stars)
2. Bob Fitzmaurice (Avenuers) 4. Bill Burke Jr. (Golden Crown)

Source: The Mummers Museum.

159 PHILADELPHIA ROCK, POP, AND NEW WAVE PERFORMING ACTS, 1970–1990

The A's, Admiral God, Alan Mann and the Free Arts Band, The Ambush Bugs, American Dream, Anvil Bitch, Ashtray, Autistic Behavior, The Autistics, Baby Flamehead, Baby Grand, The Beat-Offs, The Ben-Wah Torpedoes, Beru Revue, The Big Thing, The Bloodless Pharoahs, The Boneheads, Brick House, Bunnydrums, The Butcher Brothers, Carnival of Shame, Children's Crusade, Crash Course in Science, Cyclic Blowfield and the Funky Calypsos, DecaDance, Decontrol, Dewey Street, Doctor At Tree, Doctor Bombay, Doomed on Planet Earth, The Edison Electric Band, The Eight Balls, The Electric Love Muffin, The Electric Weasel Brothers, Elizabeth, The Endorphins, ETR Posse, Evil Seed, The Excellos, Executive Slacks, The Fabulous Fondas, The Fad, The Falling Ushers, The Five Charms, 5-Story Fall, Flight of Mavis, The Flys, F.O.D., Freight Train, The Front Street Runners, Fun City, Ghostwriters, Good God, Good News, Grey Dominion, Grisly Fiction, Headcheese, The Heathens, Hidden Combo, High Treason, Homo Picnic, Horn and Hard Art, Immaculate Hearts, The Impossible Years, Informed Sources, Initial Attack, The Jags, Jericho Seven, Jitterbops, Joey and the Pets, John Cadillac Blues Band, Johnny's Dance Band, The Johnsons, Junior Mints, King Carcass, King of Siam, Kremlin

In Bronze on Broad Street

The Philadelphia Music Alliance (PMA) was founded in 1986 to promote Philadelphia's music industry, but it's best known for its Walk of Fame on South Broad Street. Every year, bronze plaques join those already embedded in the sidewalk to commemorate individuals and groups who have enriched the city's musical life. PMA's annual galas, which honor the latest Walk of Fame inductees, have become a Who's Who of the local and national music scene.

Honorees are chosen by a committee of PMA board members and other regional experts. The public is invited to nominate those who've had a longtime association with the Philadelphia music scene. Send names and biographical information to the Nominating Committee, c/o Philadelphia Music Alliance, 250 S. Broad Street, Philadelphia, PA 19102 (phone: 790-2415; fax: 790-9427).

The Walk of Fame now consists of 59 bronzes set into the pavement along South Broad Street. Plaques have been added every year since 1987, except for 1991.

1987
Marian Anderson, opera and spirituals singer
Pearl Bailey, singer and entertainer
Chubby Checker (Ernest Evans), pop singer
Dick Clark, DJ and television personality
John Coltrane, saxophonist and composer
Dizzy Gillespie, trumpet player and composer
Bill Haley, rock musician
Mario Lanza, opera singer
Bobby Rydell, pop singer
Bessie Smith, blues singer
Leopold Stokowski, conductor

1988
Frankie Avalon, pop singer
Jim Croce, singer-songwriter
The Dixie Hummingbirds, gospel and pop vocal group
Nelson Eddy, opera and film star
Eddie Fisher, pop singer
Four Aces featuring Al Alberts, pop vocal group
Stan Getz, saxophonist and composer
Jeanette MacDonald, singer and film star

Music

Anna Moffo, opera singer
Eugene Ormandy, conductor
Ethel Waters, singer and film star

1989
Kal Mann and Dave Appell, songwriting team
Samuel Barber, composer
Stanley Clarke, bassist and composer
Ed McMahon, TV personality
Al Martino, pop singer
Harold Melvin and the Blue Notes, R&B group
Teddy Pendergrass, soul singer
Todd Rundgren, rock musician and songwriter
André Watts, classical pianist

1990
Stan Lee Broza, radio pioneer and personality
Linda Creed, songwriter
Patti LaBelle, singer and entertainer
Gerry Mulligan, saxophonist, bandleader, and composer
Arthur Tracy, singer and entertainer
Efrem Zimbalist, Sr., violinist, composer, and music educator

1992
Lee Andrews and the Hearts, R&B vocal group
Danny and the Juniors, pop vocal group
Kitty Kallen, singer and radio personality
Eddie Lang (Salvatore Massaro), jazz guitarist
Riccardo Muti, conductor
Dr. Max Rudolf, conductor and music educator
Clara Ward and the Famous Ward Singers, gospel vocal group
Grover Washington, Jr., saxophonist, composer,
    and bandleader

1993
Thom Bell, songwriter
Jerry Blavat, DJ and radio personality
Kenneth Gamble and Leon Huff, producers, songwriters,
    and musicians
Joe Grady and Ed Hurst, radio personalities
Buddy Greco, pop singer and jazz pianist
Darryl Hall and John Oates, pop and soul singer-songwriters
The Heath Brothers (Percy, Jimmy, and Albert "Tootie"
    Heath), jazz musicians, composers, and producers
Doug "Jocko" Henderson, Sr., DJ and music producer
Hy Lit, DJ and radio personality
Bernie Lowe, producer
Sid Mark, radio personality
Joe Niagara, radio personality
Molly Picon, singer and stage entertainer
Rudolf Serkin, pianist and music educator
Georgie Woods, DJ and community leader ■

---

159 PHILADELPHIA ROCK, POP, AND NEW WAVE PERFORMING ACTS, 1970–1990

continued...

Korps, Little Gentlemen, The Love Chunks, M Factor, McRad, Mama Volume, The Mandrake Memorial, Marshall Law, Marty Watt, Memo Lender and the Elements, The Mesmerons, Monkey 101, The Morrocos, Mother May I, Mr. Mehta, Napalm Sunday, The Nazz, Neighbors and Allies, Nine Firemen Nine, Nixon's Head, No Milk, The Normals, Orifice, Pagan Babies, Pay Attention, Physical Push, PILT, Poor Devil, Popular Mechanics, Pretty Poison, Pure Hell, Quincy, The Ravens, Red Buckets, The Reds, Reesa and the Rooters, The Revolvos, Robert Hazard, Rotgut, Ruin, Sadistic Exploits, Scab Cadillac, Science Fiction, Scram!, The Secret Kidds, Seeds of Terror, Sensory Fix, Separate Checks, The Serial Killers, The Sharp Nines, The She-Males, The Sic Kidz, Sick Man of Europe, Sink Manhattan, Sir Dot, The Skilly Band, The SKPs, Slant 6, Snub, Stalin's Daughter, The Stick Men, Strictly Limerance, Suzy Cosmo, Sweet Stavin' Chain, Three-Foot Acid, The Tickets, Tons of Nuns, Tornado 5, The Trace, Trained Attack Dogs, Trance Factor, Union Jacks, The Vels, The Von Cools, The Warm Jets, Wax, Whole Oats, The Wild Women of Wongo, The Wishniaks, Woody's Truck Stop, The X-Men, Y-Di, Youth Camp

---

Philadelphia Sounds

T he roots of Philadelphia's popular music go back to the 1820s, farther even. But today's Philadelphia music scene rests on a rich immediate past. The last couple of musical genera- tions have provided a meeting place for everything from classical opera to street-corner soul and cerebral jazz.

Let's roll back to the 1930s when Clara Ward and the Ward Singers earned the first gold record for gospel; Leopold Stokowski shook up Main Line Philadelphians with his daring pro- gramming at the Academy of Music and shook hands with Mickey Mouse on the Disney screen; and Eddie Lang and Joe Venuti took the guitar and violin to new heights of jazz improvisation. Local musicians could find work in the pit bands at the Royal on South Street at 16th, the Earle at 11th and Market Streets, or other of the city's entertainment palaces.

By the 1940s, such innovative South Philadelphia teacher-players as Dennis Sandole were teaching music theory to John Coltrane and a host of other jazz men and women. In North Philadelphia, a nine-year-old boy named Solomon Burke was preaching and performing to packed houses in a church founded by his grandmother. Nightclubs sprouted citywide, and even though they were sometimes intimidated by the authorities into paying kickbacks, Philadelphia had a support system for local talent.

By the mid-1940s, jazz greats including Duke Ellington, Billie Holiday, and Charlie Parker were visiting the city regularly to play—and to seek out local talent. At the Academy, Parker met Philadelphia trumpeter and future bandmate Red Rodney when Rodney climbed out of the audi- ence and onto the bandstand to jam. Failed as an opera house, the giant Metropolitan at Broad and Poplar Streets branched out with everything from gospel shows to boxing matches.

In the 1950s, gospel shouters teamed up with street-corner harmonizers in the city's poorer neighborhoods to create the doo-wop sound. Jazz musicians who soloed on R&B records (if only to pay the bills) helped shape bop music as they joined a dynamic scene of small clubs packed with hot players. Clifford Brown worked with Art Blakey and Max Roach. Benny Golson worked with Donald Byrd and led his own Jazztet. WFIL-TV's afternoon filler show, "Bandstand," became a local, then a national hit. Talent scouts scoured South Philadelphia for telegenic boys who could sing a little, com- ing up with Frankie Avalon, Bobby Rydell, and Fabian. Ernest Evans, plucked from a poultry store at the Italian Market, showed he could sing *and* dance; as Chubby Checker, he recorded "The Twist."

A number of music and nightlife centers were well established by the 1950s: in West Philadelphia, 52nd Street between Arch and Locust; in North Philadelphia, Columbia (now Cecil B. Moore) Avenue near Broad Street; in Center City, the side streets near City Hall and Broad and South Streets. The Blue Note and Clef Clubs in black South Philadelphia emerged as musical and social centers for players of jazz.

In the 1960s, organ trios—hard-swinging groups led by keyboard players backed by drums, guitar, or sax—electrified bars all over town. Shirley Scott, Jimmy Smith, and Trudy Pitts defined this technically demanding and highly listenable music during long-term gigs. A white DJ named Jerry Blavat reintroduced fifties doo-wop and R&B "oldies" to an eager audience of white baby- boomers. But active R&B performers hit tough times in the mid-sixties, when the "English inva- sion" swept the scene. Thousands of local white kids started bands—nearly to a one aping the English sound. Just a few chose to hear the beat thumping in the streets all around them, spawn- ing the "blue-eyed soul" movement. In 1967, The Soul Survivors took that formula to the Top Ten with "Expressway to Your Heart." Meanwhile, the psychedelic sounds emanating from the West Coast caught up with local artists like the Nazz (with Todd Rundgren) and The American Dream.

Hard rock and Motown seemed to own the pop charts in the 1970s. But then came the "Sound of Philadelphia"—a smooth mixture of the doo-wop vocals of the 1950s and sophisticated lyrics, backed by top musicians (among them moonlighting Philadelphia Orchestra players). The O'Jays, the Intruders, the Tramps, and the Blue Notes sold millions of records.

But jazz was in a slump, locally and nationwide. Many musicians left town or took day jobs. Teachers and performers such as Bernard Pfeiffer (the French classical jazz pianist who settled in Chestnut Hill) and his bassist Al Stauffer kept the fires going for scores of younger jazz players, such as Tommy Lawton. Classically trained bassist Stanley Clarke won fame with a jazz-rock fusion. Diehard jazz fans could see Miles Davis, Charles Mingus, and Bill Evans in intimate venues such as The Bijou Cafe on Lombard Street near Broad. With commercial success an admitted pipedream, players like McCoy Tyner and Sunny Murray were free to push at the limits of improvisation.

Up until the 1970s, Latin music was mostly an imported product, with older musicians bringing their talents to the area. But by the mid-seventies, Kipland Morris, an Edison High School music teacher inspired by the Latin sounds of his pupils, launched a Latin music program that introduced dozens of young players into a now rapidly expanding salsa circuit. In abandoned warehouses on the fringes of the campuses of Drexel and Penn, jazz and black funk music from Philadelphia's neighborhoods merged. Patti LaBelle, originally an R&B singer, bounced back on the charts 15 years after her first hit.

The Philadelphia Folk Festival was now an established stop for the stars of the folk and blues world. The Cherry Tree Music Co-Op, Bothy Folk Club, and Bucks County Blues Society all made Philadelphia a major town for traditional instrumentalists.

In the 1980s, disco and middle-of-the-road rock hurt the live music scene in Philadelphia—but not without a reaction. Punk bands like the Autistics and Pure Hell made an angry, unpolished rock. On the pop front, classic rockers such as the Hooters were balanced by The Dead Milkmen, a tongue-in-cheek punk combo. Brazilian musician Orlando Hadad established PhilaSamba, a school/troupe that taught scores of Philadelphians to play samba rhythms.

The smooth vocal sound that black Philadelphia performers pioneered in the fifties and polished in the seventies resurfaced in the 1990s. Boyz II Men effortlessly plug rap into their work, and Philadelphia is making its mark on the rap scene with artists like the Fresh Prince and The Goats. Neo-doo-wop harmony groups like New Image capture listeners from among fans of folk and blues.

Most of the nightlife strips are gone, victims of economic pressures, competition from other forms of entertainment, demographics, and changing tastes. While only a handful of clubs feature true improvisational jazz full-time, those that do pull loyal, knowledgeable audiences.

The Avenue of the Arts, the proposed, well-funded plan to make Broad Street an axis of cultural activity, will include a new Clef Club building—official acknowledgment of jazz's importance to the city.

Guitarists from the traditional bop school like Jimmy Bruno and experimental pickers like Rick Iannocone are active in a scene large enough to accommodate both. The Mill Creek Jazz Center and the Asociación de Musicos Latino Americanos are working to preserve and expand ethnic music forms, while the Folklife Center at International House and the Painted Bride, with the Philadelphia Folklore Project, are exploring the work of new musicians from Asia and the Middle East.

We move forward with an eye to the best of the past. Marion Williams, one of the original Ward gospel singers, received a MacArthur Award in 1993. And the 1993 Mellon Jazz Fest was dedicated to keyboard master Shirley Scott. ■

The vibrating dental mallet, which filled gold into cavities, was perfected in 1875 by Dr. William G. A. Bonwill. He first conceived the idea while watching a telegraph key in operation at Philadelphia's Continental Hotel.

Beneath Our Feet

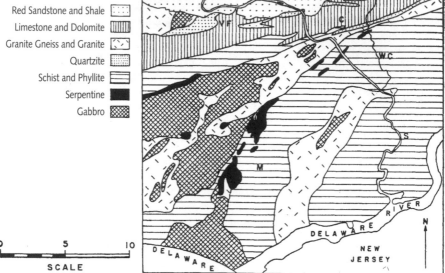

Red Sandstone and Shale
Limestone and Dolomite
Granite Gneiss and Granite
Quartzite
Schist and Phyllite
Serpentine
Gabbro

0   5   10
SCALE

Beneath the sidewalks and streets of Philadelphia are rocks older than the dinosaurs—500 million years old, give or take.

The majority of Philadelphia lies on the eastern edge of a geologic region called the Piedmont, a strip that runs along the eastern slope of the Appalachian Mountains from New York to Alabama. The primary type of rock in this part of the Piedmont is the metamorphic Wissahickon schist, a sedimentary shale subjected to enormous pressure and temperature eons ago. Wissahickon schist is so common in the city's northwestern neighborhoods, from Germantown to Chestnut Hill, that thousands of houses were built of it.

As you move south and east in Philadelphia, you leave the Piedmont and enter the coastal plain. That land is made up of material eroded from the Piedmont over the last 70 to 90 million years. In effect, the coastal plain—all the way to the New Jersey shore—is a flattened pile of debris that's fallen off or washed off a prehistoric coast of North America.

The Piedmont and the coastal plain meet at what is called the fall line. The coastal plain erodes more readily than the Piedmont, and along rivers and creeks this translates into natural waterfalls. (The term was coined by early settlers, whose river journeys were blocked by an abrupt series of falls and rapids.) The fall line crosses the Delaware River at the Trenton Falls. It crosses the Schuylkill River around Manayunk and East Falls, once called Falls of the Schuylkill—for the gentle rapids obscured since the 1820s by backup from the dam at Fairmount.

Geologically speaking, the flatlands along the Delaware River are recent. When the last Ice Age ended, between 10,000 and 12,000 years ago, the sea level rose and the Delaware Bay extended farther up the river than it does today. As a result, the part of Philadelphia that now borders the Delaware River used to be submerged under a slow-flowing estuary. Sediment accumulated. Waters receded. And flatlands of rich alluvial soil were left behind—an ideal place for forests to grow and for humans to hunt and, eventually, farm. ■

Source: Bruce K. Goodman, *Guidebook to the Geology of the Philadelphia Area* (Pennsylvania Geological Survey, 1964).

Named for Philadelphia and Pennsylvania

To the 17th-century settlers of Philadelphia, nature meant a rich wilderness whose variety could be little explained and much exploited. William Penn himself wrote home and introduced "the creatures (for profit only) that are natural to these parts...the wild catt (Panther) Otters, woolf fox (fishers) mincks, musk ratt, and of the water, the whale (for oyle) of which we have a good store." Pennsylvania was more than a new address; it would be an opportunity as close as the soil beneath one's feet. Gustavus Hesselius wrote to his mother back in Sweden in 1714: "My brother Anders planted a Peach Pit when we arrived in this country [two years earlier], now there is a tree so big that it bears fruit. If you put a stick in the ground it will soon take root."

This new world also begged to be explored and explained. And as the cosmopolitan outpost at the edge of the American wilderness, Philadelphia quickly became a center for the study of natural history. Through the 18th and 19th centuries, a cult of nature grew here. The American Philosophical Society (founded in 1743) and the Academy of Natural Sciences (founded in 1812) offered a home base to clear-minded naturalists. Over time, the scientific approach to the wilderness proved at least as powerful as the original trappers and clear cutters who had tamed nature with sheer force.

Now, more than 300 years later, we can look back at the many species of plants and animals discovered and named for this former outpost of civilization. Here are a few:

Birds
- *Larus delawarensis*, ring-billed gull. Described in 1815. Found in the Delaware River below Philadelphia.
- *Dendroica pensylvanica*, chestnut-sided warbler. Described in 1766. Found in Philadelphia.
- *Larus philadelphia*, otherwise known as Bonaparte's gull.
- *Vireo philadelphicus*, Philadelphia vireo. Pale yellow on the breast and olive green above. Nests in Eastern and Central Canada each summer and spends winter in the tropics. Best time to find one in this region is during spring and fall migrations.
- *Oporornis philadelphia*, mourning warbler. A little bird, named in 1810, with a gray hood, yellow chest, black chin, and olive green back, wings, and tail. Nests in Canada and winters in Central and South America.

Fish
- *Centropristis philadelphica*, rock sea bass. Described in 1758 and named after the city, but nowadays found from North Carolina to Florida and in the Gulf of Mexico.

Insects
- *Hydraena pennsylvanica*, Insecta:Coleoptera: Limnebiidae. Minute moss beetle.
- *Ampulex pensylvanicus*, Insecta: Hymenoptera:Sphecidae. Sphecid wasp.
- *Casnonia pensylvania*, Insecta:Coleoptera: Carabidae. Ground beetle.

Lilium philadelphicum

URBANATURA?

Although long devoid of wilderness, Philadelphia remains inseparably bound to its natural surroundings. The Delaware, source of much of the city's water, is the largest undammed river in the eastern United States. Fairmount Park not only helps protect the Schuylkill watershed but is home to both wildflowers and wildlife.

In Philadelphia's three centuries, ecosystems have been dramatically altered. Forests were cut and tidal marshes filled. Many species were driven out; others learned to coexist and even thrive. Peregrine falcons nest on the bridges spanning the rivers and atop the rare skyscraper. The deer population far exceeds its natural size. For gray squirrels, city life is a dream come true. Oak, maple, and tulip poplar abound, providing natural food; bird feeders and poorly sealed trash receptacles beckon; natural predators (such as bobcats) are gone. Opossums and raccoons pilfer gardens and nest in garages and sheds. The indigenous coexist with the introduced: sparrows, starlings, and pigeons. In the Wissahickon Valley, great horned owls and red-tailed hawks can still be seen.

These creatures, and hundreds of others, share a common bond: the ability to thrive in the patchwork of concrete, lawns, weedy lots, and snippets of forest comprising Philadelphia's natural landscape.

Natural History

- *Pentatoma pennsylvaniae*, Insecta:Hemiptera:Pentatomidae. Stink bug.
- *Agelena pensylvanica*, Arachnida:Aranaeae:Agelenidae. Funnel-web spider.
- *Apion pennsylvanicum*, Insecta:Coleoptera:Curculionidae. Snout beetle.
- *Cantharis pensylvanica*, Insecta:Coleoptera:Cantharidae. Soldier beetle.
- *Chrysis pensylvanica*, Insecta:Hymenoptera:Chrysididae. Cuckoo wasp.
- *Geotrupes pensylvanicus*, Insecta:Coleoptera:Scarabaeidae. Earth-boring dung beetle.

Plants

- *Erigeron philadelphicus*, Philadelphia fleabane. A plant of thickets and moist meadows, with pink or magenta daisy-shaped flowers.
- *Panicum philadelphicum*, a grass of rocky or sandy open ground and dry woods, with a large open seed head.
- *Polygonum pensylvanicum*, Pennsylvania smartweed. A very common plant of disturbed or cultivated ground, with bright pink cylindric flower spikes.
- *Prunus pensylvanica*, fire cherry. A small wild cherry tree of dry woods with white flowers and sour fruits.
- *Acer pensylvanium*, striped maple. A slender tree of cool, rich woods, with bark showing green and dark vertical bands.
- *Viola pensylvanica*, smooth yellow violet. Found in damp woods and shaded rocky slopes throughout this area.
- *Brachyoxylon pennsylvanianum*, fossil plant from the late Triassic period, approximately 200 million years ago. Described in 1912. Found on a farm in Woodbourne, Bucks County.
- *Lilium philadelphicum*, wood lily. A species of lily that grows in sandy soils and forest openings throughout the area. Noted for spectacular orange flowers.
- *Cardimine pensylvanica*, Pennsylvania bittercress. A small white flower that blossoms on wet ground in the spring.

Mollusks

- *Mesodon pennsylvanicus*, snail described in 1827.
- *Lucina pensylvanica*, marine clam described in 1758. Found in West Indies.
- *Lymnaea philadelphica*, fresh water snail from the Schuylkill River in Philadelphia, described in 1841.
- *Diplodon pennsylvanicus*, fossil clam or snail from the Triassic period, about 200 million years old. Described in 1921. Found in Trias, York County, Pennsylvania. ■

Sources: The Academy of Natural Sciences; William Penn, *Some Account of The Province of Pennsylvania In America* (Benjamin Clark, 1681).

Manayunk, Texas, and Smoky Hollow: The Philadelphia 389

All of Flat Rock was perplexed. After water had backed up behind the new dam at Fairmount, the Schuylkill River had risen to gently cover the great flat rocks long taken for granted. Out of sight, these submerged rocks seemed irrelevant to the villagers and to the name of their village in the northwestern section of Philadelphia County. So residents called a meeting to select a new name.

"Bridge Water," barked the curmudgeonly Captain John Towers. Logical enough, agreed others. The place had plenty of water, and it had a bridge. But someone pointed out that floods carried the bridge away every now and again, so the Flat Rockers in attendance turned to the local Greek scholar, a man named Hagner. He searched his memory for an appropriate name.

"Udoravia?" tried Hagner. Simple enough. It meant "place by the water." So then and there the Flat Rockers took a vote and decided to become Udoravians.

The next day, a subcommittee of Udoravians painted a sign bearing the name and hung it prominently on Main Street. The mill owners, who hadn't attended the meeting, vetoed the choice. Oh, these mill owners were all in favor of the Greek Revival. Their new bank down the river in the center of Philadelphia was all white marble columns and pediments. But no one could claim that "Udoravia" exactly rolled off the tongue. And that stubborn Captain Towers had printed up stationery proclaiming his address as Bridge Water. Udoravia's popularity was not unanimous.

The mill owners suggested something American—Native American. Perhaps a mellifluous, indigenous name of some significance? What about the name for the river in whose waters those Flat Rocks lay submerged? The river's name—Manayunk, "place where we drink"—was proposed, adopted, and accepted by posterity.

❖

Who thinks of Philadelphia today without Manayunk, Frankford, Port Richmond, Germantown, West Oak Lane? But few know all of the nearly 200 neighborhood names currently in use and the nearly 200 used no longer in this big city of small neighborhoods.

Anyone who sets out to make a comprehensive list of neighborhoods—as we did for this almanac—soon finds that names used by official and unofficial historians, map makers, the Postal Service, the Census Bureau, the Planning Commission, and SEPTA vary widely and sometimes conflict. What, then, makes a neighborhood a candidate for this list?

We felt most comfortable when a neighborhood name appeared many times in our sources. Bridesburg, for example, first appeared on the 1839 map we consulted and then reappeared in 15 other of our sources up to the present day. Logan, which many Philadelphia-neighborhood aficionados think of as old, appeared in none of our early sources. Of course, Logan is in this list, as are truly esoteric neighborhoods from the past such as Texas, Smoky Hollow, Beggarstown, Rose of Bath, and Saw Dust Village and more recent additions such as Bentley, Fernhill, Mount Moriah, and Penn-Knox.

In this first edition, we claim inclusiveness, not necessarily completeness. For example, many neighborhood names turned up without dates of origin in textual sources; we chose to include them, feeling certain that our readers will help us learn more. If you can add to or clarify any of our entries, we would like to hear from you. Please write to: Almanac Editor, 1314 Locust Street, Philadelphia, PA 19107.

This gazette of 389 Philadelphia names—more than anyone has previously claimed exist in a city long known as a "city of neighborhoods"—includes bits and pieces of our forgotten past that had seemed perched on the edge of oblivion. We hope this list helps pull them back from that brink.

Neighborhood names in boldface type are in current use. At the end of most entries is a date in parentheses. This indicates the earliest appearance of that name in the sources we consulted. For many of the names that have gone out of use, we also provide the last year they appeared.

Mermaid Inn (between Chestnut Hill and Mount Airy)

Abbotsford. South of 52nd Street and Baltimore Avenue.

Abbottsford. East of Schuylkill River on heights below Falls of the Schuylkill, approximately where North Laurel Hill Cemetery is situated.

Academy Gardens. Vic. Willits Road and Pennypack Park. (1970s)

Achpoquesing. See *Poetquessing.*

Adelphi. Along Indian Run, about ½ mile north of Haddington.

Allegheny West. East bank of Schuylkill River, from Allegheny to Glenwood Avenues, to railroad tracks. (1970s)

Andorra. Beyond Roxborough, between Wissahickon Creek and Schuylkill River. Named for the European principality. (1861)

Angora. Vic. Cobbs Creek around Baltimore Avenue. Settled by David Callahan. (1861)

Aramingo, Gunner's Run. The former from the Native *tumanaramingo,* or "wolf walk"; the latter from a nearby creek. Between Northern Liberties and Bridesburg. (1850)

Armentown. Derogatory name for early settlement in Germantown.

Art Museum Area. See *Fairmount.*

Arunnamink. South of Woodland Avenue and west of Schuylkill River to Cobbs Creek.

Ashton-Woodenbridge, Ashton—Wooden Bridge. Vic. North Philadelphia Airport, including Wooden Bridge Run west to Academy Gardens. (1970s)

Asoepek. Native village, west of Frankford Creek. (17th c.)

Aston, Astenville, Five Points. Intersection of Monument, Falls, and Ford Roads.

Babylon. Village ½ mile southeast of Byberry Meeting.

Badlands, The. Vic. 4th and Cambria Streets. Named by narcotics police and the media. (1991)

Ball Town, Balton. South of Port Richmond, where Cramp's Shipyard stood. (1808)

Bankahoe. North of Shackamaxon. (17th c.)

Baring. North of Lancaster Avenue and 40th Street, south of Mantua. (1990)

Bartram Gardens, Bartram Village. Vic. 56th Street and Lindbergh Boulevard. (1980s)

Bath Town, Bathtown, Rose of Bath (1808). Vic. Germantown Road near Cohocksink Creek in present Northern Liberties. (1765)

Bebberstown, Beggarstown, Dogtown, Franklinville. Vic. Mennonite Church on Germantown Avenue, Gorgas Lane to Cliveden Street. Named for the Rev. Mathias van Bebber.

Belfield. Vic. Chelten and Olney Avenues, Wister Street and Ogontz Avenue. (1980)

Bella Vista. Between Sixth and 12th Streets, Lombard Street to Washington Avenue. (1976)

Bellevue. Vic. Nicetown Lane and Westmoreland Street.

Bell's Corner. South of Pennypack Creek, north of Rhawnhurst, vic. Algon Avenue and Horrocks Street. (1980s)

Belmont. West from Schuylkill River along Parkside Avenue and north to City Avenue. Named for the 1743 (extant) Peters family house. (1853)

Bentley. Above Philmont Avenue, at border of Montgomery and Bucks Counties. (1980s)

Black Bottom. Vic. 40th and Market Streets north and east to Haverford Avenue.

Blockley. Large township on west bank of Schuylkill River, north of Kingsessing Township. Name later used for an almshouse, then a building in Philadelphia General Hospital. (1705–1861)

Blocks, The. At foot of Hays Lane, in Manayunk.

Blue Bell. Woodland Avenue and Cobbs Creek. (1939)

Blue Bell Hill. Vic. Walnut Lane and Johnson Street, north of Wissahickon Creek.

Bonnafon. Vic. Wilmington & Baltimore Railroad station along Cobbs Creek near Darby Road.

Branchtown. Named for Branchtown Hotel, Old York Road near Church Lane. (1839–1910)

Brewerytown. East bank of Schuylkill River, north of Fairmount. (1920s)

Brickyard. Irish section of Germantown.

Bridesburg, Kirkbridesburg. Along Delaware River north of Frankford Creek, named for ferry operator and bridge owner Joseph Kirkbride. (1839)

Brideton. Vic. east end of Columbia Avenue Bridge, now in Fairmount Park.

Burholme. Vic. Cottman and Oxford Avenues and Verree Road; named for mansion. (early 20th c.)

Bush Hill. Between 12th and 19th Streets, Vine Street to Fairmount Avenue; named for mid-18th century house later occupied by Andrew Hamilton. (1808)

Bustleton, Busseltown. West of Roosevelt Boulevard, north of Pennypack Creek, adjacent to North Philadelphia Airport. After mid-18th century Busseltown Tavern. (1839)

Butcherville. Vic. Haddington.

Byberry. West of Roosevelt Boulevard, above Somerton Avenue to Bucks County line. Settled by Swedes, renamed by English. (1703)

Byberry Cross, Plumbsock. Junction of Byberry and Bensalem turnpikes. (1839–1861)

Byberry Point. Where Bensalem Road branches from Bustleton Avenue. (1839–1861)

California. Vic. Swampoodle.

Callowhill. Vic. Second and Callowhill Streets. (1768)

Camac's Woods. 11th Street and Montgomery Avenue site for circuses, balloon ascensions, and athletic events. (1850)

Campington. Vic. west of Second and Green Streets, where British troops camped in the 1750s. (1808)

Carcus Hook. Vic. 84th Street (Hook Road) and Buist Avenue, north of Eastwick.

Carpenter's Island. North of Hog Island. (1750)

Carroll Park. Between Lansdowne and Girard Avenues, from 52nd to 63rd Streets. (1970s)

Castor. Vic. Castor and Cottman Avenues. (1980)

Cedarbrook. Vic. Wadsworth Avenue, Stenton to Cheltenham Avenues. (1970s)

Cedar Grove, Helltown, Pleasantville. Vic. Limekiln Pike, above Washington Lane.

Cedar Grove, Whitaker's Hollow. Vic. Tacony Creek, Olney and Asylum Roads.

Cedar Park. Larchwood Avenue between 46th and 52nd Streets south to SEPTA tracks. (1970s)

Center City. Philadelphia proper, river to river, Vine to South Streets. (1970s)

Chestnut Hill. Vic. Germantown Avenue, Cresheim Valley Road to Northwestern Avenue. (1808)

Chinatown, China Town. Arch to Vine Streets, from Eighth to 11th Streets; first Chinese business opened on 10th Street in 1850. (1926)

139

Crescentville

Chingihameng. Included Society Hill and part of Northern Liberties. (1655)

Clearview. East of Cobbs Creek to Lindbergh Boulevard, between 78th and 84th Streets. (1888)

Cloverhill. West of Frankford, south of Tacony Creek and Juniata Parks. (1808)

Cobbs Creek. Vic. Cobbs Creek Park, from Baltimore Avenue to Market Street. (1970s)

Cohocksink, Cohocksink Village. Vic. Sixth Street and Germantown Avenue. From the Native *cuweuchacsink*, or "pine woods." (1839)

Collegeville. Above Holmesburg, along Frankford Avenue north of Pennypack Creek. (1839–1910)

Comlyville. Vic. Frankford Creek, site of a powder magazine.

Cooksocky, Wood's Landing. Vic. East Falls, north of Mendenhall Ferry, on west bank of Schuylkill River.

Coopersville. See *West Kensington.*

Coquanoc, Cuwequenaku. Native village once occupying a portion of Center City.

Corktown. Irish section vic. Mantua.

Country Lane. West of Bustleton Avenue and Route 532. (1980s)

Cowtown, Kelleyville. Vic. Chelten Avenue and Morton Street, in Wingohocking Valley.

Crefelt. Tract north of Chestnut Hill to Streeper's Mill.

Crescentville, Grubtown, Grubbstown. Vic. Adams, Rising Sun, and Tabor Avenues. Named for early 19th century rope factory. (1839)

Cresheim, Kriesheim. Vic. Washington Lane to Limekiln Pike.

Crestmont Farms. Along Bucks County line, at Poquessing Creek. (1970s)

Cross Roads. Vic. Byberry Road and Dunk's Ferry Road. (1839)

Dearnley Park. Between Dearnley Street and Wigard Avenue, west of Ridge Avenue, in Roxborough. (1980s)

Devil's Pocket. South of Lombard Street, east of 27th Street and north of Washington Avenue.

Dogtown. See *Bebberstown.*

Doverville. New name chosen for Roseville (over Goosetown, Geisseville, Bridgewater, and Christian Shore) by "respectable inhabitants" of village along Frankford Road, just below Frankford Creek. (1845)

Dungan Hill. Bustleton Avenue near Sandiford.

140

Fishtown

Dunlap. Vic. Haverford Avenue and Market Street, 46th to 52nd Streets. (1980s)
Dyottsville. Vic. south of Port Richmond. Named for Dyott glass works. (1839)
East Falls, Falls of the Schuylkill, Falls Village. East side of Schuylkill River, about ½ mile south of mouth of Wissahickon Creek. Named in early 19th century for river rapids that disappeared after completion of the dam at Fairmount. (1946)
East Mount Airy. Mount Airy east of Germantown Avenue. (1970s)
East Oak Lane. Godfrey Avenue to Cheltenham Avenue, east of Broad Street. (1970s)
Eastwick, Gladwyn. Northwest of Philadelphia International Airport, vic. Heinz National Wildlife Refuge. Named for Andrew M. Eastwick. (1946)
Elmwood. North of Eastwick below Woodland Avenue. (1888)
Evergreen. South of South Street, east of Grays Ferry. (1808)
Fackenland. South of Frankford Creek; German for "fine land." (17th c.)
Fairhill. Front to 10th Street, Cumberland Street to Allegheny Avenue. (1980s)

Fairmount, Art Museum Area. West of Broad Street below Girard Avenue to Spring Garden Street. (1970s)
Falls of the Schuylkill, Falls Village. See *East Falls.*
Far Northeast. East of Roosevelt Boulevard, north of Pennypack Creek. (1970s)
Feltonville. South of Roosevelt Boulevard, vic. Wyoming Avenue. (1855)
Fenian Hill. Section of Somerville, vic. Church Lane and Limekiln Pike.
Fernhill. Vic. Wissahickon and Wayne Avenues to Manheim Street and Roosevelt Boulevard. (1980)
Fern Rock. Between Olney and Oak Lane. Named for estate of Arctic explorer Elisha Kent Kane. (1899)
Fisher's Hollow. Vic. mouth of Frankford's Mill Creek on Delaware River; reached by Fisher's Lane.
Fishtown. Along Delaware River below Kensington. Legend has it that Charles Dickens named the neighborhood in 1842, but the use is 20th century. (1920)
Five Points. See *Aston.*
Five Points. Vic. Castor and Oxford Avenues, northeast of Frankford. (1855–1910)

141

Frankford

Flat Iron. South of Devil's Pocket.

Flat Rock. See *Manayunk.*

Forepaugh's Row. South of Stenton Avenue and Wister Street, on Laveer Street, built as part of winter quarters for Forepaugh's circus. (late 19th c.)

Fox Chase. Southwest of Pennypack Park along Montgomery County border. Named for an inn whose sign depicted fox hunters. (1839)

Fraleyville. Vic. Frankford near former arsenal where in 1816 Frederick Fraley began manufacturing small arms and ammunition. (1839)

Francisville, Vineyard (1808). South of Poplar Street and Ridge Avenue, where streets run perpendicular to Ridge. (1839)

Frankford. West of Bridesburg and Wissinoming, east of Roosevelt Boulevard. Settled by Germans. (17th c.)

Franklintown. Vine to Callowhill Streets, vic. 17th Street. (1980s)

Franklinville. Vic. Erie Avenue to Westmoreland Street, between Broad Street and Sedgley Avenue. (1888)

Franklinville. Vic. Third and Butler Streets.

Franklinville. See *Bebberstown.*

Frog Hollow. Site of Wister and Smith Mills,

near Central High School.

Gander Hill. West of Swampoodle.

Garden Court. Locust Street to Hazel Avenue, 46th to 52nd Streets. (1970)

Germantown. Between East Falls, Mount Airy, West Oak Lane, and Logan. Original center: Germantown Avenue and Church Lane. (1682)

Germany Hill. Western portion of Roxborough from Parker Avenue to Fountain Street, Ridge Avenue to Schuylkill River. (1980)

Gillietown. Vic. 27th and Dauphin Streets.

Girard Estate. Between Porter Street and Passyunk Avenue. (1970s)

Girard Point. At mouth of Schuylkill River, once known for massive grain elevators.

Gladwyn. See *Eastwick.*

Glen Willow. In Manayunk, vic. The Blocks.

Glenwood. Vic. North Philadelphia Station to York Street. (1990)

Goat Hill. Germantown, east of Fenian Hill, vic. Somerville.

Godfrey. Village near Chelten Avenue and Wister Street. (1890s)

Good Intent. Vic. 46th and Market Streets, site of Good Intent Mills. (1849)

Goosetown. Locust to Pine Streets, 17th to 20th Streets. (1825–1850)

Grays Ferry. East bank of Schuylkill River above Point Breeze. (1970s)

Green Hill. Northeast of Francisville, near 17th Street and Girard Avenue. (1808–1849)

Greenland. Village on west bank of Schuylkill River near Ford Road.

Greenville. Vic. Powelton. (1839)

Greenwich Island, Greenwich Point. Formerly Drufwe Island, Isle de Raisins, or Grape Island, the eastern end of which jutted into Delaware River. (1839–1899)

Grubtown, Grubbstown. See *Crescentville.*

Gunner's Run. See *Aramingo.*

Haddington. North of Market Street between 65th and 70th Streets. (1816)

Hamilton Village, Hamilton Ville, Hamiltonville. Schuylkill River at Market Street west to 36th Street, between Lancaster and Woodland Avenues. (1809–1839)

Hamlet, The. Attempt to settle a village on Pell Hill farm, vic. Girard College. (1811)

Harisville. On York Road above Rising Sun Avenue.

Harper's Hollow. Vic. 18th Street and Olney Avenue.

Harrisburg. Vic. Welsh and Ashton Roads. Started as a settlement of freed slaves. (1839–1910)

Harrowgate. Vic. Venango Street and Kensington Avenue, between Kensington and Frankford. Named after a 1780s health resort established there. (1888)

Hartranft. Lehigh Avenue to Diamond Street, Broad to Fairhill Streets. (1970s)

Hatshop Hill. See *Sunnycliff.*

Hawthorne. Between southwest Center City and Bella Vista. (1970s)

Heartsville. Vic. Frankford Avenue and Heart (now Hart) Lane, above Somerset Street. (1839)

Helltown. See *Cedar Grove.*

Hestonville. Along Lancaster Avenue south of George's Hill, the country seat, ca. 1800, of the Heston family. (1839)

High Rue. West of Roosevelt Boulevard, between Bustleton Avenue and Welsh Road. (1980s)

Hitesville. See *Jacksonville.*

Hollinsville. Village at intersection of Bristol turnpike and road from Tacony below Holmesburg. (1839–1861)

Holme Circle. In loop of Pennypack Creek at Holme Avenue and Welsh Road. (1980s)

Holmesburg. Below Pennypack Creek, approximately at Rhawn Street and Frankford Avenue. Named for Thomas Holme, William Penn's surveyor, who settled there. (1839)

Hopkinsville. Vic. Haddington.

Hunting Park. South of Roosevelt Boulevard, east of Germantown Avenue, north of SEPTA's R7 line. (1976)

Irishtown. See *Somerville.*

Irish Tract. Vic. 18th and Wharton Streets.

Ivy Hill. Vic. Ivy Hill Cemetery, north of East Mount Airy. (1980)

Jacksonville, Hitesville. South of Nicetown, vic. Germantown Avenue. (1861)

Jewtown. Vic. Alburn and Weikel Streets, in Richmond. (1870–1940s)

Juniata Park, Juniata. South of Frankford Creek at Hunting Park and north of SEPTA's R7 line, between Feltonville and Richmond. (1946)

Kelleyville. See *Cowtown.*

Kenderton. Vic. Broad Street and Germantown Avenue. Named for Kenderton Smith, lawyer and landowner. (1808–1861)

Kensington. From Delaware River to Front Street, where Kensington Avenue bears northeast. Named by Anthony Palmer, an English sea captain. (1730)

Kingsessing. South of railroad tracks and Baltimore Avenue to Woodland Avenue, west to Cobbs Creek. From the Native term for "place where there is a meadow." (1712)

King Village, Kings Village. Between Point Breeze and Grays Ferry. (1980s)

Kirkbridesburg. See *Bridesburg.*

Knightsville. On Byberry-Bensalem turnpike at Moreland Road. Named for Leonard and Judge Jonathan T. Knight. (1839)

Knorr. Oxford Avenue and Martins' Mill Road. (1839)

Kriesheim. See *Cresheim.*

LaGrange. Between Bustleton and Holmesburg, vic. Bustleton Avenue and Pennypack Creek. (1855–1895)

Laniganville. Vic. 36th Street and Girard Avenue.

Kensington

Lansdowne Village. Failed real estate venture, 40th to 50th Streets north of Parkside Avenue, that became part of site for Centennial Exhibition. (mid-19th c.)

Lawncrest. Combination of Lawndale and Crescentville; on border with Cheltenham Township, Montgomery County. (1970s)

Lawndale. Near Rising Sun and Oxford Avenues, south of Cottman Avenue. Named by a real estate developer. (1946)

Leverington. Adjacent to Manayunk along Ridge Avenue, vic. Gorgas Lane. (1861)

Levezytown, Livezeytown. Vic. Rhawn Street and Verree Road. (1855)

Lexington Park. Bounded by Pennypack Creek on east, Roosevelt Boulevard on west, below Rhawn Street and above Cottman Avenue. (1970s)

Lindley. Village at Seventh Street and Lindley Avenue.

Little Britain. North of Wayne and Chelten Avenues, vic. West Price Street.

Livezeytown. See *Levezytown.*

Logan. Above Roosevelt Boulevard, south of Olney. (1970s)

Logan Circle. Area from Schuylkill River to near Broad Street, north to Spring Garden Street, and south to about Market Street. (1976)

Logan's Hill. See *Negley's Hill.*

Lower Tioga. Bounded by Broad Street, Westmoreland Street, and the railroad. (1980)

Ludlow. East of Broad Street, vic. Spring Garden Street. (1970s)

Lumar Park. Below Somerton, bounded by Red Lion Road, Bustleton Avenue, and Woodhaven Road. (1980)

McCartersville. South of Crescentville, along New Second Street Road. (1839–1910)

MacLean. Belmont Avenue and Conshohocken State Road.

McNabbtown. Village at SEPTA's Washington Lane station, near Awbury Arboretum.

Manatawna. Up Ridge Avenue from Andorra, near Manatawna Avenue. Native term meaning "where we drink liquor." (1888–1910)

Manayunk. North of Schuylkill River, upstream from mouth of Wissahickon Creek. From the Native term meaning "where we go to drink." Renamed from Flat Rock after a brief interlude as Udoravia. (1821)

Mantua. Across from Zoo at railroad tracks to 30th Street Station. Laid about 1809. (1839)

Martinsville. East of Front Street, between Wolf and Porter Streets, vic. Greenwich Point Road and Southwark Canal. (1861–1899)

Mayfair. Cottman and Frankford Avenues to Roosevelt Boulevard. Named by neighborhood civic association. (1929)

Maylandsville, Maylandville. Vic. Darby Road, at crossing of Mill Creek, below Woodlands

Nicetown

Cemetery. (1839)

Meadows, The. Vic. south of 84th Street, east of Darby Creek, north of Heinz National Wildlife Refuge, west of SEPTA's R1 tracks. (1980)

Mechanicstown, Mechanics Town, Pumpkinstown, Pumpkin Town (1839). Germantown Avenue, Bethlehem Pike to Bells Mill Road. (1855)

Mechanicsville. At border with Bucks County, southeast of Roosevelt Boulevard. (1839)

Middleton. Upper end of Germantown Avenue, now site of Chestnut Hill College. Named for Joseph Middleton. (1839)

Mifflin's Hollow. Along Midvale Avenue in East Falls.

Milestown. Along Old York Road, north of Branchtown, above Oak Lane. (1800–1910)

Millbrook. Below Woodhaven Road in the Northeast. (1970s)

Mill Creek. North of Haverford Avenue, south of Girard Avenue, 45th to 52nd Streets. (1970s)

Modena Park. East of North Philadelphia Airport at Morrell Avenue. (1970s)

Molesville. Vic. Haddington.

Mondal. Village near Cobbs Creek and Woodland Avenue, with a windmill and an early grist mill.

Monroe Village, Monroeville. Vic. railroad station, 48th Street and Lancaster Avenue. (1849)

Morrell Park. North of Grant Avenue, east of North Philadelphia Airport. (1970s)

Morrisville, Morris City. Vic. Callowhill Street, 22nd to 25th Streets; also vic. Kelly Drive near Girard Avenue. (1830)

Morton. South of West Oak Lane, east of East Mount Airy, west of Broad Street. (1970s)

Mount Airy. North of Johnson Street, south of Cresheim Valley Road, along Germantown Avenue. (1839)

Mount Moriah. East of Cobbs Creek, vic. Kingsessing Avenue. (1980s)

Mount Pleasant, Mount Pleasant Village. On Germantown Avenue, vic. Mount Pleasant Avenue. (1800–1910)

Mount Vernon. In Manayunk, vic. foot of Hermitage Street.

Moyamensing. South central Philadelphia, between Passyunk and Wicaco. Said to mean "unclean place" or, more literally, "place of pigeon droppings." Also "place of meeting." (18th c.)

Neck, The. Southernmost part of South

Old City

Philadelphia, below Moore Street.

Negley's Hill, Logan's Hill. Along Germantown Avenue, near Wayne Junction.

New Philadelphia. A town proposed for vic. Spring Garden Street, 19th Street to Schuylkill River. (1799)

Nicetown. Southeast of Germantown, below Wayne Junction Station. Named for de Neus, Dutch Huguenots who settled there about 1700. (1808)

Nittabaconck. Native settlement on east bank of Schuylkill River, vic. East Falls.

Normandy, Normandy Village. East of Roosevelt Boulevard, vic. Woodhaven and Byberry Roads. (1980s)

North Penn Village. Vic. north of Susquehanna Avenue, between 25th and 30th Streets. (1861–1899)

North Philadelphia. Most of area north of Center City and south of Logan.

Northeast Philadelphia. Between Shackamaxon and city limits.

Northern Liberties. North of Spring Garden Street, on Delaware River, to approximately Girard Avenue. (1680s)

Northwood. Vic. Adams Avenue at Roosevelt Boulevard, east to Frankford. (1970s)

Nya Vasa. Swedish settlement west of Schuylkill River and north of Philadelphia International Airport, opposite Girard Point. (17th c.)

Oakdale. Vic. pleasure park at 12th and Huntingdon Streets, near Lehigh and Germantown Avenues.

Oak Lane. Northeast of Broad Street and Godfrey Avenue. Named for a landmark oak tree. (1895)

Ogontz. From Ogontz Avenue to Broad Street above Olney Avenue. (1980s)

Olde City, Old City. Along Delaware River, north of Walnut Street, south of Spring Garden Street, west to Fourth Street. (1970s)

Olde Kensington, Old Kensington. Southern portion of Kensington, north of Northern Liberties, west of Fishtown. (1976)

Olney. Vic. Fifth and Chew Streets, west of railroad tracks to Fox Chase and east of Melrose Park. Named for estate of Alexander Wilson. (1855)

Orchard Park. Island Road near 81st Street, north of Eastwick. (1890s)

Oregon. Vic. Swampoodle. (1840)

Overbrook. West along City Avenue near Lancaster Avenue, where Pennsylvania

Railroad built a station in 1867. (1910s)

Overbrook Farms. West of Overbrook, along Haverford Avenue. (1895)

Overbrook Park. Vic. City Avenue and Cobbs Creek. (1970s)

Oxford Circle. North of traffic circle where Roosevelt Boulevard and Cheltenham, Oxford, and Castor Avenues intersect. (1920s)

Oxford Village. West of Oxford Avenue, south of Lawncrest. (1980s)

Packer Park. At southern end of Broad Street, north of Franklin Delano Roosevelt Park and west of Broad Street.

Panorama Hill. Section in the village from 49th to 53rd Streets, south of Girard Avenue. Now Cathedral Cemetery. (1853)

Paradise. At Hunting Park and Ridge Avenues, east of Schuylkill River bend, north of Strawberry Bridge, vic. Laurel Hill Cemetery. (1970s)

Parkside. Vic. Fairmount Park at Parkside Avenue, west of Belmont Avenue, bordering Wynnefield. (1980s)

Parkwood, Parkwood Manor. Near Bucks County border south of Mechanicsville, northeast of Woodhaven Road. (1970s)

Paschall. Vic. Cobbs Creek Park and Chester Avenue. (1970s)

Paschallville, Paschalville, Paschall Ville. Vic. Paschall Avenue and Island Road. (1861–1910)

Passyunk, Passayunk, Passyonck, Passuming, Passajungh, Perslajongh, Passajon, Paisajungh. All related to Native pachsegink, meaning "in the valley" or "place between the hills." Areas south of Tasker Avenue. The word is currently pronounced PASH-yunk. (1680s)

Passyunk Homes. Vic. 26th Street and Penrose Avenue. (1980s)

Passyunkville. Vic. Point Breeze. (1811)

Pauls Run. North of Country Lane, west of Bustleton Avenue, south of Red Lion Road. (1980s)

Pelham. Vic. Carpenter Lane and Germantown Avenue, the former Carpenter estate. (1893)

Pemichpacka. Native settlement, meaning "deep, dead water" or "a pond not having current," along Pennypack Creek.

Penn-Knox. In Germantown, from Manheim Street to Chelten Avenue between Wayne and Germantown Avenues. (1980s)

Pennsport. South of Washington Avenue, along Delaware River. (1970s)

Pennypack. Between North Philadelphia Airport and Pennypack Park. (1970s)

Pennypack Woods, Pennypack Village. Below Holme Avenue, east of Holme Circle, south of Academy Gardens. (1970s)

Pittville, Pittsville. Vic. Limekiln Pike and Haines Street. (1855–1910)

Pleasant Hill. Easternmost section of Torresdale, below Poquessing Creek. (1888)

Pleasantville. See Cedar Grove.

Pleasantville. See Somerton.

Pleasantville, Terrapin Town, Tortleberg. Vic. east of Somerton. (1839)

Plumbsock. See Byberry Cross.

Poetquessing, Poanpissing, Achpoquesing. Native for "a place abounding with mice" on banks of Poquessing Creek in the Northeast. (17th c.)

Point Breeze. East of Schuylkill River, north of Passyunk Avenue, south of Grays Ferry Avenue. (1895)

Point-No-Point. South of mouth of Frankford Creek, now Bridesburg.

Poor Island. Along Delaware River near Shackamaxon, now part of Port Richmond.

Poplar. North of Chinatown, between Spring Garden and Northern Liberties. (1970s)

Port Richmond. Along Delaware River between Kensington and Frankford Creek. In 1728 mansion "Richmond Hall" was named for a London suburb. Port added due to riverfront commerce. (1970s)

Powelton, Powelton Village. South of Lancaster Avenue and Spring Garden Street, east of 42nd Street, northwest of Powelton and Lancaster Avenues. (1839)

Princeton Station. See Rockdale.

Prospect Heights. North of Somerton. (1890s)

Province Island. In Kingsessing. (1839)

Pulaskitown. On west side of Germantown Avenue.

Pumpkin Town, Pumpkinstown. See Mechanicstown.

Queen Lane Manor. Vic. campus of William Penn Charter School.

Queen Village. Below South Street, along Delaware River, to vic. Eighth and Carpenter Streets. (1970s)

Ramcat. See Schuylkill.

Paschallville

Rhawnhurst. At Rhawn Street and Bustleton Avenue, north of Cottman Avenue, west of Roosevelt Boulevard. Named for George and William Rhawn by real estate developers. (1924)

Richmond. On Delaware River, south of Frankford Creek, east of Kensington and Frankford Avenues. (1839)

Risdon's Ferry. Vic. Torresdale on Delaware River. Named for John Risdon, whose ferry ran from foot of Fitler Street.

Rising Sun, Sunville. East of Temple University Hospital. Named for a tavern at Germantown Avenue and Old York Road. (1839–1899)

Rittenhouse. Southwest quarter of Center City, vic. Rittenhouse Square. (1970s)

RittenhouseTown, Rittenhouse Town, Rittenhouse. In Fairmount Park, vic. Lincoln Drive and Wissahickon Avenue. Site of first paper mill in America in the 1690s. (1970s)

River Park. Vic. Schuylkill River, near City Avenue, adjacent to Fairmount Park. (1980)

Rockdale, Princeton Station. Last place in Philadelphia along Schuylkill River, just before Miquon.

Rockville, Rocky Hill. Northwest of Cedar Hill Cemetery, vic. Oxford Circle. (1839–1899)

Rosehill. Vic. C Street and Indiana Avenue.

Rose of Bath. See *Bath Town.*

Roseville. On Frankford Avenue just below Frankford Creek. Renamed Doverville in 1845. (1839)

Rowlandville. Vic. Tacony Creek and Wyoming Avenue. Named for Benjamin Rowland shovel factory. (19th c.)

Roxborough, Rocksborrow, Roxborro. Between Wissahickon Creek and Schuylkill River, above Manayunk. (1706)

Ryers. North of Cottman Avenue at border with Montgomery County. (1980)

Sandiford. Between Fox Chase and Holmesburg, on Bustleton Avenue. (1855–1910)

Sandy Hill. Along Bustleton and Smithfield turnpike, north of River Road. (1839)

Saunders Park. Vic. 40th Street, Lancaster to Powelton Avenues. (1980s)

Saw Dust Village. On a hill south of the site of Central High School.

Schuylkill. East of Schuylkill River, from Christian Street to Grays Ferry Avenue, to 23rd Street, to about Pine Street. (1970s)

Shackamaxon, Shackaemuxen. Known by Swedes (40 years before English arrived) by the Native term meaning "place of eels," but considered "meeting place of chiefs." (17th c.)

Shantytown. Along Parkside (then Elm)

Avenue from 41st to 44th Streets until destroyed by a fire. (mid-19th c.)

Sharswood. East of Brewerytown, vic. Girard College. (1970s)

Shawmont. Along Schuylkill River, beyond Manayunk. (1980s)

Sherwood. At Baltimore Avenue between 50th and 56th Streets. (1990)

Smearsburg. Vic. Manheim and Wister Streets in Germantown. (1890s)

Smithfield, Smithville. See *Somerton.*

Smoky Hollow. Vic. Rising Sun Avenue and Wingohocking Street, near Greenmount Cemetery.

Society Hill. Walnut Street south to Pine Street, Delaware River west to Seventh Street. Southerly portion of original settlement by Free Society of Traders. (1681)

Somerton, Smithfield, Smithville, Pleasantville. Bustleton Avenue and Byberry Road. (1720)

Somerville, Irishtown. Church Lane and Limekiln Pike. Vic. Fenian Hill and Goat Hill. (1888–1910)

Sommerhausen, Somerhausen, Summerhausen. Now Chestnut Hill. Named by settlers of Germantown after birthplace of their leader, Francis Daniel Pastorius. Northwest along Germantown Avenue from Mermaid Lane to Chestnut Hill Avenue. (1689)

Southbrook Park. Vic. 28th Street, New Hope Street and Vare Avenue. (1980s)

South Philadelphia. South of South Street, between Delaware and Schuylkill Rivers.

Southwark. West of Pennsport from Mifflin Street to Washington Avenue, Fourth to Eighth Streets. (1762)

Southwest Center City. From Lombard Street to about Oregon Avenue, Broad Street to Schuylkill River. (1976)

Southwest Philadelphia. From Schuylkill River west to city limits, SEPTA's R3 tracks.

Southwest Schuylkill. Above Elmwood, along Schuylkill River, vic. SEPTA's R3 tracks.

Spring Brook. Northeast of Frankford and Cottman Avenues. (1855)

Springettsbury Manor. From Vine Street to Willow Street, Delaware to Schuylkill Rivers. Named for William Penn's first wife, Gulielma Springett.

Spring Garden. North of Benjamin Franklin

Parkway to Fairmount Avenue, Broad Street to Schuylkill River. (1808)

Spruce Hill. West of University of Pennsylvania, Locust Street to Woodlands Cemetery, to vic. 46th Street. (1970s)

Squirrel Hill. From Kingsessing Avenue to Windsor Avenue, vic. 46th Street. (1980s)

Stanborough. Vic. Frankford Avenue and Clearfield Street.

Stanton. Between Strawberry Mansion and Broad Street. (1970s)

Steinberg. Village along Frankford Road, laid out by Robert Brook and G. W. Steinhauer. (1815)

Stenton. Between West Oak Lane and Ivy Hill, Mount Airy to Montgomery County. (1946)

Stewards Glenn. East of Normandy, west of Academy Road. (1980s)

Stonehouse Lane. South of Fifth and Ritner Streets. (1920)

Strawberry Mansion. East side of Schuylkill River and Fairmount Park, at 33rd and Diamond Streets. Named for 18th-century mansion. (mid-20th c.)

Summerdale. East of Crescentville, between Roosevelt Boulevard, Langdon Street, and Oxford Avenue. (1970s)

Sunnycliff, Hatshop Hill. Along Green Lane in Manayunk. Highest point in Philadelphia. (before 1930)

Sunville. See *Rising Sun.*

Swampoodle. Junction of three railroad lines, vic. Lehigh Avenue and 22nd Streets. (before 1926)

Tabor. Site of Einstein Hospital. Named for biblical Mount Tabor. (1870s)

Tacony. On Delaware River west to Frankford Avenue, between Holmesburg and Wissinoming. Early Swedish records spell it Taokanink, a Native word for "forest" or "wilderness." (1677)

Taney. From Pine to Bainbridge Streets, 25th Street west to Schuylkill River. (1980s)

Terrapin Town. See *Pleasantville.*

Texas. Vic. Swampoodle. (1840s)

Thayersville. Vic. Haddington.

Tioga. North of Allegheny Avenue at Broad Street, vic. Tioga Street. (1854)

Torresdale, Torrisdale. Along Delaware River between Holmesburg and Bucks County.

Shackamaxon

Named by Charles Macalester for his Scotland home. (1850)

Tortleberg. See *Pleasantville.*

Uberville. Vic. Ridge Avenue, near Oxford Street.

Udoravia. See *Manayunk.*

Unionville. Village north of Feltonville. (1860s)

University City. Vic. University of Pennsylvania and Drexel University. (1970s)

Upper Holmesburg. Delaware River and Pennypack Creek, Frankford Avenue to Willits Road. (1976)

Upper Roxborough. Northwest of Roxborough, southeast of Andorra. (1970s)

Verreeville, Verree's Mills. Northeast of Fox Chase in Bustleton. Named for John P. Verree, politician and mill owner. (1839–1910)

Ville Hartwell. Chestnut Hill, Rex Avenue vic. Wissahickon Creek. (1855)

Vineyard. See *Francisville.*

Volunteer Town, Volunteertown. Between Frankford and Fox Chase. Named for a tavern. (1839–1899)

Walnut Hill. Market to Locust Streets, 46th to 52nd Streets. (1980s)

Washington Square. West of Society Hill from Market to South Streets. (1970s)

Washington Square West. Between Eighth and Broad Streets in Center City, south of Market Street. (1970s)

Weccacoe, Wicaco, Wichacomoca. Eastern half of South Philadelphia, originally a Native village. Name means "dwelling place." (18th c.)

West End. Vic. 61st Street and Larchwood Avenue. (1888–1895)

West Falls. See *Whitestown.*

West Kensington, Coopersville (1861–1910). Vic. Amtrak roadbed, between Front and Third Streets. (1970s)

Westminster. North of 52nd Street and Westminster Avenue.

West Mount Airy. North of Wissahickon Creek, east of Cresheim Creek. (1970s)

West Oak Lane. Stenton Avenue to Cheltenham Avenue, Broad Street toward Ivy Hill. Named by real estate developers. (1925)

West Park. Below River Park, near Belmont Reservoir, adjacent to Fairmount Park. (1980s)

West Philadelphia. From west bank of Schuylkill River along Market Street.

West Powelton. Powelton Avenue to Lancaster Avenues, vic. 42nd Street. (1980s)

Neighborhoods

West Torresdale. Near Morrell Park, adjacent to North Philadelphia Airport. (1970s)

Wharton. Along Wharton Street, west of Pennsport, east of Point Breeze. (1970s)

Wheat Sheaf. Vic. Bustleton and Cottman Avenues. (1899)

Whitaker's Hollow. See *Cedar Grove.*

White Hall. Borough northwest of Bridesburg, from U.S. Arsenal west to Frankford Creek and Little Tacony Creek. (1849–1899)

Whitestown, West Falls. West side of Schuylkill River, opposite East Falls. Named for Josiah White's wire factory. (1820s)

Whitman. South on Delaware River, below Pennsport, vic. Second and Wolf Streets. (1970s)

Whitman Park. South of Whitman, Oregon Avenue to Porter Street, Front to Third Streets. (1980s)

Wicaco, Wichacomoca. See *Weccacoe.*

Willow Grove. West of Schuylkill River, south of Girard Avenue, east of Lancaster Avenue. (1808)

Winchester Park. Vic. Pennypack Park, north of Holmesburg. (1970s)

Wissahickon. West of Wissahickon Creek, adja-

cent to Roxborough. (1910)

Wissinoming. Along Delaware River, north of Bridesburg, east of Frankford. From the Native term for "place where the grapes grew." (1895)

Wister. Bounded by Germantown Avenue, Belfield Avenue, Wister Street, and Chelten Avenue. (1970s)

Wood's Landing. See *Cooksocky.*

Woodvale Cottage. East of Broad Street, south of Columbia Avenue.

Wylietown. Part of Francisville near plant of Keystone Watch Case Company, 19th and Wylie Streets.

Wynnefield. West of Parkside Avenue, north of Lancaster Avenue, east of St. Joseph's University. Named for Thomas Wynne, William Penn's physician, who resided at 52nd Street and Woodbine Avenue. (1920s)

Wynnefield Heights. On Montgomery County line at Belmont Avenue, to George's Hill Drive. (1970s)

Wyoming Villa. Vic. D Street and Wyoming Avenue.

Yorktown. North of Poplar, west of Ludlow. (1970s) ■

Sources: Maps and atlases are listed first, in chronological order. They are followed by books and articles, listed alphabetically by author.

Hills Record & Historical Map or a Plan of the City of Philadelphia and environs (John Hills, 1808); D. H. Kennedy, *A Map of the County of Philadelphia* (Charles Ellet, Jr., 1839); J. C. Sidney, *Map of the City of Philadelphia* (Smith & Wistar, 1849); *Scott's Map of the Consolidated City of Philadelphia* (Scott & Moore, 1855); D. J. Lake and S. N. Beers, *Map of the vicinity of Philadelphia* (J. E. Gillette, 1861); *Lippincott's Pronouncing Gazetteer* (J. B. Lippincott, 1862); G. Wm. Baist, *Baist's Atlas of the City of Philadelphia Penna* (Philadelphia, 1888); George W. and Walter S. Bromley, *Atlas of the City of Philadelphia* (Philadelphia, 1895); *Official map showing the system of lines of the Union Traction Co. in Phila.* (1899); George W. and Walter S. Bromley, *Atlas of the City of Philadelphia* (Philadelphia, 1910); Philadelphia Transportation Company, *Street Map of Philadelphia & Vicinity* (1946); Hagstrom's *Greater Philadelphia/Camden Atlas* (5th ed., 1987); *SEPTA's Philadelphia Street and Transit Map* (1990); ADC's *Street Map of Philadelphia Vicinity and Delaware County, Pennsylvania* (12th ed., n.d.).

William Bucke Campbell, "Old Towns and Districts of Philadelphia," *Philadelphia History*, Vol. 4, No. 5 (City History Society of Philadelphia, 1942); John Daly and Allen Weinberg, *Genealogy of Philadelphia County Subdivisions* (City of Philadelphia Department of Records, 2nd ed., 1966); Joseph Jackson, *Encyclopedia of Philadelphia* (National Historical Association, 1931); Isadore Lichstein, editor, *The Bulletin Almanac* (The Evening and Sunday Bulletin, 1973); George Morgan, *The City of Firsts* (Historical Publication Society in Philadelphia, 1926); Christopher Morley, *Travels in Philadelphia* (David McKay, 1920); Philadelphia City Planning Commission, *Census Tracts and Blocks* (1980); Philadelphia City Planning Commission, *Philadelphia: City of Neighborhoods* (1976).

You can request a hearing if you want to dispute your parking ticket (instructions are on the back of the ticket). Otherwise, pay the fine within eight calendar days. If you don't, a $23.00 penalty is added to the fine. And remember that your car can get the boot—a tire lock—if you have three or more unpaid parking tickets.

If you're late getting to your car to feed more money into the meter and discover that you've already been ticketed, don't stuff the ticket into your pocket and put more money in the meter. If the meter expires again, you'll be ticketed again. Leave the ticket on your windshield and put your meter money back in your pocket to help pay the fine; you won't be ticketed twice for a parking violation in the same space.

If you have questions about a parking ticket and have a touch-tone phone, you can call the Parking Violations Branch Automated System at 561-3636. You'll never need to talk to a live person to learn about disputing tickets, the status of a current ticket (have it handy), changing a hearing date, paying tickets—even installment plans for fines adding up to $100 or more.

THE 1961 PARKING RIOT

Mayor Richardson Dilworth thought he had a scheme to help solve South Philadelphia's parking woes. It involved a new $40 parking fee for residents. In order to fully explain the plan, and determine neighborhood reaction, Dilworth arrived at the George Washington Elementary School at 5th and Federal Streets on July 24, 1961. He was met by more than 1,700 jeering protesters. Dilworth remained at the head of the auditorium through the melee, even as rocks smashed a few windows. After two hours, the Mayor left under heavy police guard, his case unmade.

❖

SEPTA's Schuylkill River tunnel is 74 feet below street level—about 30 feet below the actual river bed.

Ticketed Again?

Philadelphia has approximately 6,000 metered and otherwise timed parking spaces in its central business and shopping areas (and thousands more elsewhere in the city). It also has a long list of parking regulations and a highly efficient—some would say over-zealous—enforcement system. On an average day, officials write about 4,500 tickets, tow away over 60 cars, and boot almost 30 more. On that same average day, the Philadelphia Parking Authority collects close to $50,000 in coins from parking meters.

Nothing is random; it just seems that way. There is a system behind everything at the Parking Authority.

Meter rates are either $1.00 or $.50 an hour, depending upon whether the meter is in a central location—such as Center City or University City—or in an outlying area. Most meters no longer take nickels or dimes.

Meter time—one hour, two hours, or three hours (and, in a few cases, longer)—is determined by how fast the turnover should be to serve the local businesses and institutions. The Authority's parking analysts do "turnover studies" that form the basis of these decisions. On a street where there are quick ins-and-outs, with stores like cleaners and pharmacies, meters are probably timed for an hour. In areas around museums and other institutions, meters are usually good for two or three hours. If you want to complain about meters that seem too long or too short for an area, call 977-PARK and ask to speak to a parking analyst.

The green lettering on parking signs tells you when you can park. The red lettering tells you when you cannot park. The same signs will tell you how long you can park.

Many parking signs have arrows on them. They are called anchor signs, and they come in pairs, posted at some distance apart. In theory, the arrows on the signs bracketing a set of parking spaces point toward each other and tell you what you can or cannot do with your car there. Unfortunately, the signs are sometimes twisted, so you may not always know which way the arrows are pointing. ■

Source: Philadelphia Parking Authority.

CITIZENS' MANUAL

Parking

Booted or Towed?

If your car is booted:

You'll quickly recognize when a boot has been placed on your car; it makes the tire look as if it is being treated for gout. If you're like most people, your first reaction will be to walk around your car in disbelief. Do that a few times, if it helps. Then take these steps:

1. If you want to (and you have the money to) pay all of your outstanding tickets and the $50.00 boot fee, go to the Parking Violations Branch at 913 Filbert Street (574-3654). Hours are Monday–Friday 8am–7pm, Saturday 9am–1pm, closed on Sunday. After you have paid, someone will come and remove the boot.

2. If you want to request a hearing, go to the Bureau of Adjudication at 909 Filbert Street. A hearing examiner will determine how much money you have to put down and a payment schedule for the rest of what you owe. Once you've made your down payment, the boot will be removed.

If your car is towed:

You can be certain of death, of taxes, and of being towed if you park at the wrong time in a rush-hour tow-away zone such as those on Walnut, Arch, and Race Streets. When you return to your car and find it gone—and figure out that, since no other cars are there, yours has probably been towed rather than stolen—you can do this:

1. Go to the Parking Violations Branch at 913 Filbert Street (561-3636). Hours are Monday–Friday 8am–7pm, Saturday 9am–1pm, closed on Sunday. They accept Visa, MasterCard, certified check, money order, and cash. Pay the $75.00 tow fine and any unpaid parking tickets. (They will check to see if you have any.)

2. Take your receipt and go to the impoundment lot at Delaware Avenue and Spring Garden Street (923-5624; open until 8pm during the week, 4pm on Saturday, closed on Sunday). They will return your car once you show them proof of payment. Every additional day you wait, the storage cost goes up $5.

3. Of course, no transportation is provided from 913 Filbert to Delaware Avenue. Hike up to Spring Garden Street and catch SEPTA's Route 43 bus. That'll take you down to the waterfront. ∎

Source: Philadelphia Parking Authority.

PARKING FINES

$15: Expired meter; over the time limit in an unmetered space

$20: In loading zone; on sidewalk; on crosswalk; stopped or standing in bus zone

$25: Double-parked; within 20 feet of corner; in a parking- or stopping-prohibited zone

$30: Within 15 feet of fire hydrant

$100: For blocking a mass transit vehicle; in a space reserved for the handicapped

CENTER CITY PARKING COSTS

What it can cost to park your car in a lot if you:

Spend the day sightseeing in Independence National Historical Park: **$9.00**

Attend a show at the Forrest Theater: **$5.00** (enter after 5pm)

Browse for books at Borders in Center City: **$2.50** for each half-hour

Attend an all-day event at the Pennsylvania Convention Center: **$9.50**

Spend the day at Jefferson Hospital: **$15.00**

Live in Society Hill and don't want to park your Lexus on the street: **$120.00** per month

Insist on driving to work in Center City, instead of taking public transportation: **$140.00** per month

Thirteen White (Male) Authors Buried at Laurel Hill Cemetery

- **Robert Montgomery Bird (February 5, 1806–January 23, 1854)** Physician Bird wrote five plays for the John Wayne of his day, Edwin Forrest. But long before the record 1000th production of Bird's *Gladiator,* Forrest's most famous role, in 1853, the two were completely estranged. Bird also edited *The North American,* one of Philadelphia's major daily newspapers, and experimented with photography.
- **George Henry Boker (October 6, 1823–January 2, 1890)** Author of *Francesca da Rimini* and much more. "As a total contrast and equal counterweight to Whitman–the conservative to Whitman's radical–he still looms as a powerful if still only dimly visible figure in American literary history," wrote Nathaniel Burt and Wallace E. Davies.
- **Charles Brockden Brown (January 17, 1771–March 22, 1810)** Brown wrote six novels in only two years, including a graphic account of Philadelphia's yellow fever epidemic. He has been called America's first novelist to attract an international audience.
- **William Duane (May 17, 1760–November 24, 1835)** Editor of *The Aurora* and a fiery journalist who lived in Benjamin Franklin's house, having married a descendant in 1801. A friend of Jefferson, who wrote: "His passions are stronger than his prudence."
- **Thomas Godfrey, Sr. (1704–December 1749)** While at work on the scaffolding at "Stenton," James Logan's newly finished country seat, glazier Godfrey was distracted by a falling shard of glass. He descended and headed to Logan's library, pulled off the shelves one of Logan's 13 titles by Newton, and was "discovered" by Logan. But Godfrey failed to grow popular among the city's intellectual elite. Benjamin Franklin once complained that Godfrey "was forever denying or distinguishing upon trifles to the disturbance of all conversation." And Godfrey's bid at lasting fame failed, too. He improved the mariner's quadrant for determining latitude—but a Brit named Hadley got all the credit.
- **George Rex Graham (January 18, 1813–July 13, 1894)** *Graham's Magazine,* a monthly, published works by Poe, Longfellow, and others.
- **Elisha Kent Kane (February 3, 1820–February 16, 1857)** An adventurer from Philadelphia. Pioneer Kane attempted to reach the North Pole and wrote a stirring narrative of the search for a lost comrade, Sir John Franklin.
- **Morton McMichael (October 20, 1807–January 6, 1879)** A journalist (McMichael and Bird were partners at *The North American*) who became mayor and an advocate for establishing Fairmount Park, where a statue of him still stands.
- **John Kearsley Mitchell (May 12, 1793–April 4, 1858)** Among all of Jefferson College physician and poet Mitchell's accomplishments, he is best known as the father of physician/writer Silas Weir Mitchell.
- **Henry Peterson (December 7, 1818–October 10, 1891)** The quarter-century editor, beginning in 1848, of *The Saturday Evening Post.* He gave it literary leanings.
- **Thomas Buchanan Read (March 12, 1822–May 11, 1872)** One of those 19th-century painter/poets who wouldn't have survived if not for odd jobs cutting inscriptions onto tombstones, painting canal boats, and (least artistically of all) rolling cigars.
- **Richard Penn Smith (March 13, 1799–August 12, 1854)** Apparently Edwin Forrest liked plays written by young, smart urban professionals. Lawyer Smith wrote 20 by the time he turned thirtysomething.
- **Charles Thomson (November 29, 1729–August 16, 1824)** As Secretary of the Continental Congress for nearly 15 years (beginning in 1774), Thomson kept the minutes that chronicle the birth of the new nation. In retirement, he translated the New Testament. ∎

Source: An unpublished manuscript tour of Laurel Hill Cemetery by John Ashmead, ca. 1990.

Thirteen Women of Letters

- **Jane Aitken (July 11, 1764–August 29, 1832)** At age 38, in 1802, Aitken assumed her father's printing and bookbinding business—and his debts. Until she landed in the Norristown debtors' prison, Aitken published at least 60 titles. She is presumed buried in the now-destroyed cemetery of the Associate Reformed Presbyterian Church.
- **Lydia R. Bailey (February 1, 1779–February 21, 1869)** A young widow with four children, Bailey inherited her husband's printing business and paid off its heavy debts. Between 1830 and 1850 she was the first woman to hold the office of City Printer. Bailey is buried at the Old Pine Street (Third Presbyterian) Church cemetery, Fourth and Pine Streets.
- **Catherine Shober Drinker Bowen (January 1, 1897–November 1, 1973)** Bowen, descended from the first English person born in Pennsylvania, wrote books including *"Beloved Friend": The Story of Tchaikowsky and Nadejda von Meck* (with Barbara von Meck, 1937); *The Lion and the Throne*; and *Miracle at Philadelphia.* She died in Haverford about a mile from her birthplace.
- **Pearl Sydenstricker Buck (1872–1973)** Buck, winner of the Nobel Prize in Literature in 1938, was the author of *East Wind, West Wind* (1930); *The Good Earth* (1931), which won the 1932 Pulitzer Prize; *A House Divided* (1935); *The Exile* (1936); *Dragon Seed* (1942); and other works. She is buried on the grounds of the Pearl S. Buck House in Perkasie, Pennsylvania.
- **Rebecca Blaine Harding Davis (June 24, 1831–September 29, 1910)** Journalist Davis wrote about life in the steel mills of West Virginia and later covered the Civil War; she also encouraged the writing career of her son, Richard Harding Davis. Her ashes are buried in Leverington Cemetery on Ridge Road in Roxborough at the corner of Rittenhouse Lane.
- **Elizabeth Sandwith Drinker (1734–November 24, 1807)** Diarist Drinker kept a continuous journal from 1758 to 1787, recounting household affairs and eyewitness stories of warfare and hardships during the Revolution. She is listed in the Arch Street Monthly Meeting Burial Book.
- **Jessie Redmon Fauset (April 26, 1882–April 30, 1961)** Born in Lawnside, New Jersey, Fauset grew up there and in North Philadelphia. She was the first African American woman at Cornell University and the first literary editor of *The Crisis*, NAACP's monthly magazine; she wrote four novels of the Harlem Renaissance. Faucet is buried in Eden Cemetery, Collingdale, Pennsylvania.
- **Elizabeth Graeme Ferguson (February 3, 1737–February 23, 1801)** Poet and prolific letter-writer, Ferguson established a cultured literary salon at Graeme Park, the family mansion in Montgomery County. She is buried at the Christ Church burying ground.
- **Sarah Josepha Buell Hale (October 24, 1788–April 30, 1879)** Following her husband's death, Hale wrote poetry and novels, championed education and work for women, and served as editor of *Godey's Lady's Book* until she was 90. She is buried in West Laurel Hill Cemetery.
- **Sarah Ewing Hall (October 30, 1761–April 8, 1830)** One of the first famous American women writers, novelist Hall also contributed to *The Port Folio*, the Philadelphia literary magazine. She is buried at the Old Pine Street (Third Presbyterian) Church cemetery, Fourth and Pine Streets.
- **Eliza Leslie (November 15, 1787–January 1, 1858)** Author and editor Leslie wrote books on "domestic economy," as well as cookbooks, children's stories, and articles for *Godey's Lady's Book*. She is buried at St. Peter's churchyard at Third and Pine Streets.
- **Agnes Repplier (April 1, 1855–December 15, 1950)** Repplier was a rebellious student who found her literary niche with *The Atlantic Monthly.* (Her last essay appeared there in 1940 on her 85th birthday.) She also wrote five biographies and lectured. She is buried in the family vault at the Church of St. John the Evangelist, 13th Street near Market.
- **Sarah Tyson Heston Rorer (October 18, 1849–December 27, 1937)** A diet advocate and cookbook author, Rorer directed the New Century Club, opened the Philadelphia Cooking School, and established a diet kitchen at the Hospital of the University of Pennsylvania. She is buried in Hill Church Cemetery, Lebanon, Pennsylvania. ■

CARVED IN STONE

As Franklin lay dying in bed at home on Market Street near Third, folks wondered how they might remember him. On Fifth Street, just across from Independence Hall, the Library Company of Philadelphia, which Franklin had started in 1731, was building a home. Above the white-marble stairs to the front entrance blankly stood a large, empty niche. It cried out for a statue, and one larger than life. Had the library considered Minerva, the Roman goddess of wisdom, or some other bookish allegory in the Classical mode? A real person had not yet been rendered on a Philadelphia building, let alone one so real as to be still breathing, only a few blocks away.

Enter wealthy merchant William Bingham, who commissioned a sculpture of Franklin for the niche. Franklin consented to the Roman toga, and he certainly wouldn't have objected to the stack of books under the right arm or to the scepter, inverted to indicate displeasure with kings, in the left.

Sculptor Francesco Lazzarini, from Cararra, Italy, later sculpted Mars, the god of war, and Bacchus, the god of wine. He couldn't have told his clients that he had done a Philadelphia god, but he could well say he had done its patron saint—nearly eight feet tall. The statue arrived in April 1792, two years after Franklin's death.

COULD BE CARVED IN STONE

A learned blockhead is a greater blockhead than an ignorant one. (1734)

He does not possess wealth; it possesses him. (1734)

What maintains one vice would bring up two children. (1747)

The end of passion is the beginning of repentance. (1749)

All would live long, but none would be old. (1749)

Most of the learning in use is of no great use. (1749)

The first mistake in public business is the going into it. (1758)

Benjamin Franklin, Susanna Stout, and Life After Death

Benjamin Franklin harbored "some doubts" as to the divinity of Christ, though he believed in "one God, Creator of the Universe" and the soul's immortality. "I have no doubt of its continuance," Franklin wrote of life after death, "without the smallest conceit of meriting it."

An account of Franklin's own death in 1790, one that escaped the notice of his many biographers, appeared in an almanac published nearly 40 years later:

"A respectable layer-out of the dead in this city," a Mary M—, recalled that she "was called to perform this last office for the corpse of Franklin, and was surprised to see, at the foot of the bed, an old picture of the Day of Judgement—where the awful Judge was enthroned in glory, and giving sentence." Shortly before he died, the Doctor had requested the nurse "bring it and place it at the foot of his bed that he might have it always in his view."

❖

Susanna Stout, who lived with her sister and brother-in-law on Second Street, reported the following remarkable event in 1768: An angel took her up to heaven in a cloud, dressed her "with Angels Cloath and with Wings," and brought her before Christ sitting in the seat of judgment. Stout, the daughter of a stocking weaver, saw Christ give a child a "Crown of Everlasting Glory" and condemn a woman to eternal damnation. As these events were taking place, the angel told Stout of a way to later verify what she had witnessed. Plant a boiled rosemary, said the angel, it would grow as living proof.

Stout's rosemary burgeoned. ■

Sources: Kite's Town and Country Almanac for the year 1830 (Thomas Kite, 1829); *A Short and True Account of a Young Youth; Born in Philadelphia of honest and true Christian Parents; who was taken away by an Angel the 31st of January 1768, up to the Coelestial Parts, where the Lord of Hosts show'd her great Wonders and supernatural Things* (Anthony Armbruster, 1768).

Darwin and the Evolution of Photography

C harles R. Darwin, of Easton, who expects to celebrate his 99th birthday in January 1994, recently recalled when he started working for photographer William H. Rau.

Darwin described Rau, who operated a wonderful Camac Street studio, as a "Buffalo Bill type." He especially remembered the mammoth, out-of-date glass negatives Rau learned to love while official photographer for the Pennsylvania Railroad in the 1890s. When Darwin started working for Rau in the early 1910s, the older photographer was past his negative-hauling days. Each negative weighed five pounds at the bottom of the hill, Darwin remembered. At the top, it felt like much more. Having this belated experience in Civil War–era expedition photography, Darwin figured he witnessed just about the entire evolution of photography.

Darwin's employment with Rau is part of a professional genealogy that links some of today's photographers to the very beginning of the profession in America. During Rau's courtship of Louise Bell in 1874, her father William secured an expedition job for the 19-year-old. A veteran photographer of the American West, Bell had learned the trade from several pioneers, including James E. McClees, the Chestnut Street daguerreotypist. McClees had been trained by Montgomery P. Simons. Simons had been in partnership with the brothers David and Thomas Collins, who had learned the trade from Marcus Aurelius Root. Root had studied with Robert Cornelius, one of the world's first professional photographers, who opened Philadelphia's first studio on 8th Street near Chestnut in May of 1840, less than a year after Daguerre introduced the process in Paris.

Darwin has fond memories of his employment with William Rau as well as in his own shop, The Photo-Illustrators. The late Joseph Kelly ran that operation in a cavernous building on Walnut Street until the early 1980s. Kelly never much cared for small cameras, or ones with shutters. He timed exposures by carefully removing the lenscap from his large-format camera, holding it to his chest for a correct number of heartbeats, and then carefully replacing the lenscap. Is there any other way to rightfully capture an image? ■

"You have perhaps heard of the Daguerreotipe," artist and inventor Samuel F. B. Morse wrote to a newspaper in the spring of 1839. "It is one of the most beautiful discoveries of the age...the exquisite minuteness of the delineation cannot be conceived. No painting or engraving has ever approached it."

As soon as the Parisians published a recipe telling how to make daguerreotypes, Philadelphians set out to prove (or disprove) this alleged, modern miracle. Experimenters such as chemist-physician Paul Beck Goddard and brass founder Robert Cornelius joined forces and improved on Daguerre's chemistry. They reduced exposure time from minutes to seconds and made portraiture feasible. In May 1840, Cornelius opened a portrait studio on Eighth Street, just north of Chestnut.

Only about 40 of his tiny, cased portraits survive, including the one shown here. Save for a few folks who couldn't resist the latest thing in technology (or the latest thing from Paris), Cornelius found subjects only with the help of his friends. ("If convenient for you to call at the store any clear day from 10 to 3 o'clock," solicited one, "I will be happy to accompany you to his rooms..."). After a few interesting, struggling seasons, Cornelius closed shop.

Daguerreans made profits, all right—after years of advertising. Chestnut Street had several successful studios, including one run by a Barnum-like character named Marcus Aurelius Root, who bragged of having 70,000 sitters—only two blocks and one decade from where Cornelius labored.

Henry Howard Houston,
by Cornelius.

Philadelphia's First Export

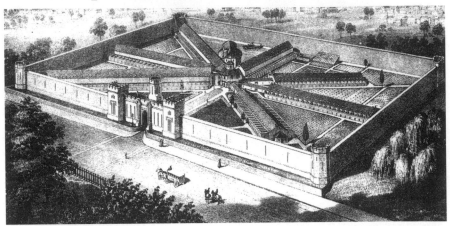

Quaker faith in all of humanity—including the so-called dregs of society—led to improved standards for prisoners. By 1790, new standards were set: no alcohol, no mixed sexes, and no mixing debtors with common criminals. The Walnut Street Prison, built in 1773, was upgraded but was hopelessly small. In 1821, when the Pennsylvania Legislature authorized a new prison, it turned out to be one of the largest American building projects to date. The Commonwealth bought a farm near Fairmount (called Cherry Hill) and selected a well-studied, well-traveled English-born architect named John Haviland.

In his design, Haviland combined the Quaker reform theory of separate confinement with a centralized, radial neo-classical design that was well received even before the first hooded prisoner was admitted on October 25, 1829. Eastern State drew thousands of visitors from around the world, including Charles Dickens and Alexis de Tocqueville. Wardens and visitors alike could stand in the center of the plan and instantly view the corridors of all seven cellblocks, comprising hundreds of 8 x 12 foot cells, with small, adjacent exercise yards. Many were impressed with the design's promise for a more humane institution. Over time, more than 300 prisons around the world would be built on the model of Philadelphia's Eastern State. ■

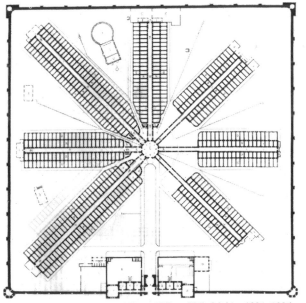

Eastern State Penitentiary (Cherry Hill) at Philadelphia, 1821–1836

Compiler: Norman Johnston.

158

Penitentiaries

Copenhagen, 1859

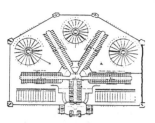

London (Pentonville), 1840

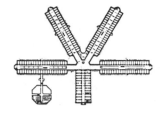

Berlin (Moabit), 1832

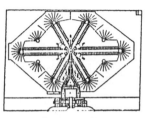

Louvain, 1856

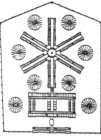

Milan, 1867

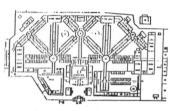

Beijing, 1909

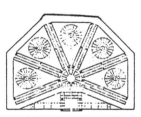

Paris (Mazas), 1843

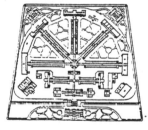

Buenos Aires, 1872

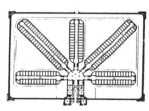

Trenton, 1833

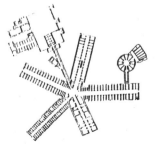

Dublin (Mountjoy), 1855

Hakodate, Japan, 1931

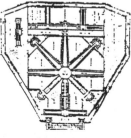

Madrid, 1954

159

The Turkish Automaton's Final Act

The Turkish Automaton in 1783.

To please the Empress Maria Theresa, the Baron Wolfgang von Kempelen, a Hungarian inventor, constructed a chess-playing pseudo-automaton in 1769. It appeared as a lifelike, elaborately costumed Turkish mannequin holding a long pipe seated behind a cabinet whose doors were opened to reveal an impressive display of wheels and gears. In performance, the apparatus was wound up, and the Turk commenced to play chess against all comers. He compiled an impressive record of victory, defeating many of the best players in Europe, and clearly articulating the word "échec" as his opponent's doom seemed inevitable. Attempted explanations and exposés of the mechanism (in truth: a secret, hidden chess expert/operator) did little to deflate its popularity, which was enhanced by matches against such worthies as Napoleon and Benjamin Franklin.

Von Kempelen occasionally exhibited the machine, always slightly embarrassed at the attention it garnered. Although his system of concealment was exceedingly clever, he felt the hidden human agent belittled his achievements as a serious inventor. After the Baron's death, musician, inventor, and itinerant showman Johann Nepomuk Maelzel purchased the machine. In 1826, Maelzel brought his automaton to America, exhibiting in New York and Boston before making Philadelphia his base of operations.

Although the Turk was a resounding success in its initial Philadelphia appearances, over the years its popularity waned due to a combination of factors. Too often the machine concealed inferior players. Too frequently its secret was revealed (once by a young Edgar Allan Poe). Knock-off versions and over-exposure of the original diminished its novelty.

Performance

After Maelzel's death in 1838, the Turk was stored in a warehouse at the Lombard Street wharf. Two years later, with the machine in a horrible state of disrepair, a group of Philadelphia investors headed by the well-known physician John Kearsley Mitchell (Poe's personal physician) came forward to purchase it. Mitchell restored the automaton and exhibited it privately. One of the Turk's hidden directors was Lloyd P. Smith, a young businessman who later became librarian of the Library Company of Philadelphia.

In 1840, the Turk was exhibited at the Franklin Institute (now the building of the Atwater Kent Museum) and thereafter at the Chinese Museum at Ninth near Sansom Streets. Its active career may have been only a few days, but it remained in the museum until July 5, 1854, when a fire that started at the nearby National Theater claimed several adjacent buildings, including the museum that housed the 85-year-old Turk. John Kearsley Mitchell's son, the dapper novelist and physician S. Weir Mitchell, entered the building before the conflagration made access completely impossible, possibly to rescue a few essential parts of the device, and witnessed a scene that he later delivered as the Turk's epitaph:

> Already the fire was about him. Death found him tranquil. He who had seen Moscow perish knew no fear of fire. We listened with painful anxiety. It might have been a sound from the crackling woodwork or the breaking window-panes, but, certain it is, that we thought we heard, through the struggling flames, and above the din of outside thousands, the last words of our dear departed friend, the sternly whispered, oft repeated syllables, "Échec! Échec!"

—*Ricky Jay* ∎

Sources: Bradley Ewart, *Chess: Man versus Machine* (A.S. Barnes and Tantivy Press, 1980); George Allen, *Proceedings of the First Annual Chess Conference* (Philadelphia, 1859).

Ruins of the Chinese Museum, July 5, 1854.

1609–1709

"We are your brothers, and intend to live like brothers with you; we have no mind to have war."

—*Native American king to the settlers of Burlington, N.J., ca. 1668*

"Pliny and Isadore wrote that there are not above 144 kinds of fishes, but to my knowledge there are nearer 300: I suppose America was not known to Pliny and Isadore."

—*John Josselyn on the New World, 1672*

"I have already taken care that none of my people wrong you, by good laws I have provided for that purpose; nor will I ever allow any of my people to sell rum, to make you people drunk. If anything should be out of order, expect, when I come it shall be mended..."

—*William Penn's letter of introduction to the Native Americans for his surveyor, Thomas Holme, 1682*

"I...[heard] people generally complaining, that they scarcely knew how time passed, nor that they hardly knew the Day of rest...for want of a Diary, or Day Book, which we call an Almanack. I was really troubled."

—*Samuel Atkins in the first almanac, 1685*

"The forest is lovely and beautiful, there is no garden in Sweden so wonderful to walk in as the forest here in America and [none] smells so good."

—*Gustavus Hesselius in a letter to his mother, 1714*

1609: In search of a faster route to Asia, Henry Hudson sails into the bay between what later became New Jersey and Delaware.

1610: On his way from Cape Cod to Virginia, Samuel Argall sails into the river and names it for his Governor: Lord De La Warr.

1615: Cornelius Hendrickson of Dutch-controlled Manhattan trades with the natives, visits the Schuylkill River, and claims the land.

1626: Dutch build Fort Nassau at Gloucester Point (near West Deptford, N.J.), the first settlement by Europeans.

1631: Zwanendael, "Valley of the Swans," settled near Cape Henlopen by 28 Dutch whalers. Before the year is out, natives massacre the whalers and burn the settlement.

1632: English party from Virginia murdered by natives at Cooper's Creek. David Pietersen DeVries forges a "treaty of amity" with the natives.

1638: Swedes make their first American settlement at Fort Christina, later Wilmington, Delaware.

1648: Fort Bevesrede, a Dutch beaver skin trading post, established along the Schuylkill River where oil tank farms now stand.

1664: Ignoring previous settlements, commissions, and claims, Britain's King Charles II grants his brother James, the Duke of York, proprietary rights to much of what the Dutch had been calling New Netherland.

1669: Near what is now Queen Village and what then was the native village of Wicaco ("a dwelling place"), Swedes build a long blockhouse. The structure is consecrated as a church in 1675 and replaced by Gloria Dei in 1700.

1677: First English Quakers settle, also near Wicaco.

1682: One year after a land grant from Charles II, William Penn's new government in Pennsylvania attracts 23 ships of immigrants, mostly Quakers, to the first unfortified settlement in the region.

1685: William Bradford publishes *Kalandarium Pennsilvaniense*, an almanac, the first book published in Pennsylvania.

1688: Citizens of Germantown protest slavery.

1690: William Rittenhouse builds America's first paper mill near the Wissahickon Creek.

1700: Population rises to the largest in the colonies with 2,200 occupying 400 houses.

1701: Philadelphia officially becomes a city on October 25.

1709: A brick building built in the center of High Street (now Market) and 2nd Street serves as Town Hall and Court House.

Philadelphia Chronology

1720–1793

1720: Swedes in Southwark tame wild beavers to fish.

1729: Benjamin Franklin opens the New Printing Office on High Street (now Market) near 3rd Street.

1731: Father Joseph Greaton begins construction of St. Joseph's Roman Catholic Church.

1732: A growing government begins construction on the new State House, now known as Independence Hall.

1733: Regular stage established between Philadelphia and New York.

1743: Clockmaker Christopher Sauer opens a printing business in Germantown and produces, among other publications, the first American German-language bible.

1747: As French warships threaten the city during the war between England, France, and Spain, Benjamin Franklin persuades Philadelphians to form a militia and build fortifications.

1752: The new State House bell, ordered from an English foundry for Philadelphia's 50th anniversary, cracks when first rung. A local foundry, Pass and Stow, recasts it.

1761: A public lottery raises funds to pave Market Street.

1766: Colonists receive with hostility the Stamp Act, passed by Parliament to raise revenues. Its repeal is largely due to efforts of Pennsylvania's agent in London, Benjamin Franklin.

1766: The Southwark Theater, the first permanent theater building, opens at the southwest corner of South and Leithgow Streets.

1773: Threats from the "Committee of Tarring and Feathering" turn away the *Polly*, a ship laden with taxable tea waiting to enter the port. This success inspires the Boston Tea Party.

1776: A month after the Provincial Convention of Pennsylvania declares the province an independent state, the Second Continental Congress adopts the Declaration of Independence.

1787: Delegates of the 13 United States agree on a draft of the Constitution.

1790: The federal government, with George Washington as first President, is established in Philadelphia, where it remains for the decade.

1791: Dollars and cents are adopted as the currency, replacing colonial shillings and pence.

1793: The Reverend Richard Allen begins the first African American congregation.

1793: J. P. Blanchard ascends in a balloon from the courtyard of the Walnut Street Prison (6th and Walnut Streets) and stays aloft for 46 minutes, landing in Gloucester, New Jersey.

"An innocent Plowman is more worthy than a vicious Prince."

—*Benjamin Franklin in* Poor Richard's Almanac, *1734*

"The poorest labourer upon the shores of the Delaware thinks himself entitled to deliver his sentiment in matters of religion or politics with as much freedom as the gentleman or scholar. ...Such is the prevailing taste for books of every kind, that almost every man is a reader."

—*Jacob Duché, 1772*

"These are the times that try men's souls."

—*Thomas Paine, 1776*

"This city was, for days, the greatest scene of distress that you can conceive; everybody but Quakers were removing their families and effects, and now it looks dismal and melancholy."

—*Robert Morris, December 21, 1776*

"Peace, Liberty, and Independence"

—*Headline on a broadside declaring the official end to the Revolutionary War, written and printed by Eleazer Oswald, March 23, 1783*

"About noon, the illustrious Washington appeared, and as he passed under the first triumphal arch, the acclamations of an immense crowd of spectators rent the air, and the laurel crown, at that instant, descended on his venerable head."

—Columbian Magazine *on Washington's arrival at Grays Ferry in May 1789*

"The eye will be gratified by a fine prospect of both shores, some handsome country seats being on the bank, and the land agreeably undulated..."

—James Mease on the view looking up the Schuylkill River from Market Street, 1811

"The days of Greece may be revived in the woods of America, and Philadelphia become the Athens of the Western World."

—Benjamin Henry Latrobe, 1811

The Earliest Commuters

"The good, respectable old-family society for which Philadelphia was once so celebrated is fast disappearing & persons of low origins & vulgar habits, manners & feelings are introduced because they are rich..."

—Sydney George Fisher, in his diary, 1837

"In whatever part of the city you go the same staid, absorbed, imperturbable placidity arrests your attention and even pervades the atmosphere. The very clock on the State House Steeple appears to be calculating how much it can make by striking. ...Like a surly tenant, it takes all the time the law allows, and then strikes only to save its character for punctuality."

—George G. Foster, Philadelphia in Slices, *1848*

Philadelphia Chronology

1794–1861

1794: Frenchman Peter Bossu introduces ice cream, later sold by street vendors as "hokey pokey."

1797: Thomas Dobson issues the last of his 18-volume *Encyclopedia,* an Americanized piracy of the *Encyclopedia Britannica.*

1812: A 340-foot, single-span covered bridge, "The Colossus," crosses the Schuylkill River at Fairmount.

1820: First coal arrives from the Lehigh River Valley.

1827: Fifty cotton manufacturing plants flourish along the Pennypack Creek, in Manayunk and in Kensington.

1831: Circus elephants Virginius and Bozzarius drown while crossing the Delaware River.

1832: Railroad service between 9th and Green Streets in Philadelphia and Germantown begins.

1833: Two baseball teams form.

1835: The State House bell (Liberty Bell) reportedly cracks irreparably as it tolls after the death of Chief Justice John Marshall.

1838: A mob sets fire to the brand-new Pennsylvania Hall, just before an anti-slavery convention convenes.

1844: Estate of Lemon Hill is purchased as the first step toward creating a park to protect the Schuylkill River's banks from industrial development and water pollution.

1845: The Chestnut Street Theater presents *Leonora,* an American-written opera by William Henry Fry.

1847: African Americans own Philadelphia real estate worth over $500,000, support 19 churches and 106 beneficial societies, and maintain their own insurance societies, cemetery associations, labor unions, and financial organizations.

1849: Cramp's shipyard launches the *Caroline,* the world's fastest propeller ship to date.

1849: Philadelphia has ten millionaires, twice the number in New York.

1850: Both Women's Medical College (now the Medical College of Pennsylvania) and the School of Design for Women (now the Moore College of Art) open.

1851: Six Philadelphia manufacturers win medals for their products at London's Crystal Palace, the first great international exposition.

1854: Consolidation of towns and villages within the 129 square miles of Philadelphia County forms a sprawling city determined to provide services more efficiently.

1857: The city's 260 mills make Philadelphia the world's largest textile manufacturer.

1861: First Confederate prisoners of war are confined in Moyamensing Prison, 10th and Reed Streets.

164

Philadelphia Chronology

1863–1904

1863: General Lee's invasion of Pennsylvania causes fear and excitement. Businesses offer employees to help dig earthworks at the city's outskirts. After victory at Gettysburg, sick and wounded pack the city's many temporary army hospitals.

1865: En route to Springfield, Illinois, the body of Abraham Lincoln lies in state in Independence Hall; 85,000 pay homage.

1867: $67,219 is collected for war-torn Southerners.

1870: A referendum determines the site of a new city hall: Penn Square (Center Square), not Washington Square. Project takes more than 30 years to complete.

1876: Centennial Exhibition, an international exhibition with 249 mostly temporary buildings on 300 acres of West Fairmount Park, proclaims America as a rising industrial giant.

1878: Bell Telephone opens its first exchange.

1881: Pennsylvania Railroad's new station across from City Hall, Broad Street Station, brings travelers by rail to the heart of the city. A decade later, the Philadelphia and Reading Railroad builds its terminal three blocks to the east.

1881: Gaslights along Chestnut Street replaced by electrical fixtures.

1882: A group of 225 Russian Jewish immigrants—refugees from the pogroms—arrive at a wharf near Old Swedes Church. Within 10 years, 40,000 settle.

1884: Bryn Mawr College, bellwether of all women's colleges, founded. University of Pennsylvania begins its school of veterinary medicine. Four years later, Temple College is chartered. Nine years later, banker Anthony J. Drexel establishes Drexel Institute.

1884: Mayor Samuel G. King appoints the first African American police officer. Christopher J. Perry founds the first newspaper for African Americans, *The Philadelphia Tribune.*

1895: A generator at 9th and Sansom Streets begins producing electricity for lighting homes and streets.

1897: Smith's Island, a longtime beer garden and popular resort in the middle of the Delaware River opposite Center City, is removed to improve port access.

1899: Optician Siegmund Lubin produces his first motion pictures in a rooftop studio at 916 Arch street.

1900: The city's Italian population rises to 18,000, up from 300 in 1870. Within another decade, the city's Italian American population is 77,000.

1901: Mummers inaugurate annual parade up Broad Street.

1904: More than 7,000 textile plants employ 35% of the city's workers. The annual output of carpet alone could belt around the earth and leave a remnant that would reach Cincinnati.

"There are in Philadelphia thousands—absolutely thousands, who rise in the morning without knowing where they are to obtain a mouthful of food, or where their wretched heads are to rest at night."

—Caspar Souder in Mysteries and Miseries of Philadelphia, *1853*

Lincoln Funeral

"Undefined sensations steal irresistible over the senses."

—D. W. Belisle on Independence Hall, *1859*

"the center of human concourse from which all things radiate and to which all things converge."

—Benjamin H. Brewster on the placement of the new Philadelphia City Hall, *1874*

"To be sure a colored man to-day can walk the streets of Philadelphia without personal insult; he can go to theatres, parks and some places of amusement without meeting more than stares of discourtesy; he can be accommodated at most hotels and restaurants, although his treatment in some would not be pleasant. All this is a vast advance and augurs much for the future."

—W. E. B. DuBois in The Philadelphia Negro, *1899*

165

1912–1993

"A demure country village...which has done the work and earned the money of a big bustling town...enjoys its luxury and hides behind its plain brick fronts."

—*Elizabeth Robbins Pennell, 1914*

"The ancient and noble city of Philadelphia is a surprisingly large town at the confluence of the Biddle and Drexel families. It is wholly surrounded by cricket teams, fox hunters, beagle packs, and the Pennsylvania Railroad."

—*Christopher Morley, 1920*

"...that perfected miracle of ugliness and inconvenience, that really remarkable combination of bulk and insignificance."

—*Agnes Repplier on City Hall, 1934*

"Without legislation and with nothing more than a gentleman's agreement, the tallest of the city's office buildings have been piously kept lower than the bronze figure atop this building."

—*Lewis Mumford on the dominance of City Hall, 1956*

"If the people planning Philadelphia's tribute to the Constitution had been in charge in 1786, we'd probably be driving on the left side of the street today."

—Newsweek *magazine, 1987*

"Image is money."

—*Sam Rogers, Convention and Visitors Bureau, 1988*

1912: Leopold Stokowski is appointed conductor of the Philadelphia Orchestra.

1917: Benjamin Franklin Parkway links Center City with Fairmount Park.

1918: In September, a devastating influenza epidemic sweeps the city. Two months later, survivors join in jubilant celebration of German surrender at the end of World War I.

1926: Delaware River (now Benjamin Franklin) Bridge completed as part of an otherwise unsuccessful celebration of the Declaration of Independence.

1929: Robin Hood Dell opens the summer before the October financial crash. The Rodin Museum, a gift of Jules Mastbaum, is dedicated one month after the crash.

1932: The Philadelphia Saving Fund Society skyscraper is completed on the former site of William Penn Charter School. It is Philadelphia's best example of the International Style building and America's first centrally air-conditioned building.

1946: J. Presper Eckert and John W. Mauchly unveil ENIAC, the world's first computer, at the University of Pennsylvania's Moore School of Engineering.

1959: Schuylkill Expressway completed. Urban renewal with federal funds begins to reshape Center City and many older neighborhoods.

1969: Philadelphia Board of Education declares January 15, the birthday of Dr. Martin Luther King Jr., a school holiday.

1974: The Delaware River is covered by a three-mile oil slick from 20,000 gallons spilled by Mobil.

1976: After the stroke of a rainy midnight on New Year's Day, Liberty Bell is moved from Independence Hall into a separate, modern pavilion. City officials had feared that anticipated crowds for the Bicentennial would wear out Independence Hall.

1984: Commuter rail tunnel and Market East station open, joining in a single system 490 miles of track laid by a pair of one-time competitors.

1985: Eleven die and 62 homes destroyed after police bomb the rowhouse headquarters of MOVE.

1986: Manufacturing jobs down 27% from 1956 and declining.

1987: Bicentennial of U.S. Constitution modestly celebrated.

1989: Median home prices are double 1975 levels. Meanwhile, as many as 600 homeless people live on the streets and thousands of houses stand abandoned.

1990: Population shrinks for the fourth consecutive census to 1.6 million, less than the number in 1920.

1993: Pennsylvania Convention Center opens with celebration addressed by President Clinton. The Liberty Medal is presented to South Africa's F. W. De Klerk and Nelson Mandela. ■

Philadelphia's Population, 1760–1990

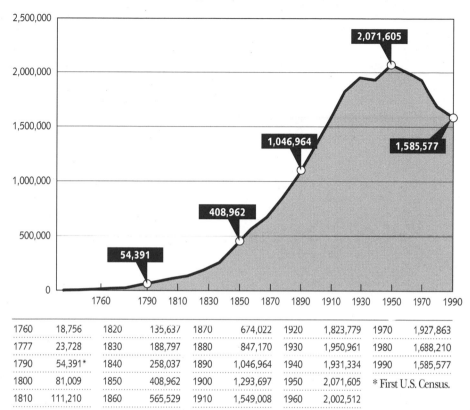

1760	18,756	1820	135,637	1870	674,022	1920	1,823,779	1970	1,927,863
1777	23,728	1830	188,797	1880	847,170	1930	1,950,961	1980	1,688,210
1790	54,391*	1840	258,037	1890	1,046,964	1940	1,931,334	1990	1,585,577
1800	81,009	1850	408,962	1900	1,293,697	1950	2,071,605	* First U.S. Census.	
1810	111,210	1860	565,529	1910	1,549,008	1960	2,002,512		

THE REGION, 1950–1990

County	1950	1960	1970	1980	1990	% change
Bucks	107,715	308,567	413,098	479,180	541,174	+402
Chester	135,626	210,608	274,214	316,660	376,396	+178
Delaware	310,756	553,154	592,200	555,023	547,651	+76
Montgomery	289,247	516,682	622,376	643,377	678,111	+76
Philadelphia	1,931,334	2,002,512	1,927,863	1,688,210	1,585,577	-181
Burlington	97,013	224,499	323,132	362,542	395,066	+307
Camden	395,066	392,035	456,291	471,650	502,824	+97
Gloucester	72,219	134,840	172,681	199,917	230,082	+219
Mercer	229,781	266,392	304,116	307,863	325,824	+42
Salem	49,508	58,711	60,346	64,676	65,295	+32
Total	**3,618,265**	**4,668,000**	**5,146,317**	**5,089,098**	**5,248,000**	

Source: U.S. Census.

Percent decrease of whites living in
Philadelphia, 1980–1990: 13.7

Percent decrease of blacks: 1.1

Percent increase of Asians: 145.0

Percent increase of Hispanics: 40.3

Whites as percent of city population
in 1990: 53.5

Whites as percent in 1980: 58.2

Blacks as percent of city population
in 1990: 39.9

Blacks as percent in 1980: 37.8

Percent of city residents under 20
in 1990: 27.0

Percent under 20 in 1980: 29.6

Percent of city residents 65 or over
in 1990: 15.2

Percent 65 or over in 1980: 14.1

Nine-county region's average number
of children per family in 1990: 1.82

Region's average children per family
in 1980: 1.86

Percent increase of Philadelphia
households headed by females,
1980–1990: 6.5

**The number of households in the
nine-county region (Philadelphia,
Bucks, Chester, Montgomery,
Delaware, Mercer, Burlington,
Camden, and Gloucester
Counties) is increasing:**

1990: 1,894,306

1980: 1,745,149

**The average household size in
the region is decreasing:**

1990: 2.66 persons

1980: 2.90 persons

**The population density is
increasing:**

2010: 2.30 persons per acre
(forecasted)

1990: 2.16 persons per acre

1988: 2.10 persons per acre

Sources: Delaware Valley Regional
Planning Commission; Center
for Greater Philadelphia.

Population

Trends in Poverty

Poverty in Philadelphia

	1990 Number	%	1980 Number	%	1970 Number	%
Total	313,374	20.3	340,515	20.6	294,429	15.1
Black	179,191	29.0	198,608	32.2	165,004	25.7
Hispanic	37,364	45.3	28,702	45.9	9,8883	7.8*
Age 65+	37,907	16.3	39,042	17.0	53,183	14.2

*1970 data for persons of Puerto Rican origin.

How Philadelphia Stacks Up — Persons Below Poverty

	1990 Number	%	1980 Number	%
Philadelphia	313,374	20.3	340,515	20.6
Chester County	17,160	4.7	19,588	6.4
Delaware County	37,171	7.0	39,848	7.4
Montgomery County	23,779	3.6	29,773	4.8
Pennsylvania	1,283,629	11.1	1,209,819	10.4
United States	33,600,000	13.5	29,300,000	12.4

The average poverty threshold for a family of four as set by
the federal government: $13,359 in 1990; $8,414 in 1980.

Families Below Poverty

	1990 No.	% of total	1980 No.	% of total	% change 1980–1990
Philadelphia	61,253	16.06	69,192	16.64	-11.47
Chester County	2,978	2.97	3,871	4.71	-23.07
Delaware County	7,142	4.97	8,332	5.75	-14.28
Montgomery County	4,089	2.25	5,670	3.30	-27.88
Pennsylvania	259,117	8.16	244,686	7.77	

Sources: Pennsylvania State Data Center; United Way of
Southeastern Pennsylvania; City Planning Commission;
Delaware Valley Regional Planning Commission.

Radio

Still the Golden Years

Whether it's the medium's unique appeal or its relatively low capital investment and operating costs, radio thrives as one of our most popular forms of mass communication. Turn the AM or FM dial and encounter an array of stations, each devoted to its specialty: call-in, all-news, all-weather, rock, folk, children, country, religion, elevator—whatever. Add to these a growing number of stations broadcasting in the many languages of Americans.

Greater Philadelphia receives nearly 200 stations. This abundance is a far cry from the memories of some (still extant) adults who remember clasping the headpiece of a crystal set clumsily to their young ears and hearing—all the way over the night mountains from Pittsburgh—the voice of KDKA. And there are others who recall Toscanini's NBC symphony broadcasts over WJZ, New York, which helped pioneer the idea of a nationwide network of stations. One of our regional stations, WWJZ in Mount Holly, New Jersey, is named for this famed predecessor.

One thing all stations have in common are call letters. These are used by the Federal Communications Commission and on-air announcers alike to identify the stations. Some were chosen by the owners; most are assigned. Stations east of the Mississippi generally begin with the letter "W"; those in the west with a "K." KYW, the local exception, was in business before the rule took effect.

Today, many call letters are anachronistic, abstract, or both. Owners and station formats have changed but the call letters often remain. Philadelphia's oldest station, WIP, retains its letters after 72 years on the air at the same frequency. Others have been dropped and reappear elsewhere. WIBG (I Believe in God), originally owned by a church in Glenside, evolved in the hands of a subsequent owner into a popular rock station. In the 1960s, listeners called it "Wibbage." WIBG is now assigned to a station in Ocean City, New Jersey. Another music station, WZZD, was promoted as "Wizzard," an acronym dropped when religious programming later replaced rock. ■

ABBREVIATIONS ON THE FOLLOWING PAGES

AM: Amplitude modulation (530–1710 kilohertz), the original technique of radio broadcasting.

FM: Frequency modulation (88.1–107.9 megahertz), the clearer, static-free form of broadcasting used also for television as well as the Weather Band (162.4–162.55 megahertz).

CC: Carrier current; unlicensed AM-type stations serving specific areas such as residence halls on a college campus.

BROADCAST FIRSTS

The first experimental radio license was granted on August 13, 1912, to St. Joseph's College.

The first radio broadcast of a ship launching took place on April 7, 1925, when several stations gave a firsthand account of the christening of the aircraft carrier *Saratoga* at the New York Shipbuilding Company in Camden, New Jersey.

The first football game televised in color was played on September 29, 1951, at Franklin Field. Penn lost to the University of California, 35–0.

The first intercity telecast using coaxial cable took place on October 5, 1936, between New York and Philadelphia.

Ten minutes of a surgical operation by Dr. Isidor S. Ravdin at the University of Pennsylvania were televised live by WPTZ on March 16, 1952, the first such program by a local station.

TONGUES OF PENNSYLVANIA

In 1993, Pennsylvania had 806,876 residents over the age of five who did not speak English at home. About 13.4% of them did not speak English well, or at all. The following is a list of the top 10 non-English languages (out of a total of 138) spoken in the Commonwealth and the number of residents who speak them as their first language.

Spanish	213,024
Italian	103,844
German	78,494
Polish	55,344
Pennsylvania Dutch	47,988
French	44,289
Slovak	23,767
Chinese	23,611
Korean	18,116
Greek	17,982

Source: U.S. Census.

169

Broadcasting Call Letters

KHB38	162.4FM	Atlantic City, NJ	National Weather Service
KIH28	162.475FM	Philadelphia, PA	National Weather Service
KYW	1060AM	Philadelphia, PA	Young Warrior
WABC	770AM	New York, NY	American Broadcasting Companies
WADB	91.7FM	Point Pleasant, NJ	Adamant D. Brown (former owner)
WAEB	790AM/ 104.1FM	Allentown, PA	Allentown Easton Bethlehem
WAMS	1380AM	Wilmington, DE	Wilmington's All-Music Station
WAYV	95.1FM	Atlantic City, NJ	WAVE
WBCB	1490AM	Levittown, PA	Bucks County's Best; BuCks Broadcasting
WBCQ	1180AM	Quakertown, PA	Bucks County—Quakertown
WBEB	560AM/ 101.1FM	Philadelphia, PA	None
WBGD	91.9FM	Brick, NJ	Brick's Greatest DJs/Green Dragons
WBMR	91.7FM	Telford, PA	BuxMont Radio
WBNJ	105.5FM	Cape May Ct House, NJ	New Jersey
WBSS	97.3FM	Millville, NJ	BoSS
WBUD	1260AM	Trenton, NJ	BUD Hardin (former owner)
WBUX	1570AM	Doylestown, PA	BUCKS County
WBVR	640CC	Glenside, PA	BeaVeR College
WBYO	88.9FM	Sellersville, PA	Play on BOYERTOWN (former city of license)
WCBS	880AM	New York, NY	Columbia Broadcasting System
WCHE	1520AM	West Chester, PA	West CHEster; West Chester Has Everything
WCHR	94.5FM	Trenton, NJ/Yardley, PA	CHRistian
WCMC	1230AM	Wildwood, NJ	Cape May County
WCOJ	1420AM	Coatesville/ W Chester, PA	COatesville
WCUR	680CC	West Chester, PA	West Chester University Radio
WCZN	1590AM	Aston, PA	Country COUSIN (formerly country format)
WDAS	1480AM/ 105.3FM	Philadelphia, PA	Dannenbaum And Steppacher (former owners)
WDBK	95.1FM	Blackwood, NJ	WooDBlacK
WDEL	1150AM	Wilmington, DE	DELaware
WDNR	89.5FM	Chester, PA	WiDNeR University
WDOX	93.1FM	Wildwood Crest, NJ	DOX Radio Partnership
WDVR	89.7FM	Delaware Twp, NJ	Delaware Valley Radio
WEEE	89.5FM	Cherry Hill/Voorhees, NJ	None
WEST	1400AM	Easton, PA	EaSTon

WEXP	530CC	Philadelphia, PA	EXPlorer (Lasalle U team)
WFAN	660AM	New York, NY	Sports FANatic
WFLN	95.7FM	Philadelphia, PA	FrankLiN Broadcasting Co (former owner)
WFMZ	100.7FM	Allentown, PA	Fine Music
WFNN	98.7FM	Villas, NJ	FUN
WFPG	96.9FM	Atlantic City, NJ	World's Favorite PlayGround
WGLS	89.7FM	Glassboro, NJ	GLaSsboro (Rowan College)
WGPA	1100AM	Bethlehem, PA	Globe Publishing Assoc (former owner)
WHAT	1340AM	Philadelphia, PA	William Penn's HAT
WHHS	107.9FM	Havertown, PA	Haverford High School
WHOL	1600AM	Allentown, PA	HOLy
WHWH	1350AM	Princeton, NJ	Herbert W. Hobler (former owner)
WHYY	90.9FM	Phila, PA/ Wilmington, DE	Wider Horizons for You and Yours
WIBF	103.9FM	Jenkintown, PA	Wm., Irwin & Benj. Fox (former owners; now owned by WDRE of NY)
WIBG	1520AM	Ocean City, NJ	I Believe in God
WIFI	1460AM	Florence, NJ	HIgh FIdelity
WILM	1450AM	Wilmington, DE	WILMington
WIMG	1300AM	Trenton, NJ/ Wash Crsng, PA	IMaGination
WINS	1010AM	New York, NY	International News Service (former owner)
WIOQ	102.1FM	Philadelphia, PA	IOQ looks like 102, the dial position
WIP	610AM	Philadelphia, PA	Wireless In Phila.; Watch Its Progress
WJBR	1290AM/ 99.5FM	Wilmington, DE	John Beauchamp Reynolds (former owner)
WJIC	1510AM	Salem, NJ	Jersey Information Center
WJJZ	106.1FM	Philadelphia, PA	Smooth JaZz
WJLK	94.3FM	Asbury Park, NJ	J. Lyle Kinmouth (former owner)
WJNN	106.3FM	North Cape May, NJ	None
WJRH	104.9FM	Easton, PA	None (Lafayette College)
WJRZ	1550AM/ 100.1FM	Toms Rv, NJ (AM)/ Manhwkn, NJ (FM)	JeRsey
WKAP	1320AM	Allentown, PA	Allentown, Pennsylvania
WKDN	106.9FM	Camden, NJ	Play on Camden
WKDU	91.7FM	Philadelphia, PA	Drexel University
WKOE	1450AM	Atlantic City, NJ	Suggests Country
WKTU	98.3FM	Ocean City, NJ	None
WKXW	101.5FM	Trenton, NJ	Kicks
WLEV	96.1FM	Easton, PA	LEhigh Valley
WLFR	91.7FM	Pomona, NJ	Lake Fred Radio (Stockton State College)

WLIU	88.7FM	Lincoln University, PA	LIncoln University
WLVR	91.3FM	Bethelehem, PA	Lehigh Valley Radio (Lehigh University)
WMGK	102.9FM	Philadelphia, PA	MaGic
WMGM	107.3FM	Atlantic City, NJ	For NYC station WMGM (Metro-Goldwyn-Mayer)
WMID	1340AM/ 99.3FM	Atl Cty (AM)/ Pleasantvl (FM), NJ	MID-Atlantic Broadcasting (former owner)
WMIZ	1270AM	Vineland, NJ	La Zeta (Spanish for letter Z)
WMMR	93.3FM	Philadelphia, PA	MetroMedia Radio (former owner)
WMPH	91.7FM	Wilmington, DE	Mount Pleasant High School
WMUH	91.7FM	Allentown, PA	MUHlenberg College
WNAP	1110AM	Norristown, PA	Norristown And Philadelphia
WNJC	1360AM	Washington Twp, NJ	New Jersey Country
WNJN	89.7FM	Atlantic City, NJ	New Jersey Network
WNJS	88.1FM	Berlin, NJ	New Jersey Network South
WNJT	88.1FM	Trenton, NJ	New Jersey Network Trenton
WNNN	101.7FM	Canton, NJ	None
WNPV	1440AM	Lansdale, PA	North Penn Valley; North Penn's Voice
WNRK	1260AM	Newark, DE	NewaRK
WOBM	1160AM/ 92.7FM	Lakewd, NJ (AM)/ Toms Riv, NJ (FM)	Ocean, Burlington & Monmouth counties
WOCC	90.5FM	Toms River, NJ	Ocean County College
WOGL	1210AM/ 98.1FM	Philadelphia, PA	Old GoLd
WOND	1400AM	Pleasantville, NJ	WONDerful
WOR	710AM	New York, NY	World Of Radio; Orpheum Radio
WPAZ	1370AM	Pottstown, PA	Pottstown Area
WPEB	88.1FM	Philadelphia, PA	West Philadelphia Educational Broadcasting
WPEN	950AM	Philadelphia, PA	William PENn Broadcasting Corp (former owner)
WPGR	1540AM	Bala Cynwyd, PA	Philadelphia Gold Radio
WPHE	690AM	Phoenixville/Phila, PA	Philadelphia Hispanic Echo
WPLY	100.3FM	Media, PA	PhiLlY
WPRB	103.3FM	Princeton, NJ	Princeton (U.) Radio Broadcasting
WPST	97.5FM	Princeton, NJ	Passport Stereo Trenton (former travel format)
WQHS	730CC	Philadelphia, PA	Quad Hill Superblock (Univ of Penn dorms)
WQNJ	89.5FM	Ocean Acres, NJ	New Jersey (simulcasts WJLK)
WRDR	104.9FM	Egg Harbor City, NJ	RoDio Radio, Inc. (owner)
WRDV	89.3FM	Warminster, PA	Radio Delaware Valley
WREY	1440AM	Millville, NJ	REY Spanish for "king"; billed King of Radio
WRFT	540CC	Ambler, PA	Radio Free Temple (University)
WRGN	88.1FM	Sweet Valley, PA	Radio Good News
WRRC	88.1FM	Lawrenceville, NJ	Radio Rider College

Radio

Call	Frequency	Location	Description
WRSD	94.9FM	Folsom, PA	Ridley School District (Ridley High School)
WRTI	90.1FM	Philadelphia, PA	Radio Temple Institute (Temple University)
WSJL	102.3FM	Cape May, NJ	South Jersey's Lighthouse
WSJR	530CC	Phila/Merion Sta, PA	Saint Josephs (University) Radio
WSKR	102.7FM	Petersburg, NJ	SCORE (sports format)
WSNJ	107.7FM	Bridgeton, NJ	We Serve New Jersey; South New Jersey
WSRN	91.5FM	Swarthmore, PA	Swarthmore (College) Radio Network
WSSJ	1310AM	Camden, NJ	Sound of South Jersey; Super Station
WSTW	93.7FM	Wilmington, DE	STeinman Enterprises, Wilmington
WTEL	860AM	Bala Cynwyd, PA	TELevision
WTMR	800AM	Camden, NJ	Where The Master Reigns; Thomas M. Roberts
WTSR	91.3FM	Trenton, NJ	Trenton State (College) Radio
WTTH	96.1FM	Margate City, NJ	The ToucH
WTTM	920AM	Trenton, NJ	The World Takes, Trenton Makes
WURD	900AM	Philadelphia, PA	As in The WORD (religious)
WUSL	98.9FM	Philadelphia, PA	USL looks like U.S. 1 (the highway)
WUSS	1490AM	Atlantic City, NJ	None
WVCH	740AM	Chester/Brookhvn, PA	Voice of the Christian Home; Voice of CHester
WVLT	92.1FM	Vineland, NJ	Vineland LighT
WVUD	93.1FM	Newark, DE	Voice of the University of Delaware
WWDB	96.5FM	Philadelphia, PA	William and Dolly Banks (former owners)
WWFM	89.1FM	Windsor Twp, NJ	West Windsor FM
WWJZ	640AM	Mount Holly, NJ	Named for old WJZ, NYC big band station
WWOC	94.3FM	Avalon, NJ	From WildWood to Ocean City
WWPH	107.9FM	Princeton Jctn, NJ	West Windsor—Plainsboro High
WXKW	1470AM	Allentown, PA	None
WXLV,39	169 4FM	Allentown, PA	National Weather Service
WXLV	90.3FM	Schnecksville, PA	EXperimental Lehigh Valley (Community College)
WXPN	88.5FM	Philadelphia, PA	EXperimental (University of) Pennsylvania Network
WXTU	92.5FM	Philadelphia, PA	None
WXVU	89.1FM	Villanova, PA	EXperimental Villanova University
WYNS	1160AM	Lehighton, PA	WINS
WYSP	94.1FM	Philadelphia, PA	We're Your Station in Philadelphia
WYXR	104.5FM	Philadelphia, PA	None
WZXL	100.7FM	Wildwood, NJ	None
WZZD	990AM	Lafayette Hill, PA	WiZZarD (used when rock; now religious)
WZZE	97.3FM	Glen Mills, PA	None (Glen Mills High School)
WZZO	95.1FM	Bethlehem, PA	ZOO

How the Delaware River Got Its Name

If not for the European predilection for claiming and naming, Philadelphia would be up the Lenapewitik, or "River of the Common People."

In 1609, Henry Hudson, the first European to worry about the shoals off Cape Henlopen, gave the river a colorless, if logical name: the South River. This distinguished it from the previously discovered North River that flowed by Manhattan. The South River's shallow waters couldn't possibly lead to the Pacific Ocean, figured Hudson, and bearing in mind his assignment—to find a passage to Asia for the Dutch East India Company—he ordered the lumbering *Halve Maen* (Half Moon) back into open sea. Then Hudson continued northward to survey the flat expanse of New Jersey for the westward passage. Shipmate Robert Juet commented in his diary that August morning: "Hee that will thoroughly Discover this great Bay, must have a small Pinasse [schooner], that must draw but foure or five foote water."

Throughout the 17th century, Dutch maps marked this place as "Zuydt Rivier" (South River). Not the British maps. Hardly a year after Hudson, Samuel Argall, an adventurer known for fast sailing and hard dealing (he later took Pocahontas hostage for the release of English arms and prisoners), had delivered Virginia's first appointed governor, Thomas West, to Jamestown. West found his fellow colonists starved, demoralized, and eager to return home. Possibly to avert an exodus, West dispatched his two best vessels, Argall's and another under George Somers, in search of food and provisions.

They set out for the Bermudas, which Somers well knew (from having been shipwrecked there) had an impressive population of wild hogs. (Shakespeare based *The Tempest* partially upon the popular story of Somers' wreck.) After yet another storm, Somers found himself back at Bermuda. Argall was driven far north, to Cape Cod, where he loaded up on fish for the sorry Virginians. Carefully wending his way back down the coast, Argall sailed into a large bay fed by a wide river, the same one Hudson had visited only a year before. He renamed Hudson's South River the "Delaware" for his governor, Thomas West, the Lord De La Warr. West never visited and, by all accounts, never gave much thought to the "discovery" made in his name. ∎

Source: C. A. Weslager, *Dutch Explorers, Traders and Settlers in the Delaware Valley 1609–1664* (University of Pennsylvania Press, 1961).

Walt Whitman and the Camden Ferry

CITIZENS' MANUAL

" T hen the Camden Ferry. What exhilaration, change, people, business, by day. What soothing, silent, wondrous hours, at night, crossing on the boat, most all to myself—pacing the deck, alone, forward or aft. What communion with the waters, the air, the exquisite chiaroscuro—the sky and stars, that speak no word, nothing to the intellect, yet so eloquent, so communicative to the soul. ...

"I don't know anything more *filling* than to be on the wide firm deck of a powerful boat, a clear, cool, extra-moonlight night, crushing proudly and resistlessly through this thick, marbly, glistening ice. The whole river is now spread with it—some immense cakes. There is such weirdness about the scene—partly the quality of the light, with its tinge of blue, the lunar twilight—only the large stars holding up their own in the radiance of the moon. Temperature sharp, comfortable for motion, dry, full of oxygen. But the sense of power—the steady, scornful, imperious urge of our strong new engine, as she ploughs her way through the big and little cakes. ...

"Such a show as the Delaware presented an hour before sundown yesterday evening, all along between Philadelphia and Camden, is worth weaving into an item. It was full tide, a fair breeze from the southwest, the water of a pale tawny color, and just enough motion to make things frolicsome and lively. Add to these an approaching sunset of unusual splendor, a broad tumble of clouds, with much golden haze and profusion of beaming shaft and dazzle. In the midst of it all, in the clear drab of the afternoon light, there steam'd up the river the large new boat, 'the Wenonah,' as pretty an object as you could wish to see, lightly and swiftly skimming along, all trim and white, covered with flags, transparent red and blue, streaming out in the breeze. Only a new ferryboat, and yet in its fitness comparable with the prettiest product of Nature's cunning, and rivaling it. High up in the transparent ether gracefully balanced and circled four or five great sea hawks, while here below, amid the pomp and picturesqueness of sky and river, swam this creation of artificial beauty and motion and power, in its way no less than perfect. ..." ∎

—Walt Whitman, *Specimen Days* (Rees Welsh, 1882–1883)

THE RIVERBUS

Crosses the Delaware between Penn's Landing at the foot of Walnut Street (SEPTA connection: Routes 33 and 21) and New Jersey State Aquarium (NJ Transit connection: "Aqualink" shuttle to the Camden Transportation Center).

Departs Philadelphia: quarter past and three-quarters past each hour of operation.

Departs Camden: every hour and half hour of operation.

Hours of operation:
Summer (Memorial Day Weekend to Labor Day):

8am–8pm	Monday, Tuesday, Thursday
8am–9pm	Wednesday, Friday
9am–midnight	Saturday
9am–9pm	Sunday

Winter (Labor Day to Memorial Day):

8am–5:45pm	Monday–Friday
9am–7:45pm	Saturday
9am–5:45pm	Sunday
Ride time:	10 minutes

Fares:

Adults	$ 2.00
Children and Seniors	$ 1.50
Twenty-ticket book	$20.00

Call **(609) 365-3300** for Aquarium hours.

Call **(800) 634-4027** for Riverbus information and group rates.

Riverbus Facts:

Built:	Rhode Island in 1972
Original name:	"Mount Mansfield"
First home:	Lake Champlain
Original capacity:	20 automobiles
Second home:	Mobile, Alabama (1979–1988)
Length:	100 feet
Current capacity:	400 people

Source: Robert J. Ravelli, ed., *Car-Free in Philadelphia: The Regional Public Transit Guide,* 1993–1994 edition (Camino, 1993).

Twenty-five years ago, when the PSFS Building was selected "Building of the Century" by the Philadelphia Chapter of the American Institute of Architects, the building was honored "for being...the first matured, significant, architectural expression of the American skyscraper."

Architects:
George Howe (1886–1955) and
William Lescaze (1896–1969)

Builder: George A. Fuller Co.

Opened: August 1, 1932

Stories: 36 stories

Height: 491 feet

Height of sign: 27 feet

Color of sign's letters: Red

Distance viewed on a clear night: 20 miles

Cost of finished building in 1932: Approximately $8 million

Amount of glass on building's exterior surface: 1½ acres

Proportion of glass on exterior surface: 1:3

Number of black face bricks on the south side: 392,000

Number of face bricks on the entire building: 1,200,000

Duration of non-stop round trip of elevator: 1 minute

Square feet of office space: 296,269

Square feet of rentable store space: 28,232

Details designed by architects: Hat and coat hooks

Wall finishes of the 33rd floor: Macassar ebony, rotary walnut, Italian travertine

Veneer on the oval boardroom table on 33rd floor: Macassar ebony

Origin of Macassar ebony: Isle of Celebes (South Pacific)

Source: PSFS Building Fact Sheet.

PSFS: The Acronyms

Now that the Philadelphia Saving Fund Society is no more a corporation, the world-famous International Style building at 12th and Market Streets stands as an all-purpose neon billboard. How so? Unlike the didactic PECO lights relentlessly flashing do-goodisms, the 27-foot-high PSFS letters require more interaction to gain meaning. When the city budget deficit rises, for instance, the sign might stand for "Philadelphia's Sordid Financial Status." When a football star signs with another city, it means "Philadelphia Sports Fans Suffer." The Center City District's Make It a Night campaign urges us to "Please Stay For Supper" on Wednesdays. (Philadelphians have known the sign meant that for decades. They also knew it meant "Philadelphia Slowly Facing Starvation.") And in those down times—when imagination fails—we might look up and read the all-purpose utility motto: "Philadelphians Savor Fried Scrapple." ∎

The potential acronyms are endless. Here are only a few messages that may apply:

Prominent Sign Falters Sadly

Please Save Foundering Sign

Philadelphia's Significant, Famous Symbol

Precarious Situation Forced Sellout

Parsimonious Suburbanites Fight SEPTA

Partisan Serbians Favor Slivovitz

Police Shoot First Sometimes

Perplexed Statesmen Finesse Sanctimoniously

Pathological State Finance Statistics

Pastrami Sandwiches For Sale

Prominent Symbol Fading Soon?

Baseball: 1871–1909

October 30, 1871: In the last game of the season, the Philadelphia Athletics beat the Chicago White Stockings, 4–1, to become the first undisputed champion of the newly emerging professional baseball world. Chicago's stadium had burned down in the Great Fire, only a few weeks before, so the game is played in Brooklyn. Thousands of fans greet the Athletics on their return to Philadelphia.

April 22, 1876: A crowd of 3,000 watches the Boston Red Stockings defeat the Philadelphia Athletics, 6–5, in the first-ever National League game. It is played at Athletics Park, bounded by Master Street and Jefferson Avenue, 25th and 29th Streets.

1883: The Phillies' initial year. They win 17 games and lose 81.

April 30, 1887: The Phillies defeat the New York Giants, 19–15, before an overflow crowd in the inaugural game at the recently completed Philadelphia Base Ball Park (capacity 18,000) at the northeast corner of Broad Street and Lehigh Avenue. When New Yorker William F. Baker purchases the Phillies in 1913, the stadium becomes known as the Baker Bowl. In its intimate confines, fans hurl insults (and objects) at opposition players, and Phillies fans gain a reputation as "the league's most abominable."

July 13, 1896: In one away game, and in three consecutive at-bats, Ed Delahanty of the Phillies hits four inside-the-park home runs. Nonetheless, they lose to the Chicago Cubs, 9–8.

August 6, 1903: The most disastrous day in Philadelphia spectator sports. In the top of the fourth inning of the second game of a double-header at the Baker Bowl (Phillies vs. Boston Braves), fans hear a brawl on the street outside. Hundreds rush to the top of the stands, and their collective weight cracks rotten timbers. The stadium collapses to the street, killing 12 and injuring 232.

October 6, 1905: The Athletics win the American League pennant. Due to a shoulder injury incurred while horsing around with fellow Athletics pitcher Andy Coakley, ace "Rube" Waddell is unable to play in the World Series. The Giants' incomparable Christy Mathewson shuts out the Athletics in three games as the Giants take the series, four games to one.

April 12, 1909: Shibe Park, the first of the great American concrete-and-steel arenas and the showplace of the American League, opens. It is about six blocks from the Baker Bowl, bounded by Lehigh Avenue and Somerset Street and 20th and 21st Streets. Benjamin Franklin Shibe, a Fishtown native and partner in Shibe and Reach, Kensington manufacturers of baseball and athletic equipment, owns 50% of the Athletics. On opening day an overcapacity 31,160 fans watch Eddie Plank defeat the Boston Red Sox, 8–1.

LEARNING TO ROW

I chose crew for my spring sport. An old master named Mr. Church took us new girls out to the Lower School boat docks to learn the basics: how to get the boat off its shelf, down the dock, and into the water; how to step into the boat and strap our feet into the stirrups; how to position our oars in the oarlocks and where to grip the smooth butt of the oar. He taught us port from starboard, how deep to dip our oars into the water and how high to carry them when we pulled them out. ...

Once we learned how to get the boat into the water without ruining the shell or hurting ourselves, he led us into the calm water. We rowed clumsily, scooping deep into the water or glancing the surface. ...

I watched the back of the girl in front of me and moved my body with hers. The oars dipped, and I listened to the sound in order to hit the rhythm. Crouch and pull. Make the pull smooth, hard, long as you could. The trick was to hit a balance between thinking and not thinking. Once I'd gotten the oar into the water just right, I had to stop thinking about it and put my arms just there again, pull just so hard with my back, slide with just the same force from my thighs and calves. It took thinking about each part, and then letting go of the thought so that the parts could work together. Now and then I hit the balance. My body moved, and my mind was clear, focused on nothing but the rhythm and the sounds of the oars, the repetition, and Patty Glovsky's voice shouting hoarsely: Stroke! Stroke! Stroke! Wood and metal and water made their own sounds, and we were silent.

—Lorene Cary, *Black Ice.*

CITIZENS' MANUAL

SCHUYLKILL NAVY

The Schuylkill Navy of Philadelphia was founded in 1858, with Charles M. Prevost as the first Commodore. Today, the 10-club organization claims to be the oldest continuous sports-governing body in the country, responsible for organizing Schuylkill River regattas nearly every weekend throughout the year. And it hosts two of the largest regattas in the country.

The Dad Vail Regatta is the largest independent competitive collegiate rowing event in the world, with more than 100 colleges and universities participating each year. Founded in 1934 to help encourage rowing on small college campuses, it moved from city to city before coming to Philadelphia for keeps in 1952. The Dad Vail was started by Rusty Callow, former crew coach at the University of Pennsylvania, and is named in honor of former Coach Harry Emerson Vail, known as Dad Vail to his crew at the University of Wisconsin. The two-day event is always held the Friday and Saturday before Mother's Day.

The Stotesbury Cup started out as a single race in 1926, when Philadelphian Edward T. Stotesbury offered a cup to the winner of a regatta. Over time, the Stotesbury Cup has become its own two-day regatta for high-school rowers. Now known as the largest secondary scholastic regatta in the world, it is always scheduled for the weekend after the Dad Vail.

1994 REGATTAS OF THE SCHUYLKILL NAVY

January 15: Annual scholastic meeting

February 6: Vesper indoor rowing (Memorial Hall)

February 19: High-school water practice; Annual referee meeting

March 13: Many Flick Regatta (first in a series of high-school regattas named for Flick, whose sons rowed for Monsignor Bonnor High School)

March 20: Many Flick Regatta

March 21: Schuylkill Navy meeting

Baseball: 1910–1915

October 23, 1910: Philadelphia's first World Series victory. In the eighth inning of the fifth game, the Athletics score five runs to defeat the Chicago Cubs, 7–2.

October 26, 1911: In the sixth game of the World Series, Connie Mack's Athletics batter John McGraw's New York Giants, 13–2, at Shibe Park to again become world champions. Ever since it started in 1903, the World Series has drawn large crowds, but the 1911 series attendance of 180,000 sets a record. The players receive highest-ever pay: $3,655 each for the Athletics and $2,436 each for the Giants. The modern stadiums of both teams are packed and, for the first time, those who can't purchase tickets are prohibited from standing on the field. Scores of telegraph operators tap out play-by-play reports to fans throughout America and as far away as Havana.

May 18, 1912: A few days earlier, in New York, Detroit Tiger Ty Cobb had been suspended for charging a heckler in the stands, and his teammates had vowed not to play until the suspension was lifted. When the Tigers take the field at Shibe Park to play the Athletics, umpire Bill Dinneen orders Cobb off, and the entire team leaves in protest. Anticipating this turn of events, Connie Mack and the Detroit manager are prepared with a team recruited by Aloysius Travers from the St. Joseph's College squad and the sandlots of Fairmount Park. The Tigers turn over their uniforms to the amateurs, who amuse the Athletics, 24–2, before 20,000 disgruntled fans. Travers later is ordained a Jesuit priest and eventually returns to St. Joseph's as a member of its faculty.

August 30, 1913: A brouhaha flares up at the Baker Bowl between the Phillies—who have seen a comfortable National League lead held for almost half the season wither away—and the New York Giants, with whom they are locked in a do-or-die struggle for first place. With the Phillies holding an 8–6 lead at the top of the ninth, hundreds of fans move to the empty centerfield bleachers and wave newspapers, programs, handkerchiefs, and hats to distract the Giants batters. New York manager John McGraw convinces home plate umpire Bill Brennan to order the centerfield bleachers cleared, but neither the Phillies manager nor the police take action. Brennan declares the game forfeited to the Giants, and an angry mob of Phillies fans harass Giant players as they enter North Broad Street Station. National League officials order the two teams to resume the game, but the Phillies win comes after the Giants have the pennant wrapped up.

October 8, 1915: In the first game of the World Series, the Phillies, with Grover Cleveland Alexander on the mound, defeat the Boston Red Sox, 3–1. The Phillies will not win another World Series game for 65 years.

Baseball: 1917–1949

September 3, 1917: The Phillies' Grover Cleveland Alexander pitches two games against the Brooklyn Dodgers in the same day and wins them both. For the third straight year, he will finish the season with at least thirty wins.

October 3, 1924: The first game of the first "Colored World Series" is played at the Baker Bowl before a capacity crowd of 18,500. The Kansas City Monarchs beat the Philadelphia Hillsdale team, and KC goes on to capture the series.

October 12, 1929: At Shibe Park in the seventh inning of the fourth game of the World Series, Connie Mack's Philadelphia Athletics trail the Chicago Cubs, 8–0. Al Simmons homers to begin one of the most spectacular comebacks in the history of post-season play. The Athletics explode for nine more runs, and Connie Mack brings in Robert Moses "Lefty" Grove to shut down the Cubs the rest of the way. The A's go on to win the next game and take the series, four games to one.

May 28, 1930: At the age of 43, the incomparable Grover Cleveland Alexander appears in a major league game for the last time, pitching the seventh and eighth innings for the Phillies against the Braves in Boston.

October 8, 1930: George Earnshaw wins the final game as the Philadelphia Athletics win the World Series for the second year in a row, beating the St. Louis Cardinals four games to two. Some still consider this team, with its slick infielding, hard-hitting outfield, and outstanding pitching staff, the greatest team in baseball history.

1932: Jimmie Foxx of the Athletics hits 58 home runs, the most ever hit in one season by a Philadelphia major league player.

July 10, 1936: The Phillies' Chuck Klein hits four home runs in a 10-inning game against the Pittsburgh Pirates at Forbes Field as the Phillies win, 9–6.

June 30, 1938: The Phillies play at the venerable Baker Bowl for the last time, losing to the New York Giants, 14–1. Their next game, on the Fourth of July, is played at Shibe Park.

May 17, 1939: The first night game is played at Shibe Park as the Cleveland Indians defeat the Athletics, 8–3. At exactly 8:36pm, the floodlights are switched on in unison, stunning the crowd of 15,109 with their brilliance (but unfortunately failing to warm the chilly 54° temperature). A reporter for the *Evening Bulletin* complains that the "perfect illumination" exposes but does nothing to improve the Athletics' lackluster skills; the game is their fifth straight loss.

June 15, 1949: Phillies' first baseman Eddie Waitkus is shot and severely wounded in a Chicago hotel by Ruth Steinhagen. Waitkus recovers to play the following season. The scene inspires Bernard Malamud for a major incident in his novel, *The Natural.*

REGATTAS continued...

March 26 or April 2: College regattas begin

March 27: Many Flick Regatta

April 9: Childs Cup (Penn, Princeton, Columbia)

April 10: Many Flick Regatta

April 16: Murphy Cup; Penn/Princeton

April 17: Many Flick Regatta

April 18: Schuylkill Navy meeting

April 23: Kerr Cup (always in Philadelphia; named for the first crew coach at Drexel, Thomas Kerr); Adams Cup (rotates among cities)

April 24: Catholic high-school championship

April 30: Bergen Cup (Drexel, LaSalle, Saint Joseph's, Temple, Villanova)

May 1: City championship (high school)

May 13–14: Dad Vail collegiate championship

May 15: Shipley Regatta (high school)

May 16: Schuylkill Navy meeting

May 20–21: Stotesbury Cup (high school)

May 29: Middlestate Regatta (colleges, high schools, clubs)

June 18: Schuylkill Navy Regatta (clubs)

June 20: Schuylkill Navy meeting

July 2–3: Independence Day Regatta

September 10: Bayada Regatta (for the disabled)

September 19: Schuylkill Navy meeting

October 8: Navy Day Regatta

October 17: Schuylkill Navy meeting

October 29: Head of the Schuylkill

November 5: Drexel Regatta

November 12: Frostbite Regatta

November 13: Braxton Memorial Regatta

November 21: Schuylkill Navy meeting

November 24: Thanksgiving Day Run

Source: Stephen Orova, Drexel University Coach and current Commodore, Schuylkill Navy.

CITIZENS'
MANUAL

A TRIP TO THE MINORS

Minor League Baseball Teams Within 200 Miles of Philadelphia

28 MILES
Wilmington Blue Rocks—
Carolina League, Class A
Affiliation: Kansas City Royals
Judy Johnson Field at Legend Stadium
Wilmington, Delaware
Phone: (302) 888-2583

63 MILES
Reading Phillies—
Eastern League, Class AA
Affiliation: Philadelphia Phillies
Municipal Memorial Stadium
Reading, Pennsylvania
Phone: 375-8469

107 MILES
Harrisburg Senators—
Eastern League, Class AA
Affiliation: Montreal Expos
RiverSide Stadium
Harrisburg, Pennsylvania
Phone: (717) 231-4444

130 MILES
Scranton/Wilkes-Barre Red Barons—
International League, Class AAA
Affiliation: Philadelphia Phillies
Lackawanna County Multi-Purpose Stadium
Scranton, Pennsylvania
Phone: (717) 963-6556

138 MILES
Bowie Baysox—
Eastern League, Class AA
Affiliation: Baltimore Orioles
Stadium under construction
Bowie, Maryland
Phone: (410) 467-2297

Sports

Baseball: 1950–1957

October 1, 1950: On the final day of the season, the Phillies beat the Brooklyn Dodgers in a 10-inning game at Ebbets Field to capture their first National League pennant since 1915. Rich Ashburn throws out Dodger leftfielder Cal Abrams at the plate, and Robin Roberts becomes the first Phillie since Grover Cleveland Alexander to win 20 games.

October 18, 1950: Connie Mack announces his retirement. During his 50 years in Philadelphia, he has achieved 3,776 victories and 4,025 defeats, both records that are likely to go unchallenged as long as baseball is played. Mack also won nine American League pennants and five World Series.

August 28, 1952: Robin Roberts pitches a complete game, and for the rest of the year he finishes every game he starts. During the first half of the next season, his streak of complete games continues, finally ending at 28 games on July 9, 1953, when he is relieved in the eighth inning in a game against the Brooklyn Dodgers.

September 29, 1952: Robin Roberts defeats the New York Giants, 7–4, for his 28th victory of the season.

1952: Bobby Shantz wins 24 of the 79 games the Philadelphia Athletics win during the season, and baseball writers name him the American League's Most Valuable Player.

1953: Before the start of the season, Shibe Park is renamed Connie Mack Stadium.

August 30, 1953: Philadelphia-born Roy Campanella knocks in five runs as his career team, the Brooklyn Dodgers, defeats the Cardinals, 20–4. By season's end, Campanella has scored 103 runs, knocked in 142 runs, and batted .312. He is voted the National League's Most Valuable Player, an honor he will achieve twice more.

September 13, 1953: Left-handed pitcher Bob Trice, the first African American to play for the Athletics, goes eight innings against the St. Louis Browns at Connie Mack Stadium before a sparse, late-season crowd of 8,477. He displays remarkable control, walking not a single one of the 31 batters he faces, but allows eight hits, including two home runs. The Athletics lose, 5–2, but Trice pitches twice more before season's end and wins both games.

November 9, 1954: The American League grants the Philadelphia Athletics permission to move to Kansas City.

April 22, 1957: Phillies infielder John Kennedy enters the game as a pinch runner for Solly Hemus and becomes the first African American to play for the Phillies, the last National League team to integrate. (Only the American League's Boston Red Sox took longer, waiting until 1959.)

Baseball: 1959–1976

April 16, 1959: The Phillies' Dave Philley achieves a record nine consecutive pinch hits by ending his 1958 season with eight and beginning with another at his first at-bat of the new season.

August 7, 1961: Beer is sold at Connie Mack Stadium for the first time.

August 20, 1961: The Phillies win their first game since July 28 and fly home to be greeted by a small, affectionate crowd at the airport. Their 23 consecutive game losing streak sets a modern National League record.

June 21, 1964: On Father's Day, in the first game of a double-header at Shea Stadium in New York, Jim Bunning pitches a perfect game as the Phillies defeat the Mets, 6–0. The Phillies go on to win the second game behind the pitching of 18-year-old rookie Rick Wise, who will pitch a no-hitter for the Phillies almost exactly seven years later.

September 20, 1964: The Phillies defeat the Dodgers, 3–2, in Los Angeles and fly home with a 6½–game lead with only 12 games remaining in the season. They lose the next 10 games, and the St. Louis Cardinals win the pennant.

June 15, 1968: Gene Mauch is fired by the Phillies after having managed the team for 1,331 games, more than any other manager in the history of the franchise.

October 1, 1970: The Phillies win their last game played at Connie Mack Stadium, defeating the Montreal Expos, 2–1, in 10 innings. Upon entering the gates, fans are given wooden slats as souvenirs, which they use to create a terrifying din by beating the stadium in unison. Others rip out seats as additional souvenirs; many fights start. When the game finally ends, fans run amok on the field.

April 10, 1971: A crowd of 55,352 attends the Phillies' opener against the Montreal Expos, the first baseball game played in Veterans Stadium. The Phillies win, 4–1.

June 23, 1971: Phillies righthander Rick Wise pitches a no-hit game against the Cincinnati Reds, hitting two home runs and becoming the fourth Phillie to pitch a no-hitter—and the only one to do it wearing glasses.

February 25, 1972: The Phillies trade Rick Wise for Steve Carlton from the St. Louis Cardinals. He wins 27 games, nearly half of the 57 games won in the Phillies 1972 season. Carlton compiles a 15-game winning streak and receives the Cy Young Award for the first time.

July 17, 1976: Mike Schmidt hits four home runs as the Phillies defeat the Chicago Cubs, 18–16, at Wrigley Field. Schmidt hits his first homer off Rick Reuschel and his fourth homer off Rick's brother, Paul.

A TRIP TO THE MINORS
continued...

150 MILES
Frederick Keys—
Carolina League, Class A
Affiliation: Baltimore Orioles
Harry Grove Stadium
Frederick, Maryland
Phone: (301) 662-0013

173 MILES
Hagerstown Suns—
South Atlantic League, Class A
Affiliation: Toronto Blue Jays
Municipal Stadium
Hagerstown, Maryland
Phone: (301) 791-6266

188 MILES
Binghamton Mets—Eastern League, Class AA
Affiliation: New York Mets
Binghamton Municipal Stadium
Binghamton, New York
Phone: (607) 723-6387

❖

THE FOUR PHILLIES WHOSE NUMBERS HAVE BEEN RETIRED:

Richie Ashburn,	#1
Steve Carlton,	#32
Robin Roberts,	#36
Mike Schmidt,	#20

1980 REMEMBERED

October air glistens with victory. Shocks of fodder, piles of pumpkins, the traditional assemblies of harvest home stand in the cool air, marking the end of the farmer's long war with earth. Clear and bright, autumn at its best, is how we recall the city's day of triumph. It had been a long season, a tense playoff, a hard series, but Greg Gross laid down the perfect bunt, Manny Trillo made the perfect throw, Tug McGraw leapt and patted, and a Whitmanesque babble of humanity overflowed the streets, crowding joyously to let us feel for one day how civic life might be. Divisions dissolved: bankers, bums, secretaries, newsboys, and housewives, we smiled and touched and traded small gifts like kids at an antiwar rally. Packed close, standing, dancing, yelling, we reached toward the trucks moving slowly along the route of the Pope's flash. On the trucks rode the men whose intensity yielded this bounty. They were not cool. Like heroes loosed from some old epic, they gave completely, Carlton in lonely discipline, Bowa boyishly, McBride bravely, Schmidt with the body that would have won him laurels in any sport in any age. Rose had come from the west to provide the missing link; we unified in the rhythm—Pete, Pete, Pete, Pete—when he set records and watched the man on the field, made for baseball as Eakins was made for painting. But it was, at the heart, Garry Maddox, spread at the plate into an image of concentration, Maddox doubling to center, Maddox moving stealthily to the last catch, Maddox sitting above us now. He should have been wearing embroidered robes of fawn-colored silk and riding a white charger. It was only a truck, only a game, but he was our hero, the prince of a city named Brotherly Love.

—Henry Glassie

Baseball: 1976–1993

September 26, 1976: Greg Luzinski hits the game-winning home run as the Phillies defeat the Expos at Montreal to become champions of the National League East. The Cincinnati Reds take the National League pennant.

October 8, 1977: Although Steve Carlton is on the mound, the Phillies again lose the pennant, this time to the Los Angeles Dodgers in a dreary, rain-soaked final fourth game.

September 30, 1978: Once again, Greg Luzinski hits a winning home run as the Phillies defeat the Pittsburgh Pirates, 10–8, to become champions of the National League East for the third straight year. Once again, they lose the pennant to the Los Angeles Dodgers.

October 21, 1980: For the first time in history, the Phillies are World Champions. Steve Carlton allows four hits over seven innings and Tug McGraw pitches scoreless relief as the Phillies defeat the Kansas City Royals in the sixth and final World Series game. The regular season was a cliffhanger. The high point: squeezing out an 11-inning victory over the Expos in Montreal on October 4 to clinch the Eastern Division title. In a first-ever playoff defeat of the Western Division champions, the Phillies subdue the Houston Astros in five games. Mike Schmidt hits a career-high 48 home runs during the regular season and is voted Most Valuable Player of both the National League and the World Series.

September 20, 1992: In a game against the Pittsburgh Pirates at Three Rivers Stadium, Phillies second baseman Mickey Morandini turns the first unassisted triple play in the National League since May 20, 1927. With Andy Van Slyke on first and Barry Bonds on second, the Pirates' Jeff King hits a line drive straight up the middle. Morandini catches it, steps on second to double up Van Slyke, and then tags Barry Bonds, who has strayed off second.

September 4, 1993: Darren Daulton's fourth-inning sacrifice fly allows John Kruk to score and the Phillies to break a 49-year-old National League record (previously held by the Pittsburgh Pirates) of 150 consecutive games without being shut out. With a comfortable 8½ game lead over Montreal, the first-place Phillies lose to the Cincinnati Reds, 6–5. Their record ends on September 30 at 174 games, with a 5–0 loss to Pittsburgh. By then, the Phillies have secured the division championship.

October 13, 1993: Phillies win National League pennant. ∎

Sources: Richie Ashburn with Allen Lewis, *Richie Ashburn's Phillies Trivia* (Running Press, 1983); Bruce Kuklick, *To Every Thing a Season: Shibe Park and Urban Philadelphia, 1909–1976* (Princeton University Press, 1991); Philadelphia Daily News, *Philadelphia's Record Breakers and Legend Makers* (Running Press, 1989); Rich Westcott and Frank Bilovsky, *The New Phillies Encyclopedia* (Temple University Press, 1993).

How Telephone Exchanges Got That Way

Not long after Alexander Graham Bell demonstrated his new invention at the Centennial in 1876 ("My God, it talks!") the Bell Telephone Company of Philadelphia began to provide service in Center City. Callers gave the operator the one-, two-, or three-digit number of the party being called, a system that remained unchanged until 1923.

At first, telephones were considered business instruments and the earliest neighborhoods wired were those most industrialized: Frankford, Germantown, West Philadelphia, and Manayunk. Callers announced a number followed by the neighborhood abbreviation: WP for West Philadelphia, GN for Germantown. To call the United Cab and Carriage Company at 40th and Locust Streets, for example, you would request "31 WP."

By 1882, two city pharmacies boasted pay phones. Callers from H. C. Manlove at 16th and Pine Streets and H. B. Lippincott at 20th and Cherry Streets paid the proprietor.

Exchange designations were replaced with numbers in series by 1895. Germantown, for example, became 9000; Frankford, 8000.

Just after the turn of the century, with more than 36,000 phones in use, Bell reverted to exchange name prefixes such as Walnut and Market. Even though digits have since replaced those exchange abbreviations, a vestige of those first years remains in the printed alphabet on the pad of nearly every telephone. ■

The current exchanges in Philadelphia have their origins in the 125 exchanges named here:

221:	BAldwin 1	324:	DAvenport 4	426:	GArfield 6
222:	BAring 2	329:	DAvenport 9	427:	GArfield 7
223:	BAldwin 3	331:	DEvonshire 1	438:	GErmantown 8
224:	CApital 4	332:	DEvonshire 2	455:	GLadstone 5
225:	BAldwin 5	333:	DEvonshire 3	456:	GLadstone 6
226:	BAldwin 6	334:	DEwey 4	457:	GLadstone 7
227:	BAldwin 7	335:	DEvonshire 5	462:	HOward 2
228:	BAldwin 8	336:	DEwey 6	463:	HOward 3
229:	BAldwin 9	338:	DEvonshire 8	464:	HObart 4
232:	CEnter 2	339:	DEwey 9	465:	HOward 5
235:	CEnter 5	342:	FIdelity 2	467:	HOward 7
236:	CEnter 6	382:	EVergreen 2	468:	HOward 8
242:	CHestnut Hill 2	386:	EVergreen 6	471:	GRanite 1
247:	CHestnut Hill 7	387:	EVergreen 7	472:	GRanite 2
248:	CHestnut Hill 8	389:	FUlton 9	473:	GReenwood 3
263:	COlfax 3	423:	GArfield 3	474:	GRanite 4
288:	CUmberland 8	424:	HAncock 4	476:	GRanite 6
289:	CUmberland 9	425:	GArfield 5	477:	GReenwood 7

183

KEYSTONE: THE OTHER PHONE COMPANY

Competition is healthiest—for the winner.

With the hope that competition for Bell would lower telephone rates, at the turn of the century the Keystone Telephone Company was allowed to erect poles and use city-owned conduits for its wires. Service began March 1, 1902, with one operator and one exchange. Keystone grew, if fitfully, providing limited long-distance service and introducing the first dial telephones in 1913 (two years ahead of Bell).

In 1930, Keystone bitterly opposed Bell's campaign to obtain exclusive rights to Harrisburg. But the Public Utilities Commission approved the arrangement. Four years later, when Bell had 345,000 telephones in Philadelphia and Keystone only 39,000, Bell and its sister company in New Jersey proposed buying out Keystone. Executives at Keystone turned their back on the offer.

Bell attempted a second buyout in 1941 and still a third in 1943. A merger, Bell argued, would immediately yield a massive amount of salvage for the war effort: 1,500 tons of copper, 47 tons of zinc, 8 tons of tin, and 2½ tons of aluminum. In this light, preserving Keystone (and its competition) suddenly seemed unpatriotic. The merger finally took place, ironically, on September 17, 1945—two weeks after the war's end.

Today, all of Keystone that remains is a citywide multitude of keystone-embossed manhole covers, memorials to an early era of deregulation and medallions commemorating Bell's success.

Telephone

482:	IVy Ridge 2	728:	RAndolph 8
483:	IVy Ridge 3	729:	SAratoga 9
487:	IVy Ridge 7	732:	PEnnypacker 2
523:	LAfayette 3	735:	PEnnypacker 5
528:	JAckson 8	739:	REgent 9
533:	JEfferson 3	742:	PIlgrim 2
535:	JEfferson 5	743:	PIoneer 3
537:	JEfferson 7	744:	PIoneer 4
545:	KIngsley 5	745:	PIlgrim 5
546:	KIngsley 6	747:	SHerwood 7
548:	LIvingston 8	748:	SHerwood 8
549:	LIvingston 9	753:	PLateau 3
561:	LOcust 1	763:	POplar 3
563:	LOcust 3	765:	POplar 5
564:	LOcust 4	769:	POplar 9
567:	LOcust 7	787:	STevenson 7
568:	LOcust 8	835:	TEnnyson 5
569:	LOcust 9	839:	TEnnyson 9
624:	MAyfair 4	842:	VIctor 2
625:	MArket 5	843:	VIctor 3
627:	MArket 7	844:	VIctor 4
629:	MArket 9	846:	TIme 6
632:	NEptune 2	848:	VIctor 8
634:	NEbraska 4	849:	VIctor 9
637:	NEptune 7	871:	TRinity 1
671:	ORchard 1	877:	TRinity 7
673:	ORchard 3	878:	TRinity 8
676:	ORchard 6	879:	TRinity 9
677:	ORchard 7	922:	WAlnut 2
685:	MUnicipal 5	923:	WAlnut 3
686:	MUnicipal 6	924:	WAverly 4
722:	RAndolph 2	925:	WAlnut 5
724:	SAratoga 4	927:	WAverly 7
725:	RAndolph 5	928:	WAlnut 8
726:	SAratoga 6	937:	WEather 7
727:	SAratoga 7		

Tourism

Profile of a Tourist

hiladelphia was the destination for 24 million visitors in 1991. The 12 million visitors who were here for pleasure (about the same number came for business) included nine million "day trippers" from within the region and three million true tourists—those from outside the Philadelphia area.

According to a 1988 survey, about 43 percent of all tourists to major attractions in Philadelphia come for about a day's round trip. Foreign tourists comprise 15 percent of all tourists, a larger share than for either Boston or Baltimore. The remaining 40 percent come from other parts of the United States.

Independence National Historical Park is the most important tourist attraction, with the Liberty Bell the most highly visited of the park's individual sites.

Thirty-two percent of tourists in Philadelphia visit all three of the city's top cultural attractions: the Philadelphia Zoo, the Franklin Institute, and the Philadelphia Museum of Art.

Thanks to an aggressive marketing strategy, Philadelphia is the top city in the nation for minority tourism.

The travel industry is concerned with the city's lack of a clearly defined image. Philadelphia is generally considered a quick stop whose tourism industry is still small and growing more slowly than those of other metropolitan areas. ∎

Sources: "Destination Philadelphia," Philadelphia City Planning Commission, 1993; "Tourists in Philadelphia, 1989," Coughlin, Keene, and Associates; Center for Greater Philadelphia.

❖

President Ronald Reagan, shot in 1981 by a would-be assassin, underwent surgery for an explosive bullet lodged in his lung. "All in all," wrote Reagan on a pad while a tube was still in his throat and he was still partially anesthetized, "I'd rather be in Philadelphia."

ANNUAL VISITATION AT SELECTED LOCAL SITES

Site	Visitors
Academy of Natural Sciences	230,688
Afro-American Historical and Cultural Museum	90,000
Balch Institute for Ethnic Studies	85,000
Betsy Ross House	414,294
Brandywine River Museum	200,000
Pearl S. Buck House	16,000
Eastern State Penitentiary (open 4 days)	2,500
Fort Mifflin	14,500
Franklin Institute	1,200,000
Franklin Mint	81,650
Grange Estate	15,000
Harleigh Cemetery (Walt Whitman tomb)	1,100
Mario Lanza Museum	2,000
Liberty Bell	1,500,000
Longwood Gardens	800,000
Thomas Massey House	26,000
Mercer Museum	50,230
James A. Michener Art Museum	25,000
Mill Grove/Audubon Wildlife Sanctuary	1,552
Mummers Museum	12,000
New Jersey State Aquarium	1,200,000
Old Mt. Holly Prison	1,700
Pennsbury Manor	50,512
Pennypacker Mills	314
Philadelphia Museum of Art	600,000
Philadelphia Zoo	1,300,000
Pottsgrove Manor	281
Tyler Arboretum	26,704
U.S. Mint	293,000
Valley Forge National Historic Park	4,500,000
Walt Whitman House (Camden)	3,000
Washington Crossing Historic Park	386,510
Peter Wentz Farmstead	566

Source: Listed Institutions.

185

CITIZENS' MANUAL

HERE'S WHAT YOU NEED TO KNOW BEFORE YOU GO SIGHTSEEING ON THE CAMPUSES:

- **Beaver College,** 450 S. Easton Road, Glenside, 572-2969. Self-guided tours are permitted on Grey Towers' first floor. Check in with the security guard on duty. Ask for a brochure on Grey Towers' history.

- **Rosemont College,** Montgomery and Wendover Avenues, Rosemont. Call the public relations office to request a tour of "Rathalla"; 527-0200, ext. 235. The college has published a booklet on the mansion's history.

- **Eastern College,** 10 Fairview Drive, St. Davids, 341-5800. The house may be viewed from the grounds. For more about the Walton estate's construction, read *Great House* (Eastern College, 1984) by John Baird, an Eastern vice president.

- **Cabrini College,** 610 King of Prussia Road, Radnor, 971-8255. "Woodcrest" is open to the public once a year in spring. At other times, visitors are welcome to inspect the exterior.

❖

Between Mifflin Street and Pattison Avenue, nearly every major east-west street is named for a former governor (with the notable exceptions of Jackson Street and Oregon Avenue). In North Philadelphia, many of the east-west streets are named for counties in the Commonwealth.

Contrary to popular belief, Broad Street is not the longest straight street in the world or the nation. Chicago's Western Avenue holds the world title at 23-plus miles, while Broad Street runs only about 12, if you forgive the placement of City Hall in the middle and a somewhat bent extension into the Navy Yard.

Matriculated Mansions

Grey Towers Castle in 1923.

Once they were the opulent "country" estates of Philadelphia tycoons. Today, four of the suburbs' grandest old showplaces live on as campuses of small liberal arts colleges.

For most people, the original owners are long forgotten and the estates are best known as Beaver, Rosemont, Eastern, and Cabrini. Still, a stroll on the campus among the students conjures up images of that bygone era, when you could build yourself a fortune in sugar and then a castle with your fortune.

Our tour begins north of the city at Beaver College in Glenside, where the historic Grey Towers Castle is visible over the treetops from Route 309. You're looking at the turreted home of William Welsh Harrison, a Philadelphia sugar refiner.

The castle, a National Historic Landmark, was modeled after England's medieval Alnwick Castle, the seat of the Duke of Northumberland. Harrison hired Horace Trumbauer, then just a young architect with no formal training, to design the mansion. It was completed in 1896.

The building is now used for administrative offices, dorm rooms, and the occasional social function, but visitors are permitted to view the downstairs. The grandest sight is the Mirror Room, a ballroom that was shipped ready-to-assemble from France along with the workers to put it together.

After you see the castle, you want to stroll the campus to see the former stables and clock tower. Then it's on to the Main Line to our other stops.

Just off Montgomery Avenue in Rosemont, Rosemont College occupies the former estate of the Joseph Sinott family. The French Gothic mansion, "Rathalla," is on the National Register of Historic Places, and the college is happy to offer tours by appointment.

Joseph Sinott was a classic American success story. He came to the United States from Ireland at 17 and made his fortune in the distillery business in Philadelphia. "Rathalla" means "home of the chieftain upon the highest hill." (A Sinott relative reportedly once joked that "Rum done it" would have been a more accurate name for the estate.)

The Sinott family lived here until 1918. Now the college uses the house's public areas for meetings and college functions. Among the interior details are a main hall that's open three stories up to a beautiful stained glass skylight. It's a Rosemont legend that the German stonecutter who created the gargoyles for the outside of the building was caricaturing his Irish co-workers.

Just a short ways west in Radnor Township, you'll find Eastern College and Cabrini College, the last two estates-turned-campuses on our tour.

Eastern College occupies the former estate of Charles S. Walton, a millionaire businessman in the tannery business. Walton decided to build a country estate in 1910 when doctors told him to slow down after a heart attack at the age of 48.

The house was designed by architect D. Knickerbacker Boyd and was completed in 1913. It had 55 rooms, 7 gables, and 18-inch-thick stone walls. The wrought iron and the tile roof gave it an unusual Spanish mission style. Walton lived in his grand home for just three years, dying of a stroke on Christmas Day 1916.

The estate was converted to a college in 1952. Walton Hall, as the mansion is now known, houses offices and the college dining facilities. Visitors may view it from the outside and stroll the grounds to see the estate's picturesque waterwheel, log cabin, and gatehouse.

Just across Eagle Road, you'll find Cabrini College, the former "Woodcrest" estate, another Horace Trumbauer design. The 51-room, half-timbered mansion was built in 1902 for banker James W. and Fanny Drexel Paul. Notice the courtyard large enough for carriages to turn around. The building that looks like the mansion is the former stable.

According to Cabrini legends, the ghost of a young woman with long blond hair haunts the campus. According to one version of the story, the woman had a love affair with a stable hand and became pregnant, then killed herself by jumping off the balcony inside the mansion. It is said that bloodstains appear upon the floor there when carpets are rolled back for college social functions. ∎

BRIT HIST 101

It's not a campus, but Penn's Wharton Sinkler Conference Center may be the most spectacular old estate owned by a university.

Once it was known as Lane's End, the home of Allethaire and Samuel Rotan and, later, Louise and Wharton Sinkler. The 40-room Elizabethan mansion and 40-acre estate are tucked away on quiet Gravers Lane in Wyndmoor, just over the city line from Chestnut Hill.

The 1925 house looks like the half-a-millennium-old Sutton Place in England, built for a friend of Henry VIII. It is constructed largely of salvaged materials. The 1000-year-old paneled entrance, for instance, originated in a monastery founded by Alfred the Great's grandson. The living room once belonged to Queen Elizabeth's lover, the Earl of Essex. (In a window panel is a stained-glass Tudor rose, the traditional symbol of a visit by the Queen.) The cedar-paneled library is the (transported) spot where Alexander Pope penned *The Rights of Man*.

The university holds conferences here and, to help pay the $10,000-a-month utility bills, will rent it out for weddings and receptions. (For information, call 233-1414.) Interested members of the public must wait for tours offered a few times a year by the Springfield Township Historical Society.

❖

In 1984, the Lancaster County Visitors Bureau fielded 60,000 requests for information. That number rose to 151,000 after the release of the popular film *Witness* the next year.

Stainless Steel Storefronts

Small family-run shops of the mid-century created magnificent commercial façades influenced by contemporary and very popular diner styles. By hand, mechanics rolled stainless steel sheets into fluted columns. They bent them into sunburst and quilted patterns. They sheared them into fancy geometric borders. All over Philadelphia, bars, bakeries, and other neighborhood institutions proclaimed permanence and style by transforming plain brick façades into new-clad stainless.

These specimens tended to be the sideline of sign craftsmen as well as kitchen equipment fabricators. Professional architects devoted to the International Style sometimes dabbled in stainless steel on paper, but stainless was a shop craft. Only its practitioners could master the gleaming vernacular.

What killed stainless as a choice for new façades? Cost, and the decline of neighborhood-based family businesses. As developed suburban malls replaced urban shopping strips, the family business ethic faded along with its mid-century icon, the neighborhood commercial show palace. A few of these gems stand abandoned; others have been ruined with renovations in cheaper (and duller) aluminum.

The men of steel who transformed Philadelphia's neighborhoods are long retired, and the tricks of the trade by which they once transformed simple storefronts are fading memories. But the few craftsmen who remain sometimes recall those years when the marriage of steel and the 20th century meant more, much more, than mere skyscrapers.

- **Termini Bakery, 1523 S. 8th Street.** One of the best remaining façades in the city. Meticulously maintained in its original 1930s form, Termini's features beautiful symmetry and an exquisite door.

- **Ostroff Candy, 1706 Point Breeze Avenue.** Enjoy the scalloped borders and sunburst pattern.

- **Golden Bar, 5206 Frankford Avenue.** The rippled glass was once backlit, and an air conditioner resides where letters once proclaimed this "BAR" entrance.

- **The Little Spot Bar, 4507 Frankford Avenue.** Nicely quilted and bordered in stainless with a backlit entrance and handsome door.

- **Clyburn Bar, 2741 N. Broad Street.** A contender for the stainless steel Hall of Fame.

Clyburn Bar.

- **Goll's Bar, Front and Berks Streets.** A classic. Steel plates cover the rippled glass entry panels.

- **Party Cake Bakery, 6906 Torresdale Avenue.** A once-beautiful façade still worth a visit.

- **Doctor's office, 2345 E. Allegheny Avenue.** A tavern turned doctor's office. The entry alcoves are still intact.

- **Law offices, 2958 N. 22nd Street.** The quilted work won't quit.

- *In memoriam:* **Club 421, 56th Street and Wyalusing Avenue.** This craftsman's tour de force has a magnificent ladies entrance alcove on the side. After storm damage in the winter of 1993, new owners removed all the stainless steel from this ultimate corner façade. ■

Compiler: Len Davidson.

Club 421.

Ostroff Candy.

189

Painted-Wall Advertisements

Keen-eyed commercial archaeologists can still spot the ghostlike commercial signs fading on the city's myriad of brick walls. Although a limited amount of commercial wall painting continues to this day, the older signs are distinctive kitsch. Their unique, funky designs created by sign painters and store owners lack the polish of professional ad agencies. That is why we like them so much.

Unlike billboards, which are enlarged under controlled shop conditions, these wall graphics were painted in situ from sketches. The texture of the brick, the need to work rapidly (we're not making any comparisons to the Sistine Chapel), and the inconvenience of scaffolding all contributed to degrees of difficulty. These wall paintings are naive. And we say, the more naive, the better.

Earlier in this century, particularly during the hard economic times of the 1930s and 1940s, salesmen canvassed neighborhoods for buildings with walls exposed to traffic and owners willing to part with rights to them. Today, homeowners are less interested in renting out their walls, and sign painters are less willing and able to paint them. But even if they were, these fading signs would constitute a non-renewable resource of American popular culture.

- **"Live in safety and comfort with LATH & PLASTER,"** Ridge Avenue between Broad and 13th Streets. A working plasterer, with his trowel.

- **"I prefer Esslinger,"** 11th and Bainbridge Streets. The red-hatted Esslinger Beer man holds a glass of pilsner.

- **"Shuman's Upholstery,"** 4th and Fitzwater Streets. Faded fabric (the paint, that is) atop an overstuffed chair.

- **"EAGLE shoes store featuring Buster Brown, America's Favorite Children's Shoes,"** 7th and Ritner Streets. Buster and his dog Tige.

- **"Nat King Cole says: Cool Man, Go-Go for Margo Sherry,"** 46th Street and Woodland Avenue. An advertisement with a portrait of the performer.

- **"COLEBY TAILORING, made to measure clothes,"** 57th and Market Streets. Like an old-fashioned barker's call.

- **"Atlantic Glass & Mirror Works since 1945, Custom wall mirrors at BIG SAVINGS,"** 63rd Street and Haverford Avenue. A 1950s interior: table, lamp, and a mirrored wall.

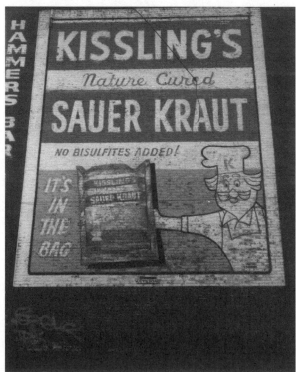

- "This is! Vincent's Cafe, we specialize in TOMATO PIES & sandwiches," Lancaster Avenue and Master Streets. The chef offers his specialty.

- "Beardsley & Son PAINTERS," 9th and Tioga Streets. A painter climbs a ladder with a bucket of paint.

- "BOBMAN UNDERWEAR, If it doesn't fit, it isn't HANES," behind 6184 Ridge Avenue. Sports a gentleman in boxer shorts.

- "See fabulous Caloric matchless gas range," Orthodox and James Streets. Depicts a 1950s range.

- "LAMPS AND LAMPSHADES, Brightlight Electric," 2nd Street and Allegheny Avenue. Vintage lamps.

- "Westmoreland 2 Trouser Suits," 3rd Street and Allegheny Avenue. A suited man holds an extra pair of pants.

- "John B. Stetson Savings and Loan Association 4¼%," 6th Street and Germantown Avenue. Near the site of the former Stetson Hat Factory.

- "Est. 1898, H. Henssler, any lock any key. EXPERT LOCKSMITH," 926 N. 11th Street. Features painted keys.

- "Muntz TV, no down payment," 27th Street and Girard Avenue. Mr. Muntz as a pirate.

- "CONVERTIBLE TOPS immediate installation, AUTO SEAT COVERS styled by Sid," 1501 N. 33rd Street. Sid is depicted at work.

- "OAK LANE CORSET SHOP," 5913 Old York Road. A girdled woman.

- Gone, but not forgotten: For decades, the mustachioed Kissling's Sauerkraut man held his bag aloft on the side of Hammer's Bar, 6th Street near Callowhill. He told passersby, "It's in the bag"—until the Vine Street Expressway came along and claimed bar, bag, and all. ∎

Compiler: Len Davidson.

❖

Each year, SEPTA'S City Division uses 11.9 million gallons of diesel fuel for its buses; 167 million kilowatt hours of electricity to power the subway, light-rail, and trackless trolley vehicles; and 164.7 million kilowatt hours of electricity to power the Regional Rail trains.

The Neon Museum

Philadelphia signmakers once painted the town neon. Before 1960, when the neon trade was exceptionally competitive, shops upped the stakes from one job to the next. Small taverns sported neon cocktail glasses, beauty salons drew clientele with neon silhouettes, and neon keys illuminated the locksmith's window. On the busiest commercial streets, competition was enhanced by animated monuments made of porcelain, enamel, and neon. Spectaculars like the giant, wing-flapping Eagle on Market Street East, of course, were the first casualties.

An extant, though threatened sign—one of the greatest porcelain and neon extravaganzas ever constructed—is Pat's King of Steaks, a giant, rooftop masterpiece at 33rd Street and Ridge Avenue. Ajax Signs, a company known for lavish neon creations, produced it in 1952 for the South Philadelphia location; a few years later it was moved to Strawberry Mansion. The panel reads "Pioneer & Originator of the Steak Sandwich" and is surmounted by a crown, covered with glowing neon rubies and diamonds.

If it can be saved, this neon masterpiece will be the literal and figurative crown for a museum-without-walls: the Neon Museum of Philadelphia. The Museum is the brainchild of Len Davidson, who has been devoted to the project for more than a decade. Davidson salvages these specimens, restores them, and installs them for display at sites throughout the city. Saving the Pat's Crown will be a matter of brinksmanship: last winter, one porcelain panel fell off during a storm. Davidson hopes the Neon Museum will be able to obtain the sign before any more damage is done. And he hopes to loan it to the new Pennsylvania Convention Center. The collection includes the following:

- **Animated Neon Fish at CopaBanana, 4th and South Streets.** This animated 1930s sign was found in an old sign shop in Chinatown.

- **Beauty Shop Silhouette at Rockerhead, 3rd Street near South.** A relic of the 1930s from Rising Sun Avenue.

- **Bulova Watches at Diner on the Square, 19th and Spruce Streets.** Found in a South Philadelphia jewelry store—still in the original 1930s boxes.

- **Buster Brown and Tige at Jim's Steaks, 4th and South Streets.** When City Shoes (just up the block) modernized, this winging, 1950s neon-on-porcelain enamel no longer worked. So its owner donated it to the Museum.

- **Club Bali Nude in Cocktail Glass at Club Bali, 52nd Street and Haverford Avenue.** Restored for its original location, this 1940s nude silhouette reclines atop a giant martini glass.

- **The Lamplighter (Howard Johnson's) at North Star Bar, 27th and Poplar Streets.** This classic 1950s neon-on-porcelain enamel is installed inside the restaurant.

- **Mobilgas Pegasus at Diner on the Square, 19th and Spruce Streets.** In the 1930s, Mobil offered its service stations this stationary version of the flying horse, in neon-on-porcelain enamel. They also had another, with animated wings.

- **Pontiac Indian at American Diner, 42nd and Chestnut Streets.** A 1940s, neon-on-porcelain enamel treasure brought out of retirement from a South Jersey neon graveyard.

- **Sherwin-Williams Cover the Earth at Northern Liberties Neighborhood Association, 733 N. 2nd Street.** This 1930s neon-on-porcelain enamel logo, obtained from a defunct hardware store on Lehigh Avenue, depicts red neon paint splashing over a green neon globe.

- **Simple Simon and the Pieman (Howard Johnson's) at Down Home Grill, 18th and Spring Garden Streets.** The ancient nursery rhyme about a boy, his dog, and a man selling pies comes alive in this 1950s neon-on-porcelain enamel icon.

- **Three-Color Neon Candle at Franklin Institute (electricity exhibit), 19th Street and the Parkway.** A vibrant 1940s specimen.

- **Trico Wiper Service at Art á la Carte, 1911 Chestnut Street.** A 1940s pictograph in glass.

- **In limbo:** And then there's Levis' Hot Dogs. From the 1930s to the early 1990s, uncounted Philadelphians dined (in a standing position) on a now-extinct combination of hot dogs and fish cakes (mashed together in a roll) beneath this 13-foot, neon-on-metal sign. Now Levis' (pronounced "Lev-is-es") is gone from 6th Street. Its sign? In storage, and looking for a home. ∎

Compiler: Len Davidson.

CITIZENS' MANUAL

THE GULPHS

Old Gulph Road begins innocently enough. Not two miles beyond Philadelphia's comforting grid, North Narberth Avenue crosses Montgomery Avenue, takes on a new name, and springs to life as one of the region's most challenging byways.

At first, Old Gulph Road heads due north, gestures toward Gladwyne (where it is pronounced "Golf" Road) and curls above Wynnewood by fording (ever so quaintly) Mill Creek. Just as the motorist breezes by some picturesque, twisted roots, of ancient vintage, the narrow road begins to head back to Montgomery Avenue.

Where Old Gulph passes Lower Merion Baptist Church (just behind Bryn Mawr College), some signage presents three options. Go straight to Montgomery Avenue—on Roberts Road. Go left to Montgomery Avenue—on New Gulph Road. Or go right to continue your tour of the Main Line—on Old Gulph Road. Now Old Gulph turns northwestward and sprints, parallel to Montgomery Avenue, past much significant real estate for about two miles. Here, Old Gulph seems to enjoy some unbridled clarity.

After a jog to the left near Calvary Cemetery (and a spectacular view) comes uncertainty. Old Gulph crosses over the Blue Route (I-476), glances by the community of Gulph Mills, and intersects with Montgomery Avenue. Old Gulph transforms into Upper Gulph here, intersects twice with a looping residential street called Gulph Hills, and begins a westward meander over Wayne, through St. David's Country Club, and out to Conestoga Road in Devon.

Still more: There is another Gulph Road (called Gulph Road) north of Gulph Mills that runs north of I-76 (the Schuylkill Expressway) as it approaches Route 202. West of 202 this becomes North Gulph Road, which slices into Valley Forge National Historical Park.

Driving Distances

Getting from Here to There

Destination	Miles	Time (hr:min)	Major Routes
Atlantic City, NJ	63	1:20	AC Expwy
Baltimore, MD	105	2:37	I95 S
Batsto, NJ	50	1:00	AC Expwy
Bethlehem, PA	63	1:15	76, 476 N, Pa Tnpk E, NE Ext
Bird-in-Hand, PA	58	1:00	676, 76 W, Pa Tnpk W
Burlington, NJ	20	0:45	B. Franklin Br. 130 N
Cape May, NJ	88	2:03	AC Expwy, NJ Pkwy S
Chadds Ford, PA	26	0:50	I95 S, 322, 1 S
Cherry Hill, NJ	9	0:20	38 E
Chester, PA	15	0:20	676 E, I95 S
Dover, DE	76	1:48	I95 S, 13 S
Doylestown, PA	26	0:50	76 W, 1 N, 611 N
Flemington, NJ	45	0:55	I95 N, 31 N, 202 N
Gettysburg, PA	128	2:40	Pa Tnpk W, 15 S
Harrisburg, PA	108	2:21	Pa Tnpk W
Hershey, PA	92	2:00	Pa Tnpk W
Jim Thorpe, PA	79	1:35	Pa Tnpk E, NE Ext
Kennett Square, PA	35	1:00	95 S, 322, 1 S
King of Prussia, PA	17	0:30	676, 76 W
Lahaska, PA	40	1:00	95 N, 32 N
Levittown, PA	27	0:45	95 N, 1 N
Media, PA	18	0:30	1 S
Moorestown, NJ	13	0:30	38 E
Mount Holly, NJ	25	0:45	38 E
New Hope, PA	38	1:00	I95 N, 32 N
New York City, NY	97	2:32	NJ Tnpk N
Phila. Int'l Airport	6.5	0:15	676, 76 E or I95 S
Princeton, NJ	47	1:00	I95 N, 1
Reading, PA	55	1:15	76 W, 422 N
Scranton, PA	139	2:46	Pa Tnpk E, NE Ext
Seaside Heights, NJ	63	1:20	70 E, 37 E
State College, PA	230	4:30	Pa Tnpk W
Stroudsburg, PA	89	2:04	Pa Tnpk W, NE Ext, 78E
Trenton, NJ	32	0:50	I95 N, 1 N
Valley Forge, PA	21	0:30	76 W
West Chester, PA	28	0:45	3 W
Washington, DC	144	3:44	I95 S
Wildwood, NJ	90	2:00	AC Expwy, NJ Pkwy S
Wilmington, DE	28	0:53	I95 S

All mileages are calculated from City Hall and do not include rest stops. ∎

Source: AAA Mid-Atlantic.

194

Transportation / Automobile

Auto Registrations

Passenger Car Registrations in Pennsylvania, New Jersey, and Delaware, 1953–1991

	Pennsylvania	New Jersey	Delaware
1991	6,415,000*	5,192,000*	409,000*
1990	6,384,121	5,179,511	406,240
1989	6,347,133	5,154,365	402,666
1988	6,253,550	5,222,761	397,286
1987	6,180,970	4,957,598	383,174
1986	6,090,520	4,769,000	378,639
1985	5,889,416	4,667,495	369,407
1984	5,805,361	4,402,243	366,024
1983	5,705,189	4,365,532	337,979
1982	5,584,455	4,342,148	330,228
1981	5,887,972	4,131,650	322,569
1980	5,789,261	4,211,489	317,973
1979	5,659,102	4,186,171	315,196
1978	5,623,469	4,055,706	311,376
1977	6,856,938	3,934,891	304,366
1976	6,921,160	3,796,581	294,473
1975	6,589,466	3,735,985	289,164
1974	6,137,529	3,723,178	282,161
1973	5,718,288	3,643,687	274,531
1972	5,460,277	3,463,443	269,676
1971	5,214,078	3,357,866	264,079
1970	5,039,923	3,197,824	260,758
1969	5,006,893	3,112,571	248,189
1968	4,828,346	2,968,733	237,177
1967	4,646,642	2,850,239	224,927
1966	4,528,343	2,777,566	215,875
1965	4,325,773	2,644,160	203,315
1964	4,188,517	2,539,478	168,949
1963	4,019,986	2,430,996	160,201
1962	3,901,105	2,304,933	152,194
1961	3,791,461	2,240,117	146,222
1960	3,712,944	2,115,195	142,297
1959	3,586,804	2,020,206	137,421
1958	3,479,210	1,959,867	132,525
1957	3,421,348	1,881,971	129,885
1956	3,336,963	1,872,432	126,281
1955	3,198,430	1,800,663	120,324
1954	3,010,900	1,677,717	110,105
1953	2,897,059	1,593,759	106,228

*Estimated.

Figures are for private and commercial vehicles, including taxi cabs; publicly owned vehicles are excluded. ∎

Source: Ward's Automotive Yearbooks.

SOME ROADS WITH BAD SUN GLARE

Motorists will encounter hazardous sun glare in the morning on the following roads and in the evening heading in the opposite direction:

I-76 East at Lee Tire curve, 2 miles east of Conshohocken, Montgomery County.

422 East between Oaks and Betzwood Bridge, Montgomery County.

73 East at Skippack, Montgomery County.

202 North at Great Valley, Chester County.

U.S. Route 1 North in Glen Riddle Hospital area, Delaware County.

DRIVE LESS, GRUMBLE MORE

Since automobile exhaust is the single greatest cause of air pollution in the Philadelphia area, it seems only logical to reduce the number of cars on the roads. That's just what Pennsylvania is trying to do through a new set of laws collectively called the Employee Trip Reduction Program.

Over the next few years, companies with more than 100 employees in the five-county region must get their employees to drive to work less and use alternative transportation more. They can do this in a number of ways: organizing car pools, subsidizing the cost of SEPTA passes for workers, even taking away formerly free parking space at the office. Companies in the region must slash the number of miles each worker travels during rush hour by 25 percent.

The plan is a source of tension between the city and the suburbs, with each side wanting the other to bear the greater burden. Philadelphia feels the suburbs should cut back more, since city residents are more likely to walk or take SEPTA to their jobs. Suburbanites retort that pollution is synonymous with the slow traffic of Philadelphia. Besides, anyone commuting from, say, Bucks County to Center City will never walk to work. Regardless of how the pollution-responsibility pie gets sliced, those receiving the largest pieces will have to relearn their roles in the region.

CITIZENS' MANUAL

Smart Bicycling

ROLL, RIDE, AND ROLL

Those rare, jointed oddities called folding bicycles are permitted on SEPTA vehicles at all times. New Jersey's PATCO High-Speed Line, on the other hand, prohibits all bicycles during peak hours. Both agencies allow the more usual, jointless models during off-peak hours with riders holding special permits. Both systems define off-peak hours as 10am–3pm and 7pm–6am on weekdays, plus all day Saturdays, Sundays, and holidays.

Both SEPTA's Bike On Rail program and PATCO's Bicycle-on-Rail program sell riders 18 or older permits for $5, good for one calendar year. Permits can be purchased at SEPTA's Customer Relations Office, 841 Chestnut Street, and at PATCO's Broadway Station office, 100 S. Broadway, in Camden. (PATCO permits can also be purchased by mail, if you have your application notarized.) SEPTA requires a photo ID with your date of birth and the serial number of your bicycle; PATCO requires proof of ID and date of birth, and the bike's serial number.

For more information, call:

SEPTA at 580-7800 and

PATCO at 922-4600, ext. 7998, or (609) 963-7998.

MAYOR'S TASK FORCE ON BICYCLE SAFETY

The task force was formed in March 1993 to help city agencies and bicyclists' groups work together more closely. To find out more, call the Bicycle Coalition of the Delaware Valley at 242-9253 (BICYCLE) or Tom Branagan of the Philadelphia Department of Transportation at 686-5514.

Philadelphia is a good city for bicycling: relatively flat, with a temperate climate, both wide and narrow streets, and a gigantic park cutting right into the center of town.

In recent years, the picture has gotten even brighter, with better relations between local government and bike groups, more high-quality bike shops opening, and, of course, the CoreStates U.S. Pro Cycling Championship, the richest one-day bike race in the world.

For the rest of us, it's a matter of riding smart day to day. Here are some tips:

Wear a helmet, equip your bike with reflectors and lights, and wear light-colored clothing. Make sure your bike fits you properly and is in good condition. If you're not sure, ask a more experienced rider or your local bike shop.

Obey traffic regulations and ride in a smooth and predictable manner. Don't ride against traffic. Don't ever ride wearing headphones.

Contact your local bike club to get more tips and to find a bike commuting partner.

Always use a good-quality U-lock, but remember no lock is invulnerable. Avoid leaving your bike out overnight, and lock your bike inside the house—many bikes are stolen during burglaries.

Photograph your bike, record the serial number, and roll a card with your name and Social Security number inside the seat post and/or handlebar.

Report thefts to the police. Report incidents of harassment by drivers—this may help police take bike riders' problems more seriously.

Buy a well-made bicycle. A new, well-made three-speed should cost about $150 to $200. The 18-speed "mountain" bikes sold in this price range tend to have cheap shifting and braking mechanisms and carelessly assembled wheels. That adds up to an unpleasant ride and mechanical problems all too soon. A well-designed mountain or city bike will cost at least $250—and can last decades with proper care. You can often do just as well with a good used bike.

Avoid "hot" bikes. Buying a bike for a ridiculous price from a thief isn't smart—it's illegal. You could wind up losing both your bike and your money.

Learn to use gears properly. Multi-speed shifting may seem mysterious, but its purpose is simply to even out the work. A good pedaling cadence for beginners is about 60 rpm. If you are pedaling too fast, shift into a higher gear. If you are pedaling too slow or straining, shift down. ■

Transportation / Bicycling

Events

CoreStates U.S. Pro Cycling Championship

Contenders in the six-hour, 10-lap, 156-mile race roll past Logan Circle's Swann Fountain, speed by Fairmount Park's mansions and meadows, and climb the "Manayunk Wall"— Levering Street and Lyceum Avenue—a grueling 285-foot hill. The race, held on an early June Sunday, has become the finale to the CoreStates Championship Festival, two weeks of bike-related celebrations and amateur races. An estimated 100,000 spectators turned out for the first CoreStates race in 1985, won by Olympic speedskater and gold medalist Eric Heiden. Ever since, the event has become part of Philadelphia's summer and a television showcase for Fairmount Park. In 1993, nearly 500,000 spectators came out to see the world's top riders battle for the largest prizes of any one-day cycling event.

Year	Winner	Team	Country	Finishing time
1985	Eric Heiden	7-Eleven	USA	6:26:39
1986	Thomas Prehn	Schwinn — Icy Hot	USA	6:22:15
1987	Tom Schuler	7-Eleven	USA	6:40:43
1988	Roberto Gaggioli	Pepsi-Fanini	Italy	6:17:32
1989	Greg Oravetz	Coors Light	USA	6:23:39
1990	Paolo Cimini	Gis-Benotto	Italy	6:01:54
1991	Michel Zanoli	Tulip	Holland	6:15:15
1992	Bart Bowen	Subaru-Montgomery	USA	6:10:51
1993	Lance Armstrong	Motorola	USA	6:19:39

The Philadelphia Museum of Art President's Bike Ride

Daily, Robert Montgomery Scott shuttles on a battered 1950s Raleigh from the train to his job at the city's largest museum. In 1981, he and Fairmount Park House Guides launched a group ride through Fairmount Park. It takes place twice a year: on the first Sunday in May and again in October. The route, different each time, passes the mansions and monuments in the Park, ending with a light repast of lemonade and cookies. Depending on the weather, this family event usually attracts 200 to 500 riders. For more information, call the Park House Guides at 684-7926.

Freedom Valley Bike Ride

This annual fundraiser, usually held the Sunday preceding the CoreStates race, attracts cyclists from all over the East Coast. Their ride fees contribute to an auto-free bike route from the Philadelphia Museum of Art to Valley Forge. With rides from 8 to 62 miles long, the Freedom Valley ride is geared to all manner of wheelpersons. Since its start in 1980, this has grown into one of the biggest annual social events in local cycling. ■

FOR MORE READING

- Adams, Dale and Dale Speicher. *25 Bicycle Tours in Eastern Pennsylvania.* Woodstock, VT: Backcountry Publications, 1989. Offers good historical background along with ride information.

- Bicycle Coalition of the Delaware Valley. *Delaware Valley Commuters Bike Map.* Philadelphia: BCDV, 1982. Shows preferred bike routes from New Castle, Delaware to Trenton, New Jersey. It's best when used with a more detailed map, like SEPTA's Suburban Transit Map.

- Commonwealth of Pennsylvania. *Bicycling in Southeastern Pennsylvania.* This free map shows the southeastern region of the state in relief, with recommended bike routes and bridges. The reverse side lists youth hostels, campgrounds, organizations, and emergency telephone numbers. Call the Pennsylvania Department of Commerce, (800) VISIT-PA.

- Forester, John. *Effective Cycling.* Cambridge, MA: MIT Press, 1993. This compendium covers all aspects: from choosing a bike to riding it properly and repairing it.

- Leccese, Michael and Arlene Plevin. *The Bicyclist's Sourcebook.* Rockville, MD: Woodbine House, 1991. How-to information and an extensive list of places to ride, annual events, and vendors.

- Powers, Peter. *Touring the Pennsylvania Countryside by Bicycle.* Eugene, OR: Terragraphics, 1992. A pocket-sized book that lets you see, for planning purposes, the terrain you'll face.

- Zatz, Arline, and Joel Zatz. *25 Bicycle Tours in New Jersey.* Woodstock, VT: Backcountry Publications, 1988. Offers good historical background along with ride information.

Bicycling Groups

Anyone, from beginners to experienced riders, can benefit by joining one of the area's bicycling organizations.

American Youth Hostels

The Delaware Valley Council of this international travelers' group sponsors bike rides, as well as hiking, sailing, and canoeing excursions. A $25 adult membership is good for accommodations at AYH hostels and campgrounds around the world. For information, call 925-6004, or write or visit their office at 624 S. 3rd Street, Philadelphia, PA 19147.

Bicycle Club of Philadelphia

The BCP's emphasis is on riding and racing. They organize rides year-round—almost every day in the warmer months. Rides range from 5- to 10-mile jaunts to 50-mile or longer training rides and tours. BCP publishes a monthly newsletter, mailed to members and distributed through bike shops, which carries ride information and advertisements for used bicycles. For information, call 440-9983, or write: Bicycle Club of Philadelphia, PO Box 30235, Philadelphia, PA 19103.

Clubhouse and members of the Pennsylvania Bicycle Club, 3940-42 Girard Avenue, in 1884.

Bicycle Coalition of the Delaware Valley

With over 1,000 members, this group works to protect and expand riders' rights. The Coalition helped get bikes on SEPTA and PATCO trains, improved bike paths in Fairmount Park, and encourages bike commuting and planning. This is not a recreational group; the Coalition has staged a number of high-profile protests for increasing bike safety, and it publishes a bimonthly newsletter featuring local and regional bike news. For information, call 242-9253 (BICYCLE), or write: Bicycle Coalition of the Delaware Valley, PO Box 8194, Philadelphia, PA 19101.

Bicycling Federation of Pennsylvania

This advocacy group performs much the same function as the Bicycle Coalition of the Delaware Valley, but on a statewide and a national scale. Their quarterly newsletter carries legislative updates and a calendar of bike events up and down the East Coast. For information, call (717) 761-3388, or write: Bicycling Federation of Pennsylvania, 413 Appletree Road, Camp Hill, PA 17011.

International Human-Powered Vehicle Association

The newly formed Philadelphia branch of the IHPVA explores the radical edge of bicycling: streamlined, recumbent, and other pedal-powered vehicles. For information, call 640-1876. ■

Trains and Buses

CITIZENS'
MANUAL

Destination	Trips	Mode	Cost (week days)	Travel Time (varies)
Asbury Park, NJ	6	NJ Transit	$12.40	3:39
Atlantic City, NJ	3	Greyhound	$13.50*	1:30
Atlantic City, NJ	2	Amtrak	$15.00	1:30
Baltimore, MD	4	Amtrak	$27.00	1:12
Baltimore, MD	6	Greyhound	$15.50	2:15
Boston, MA	20	Greyhound	$39.50	7:30
Boston, MA	10	Amtrak	$65.00	6:56
Buffalo, NY	2	Capitol	$56.00	13:45
Camp LeJeune, NC	3	Grey/Carol.	$99.00	13:40
Cleveland, OH	7	Greyhound	$49.00	12:30
Elmira, NY	1	Capitol	$54.00	8:05
Ephrata, PA	3	Capitol	$10.70	1:25
Fort Dix, NJ	8	NJ Transit	$ 6.50	1:27
Goshen, NJ	4	NJ Transit	$11.20	2:25
Harrisburg, PA	2	Capitol	$13.35	4:05
Harrisburg, PA	7	Amtrak	$18.00	1:53
Hershey (PA) Medical Center	1	Capitol	$13.35	3:30
King of Prussia, PA	2	Martz	$ 3.00	0:40
Miami, FL	2	Amtrak	$153.00	26:06
Montreal, Quebec	2	Amtrak	$78.00	16:43
Mt. Laurel, NJ	16	Greyhound	$ 8.00	0:30
Mt. Laurel, NJ	8	NJ Transit	$ 4.15	0:45
Niagara Falls, NY	3	Amtrak	$90.00	11:35
Norfolk, VA	4	Carolina	$59.50	9:55
Pittsburgh, PA	7	Greyhound	$44.50	7:40
Pittsburgh, PA	1	Amtrak	$64.00	7:18
Reading, PA	3	Capitol	$ 8.40	1:40
Richmond, VA	7	Greyhound	$45.50	5:30
Richmond, VA	7	Amtrak	$45.00	4:40
Scranton, PA	2	Martz	$17.00	2:45
Sea Isle City, NJ	2	NJ Transit	$10.60	1:55
Trenton, NJ	26	Amtrak	$15.00	0:38
Trenton, NJ	25	SEPTA	$ 4.75	0:49
Washington, DC	41	Amtrak	$34.00	2:03
Washington, DC	7	Greyhound	$20.00	3:00
Wilkes-Barre, PA	2	Martz	$17.00	2:30
Williamsburg, VA	2	Amtrak	$58.00	6:22
Williamsburg, VA	1	Carolina	$55.50	8:30

Note: All train departures listed are from 30th Street Station. All bus departures listed are from the Greyhound Bus Terminal, 10th and Filbert Streets. All fares listed are one-way, advance-purchase. SEPTA fares are during peak hours. Fares subject to change.
* Round trip.

SOUTHEASTERN PENNSYLVANIA TRANSPORTATION AUTHORITY

Routes & Schedules:	580-7800
Routes & Schedules (hearing-impaired):	580-7853
Dial-A-Schedule:	580-7777
Paratransit Registration:	580-7000
Paratransit Trip Reservation:	580-7700
Paratransit Registration/ Reservation (hearing-impaired):	580-7712
Customer Service:	580-7852
Lost & Found:	580-7800
Visitor Route Network (Center City routes):	580-7676

MORE INFORMATION

Amtrak: 824-1600

Metroliner Service: (800) 523-8720

SEPTA: 580-7800

NJ Transit: 569-3752; (800) 582-5946 from New Jersey; (800) 772-2287 for hearing-impaired.

Greyhound Lines: 931-4000; 922-6390 for Atlantic City only; 922-6393 for New York City only; 922-6410 for Baltimore-Washington only.

Martz Trailways: 931-4000 (uses Greyhound Terminal), Martz Bus Terminal, Wilkes-Barre: (717) 821-3800.

Capitol Trailways: 931-4000 (uses Greyhound Terminal); (800) 444-BUSS. Capitol Trailways Bus Center, Harrisburg: (717) 232-4251.

Carl R. Bieber Tourways: 931-4000 (uses Greyhound Terminal); Bieber Bus Terminal, Kutztown: 683-7333.

Carolina Trailways: 931-4000 (uses Greyhound Terminal); headquarters Raleigh, NC: (919) 833-3601.

SEPTA Ridership

Fiscal year 1992 marked the fourth straight year of SEPTA ridership decline. Since 1988, ridership plummeted 14.8 percent—about 128,000 daily trips, according to SEPTA's 1992 "Ridership and Statistics Report."

The City Transit Division, which carries over 80 percent of all SEPTA passengers, experienced the most severe and sustained period of decline. Since FY 1988, it declined by 15.8 percent. The Suburban Transit Division, which recorded slight growth in FY 1989, declined by 8 percent between FY 1989 and FY 1992. The Regional Rail Division was the last to experience decline, growing through FY 1990 but then declining by a total of 12.9 percent in the following two fiscal years.

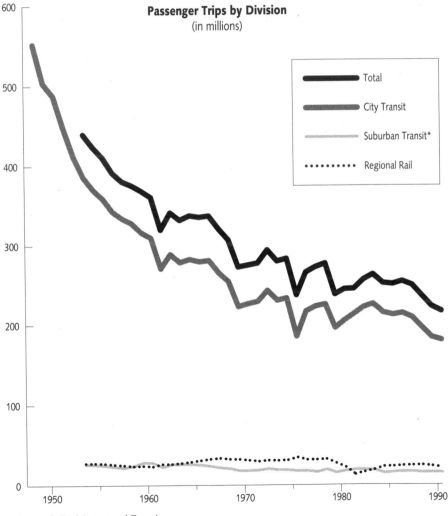

Passenger Trips by Division
(in millions)

Legend:
- Total
- City Transit
- Suburban Transit*
- Regional Rail

*Formerly Red Arrow and Frontier.

Source: SEPTA.

SEPTA Fare Schedules

City Transit Division (buses, trolleys, subways)

Date	Base Fare	Date	Base Fare
May 27, 1990	$1.50	May 18, 1977	$0.45
July 6, 1986	$1.25	January 28, 1971	$0.35
August 4, 1985	$1.00	February 2, 1969	$0.30
July 1, 1985	$0.95	February 5, 1963	$0.25
July 1, 1984	$0.85	January 15, 1962	$0.23
July 18, 1982	$0.75	October 25, 1960	$0.22
July 5, 1981	$0.70	December 18, 1955	$0.20
July 25, 1980	$0.65	January 5, 1955	$0.18
January 1, 1979	$0.50	February 6, 1951	$0.15
		December 12, 1950	$0.12

Regional Rail Division: Fares by Zones

	Zone 1	Zone 2	Zone 3	Zone 4	Zone 5
Miles from City Hall	(5.6)	(8.5)	(11.3)	(24.5)	(37.4)
Date					
May 27, 1990	$2.75	$3.25	$3.75	$4.25	$4.75
April 12, 1989	$2.50	$3.00	$3.50	$4.00	$4.50
July 6, 1986	$2.00	$2.50	$3.00	$3.50	$4.00
August 4, 1985	$1.75	$2.25	$2.75	$3.25	$3.75
September 1, 1984	$1.50	$2.00	$2.50	$3.00	$3.50
January 1, 1981	$1.30	$2.05	$2.45	$3.40	$4.35
July 25, 1980	$1.05	$1.65	$2.00	$2.70	$3.50
April 1, 1980	$0.80	$1.25	$1.50	$2.10	$2.70
April 1, 1979	$0.75	$1.10	$1.30	$2.00	$2.45
May 1, 1978	$0.70	$1.05	$1.15	$1.75	$2.20
April 1, 1977	$0.60	$1.00	$1.15	$1.50	$2.20
May 1, 1974	$0.50	$0.85	$0.95	$1.25	$1.85

DOWN TIMES FOR ·SEPTA LINES

Regional Rail Lines: 12:30–5am

Rapid Transit Line (subways): midnight–5am. Buses substitute on Broad Street and Market-Frankford routes during this time, so there's 24-hour service.

Buses: midnight–5am. Limited service is available after midnight on some routes.

Politically Incorrect Ditty that Once Helped Folks Remember Stops Along the Main Line:
(read down)

Old	(Overbrook)
Maids	(Merion)
Never	(Narberth)
Wed	(Wynnewood)
And	(Ardmore)
Have	(Haverford)
Babies	(Bryn Mawr)

Tough Enough: Top Ten Street Trees

I f only God could make a city tree. A beautiful species to provide a green canopy of welcome shade and cool breezes on hot summer nights, a peaceful relief in an urban landscape. A real streetwise kind of tree, resistant to pollution, soil compaction, car knocks, cramped space, and all kinds of city salts. A tree that wouldn't litter the neighborhood with giant leaves and bark peelings (like the London plane tree), drop fruit with a lingering stench (like the female ginkgo), heave pavement with its roots (like the red maple), or rot and die all too soon (like the Norway maple).

Too much to ask? Maybe not. Over the last decade, as public and private ventures led by Philadelphia Green (a wing of the Pennsylvania Horticultural Society) have joined in efforts to reforest Philadelphia, a new breed of urban arborists has developed preferences for certain species that are not only tough enough to thrive in urban environments but are city-friendly, too.

Here are the top ten street trees, and why they work:

Species: **Zelkova (*Zelkova serrata*, also known as Green Vase and Village Green).**

Site requirements: Needs wide-open site and full sun.

Qualities: Exceptional fall colors ranging from yellow to reddish-purple. Handsome smooth grey bark. Many ascending branches with vase-shaped habit. Mature height ranges from 60 to 80 feet.

Comments: Can tolerate dry soil.

Species: **Ginkgo (*Ginkgo biloba*, also known as Princeton Sentry or Magyar).**

Site requirements: Upright varieties are great for older, narrow streets or alleys.

Qualities: Brilliant fall colors.

Comments: Very few insect and disease problems. Leaf extract is getting much attention from herbalists. Plant male specimens to avoid aromatic fruit. Adapts to alkaline soil.

Species: **Chinese Elm (*Ulmus parvifolia*).**

Site requirements: Best suited to wider, open streets.

Qualities: Bark has an interesting mottled and flaky appearance. Grows from 30 to 50 feet.

Comments: Super tough; accommodates to a wide range of inadequate urban soils. Probably will need regular pruning in its early years to establish branch structure. Fast grower if given some TLC.

Species: **Thornless Cockspur Hawthorne (*Crataegus crus-galli inermis*).**

Site requirements: Plant under utility lines.

Qualities: White flowers in spring and crimson color in fall. Grows to about 30 feet.

Comments: Tolerates salts, drought, and high pH. Explore other varieties with over-wintering berries to attract birds.

Species: **Hedge Maple (*Acer campestre*).**

Site requirements: Use as a small tree where space is limited, in full sun or moderate shade.

Qualities: Corky twigs and often low-branched. Can easily be pruned to maintain a desired height. Grows to about 30 feet.

Comments: Adapts to acidic and alkaline soils. Shows good tolerance to pollution. Easily transplanted.

Trees

Species: Sweetgum (*Liquidambar styraciflua*).

Site requirements: Sunny location. Regular watering will help. Needs room for roots.

Qualities: Fall coloring is awesome: purples, reds, and yellows. Uniformly pyramidal branch habit and straight trunk. Growth rate is considered medium to fast.

Comments: Some consider the fruits a nuisance. A native Pennsylvania tree. Prefers acidic soils.

Species: Flowering Crabapple (*Malus species*).

Site requirements: Where a flowering tree is desired for a generally small, tight location.

Qualities: Offer sensational flowering and often brightly colored (and usually inedible) fruit. Trees will mature from 10 to 35 feet in height.

Comments: Choose varieties that have resistance to apple scab. Crabapples can also be susceptible to fire blight and powdery mildew. Tolerant of occasional drought conditions and a range of soil types.

Species: Amur Maackia (*Maackia amuremis*).

Site requirements: Use where overhead wires are a factor.

Qualities: Clean foliage often observed on specimens. White summer flowers; bark peels to shining brown on mature trees. Small, very rounded habit. Grows vigorously.

Comments: A tree to use more often. Handsome branch profile on dormant trees.

Species: Japanese Tree Lilac (*Syringa reticulata*).

Site requirements: Suitable small tree for restricted locations.

Qualities: Large, cream-colored flowers, dark green leaves, cherry-like bark. Very rounded habit.

Comments: A very tough lilac that can be set in large containers.

Species: Katsuratree (*Cercidiphyllum japonicum*).

Site requirements: Needs loose, evenly moist soil. Can be planted in slightly shaded locations. Avoid exposed locations where winds prevail.

Qualities: Emerging leaves offer reddish-purple color. Fall coloring is usually a dramatic yellow to apricot. Grows to about 50 feet with a spreading, rounded habit.

Comments: Relatively free of pests and disease. ∎

Source: Harold M. Rosner.

❖ The first national lip-reading tournament was held in Philadelphia on June 23, 1926, during the seventh annual meeting of the American Federation of Organizations for the Hard of Hearing.

GREENING AND GILDING PHILADELPHIA

It all started 20 years ago with a couple of tomato plants. Since 1974, when the Pennsylvania Horticultural Society became involved in a neighborhood vegetable garden project, Philadelphia Green has sponsored over 1,000 vegetable and flower gardens, developed garden and tree programs for 800 city blocks, rehabilitated the well-known Azalea Garden behind the Philadelphia Museum of Art, and helped city organizations plant "Ribbons of Gold" along highways and river banks.

An activist arm of the Pennsylvania Horticultural Society, Philadelphia Green works with civic associations and informal groups to beautify the city, generate local pride, and save tax dollars. (First there is the savings of the cost to clean the lot, then there is the indirect impact of transforming an eyesore into an oasis.) Such greening is often a critical step toward neighborhood revitalization.

Philadelphia Green is the largest urban greening program in the United States, with four target areas in North Philadelphia for tree plantings and seven neighborhoods cooperating to make "Greene Countrie Townes." Funds for its work come from the proceeds of the renowned Philadelphia Flower Show, corporate and foundation gifts, and other activities of the Pennsylvania Horticultural Society. These include the City Gardens Contest, a citywide annual event with over 500 contestants; the Harvest Show, a competition of displays at the Horticulture Center; the Junior Flower Show, an annual event with more than 1,200 entries, held at the First Bank of the United States; and the Spring Plant Sale at the Horticulture Center, offering wholesale prices for participating communities.

For more information, call the Pennsylvania Horticultural Society at 625-8250.

CITIZENS' MANUAL

WHERE TO START

Hundreds of organizations in Philadelphia and its suburbs are eager to welcome you as a volunteer. Perhaps you already know where you would like to volunteer. If so, make that telephone call!

If not, consult an organization that specializes in matching people with volunteer jobs they will enjoy. Two centers sponsored by the United Way have as their credo: "We'll help match your abilities, interests and time with a volunteer position that's right for you." They are:

Volunteer Action Council of Philadelphia
United Way Building
Seven Benjamin Franklin Parkway
Philadelphia, PA 19103
665-2474

Volunteer Center of Chester, Delaware, and Montgomery Counties
Neumann College Life Center
Aston, PA 19014
558-5639

Their up-to-date computer bank lists hundreds of opportunities. If you make an appointment and visit one of the centers, a counselor will inquire about your areas of interest and then suggest a variety of possibilities. There is no charge for the service and absolutely no obligation to act on any of their recommendations.

❖

February 1892: To help relieve a severe famine in Russia, Americans contribute 3,000 tons of food, which is loaded aboard the American Lines' *Indiana* in Philadelphia. Interfaith services are held at dockside.

Help Wanted: Time and Talent

Many volunteers say the time they work for free is more rewarding than the time they work for pay. A volunteer job may provide a feeling of accomplishment and service that a paid job simply does not offer.

Here is a only a fraction of the Greater Philadelphia organizations in need of volunteers. From this sampling, though, you can imagine the broad range of available opportunities:

Action AIDS, 1216 Arch Street, 4th floor, Philadelphia, PA 19107, 981-0088. Contact person: Beth Varcoe.

This service organization is dedicated to stopping the epidemic of Acquired Immune Deficiency Syndrome and helping those who suffer from it. Volunteer opportunities include: offering help and support to individuals living with AIDS, participating in advocacy groups, and working in administration and public relations.

American Red Cross, Southeastern Pennsylvania Chapter, 23rd and Chestnut Streets, Philadelphia, PA 19103, 299-4000.

The Red Cross Office of Human Services assembles Disaster Action Teams that assist victims on the scene of fires, floods, or whatever else may strike. Volunteers help provide food, clothing, and medical care at emergency shelters, serve on Bloodmobiles, and teach first aid and other health and safety courses. In addition, volunteers help families contact loved ones serving in the armed forces. (Consult suburban telephone directories for the many other Red Cross offices.)

Amnesty International USA, 3601 Locust Walk, Philadelphia, PA 19104, 387-9331.

Amnesty International is dedicated to freeing men, women, and children imprisoned solely for their beliefs, race, or ethnic origins. It seeks prompt and fair trials for all political prisoners and works toward the abolition of torture and execution. Letter writers are needed to participate in appeals aimed at the release of unjustly detained prisoners. Volunteers in local Amnesty groups help promote human rights issues.

Associated Services for the Blind, 919 Walnut Street, Philadelphia, PA 19107, 627-0600. Contact person: Linda Gaffney.

Sighted volunteers assist the visually impaired by paying home visits to read people their mail or read journals to professional men and women. Others record books and articles on audiotape and read the daily newspaper on a radio station that broadcasts to the blind.

Volunteerism

Carpenters' Hall, 320 Chestnut Street, Philadelphia, PA 19106, 925-0167. Contact person: Ruth O'Brien.

In 1770, an association of master carpenters broke ground for this gemlike building. Four years later, the First Continental Congress met within its walls, and it has been home ever since to a variety of Philadelphia institutions. Volunteers help staff the gift shop, inform the many visitors about the hall and its history, assist in the building's maintenance, perform archival work in the library, and welcome guests on special occasions.

The Free Library of Philadelphia, Community Participation Program, 1901 Vine Street, Philadelphia, PA 19103, 686-5340 or 5341. Contact person: Mary L. McGuire.

Shelving books is only one of many jobs that volunteers perform at the Free Library. Some help with summer reading programs for children. Others assist at circulation desks and conduct tours. Still others make signs, posters, and displays, assist students with their homework, and even help take care of the grounds surrounding library branches. With a branch in almost every neighborhood, the Free Library usually can find work for volunteers within a short distance of their homes.

Habitat for Humanity. North Central Philadelphia Chapter: 1829 N. 19th Street, Philadelphia, PA 19121, 765-6070. Contact person: Patricia Alex. West Philadelphia Chapter: 4948 W. Stiles Street, Philadelphia, PA 19131, 477-4639. Contact person: Jon Hoffman.

Habitat is dedicated to its founder's belief that "All of God's people should have at least a simple, decent place to live." Working in partnership with Philadelphia residents unable to afford decent shelter, volunteers construct new homes and rehabilitate old ones. Whether your carpentry skills are rudimentary or advanced, you can be of service. Help is also needed with other kinds of work, such as site selection, public relations, and fund raising.

Mayor's Commission on Literacy, 1500 Walnut Street, 18th floor, Philadelphia, PA 19102, 875-6600. Contact person: Donna Cooper.

If you are serious about becoming a tutor, call the Mayor's Commission and tell them so. If you're qualified, they'll sign you up for a series of three training sessions, each three hours long. Then you'll be referred to a site (most likely a church or school) near where you live, where you'll meet an adult student eager to learn how to read.

Philadelphia Futures, 230 S. Broad Street, Philadelphia, PA 19102, 790-1666. Contact person: Romayne L. Sachs.

Philadelphia Futures helps you "make a difference in one kid's life." Its volunteers counsel and advise individual

RSVP

Another referral service, the Retired Senior Volunteer Program (RSVP), finds volunteer jobs for people over sixty years of age. There are two Philadelphia offices:

RSVP
6600 Bustleton Avenue
Philadelphia, PA 19149
331-7787

RSVP
222 N. 17th Street
Philadelphia, PA 19103
587-3583

RSVP is a division of ACTION, the federal agency that administers VISTA and the Peace Corps. The Northeast Center is sponsored by Catholic Social Services, the Center City Center by Jewish Community Centers, but both offices welcome all senior citizens regardless of their religious or ethnic background.

When you register at one of the centers, a counselor will interview you and suggest interesting opportunities for community service. If you agree to volunteer, you will be expected to commit a minimum of four hours a week to your job. If transportation to and from the work place is a problem, the centers can help with the cost. The centers also provide on-the- job accident insurance for the clients they place in volunteer jobs.

❖

August 1899: A military transport sails from Philadelphia with $50,000 in relief supplies for hurricane victims in Puerto Rico.

September 1932: A "food conservation committee" announces it has canned 41,476 quarts of food for winter use at a shelter for the city's homeless, victims of the Great Depression.

205

high-school students who need a mature adult to count on as they face new challenges. Volunteers also tutor students, help operate a college financial aid hotline, participate in career days, and take on other assignments designed to help students succeed.

Schuylkill Center for Environmental Education, 8480 Hagy's Mill Road, Philadelphia, PA 19128, 482-7300.

After attending training sessions, volunteers talk to visiting classes about nature (in a natural setting), provide backup at the Information and Research Center, or work at the Wildlife Rehabilitation Center, where they nurse back to health thousands of orphaned and injured wild animals.

Veterans Affairs Medical Center, Department of Volunteer Service, University and Woodland Avenues, Philadelphia, PA 19104, 823-5868. Coatesville Veterans Affairs Medical Center, Department of Volunteer Service, 1400 Black Horse Road, Coatesville, PA 19320, 384-7228.

One of the urgent needs at Veterans Hospitals is for friendly visitors—people to come in and chat with patients. Coatesville has a Silver Spoons Program in which volunteers feed patients who are unable to feed themselves. Volunteers participate in many other activities as well, from assisting with Special Olympics programs to visiting patients with a cart of books from the library.

Wagner Free Institute of Science, 1700 W. Montgomery Avenue, Philadelphia, PA 19121, 763-6529. Contact person: Susan Glassman.

The Wagner Free Institute is a museum's museum, a long-standing neighborhood monument on the must-see list for the best-informed visitors to Philadelphia. Its breathtaking Victorian architecture houses thousands of natural specimens. In addition, the Institute sponsors lectures at conveniently located auditoriums throughout the city. Volunteers are needed to help with programs for children, tours for visitors, library work, and public relations.

Women in Community Service (WICS), 3535 Market Street, Room 2250, Philadelphia, PA 19104, 238-3949. Contact person: Carol Seeley.

Women in Community Service, a coalition of five national groups, helps young, at-risk women break the cycle of poverty. Volunteers mentor young women as they return to the community after graduating from a federal Job Corps program aimed at self-sufficiency. Volunteers also speak to community groups about Job Corps opportunities, interview applicants, and help with public relations. ∎

❖ Only one Philadelphia street's name reads the same forwards as backwards. The palindromic street is Camac.

The Four Faces of Philadelphia Weather

Philadelphia may not do things fast, but we do them well. Two hundred and fifty million years ago, give or take a week, Africa and North America collided and set the stage for the four geographic factors that control Philadelphia's weather today.

The Appalachian Mountains were scraped off the Iapaetus Ocean floor and stood up on end west of where City Hall would rise a quarter of a billion years later. These mountains protect us from the raging storms that characterize Middle America's weather. Here, tornadoes are almost nil, blizzards make the history books, and winter temperature readings below zero occur only a few days a year. The Appalachians also filter out snowstorms from the West. If it is snowing in Harrisburg, don't worry. If it is snowing in Washington, buy stock in snow shovels.

The Atlantic Ocean has made Philadelphia's four seasons distinct, if unequal. Water holds heat for a long time and surrenders it slowly. Philadelphians begin the summer season on Memorial Day, when ocean temperatures are still in the low 50s.

The Atlantic's weather effects continue into the summer, when humidity is added to the mix. The ocean warming that peaks in September makes autumn a long, delightful season. Summer heat lingers, and the warm ocean air flow keeps winter at bay until mid or even late December. Philadelphians declare summer over on Labor Day. Real meteorologists take September vacations.

The Atlantic and the Appalachians combine to create Philadelphia's winter weather. Storms forming over the warmer ocean move along the coast and generate intensive storms held in place by the mountains. The resulting funneling effect allows the storms to grow suddenly into massive coastal storms known as "bombs." They are most likely to occur from mid-February until the last days of March, the month that holds the records for the most severe winter storms. With winter and spring never quite separate, from March to May you can have winter one day and spring the next.

Philadelphia's precipitation pattern reveals two more subtle faces of our climate. The Piedmont Plateau divides the high elevations of the northern and western sections of the city from the lowlands of the Atlantic coastal plain known as South, Central, and Northeast Philadelphia. Rocky Balboa's view from the Art Museum steps was actually from the hill of the Piedmont (Fairmount), looking southwest over the coastal plain. Elevations range from over 450 feet in the northwestern portions of the city to five feet above sea level at Philadelphia International Airport.

The changes in elevation mean more snow in the northwestern portion of the city. Philadelphia's famous "snow line" is actually a temperature line of warmer air that changes snow to rain in lower elevations—that is, the coastal plain, or Center City.

The same differences of elevation tend to make Northwest Philadelphia drier in the summer, because the drop in elevation moves storms through the area more quickly. In contrast, thunderstorms strengthen and linger in the flat, warmer areas of the city where they have an ample supply of heat and moisture supplied by the rivers. (Just ask any Phillies fan about rain delays at the Vet.) ∎

THE HOTTEST
Day: July 4, 1966 (104° F)
Month: July 1955 and July 1993 (tied) (average temperature 81.4° F)
Year: 1931 and 1991 (tied) (average temperature 58.1° F)
Stretch: 52 days in 1991 above 90° F

THE COLDEST
Day: February 9, 1934 (-11.0° F)
Month: January 1977 (average temperature 20.0° F)
Year: 1963 (average temp. 51.9° F)
Stretch: 31 days in January 1984 below 32° F

THE DEEPEST
Day: February 11–12, 1983 (21.3 inches of snow)
Month: February 1899 (31.5 inches of snow)
Year: 1977–78 (54.9 inches of snow)
Average year: 21.6 inches of snow

THE WETTEST
Day: August 3–4, 1898 (5.89 inches of rain)
Month: August 1911 (12.10 inches of rain)
Year: 1983 (54.41 inches of rain)

THE FIRST
"Official" weather record: 1871, when the Department of Commerce established the U.S. Weather Bureau.

THE HIGHEST
Barometer reading: February 13, 1981 (31.10 inches)
Wind: October 23, 1878 (75 miles per hour Southeast)

THE LOWEST
Barometer reading: March 13, 1993 (28.43 inches), breaking the old record of March 6, 1932
Yearly snowfall: Winter 1972–73 (none)

Who's Who

If you look inside enough animal habitats in and around Philadelphia, you can find: Jingga Gula riding around on mom Rita's head (they're both Bornean orangutans); a bald eagle from Alaska that's recovered from a gunshot wound (but he still can't fly); endangered Siberian tigers (roaming around in the midst of 180 acres in Brandywine Park); a collection of exotic cats (on your way to Cape May); and smooth dog fish sharks for petting (their teeth are suited for crushing crustaceans, not snipping at hands).

Bear Pits in 1900.

And these are but a few of the more than 5,000 animals living inside one of the area's four zoos and one aquarium—zookeepers distinct both in purpose and population.

The Philadelphia Zoo is the country's oldest, dating back to March 21, 1859, when the Zoological Society of Philadelphia was chartered. Today, a walking tour of the 42-acre animal kingdom meanders past 1,700 animals in Bear Country, Carnivore Kingdom, Lions' Lookout, the Children's Zoo, Bird Lake, the Treehouse, the World of Primates (where Jingga Gula lives), the Reptile House, and the Rare Animal house. The zoo participates in 21 "Species Survival Plans" sponsored by an international organization dedicated to the survival of endangered species.

Founded in 1924, the Elmwood Park Zoo in Norristown is a precious, intimate zoo for young children, with 200 North American animals housed in over 7.5 acres. About 20 percent of the animals are located here because they have been previously injured and need a safe place to recuperate and live. The zoo's ground-bound bald eagle, for example, came from Alaska after being shot. One owl had been hit by a car, another by a truck. And while the zoo plans to expand a bit, it likes being small and welcoming, a place where all young visitors know owls Chestnut and Acorn and who sits behind whom.

Delaware's only zoo is owned and operated by New Castle County inside the 180 acres known as Brandywine Park. The Brandywine Zoo in Wilmington spotlights 150 animals native to North and South America. Featured are tigers, including a pair of Siberians, which is considered an endangered species. Since 1905, this zoo has been open to animal lovers 365 days a year.

On the way to Cape May, you can fall in love along Route 9 with a 25-acre zoo that has eight species of exotic cats. The Cape May County Park Zoo, noted for its botanical gardens, also offers 350 animals that range from zebras and giraffes to Bengal tigers and ocelots, those small cats from South America. The 14-year-old zoo will soon expand to 50 acres of the 120-acre park, which includes the Cape May Court House.

And at the newest aquarium to open along the East Coast, you can take a finger or two and rub the back of a smooth dog fish shark. Inside the Thomas H. Kean New Jersey State Aquarium at Camden, the sharks that circle close to the sides of the "Touch a Shark Tank" are bottom feeders and don't view splashing water as a signal for food. So relax and touch, before you venture off to gaze at the delightful underwater show inside the nation's second-largest open ocean tank. It is up to 24 feet deep, holds 760,000 gallons of sea water, and is home to the majority of the saltwater fish found off the coast of New Jersey. ■

CITIZENS' MANUAL

Zoo

Going to the Zoo(s) and Aquarium, Too

The Philadelphia Zoo
3400 West Girard Avenue
Philadelphia, PA 19104
243-1100
Open daily year-round; closed Thanksgiving, December 24, 25, 31, and January 1.

Hours, zoo grounds: Weekdays: 9:30am–5:45pm year-round. Weekends: April–October, 9:30am–6:45pm; November–March, 9:30am–5:45pm.

Admission: Adults, $7; children 2–11, $5.50; children under 2, free. Free admission on Mondays in December, January, and February (excluding holidays). Groups rates available for 15 or more. Treehouse, $1 additional fee.

Parking: $4.

The Elmwood Park Zoo
1616 Harding Boulevard
Norristown, PA 19404
277-3825
Open daily year-round; closed Christmas Day and New Year's Day.

Hours: 10am–4pm.

Admission: Adults, $2; children under 12, $1; children 2 and under, free; $1 per person in groups (registration required).

Parking: Free.

Brandywine Zoo
1001 North Park Drive
Wilmington, DE 19802
(302) 571-7747
Open daily year-round, 365 days.

Hours: 10am–4pm.

Admission: November–March, free; April and October, free except weekends; May–September, daily admission charged. Adults, $3; children 3–11, $1.50; children under 3, free; senior citizens (62 and over) $1.50.

Parking: Free.

Cape May County Park Zoo
Route 9, Cape May Court House
Cape May, NJ 08210
(609) 465-5271
Open daily year-round, 364 days; closed Christmas Day.

Hours: 9am–5pm.

Admission: Free for all ages; donations accepted.

Parking: Free.

Thomas H. Kean New Jersey State Aquarium at Camden
1 Riverside Drive
Camden, NJ 08103-1060
(609) 365-3300
TDD (609) 541-8861 (for the hearing-impaired)
Open daily year-round; closed Thanksgiving, Christmas, New Year's Day, Easter.

Hours: 9:30am–5:30pm.

Admission: Adults, $8.50; children 2–11, $5.50; children under 2, free. Students with ID, $7. Senior citizens (65 and over), $7. Special rates for groups of 15 or more (reservations required).

(left) White Deer in 1876.

PHILADELPHIA ZOO FACTS

Number of inmates: 1,733

Annual cost of food: $320,000

Nourishment for vampire bats: Blood cocktails laced with baby vitamins

Fast day for tigers: Monday

Fast day for lions: Tuesday

Animals considered most susceptible to human diseases and colds: Primates

Animals most likely to be seen and heard mating: Giant tortoises and rhinos

Second most popular zoo souvenir in 1992: Peacock feathers

Favorite souvenir in 1992: Punch balls (more than 125,000 sold)

Gallons of water in the Bear Country polar bear pool: 200,000

Last escape: Red panda, after a wind storm knocked down a tree and the panda walked up and out of the Carnivore Kingdom in the fall of 1992

Duration of escape: About an hour

Range of escape: Within zoo's walls

Destination of Zoo Doo: City compost piles in Fairmount Park

Destination of gorilla Massa's brain: Johns Hopkins University and the University of Pennsylvania

AMERICAN FIRSTS:

Male Indian rhinoceros exhibited in a zoo: Pete, 1875

Adult bull elephant: Bolivar, Christmas Day, 1888

Gorilla: Bamboo, 1927

Chimpanzee born: Julius, October 1, 1928

White lions in America: Jezebel and Vinkel, June 1993

WORLD RECORDS:

First orangutan born in captivity: Lucky, September 28, 1928

Believed oldest captive gorilla at death: Massa, age 54 in 1985

Oldest breeding Indian rhinoceros: Billy, age 40

First bred in captivity: Naked mole-rats, January 18, 1992

Source: The Philadelphia Zoo.

209

Index

Pennsylvania Dutch Farmers
Market, 80
Pennsylvania Environmental
Council, 69
Pennsylvania Hall, 164
Pennsylvania Horticultural Society,
82, 203
Pennsylvania Hospital, 56, 106
Pennsylvania House of
Representatives, 38–40
Pennsylvania, plants and animals
named for, 135, 136
Pennsylvania Railroad, 61
Pennsylvania Resources Council, 69
Pennsylvania state parks, 51
Pennsylvania State Senate, 42
Pennypack, 147
Pennypacker, Heinrich, 60
Pennypacker, Samuel W., 98
Pennypacker Mills, 98, 185
Pennypack Woods, 147
Pepper, George Wharton, 11
Pet cemetery, 51
Peterson, Henry, 154
Pettit, Henry, 5
Philadelphia: elected officials, 34;
health districts, 90; history of,
162–166; image of, 185; loca-
tion in relation to China, 51;
plants and animals named for,
135, 136; ward leaders, 36–38;
words composed from, 53. *See
also* Firsts, Philadelphia
Philadelphia and Reading
Railroad, 165
Philadelphia Area Consortium of
Special Collections Libraries,
109–111
Philadelphia Art Alliance, 98
Philadelphia Athletics, 177–180
Philadelphia Award, 10
Philadelphia Board of Elections, 38
Philadelphia City Building Code, 49
Philadelphia City Charter, 49
Philadelphia City Commissioners, 34
Philadelphia City Council, 112
Philadelphia City Hall, 8, 66, 106,
124, 165
Philadelphia City History Society, 1
Philadelphia College of Bible,
62, 63

Philadelphia College of Pharmacy
and Science, 62, 63
Philadelphia College of Textiles and
Science, 62
Philadelphia Contributionship for
the Insurance of Houses from
Loss by Fire, 17, 106
Philadelphia Cultural Council, 114
Philadelphia Electric Company, 68
Philadelphia Festival of World
Cinema, 73
Philadelphia Folk Festival, 133
Philadelphia Folklore Project, 133
Philadelphia Futures, 205
Philadelphia Gas Works, 68
Philadelphia Green, 82, 203
Philadelphia Hillsdale baseball
team, 179
Philadelphia Historic Preservation
Corporation, 3
Philadelphia Maritime Museum, 111
Philadelphia Masonic Temple, 4, 106
Philadelphia Museum of Art, 49, 125,
185; President's Bike Ride, 197
Philadelphia Music Alliance, 130
Philadelphia Orchestra, 44
Philadelphia Parking Authority, 154
Philadelphia Phillies, 177–182
Philadelphia Record Building, 5
Philadelphia Saving Fund Society
skyscraper, 106, 166, 176
Philadelphia School Board, 66–67
Philadelphia Tribune, 165
Philadelphia Unemployment
Project, 45
Philadelphia Zoo, 51, 185, 208, 209
PHILAFILM, 73
Phil-Ellena, 5
Philley, Dave, 181
Photography, history of, 157
Physick, Philip Syng, 104
Pickett, Clarence E., 11
Pine Barrens, 58
Pittville, 147
Plastics, 52
Pleasant Hill, 147
Pleasantville, 147
Plumbsock, 147
Plumsted, Clement, 119, 120
Plumsted, William, 119, 120

Plunkett, James, 126
Poe, Edgar Allan, 106, 160; National
Historic Site, 98
Poetquessing, 147
Poetry Center, 114
Poetry Forum, 115
Poetry Plus, 115
Poetry readings, 113, 114
Poets & Prophets, 115
Point Breeze, 147
Point-No-Point, 147
Pollution, 166, 195.
See also Environment
Pomona Hall, 98
Poor Island, 147
*Poor Richard's Almanac.
See* Franklin, Benjamin
Poplar, 147
Population trends, 167–168
Port Folio, 3
Port Richmond, 147
Postal zip codes, 117
Potholes, 50
Potts, John, 98
Pottsgrove Manor, 98, 185
Poverty, 168
Powel, Samuel, 121
Powell, W. Bleddyn, 8
Powelton, 147
Presbyterian Historical Society, 111
Presbyterian Ministers' Fund, 17
Preservation, 3
Preservation Coalition of Greater
Philadelphia, 3
President, U.S., 32
President's House, 4
Preston, Samuel, 118, 119
Pretzels, 46, 77
Price, Eli Kirk, 10
Price, Franklin H., 11
Primitive Hall, 98
Princeton Station, 147
Prisons, 4, 6, 95, 185
Prospect Heights, 147
Province Island, 147
PSFS, 176
Ptolemeis, Adalberte Benedictis, 120
Public gardens, 84–87
Public meetings, 54

Colophon: *The Philadelphia Almanac and Citizens' Manual for 1994* was designed and produced at AdamsGraphics, Inc. using Apple® Macintosh™-based systems. The cover illustration was scanned on a Howtek® D4000 drum scanner, retouched in Adobe® Photoshop™, and combined with Adobe Illustrator® blends. The halftones were scanned into Adobe® Photoshop™ using a Microtek® 600 dpi scanner. Graphs, maps, and graphic elements were created in Adobe Illustrator®. Borders, dividers, and logos were adapted from sources at the Library Company of Philadelphia: Alexander Robb, *Specimen of Printing Types and Ornaments* (Philadelphia, 1844) and Elihu White, *A Specimen of Printing Types* (New York, 1818). Page layout, typesetting, and page assembly were performed using QuarkXPress® (Adobe Syntax, Syntax Black, New Baskerville, and Bitstream Industrial 736 fonts). The cover was color proofed on a 3M Rainbow™ proofer; the text pages were proofed on a Varityper® 600W laser printer. The final film was output to a Varityper® Series 6000/5300B imagesetter. The almanac was printed by BookCrafters on 80 lb. Carolina coated cover stock and 60 lb. Enviro Text.